MARY AUSTIN'S REGIONALISM

MARY AUSTIN'S REGIONALISM

Reflections on Gender, Genre, and Geography

Heike Schaefer

UNIVERSITY OF VIRGINIA PRESS
CHARLOTTESVILLE AND LONDON

University of Virginia Press
© 2004 by the Rector and Visitors of the University of Virginia
Printed in the United States of America on acid-free paper

First published 2004

1 3 5 7 9 8 6 4 2

LIBRARY OF CONGRESS CATALOGING-IN-PUBLICATION DATA

Schaefer, Heike, 1969–
   Mary Austin's regionalism : reflections on gender, genre, and geography /
Heike Schaefer.
      p.   cm. — (Under the sign of nature)
Includes bibliographical references (p.) and index.
   ISBN 0-8139-2273-9 (cloth : alk. paper)
      1. Austin, Mary Hunter, 1868–1934—Criticism and interpretation. 2. Austin,
Mary Hunter, 1868–1934—Knowledge—Natural history. 3. Austin, Mary
Hunter, 1868–1934—Knowledge—West (U.S.) 4. Natural history—West
(U.S.)—History. 5. Women and literature—West (U.S.) 6. West (U.S.)—In
literature. 7. Regionalism in literature. 8. Nature in literature.
I. Title. II. Series.
PS3501.U8Z89 2004
818'.5209—dc22

                                                            2003022890

To Hilde Ordemann
who taught me to care

CONTENTS

ACKNOWLEDGMENTS

This book was written in many places and with the help of generous people whom I wish to thank here. I began writing about Mary Austin and environmental perception as part of my graduate work at the University of Hamburg, Germany. Through the support, advice, and gentle nudging of my advisors, Bettina Friedl and Joseph Schoepp, the project eventually grew into a dissertation. I thank them both and am particularly grateful to Bettina for her emboldening guidance of my development as writer and critic.

The first chapters of this study took shape during a year of independent research at the University of Oregon, Eugene, where I had the good fortune to meet Suzanne Clark, Bill Rossi, and Molly Westling. They introduced me to writers and theories that transformed my way of thinking about Austin and the relation of culture and environment. I also am indebted to the Mesa Verde group at the English department in Eugene. It was a joy to finally meet others who were interested in environmental literature and who would talk with me about Austin and the promises and pitfalls of ecocritical practice. I owe many insights and a general enthusiasm for ecocritical questions to my conversations and outings with members of the Mesa Verde group.

Important for the writing of this study were also two summers I spent at the Huntington Library in San Marino, California, where I read my way through hundreds of boxes, or so it seemed, of the Mary Hunter Austin Collection. I thank the staff of the Huntington for the expertise and friendliness with which they made my time there as productive as pleasant. I am grateful to the Huntington Library for supporting my research with a fellowship and the permission to quote from the materials in the Austin collection.

Several colleagues and friends who read parts of the manuscript have helped me clarify my argument. I thank Catrin Gersdorf, Christa Grewe-

Volpp, Michaela Krug, Antje Mannsbruegge, and Sylvia Mayer for their ideas, recommendations, and queries. The thoughtful questions and suggestions of the members of my doctoral advisory committee, of the members of the conference workshops in which I first tested my ideas, and of the two anonymous readers for the University of Virginia Press have helped me think and write more precisely about Austin, sense of place, and regionalist literature. To Boyd Zenner, Ellen Satrom, and Toni Mortimer, my editors at the University of Virginia Press, I am thankful for their interest in my work and the kindness with which they have guided me through the publishing process.

I gladly acknowledge the support I received in the form of scholarships from the German Academic Exchange Service (DAAD) and the City of Hamburg. I also thank the editors of the e-journal *Current Objectives of Postgraduate American Studies* and of the essay collections *The Sixties Revisited: Culture—Society—Politics; Übergänge-Transitions; Millennial Perspectives: Lifeworlds and Utopias;* and *From Landscape to Technoscape: Contestations of Space in American Culture* for permission to reprint material.

At home, I am grateful to my parents, Irmgard and Egon Schaefer, who first taught me to be curious about the world. With their bountiful support, they encouraged me throughout my studies and their loving interest keeps anchoring me today. I owe my love of travel, reading, and thinking to them. They showed me how to home in on a place and how to garden. A thank you also goes to Ulrike Mann, who has accompanied me through difficult terrain and helped me trust my imagination. Finally, I happily acknowledge my gratitude to Ralph Drews. His love, clearhearted company, and tireless support have enabled me to write this book and to enjoy the process. Ralph's confidence, clarity, and sense of humor have kept me sane and growing. Thank you.

MARY AUSTIN'S REGIONALISM

INTRODUCTION

"What I see in nature is mind," Mary Austin once jotted in her journal, "conscious mind reacting on mind shaping the world. Mind in trees and birds and insects, mind in flowers."[1] In Austin's work the world is a fundamentally unified place that unfolds in differences. Life expresses itself in a multitude of interrelated forms—different variations on the themes of matter, sentience, and consciousness, only one of which is human. Our lives, Austin held, grow out of and into an environmental matrix that extends beyond the human. Since our interactions with the world around us sustain and transform us, "conscious mind reacting on mind shaping the world," Austin reasoned, it makes sense to think of subjectivity as reciprocal rather than as autonomous, as processual rather than as stable, as emplaced rather than as self-enclosed. Our sense of self depends on our participatory relations with our surroundings. There "is communication between all living things," Austin asserted. "Once I lost it and the tree was only a vegetable growth to me and the world was a strange cold place very lonely. I feel this communication physically, between my shoulders in the back of the neck. I feel it psychically after sitting a long time silent. I almost understand what it says" (AU 363). Austin traced the ongoing conversation between self and the environing world in her essays, stories, and novels about the American desert Southwest. Her exploration of relational selfhood and environmental bonding eventually became the ground for her regionalist call for far-reaching cultural and sociopolitical reforms.

As a regionalist writer and critic, Austin sought to contribute to the formation "of an America which is the expression of the life activities of the environment."[2] She advocated the development of sustainable regional cultures that would evolve out of and consequently express their close relations to their land base. Taking the West and Southwest as her point of reference, Austin envisioned a synthesis of European American,

Native American, and Hispanic cultures that would serve as a model for America's future development. She was convinced that a cultural syncretism that aimed at regional adaptation offered the nation the greatest chance for developing an ecologically sound economy as well as a genuinely democratic culture. It was the "one best bet" Americans had "of realizing the utmost potentiality of the American idea."[3]

Austin's interest in sense of place, sustainability, and cultural geography, as we would call it today, not only put her at odds with those of her contemporaries who mistook their land base for a cornucopia of natural resources but her environmental sensibilities also signaled a departure from late nineteenth-century gender codes. For Austin had grown up, as she explains in her autobiography, *Earth Horizon,* with the admonishments of her mother that it was inappropriate for a young lady to be curious about the natural world. Austin's mother had instructed her: "Especially you must not talk appreciatively about landscapes and flowers and the habits of little animals and birds to boys; they didn't like it. If one of them took you walking, your interest should be in your companion, and not exceed a ladylike appreciation of the surroundings, in so far as the boy, as the author of the walk, might feel himself complimented by your appreciation of it. You must not quote; especially poetry and Thoreau" (112). Austin did not heed this advice. Instead, she responded to the lingering Victorian ideology of True Womanhood by assuming the posture of a "Master of the American Environment."[4] She became an accomplished and often fiercely ironic environmental writer who developed her regionalist vision in dialogue with the emerging cultural feminism.

Due to the combined environmentalist, pluralist, and feminist impetus of Austin's regionalism, her work became a nodal point in the cultural field of her times. Her theoretical and literary writing contributed to contemporaneous conversations on the direction of American literature and society. Spanning from 1889 to 1934, Austin's published work is roughly bounded by the inception of Turnerian interpretations of the West and the New Deal. It coincided with the professionalization of the conservationist movement and participated in debates about the national significance of the frontier. Analyzing mythic images of the West as well as federal reclamation policy and land use conflicts, Austin sought to influence the regional development of the Southwest. Drawing on the newly established science anthropology, she described Native American society and presented place-based Indian cultures as learning models in regional adaptation to her European American readers. She explored the processes of cross-cultural communication and commented on questions of Americanization. Rejecting forced assimilation, she advocated ethnic and cultural diversity.

Over the first three decades of her writing life, Austin developed the vision of a land-based American democracy that eventually secured her a prominent position within the regionalist movement of the twenties and thirties. Like Lewis Mumford, B. A. Botkin, Donald Davidson, and other regionalists of the time, Mary Austin sought "to fashion regionalism into a democratic civil religion, a utopian ideology, and a radical politics," as Robert L. Dorman has argued.[5] Like her peers, Austin considered regionalism a form of cultural pluralism. She defined *regionalism* as an aesthetic and political program that promoted the development of "several Americas, in many subtle and significant characterizations."[6] In this respect Austin stands representative for the regionalism of the interwar years, and it is appropriate that one of the first studies of the movement, Carey McWilliams's *The New Regionalism in American Literature* (1930), is dedicated to Austin.

Austin's later work also can be read in the context of the artist communities that flourished at Taos and Santa Fe after World War I. Austin shared, for instance, the commitment to cross-cultural communication with many of her friends and colleagues in New Mexico. Like Mable Dodge Luhan's effort to involve the artists, intellectuals, and activists flocking to her house in Taos in the struggle for Native American rights, much of Austin's work was inspired by the vision of a multi-ethnic egalitarian American society in harmony with its natural environment. In this sense Austin's writing belongs to the tradition of transcendental modernism, which Lois Palken Rudnick has described as the common ground of the writers and artists who gathered at Luhan's home in Taos.[7]

Yet Austin was also a courageous thinker who routinely challenged ready-made positions and neither unquestioningly accepted as her own the status quo nor the consensus of any one group. For Austin the creation of a regionalized American democracy hinged not only on the acknowledgement of geographical conditions and regional cultures but also depended on the willingness to negotiate across ethnic, economic, and other social boundaries the different options Americans had of inhabiting the land. The persistence, ingenuity, and humor with which she combined environmentalist advocacy, mystical practice, and the exploration of the race, gender, and class dynamics informing the European American colonization of the land render Austin unique among her regionalist contemporaries and her peers in New Mexico. Because she focused in her regionalist writing on the interplay of environmental perception, literary traditions, and social dynamics, Austin significantly contributed to the development of American environmental literature. Her regionalist narratives draw our attention to the cultural training of our perceptual habits and aesthetic preferences; and they invite us to inquire which conceptual frameworks can help us to acquire and apply place-based democratic knowledges.

Some Reasons for Reading Austin

Austin's focus on the confluence of social and ecological issues recently has earned her a double comeback as a politically and environmentally committed writer. Over the past two decades, Austin has been recanonized both as a feminist regionalist writer and as an author in the Thoreauvian tradition of American nature writing. As a regionalist, Austin is thought to represent a female-dominated branch of realist writing, which celebrates communal ways of living and "women's culture." As a nature writer, by contrast, Austin is seen to work in a male-dominated tradition of environmental nonfiction, producing scientifically based and philosophically inspired texts.[8]

The bifurcation of Austin criticism is unfortunate, because it inadvertently has worked to obscure her achievement as a regionalist author. What renders the reading of Austin's work rewarding for us today is not only that she addressed feminist, pluralist, and environmentalist concerns but that she used her artistry, imaginative powers, and humor to reveal how these concerns intersect. Austin's writing invites us to consider how geographical forces as well as our social and historical situation affect who we are and how we behave. It allows us to view our lives within both an ecological and a sociocultural matrix and thus may help us rethink what it means to be human in a world of extreme environmental degradation and uneven power relations.

Granted, Austin's specific predictions proved false in that federal reclamation policy, military testing, and urban sprawl rather than bioregional considerations dictated the development of the Southwest in the twentieth century. Her work, nevertheless, remains relevant, because it presents us with an integrated way of thinking that may help us recognize how the natural and cultural aspects of our lives and the human and non-human dimensions of the world intertwine. If we took seriously Austin's idea that cultural development in part "depends upon the nature of an adjustment between the land and its people," we would reorient not only our environmental politics but also many of our cultural practices that disconnect us from the places we inhabit.[9]

Austin's regionalist work is particularly intriguing, because her understanding of culture as an interplay of environmental, economic, biological, and social factors challenges our habit to imagine nature and culture as some sort of parallel universes. Austin's essays and stories urge us to attribute equal significance to the natural and the cultural dimensions of our lives. I stress this point because the current critical climate tends to encourage us either to be wary of essentialism and to privilege the cultural as the realm in which meaning, order, and identity are generated or to respond to the prior devaluation of the natural world with a reversal maneuver that seeks to instate natural laws or ecological prime notions as organizing principles for social processes and cultural practices. Austin's work asks us to abandon this either/or logic and to consider how social and environmental issues overlap. Several of her narratives dramatize, for instance, that our ideas about gender and race are intimately linked to our definitions of the natural and that our perception of the natural world frequently reveals as much about our cultural identity as about the unbuilt environment. As a feminist and interculturally oriented regionalist, Austin sought to extend the ecological literacy and place consciousness of her readers without rendering the natural environment as a self-evident source of individual identity and national history.

Austin's concern with the ramifications of defining someone or something as natural is especially pertinent, because the notion that indisputable, naturally given parameters exist for our behavior has served in regionalist and environmental discourse to justify nativist agendas. Consider, for instance, the anti-immigration arguments recently put forth by prominent environmentalists such as Dave Foreman, the EarthFirst! cofounder, and George Sessions, the influential Deep Ecologist. In 1998 a group of environmentalists lobbied the Sierra Club, America's largest environmental organization, to adopt an anti-immigration position. The group argued that a drastic reduction of immigration represented the most effective measure to curb population growth within the United

States, which they identified as a main source of environmental degradation. Giving the-boat-is-full logic an environmentalist update, the Sierrans for U.S. Population Stabilization insisted that a further influx of immigrants had to be prevented because the limits of ecological carrying capacities had been reached on American ground. Following months of heated debate on the issue, the Sierra Club membership rejected the proposal on their annual ballot. Still, it was alarming to see how many environmentalists and academics, who would not consider themselves susceptible to racist thought, succumbed to the appeal of this seemingly objective, scientific argument. The Sierra Club episode attests to the continuing attraction of the idea that our studies of the natural world could provide us with a value-neutral basis for our politics that would deliver us from the task of negotiating conflicting political interests and economic needs.[10]

Austin's critical and literary writing on the race, gender, and class dynamics of regional acculturation and national development suggests the hazards of such an approach to environmental policy. Anticipating the current environmental justice movement, Austin envisioned the creation of a sustainable American democracy not as a return to a naturally given order but as an intercultural learning process in environmental adaptation and economic cooperation. Her regionalist work insists that we confront the social, political, and economic differences that shape our lives, including our ways of inhabiting particular places.

One of the questions guiding my study of Austin's work, then, is how her regionalist narratives describe the interplay of forces such as gender, race, or class in the development of regional cultures and place-based senses of selfhood. How can texts that focus on the influence of the biophysical environment on human identity describe socially acquired components of subjectivity and account for the cultural conditions of regional identity formation and community building? To what extent does Austin's regionalist insistence on the environment as a primary factor in sociocultural processes help to advance an environmentalist transformation of American society, and to what extent does it work to promote a naturalized understanding of sociopolitical power dynamics and historical processes?

Critical Readings of the Regionalist Tradition

Since Austin's fiction and nonfiction about the arid regions of the West and Southwest cannot be meaningfully discussed separate from the larger regionalist project of which they are a part, this section offers a brief excursion into critical discourse that will clarify what I mean when I use the term *regionalism*. What exactly is regionalism and how have critics defined its place in American literary and cultural history?

In this study I distinguish between the terms *region* and *regionalism* and between *regional* and *regionalist*. I use the words *region* and *regional* to refer to geographically and historically defined segments of natural and social environments, whereas I use the terms *regionalism* and *regionalist* to refer to aesthetic practices and sociopolitical agendas that identify with regional interests, affirm regional particularities, and advocate place-based political and cultural developments.[11] Regionalism, as I understand it, is both a literary and a sociopolitical tradition.

Given the scope of regionalist concerns, it is not surprising that regionalism has been classified in numerous ways. It has been called a "literature of difference" and a "literature of the heart"; it has been characterized as a "literature of memory" and as a "utopian ideology."[12] Although critics disagree on the cultural function that the different forms of regionalism served in nineteenth- and twentieth-century America, the diverse critical interpretations frequently share one assumption: regionalism developed in reaction to the technological advances and social developments of modern America that furthered social homogenization, cultural standardization, and a general sense of dislocation. Chief among the socioeconomic and cultural pressures with which the regionalists grappled were forces such as industrialization and urbanization; an improving national infrastructure of commerce, transportation and communication; environmental degradation; mass migrations within and across national borders; political movements that changed gender, race, and class relations; increasing social mobility; and the rise of a popular culture based on industrial mass production. While regionalists responded to specific sociohistorical circumstances and places, the overarching concern of regionalism as a cultural phenomenon has been the formation of individual and collective identities within particular environments and the sociopolitical dynamics governing the relations between environmental or societal entities and their constitutive segments.

How can we determine the significance, then, that the regionalist project assumes within American literary and cultural history? This proves a difficult task, since the academic debate over the aesthetic and political merit of regionalism has been long, thorough, and inconclusive. On one end of the spectrum, critics caution that regionalism constitutes at its best a harmless provincialism and golden-age nostalgia and that it amounts at its worst to an unproductive antimodernism and a nativist ideology with racist implications.[13] On the other end of the spectrum, however, critics stress the disruptive potential that regional sensibilities hold in a homogenized, oppressive, environmentally destructive, and imperialist American society.[14] The inherent pluralism of regionalist conceptions of subjectivity and nationality obviously resonates well with postcolonial concepts of borderlands and contact zones, with the feminist call for situated knowledges, and with the revisionary impetus of New West historiography.[15] Equally important, its environmental orientation links regionalism to the burgeoning field of environmental literary criticism. Many ecocritics share the conviction voiced by earlier regionalists such as Austin that we need nonanthropocentric ways of thinking about and interacting with the natural world, if our societies are to become sustainable.[16]

Among American literary critics, the debate on the cultural function of regionalism frequently has focused on the tradition of nineteenth-century women's local color literature. Here the spectrum reaches from Richard H. Brodhead's focus on the nativism and elitism of women's regionalist *Cultures of Letters* (1993) to the arguments of feminist critics that regionalism offered women writers in the nineteenth century a liberating perspective. Judith Fetterley and Marjorie Pryse stress in their introduction to the Norton anthology *American Women Regionalists* (1992) that regionalist writing, since it was based on the authors' lived experience, allowed women writers to question the organization, value systems, and gender codes of their communities (xi–xx). Likewise, Sherrie A. Inness and Diana Royer, the editors of the anthology *Breaking Boundaries* (1997), define the female tradition of regionalism as a "legacy of subversion" (3).

In recovering regionalism as "a distinctly feminine tradition," feminist critics have sought to redefine previously devalued aspects of the feminine gender role as cultural assets.[17] In the spirit of the cultural feminism of the seventies and eighties, these critics read women's regionalist writing for images of nurturing female friendships, emphasizing the strength and self-determination of female characters, that is, their resistance to patriarchy, and affirming the supportive domestic communities they formed, that is, their women's culture.

The attention that early feminist critics of regionalist literature paid to the gendering of values and the possible confluence of gender and genre has been instrumental in bringing about a positive reconsideration of the female regionalist tradition. It has heightened the critical acclaim of female regionalist authors. Yet, in the long run, the reclamation of regionalist women writers along the lines of cultural feminism is prone to perpetuate both the marginal status of regional writing and essentialist concepts of femininity. Once regionalism is narrowed down to a "'regionalism' of female consciousness," the scope of the regionalist project can be reduced to an act of female bonding.[18] Its sociopolitical and literary potential then depends on the reader's willingness to respond in familial and gendered terms, "like a good daughter, practiced [in] the art of empathic imagination herself."[19] To think of the writing and reading of regionalist fiction as a sharing of stories among family members, however, is to gloss over the efforts that female regionalists undertook to gain literary authority and public influence. Despite the traditional relegation of white middle-class women to the domestic sphere, these writers self-consciously worked within a public literary market.

Since our situated perspectives influence which connections we posit between the gender of the authors working in an identifiable literary tradition and their mode of argumentation and writing, our observations frequently disclose as much about our theoretical preferences and present notions of femininity and masculinity as about the choices the authors made in response to the gender politics of their time. It hardly surprises, then, that the celebratory view of regionalism's "women's culture" has given way to a more ambivalent stance among many feminist critics in the nineties. As cultural studies and postcolonial theory shifted critical interests, feminist critics began to concentrate on the implication of regionalism in the formation of American elite culture and the processes of nation building. When critics began to apply the triad categories of race, gender, and class to the study of regionalism and to look at it in the context of genres and cultures other than "women's," they addressed not only the essentialism but also the racism and classism inherent in identifying the realities and struggles of white middle-class women as the epitome of femininity and emancipation.[20]

In response to this critical conversation, I explore in this study how the regionalist tradition and its cycles of critical appraisal and denigration intersect with gender politics, shifting definitions of "Americanness," and changing concepts of human and nonhuman relations. Since I share the regionalist interest in the interplay of social and geographical forces, I address regionalism not only as a gender-, race-, or class-specific tradition but describe it more inclusively as a literature of community and place. I am convinced that regionalist writing—because it envisions human life as inextricably linked to both a social and an environmental matrix—can provide relevant insights to current conversations on the shifting categories of nature and culture, subject and object, particular and universal, self, community, and nation. In my examination of the social and environmental implications of regionalist literature and thought, I focus on an author and cultural critic whose work constitutes both a representative instance and an innovative redirection of the confluence of gender, genre, and geography in nineteenth- and twentieth-century regionalism: Mary Hunter Austin.

Austin and the Critical Reception of Her Work

Mary Austin was a feminist, mystic, environmentalist, and a student of Native American and Hispanic cultures. Her literary ambition was to "write imaginatively, not only of people, but of the scene, the totality which is called Nature" (*EH* vii). Giving herself "intransigently to the quality of experience called Folk, and to the frame of behavior known as Mystical," she was a prolific writer (vii). During her lifetime, 1868 to 1934, Austin published more than thirty books and more than two hundred articles in over sixty-five periodicals.[21] Her interests and talents were wide ranging. She wrote short stories, essays, poems, novels, children's literature, and plays. She lectured extensively in women's clubs and at universities such as Berkeley and Yale, covering mostly subjects that we today would associate with cultural studies—for example, "American Literature as an Expression of American Life," "The Novel as Social Force," "Community Culture and Psychology in America," and "The Culture and Primitive Arts of the Southwest" (*AU* 294, *AU* 467). Austin walked in suffrage parades in England and worked for the women's movement in New York. She contributed significantly to the southwestern revival of Native American and Hispanic arts by helping to organize the Indian Arts Fund and the Spanish Colonial Arts Society. She also was a committed environmentalist with conservationist leanings. As a well-known author and prominent public figure, Austin served as a New Mexican representative to the Second Colorado River Conference in 1927.

At the beginning of her writing career Austin was a member of the Arroyo Seco group around the author and editor Charles Lummis in Pasadena, California. Later, Austin cofounded the artists' colony at Carmel, where she lived among writers such as Jack London, Lincoln Steffens, and George Sterling. She traveled extensively through Italy and England, where she associated with the Fabians and befriended H. G. Wells. From 1910 to 1924 Austin dappled in the intellectual scene of New York City but never felt at home there. Nevertheless, she gradually won the respect of the literary establishment and was recognized with a National Arts Club dinner given in her honor in 1922. When Austin settled in the last decade of her life in Santa Fe, New Mexico, she became a prominent member of Mabel Dodge Luhan's salon in Taos. She opened her house to Willa Cather, collaborated with Ansel Adams on their book *Taos Pueblo* (1930), and was awarded an honorary doctoral degree by the University of New Mexico in 1933.

Although Austin voiced strong opinions on a dazzling number of subjects, she still is best known for her first book-length publication, *The Land of Little Rain* (1903). This collection of essays and stories about the desert ecosystem and its human inhabitants established her literary reputation as a western nature writer. Austin did not become a westerner by choice, however. "Mary had not been consulted," Austin comments dryly on her move to California in her autobiography (*EH* 177). Following her graduation from Blackburn College in 1888, the Hunters moved to a homestead in the Tejon district of southern California. Austin, born and raised in Carlinville, Illinois, had difficulties adapting to the desert environment. She "succumbed to malnutrition and nervous collapse within months."[22] Still, Austin's "years of reluctant pilgrimage" in the California deserts, 1888 to 1905, were to provide the foundation for her creative and social work.[23] Several of her stories are based on local tales she heard and "filed for reference" during her first years in California (*EH* 215). Some of her protagonists are modeled on people she knew while living in the California deserts. The narrators and characters often appear as Austin's alter egos. Not surprisingly, Austin considered her work also a record of her personal experience. "I wrote what I lived, what I had observed and understood" (*EH* 320).[24]

Austin's inquiry into the importance of a regional sense of place for American society often provoked heated critical responses. Whether positively or negatively received, her regionalist philosophy and literature rarely elicited neutral reactions from her contemporaries. While B. A. Botkin detected "prophetic genius" in Austin's work, another critic considered her regionalist theory and practice "a magnificent failure."[25] Although Henry Nash Smith regarded Austin as "an early member of the society of the future" and Robert Penn Warren conceded that the "theoretically perfect regionalist must be someone like Mary Austin," other critics heartily disagreed with Austin's argument.[26] Still, they appreciated the depth and scope of her vision. As Lewis Mumford qualified his objections to Austin's line of reasoning, "Mrs. Austin's errors, however, have a certain fertility and vigor that a great many truths lack."[27]

Whether they agreed with her concept of regionalism or disapproved of her vision of a regionalized America, Austin's critics were in accord on the potential relevance that her regionalist perspective held for the contemporary culture and intellectual life of the nation. They were fascinated with the question of whether Austin was "an advance-notice of the formation of an American race," as Henry Nash Smith contended.[28] Was she "the herald of an American acculturation"?[29] Or was "the land still wait[ing] for that prophet who, by his vision, will set the people on the road to fulfillment of Mary Austin's momentary and wavering vision"?[30] What was at stake in the reception of Austin's theory and practice of regionalism, in other words, was the direction of American cultural history. Early Austin critics wondered which options Americans had for developing a distinct national identity. They were less interested in the general epistemological questions that Austin's assertions of geographical determination raised than in the ramifications of Austin's regionalism for conceptualizations of the American nation. Rather than focus on the relation of self and world, Austin's early critics stressed the relation of environment and nation.[31]

Austin was convinced that her southwestern regionalist work would become part of the literary canon. She self-confidently declared that it "had a permanent hold on the future. It could not be overwritten nor left to one side" (EH 349). Yet after her death, most of Austin's books went out of print. Like other women writers, Austin was marginalized when the conservative backlash against feminism gathered force in the twenties and thirties.[32] She was among the female authors excluded from the canon when American literary criticism underwent a process of professionalization and concomitant masculinization in the thirties and forties.[33]

In recent decades, feminist literary critics such as Melody Graulich, Marjorie Pryse, Vera Norwood, Lois Rudnick, and Esther Lanigan Stineman have initiated a reemergence of critical interest in Austin. Thanks to their research, critical attention to Austin's work has increased and the consequent republication of several of Austin's books has made her writing available again to a wider readership. With *Exploring Lost Borders* (1999), edited by Melody Graulich and Elizabeth Klimasmith, a first collection of critical essays on Austin's work has appeared, and recently two monographs on Austin's writing have been published. Mark T. Hoyer offers an in-depth study of Austin's reception of Native American cultures in *Dancing Ghosts* (1998). Barney Nelson sides with Austin's regionalist vision of rural development in *The Wild and the Domestic* (2000). Blending literary criticism and personal essay, Nelson examines Austin's animal stories as she seeks to dissolve the dichotomous views of domestic and wild nature that have worked to devalue rural ways of life. While these books by Hoyer and Nelson open trails through particular areas of Austin's varied terrain, the collection *Exploring Lost Borders* presents a wide range of critical perspectives on Austin's writing. Taken in their entirety, the collected essays reflect the diversity of Austin's interests. Yet, unfortunately, Austin's regionalism is not examined, and the collection format allows no other unifying framework to emerge that would allow readers to relate the various aspects of Austin's writing to one another. For me it is Austin's regionalist orientation that best explains how her feminist perspective, environmentalist agenda, interest in Native American cultures and European American and Hispanic folk traditions, and mysticism cohere. By focusing on her regionalist theory and practice, then, I offer in this study a comprehensive account and synthesizing view of Austin's multifaceted work.

Outline of This Study

This book examines Austin's regionalist reworking of several traditions of American environmental literature at the intersection of Progressive Era realism and modernism—chief among them the traditions of nature writing, women's regionalism, and wilderness quest narratives. It analyzes how Austin's regionalist fiction and nonfiction describe the development of individual and collective senses of place. How does place affect human identity and how do social dynamics, such as gender and race politics or the negotiation of regional and national interests, affect human relations to the land in Austin's texts?

In analyzing Austin's concept and practice of regionalism, this study examines representative instances of her work across the genres—reaching from her first to her last book-length publication, from *The Land of Little Rain* (1903) to *One-Smoke Stories* (1934). The analysis of well-known early collections of essays and stories, such as *Lost Borders* (1909), is complemented by the reading of books that have received comparatively little critical attention, such as Austin's novel on the complications of regional planning, *The Ford* (1917); her biocultural history of the Southwest, *The Land of Journey's Ending* (1924); and her posthumously published novella on feminist regionalist politics, *Cactus Thorn* (1927). Besides her literary work, Austin's critical articles and her theoretical writings are discussed—for instance, her study of the Native American and place-based origins of American literature, *The American Rhythm* (1923, 1930). To round out my analysis of Austin's regionalism, I also draw on unpublished material, on letters, journals, lectures, and notes that allow for a fuller comprehension of Austin's regionalist thought and writing. Whenever pertinent, I refer to Austin's self-fashioning in her autobiography, *Earth Horizon* (1932). My comments on the biographical background of Austin's work will be brief, however, since the life and personality of this unruly, eccentric, and influential woman writer already have received a disproportional amount of critical attention.

This study begins with a chapter on Austin's regionalist theory and aesthetics, surveying the diverse aspects of Austin's regionalist thought and practice and thus providing a context for the following in-depth study of her work. The chapter's first part analyzes the implications of Austin's conviction that cultural identity to a large extent is geographically determined. Its second part more specifically deals with her concept of regionalism as an aesthetic tradition. The chapter portrays Austin's environmentalist and pluralist agenda and her effort to develop an experiential, embodied, and spiritual poetics that would contribute to the regionalist transformation of American culture. The chapter links Austin's regionalism to earlier arguments and also relates it to the current field in American literary criticism that brings the relation among the natural world, environmental perception, and literary practices into focus: ecocriticism.

The second chapter examines Austin's contribution to the field of American environmental literature. The first part traces the concern of Austin's precursors and contemporaries with accurately gendered voices in natural history writing. It asks how we can acknowledge the influence of gender politics, particularly the ideology of separate spheres, on the production and reception of nature writing, without perpetuating essentialist concepts of gendered identity and literary authority. The second part of the chapter examines Austin's environmental nonfiction in the context of her regionalist aesthetic and the Thoreauvian tradition of nature writing. It offers a comparative reading of Austin's *The Land of Little Rain* and Thoreau's natural history essays to delineate the influence that a regionalist orientation can exert on the confluence of scientific, philosophical, and personal perspectives in the nature writing genre. Both authors are shown to encode in their environmental writing the cognitive, experiential, and communicative processes that produce place-based knowledges. The chapter demonstrates that Austin's biocentric perspective, her recognition of the permeable boundaries between subjective and objective modes of nature study, and her insistence on the democratic purpose of scientific research set her apart from most of her contemporaries, who still relied on anthropocentric frameworks, believed in absolute standards of truth, and were deadlocked in a debate on "nature faking."

The third chapter has as its subject the experiences of place of Austin's narrators and their mystical communion with nature. Its first part describes Austin's processual concept of experience and art, linking her regionalist poetics to the notion of environmental resistance and participatory experience that John Dewey later developed in *Art as Experience* (1934). The second section further delineates Austin's biocentric understanding of the place of humans in a world that extends beyond human concerns. It examines Austin's environmentalist use of the tragic desert convention to portray human life as dependent on a nonhuman support system. The third section explores Austin's phenomenological descriptions of mystical union. Her narrators are shown to test their experiential knowledge and spiritual view of their regional environments against the conventions of mechanistic science, orthodox Christianity, and romantic landscape perception. The chapter concludes with a consideration of Austin's ideal of embodied spirituality as the basis for place-centered aesthetics and politics.

The following chapters shift the emphasis from a concern with the processes of individual identity formation to an analysis of the dynamics of regional community building. The fourth chapter analyzes several of Austin's fictional narratives that explore how ideas about the nature of gender and the gender of nature intersect. Particular attention is given to the connections that the texts establish between human and nonhuman relations and the gender codes and racial politics of regional and dominant society. As a regionalist and cultural feminist, Austin objected to the wilderness cult of the Progressive Era. She identified the andropocentric myth of the frontier and an anthropocentric resource mentality as part of a sociocultural framework that interfered with the democratic restructuring and environmental acculturation of American society. Accordingly, Austin joined an ironic critique of masculinist desires to colonize the wilderness with a refutation of both traditional feminized images of the land and the prevalent gender code. This chapter shows that diverse works such as *Lost Borders, Cactus Thorn,* and *One-Smoke Stories* unfold a feminist and environmentalist revision of the association of woman and nature, while asserting the transformative potential of regionalism.

The fifth chapter concentrates on Austin's call for the creation of ecologically sustainable regional communities. Its first section outlines Austin's notion of environmental communalism, especially the concept of indivisible public utilities that she derived from her study of southwestern Pueblo economy. Since Austin developed her vision of a regionalized America in response to her observation of Native American society, the second section takes a closer look at her conception of Native American cultures, examining her critical essays on these cultures in the context of contemporaneous discourses on racial essences and the evolution of national character—noting both Austin's primitivism and her cultural pluralism. The next section returns to the issue of regional economies and land use. It traces Austin's ambivalent response to the extensive European American development of the arid regions in *The Land of Little Rain* and *Lost Borders.* Austin's conservationist orientation, her regionalist reaction to the emerging era of gigantic hydraulic "reclamation" projects, and her concern with the cultural, political, and economic implications of regional planning also provide the focus of the fourth section. In this part Austin's novel *The Ford* is read as a regionalist *Bildungsroman* that dramatizes the masculinist and individualistic bias of mythologized images of the frontier, rejecting golden-age nostalgia, provincial narrow-mindedness, and the capitalist drive behind the development of the rural West. The novel argues for communitarian regional economics and the reconciliation of rural and urban interests.

Austin's democratic ethics also provide the vantage point for the examination of her place- and community-oriented literary practices in the sixth chapter. It is given to the study of Austin's concept of regionalist literature and of her narrative strategies in her early work in comparison with two of her later pieces, *The Land of Journey's Ending* and *One-Smoke Stories*. The last chapter thus returns to the discussion of the relation between language and world, myth and history, self and community with which I began in the first chapter of this study. Chapter 6 details how the composition of Austin's texts reflects the feminist, environmentalist, and pluralist impetus of her regionalism. Tracing the regionalist conversations represented in and enacted by her narratives, the chapter comments on the relation among the authors, narrators, characters, and readers of regional literature. It presents Austin's development from a writer working in the tradition of nineteenth-century women's regionalism to a regionalist author who drew on folklore and Native American concepts of storytelling to create regionalist works that express communal values and envision a democratic, environmentally sound American culture. A brief survey of Austin's regionalist aesthetic and her innovative use of diverse literary traditions concludes the study.

I wrote *Mary Austin's Regionalism: Reflections on Gender, Genre, and Geography* to further the critical appreciation of the scope, complexity, and ambivalences of Austin's work. I am convinced that Austin's regionalism offers insights into the aesthetic and sociopolitical implications of environmental perception and representation that are pertinent to current conversations on place, sustainability, experiential knowledges, the construction of human and nonhuman nature, the ethics of scientific practice, feminist politics, and the dynamics of cross-cultural communication. I have linked my reading of Austin's regionalist work to an examination of the premises that to date have guided critical constructions of regional and environmental traditions in American literary history to offer a reconsideration of regionalism as a democratic literary and political practice of community and place.

1

"THE LAND SETS THE LIMIT"

Austin's Concept of Regionalism

Regional Identity Formation and Community Building

For Mary Austin regional differentiation represented a universal fact of life. She believed with William Carlos Williams that "[t]he locale is the only thing that's universal."[1] In her essay "Regionalism in American Fiction" (1932), Austin argues that regionalism is one of the general principles governing life on earth. "Regionalism, since it is of the very nature and constitution of the planet, becomes at last part of the nature and constitution of the men who live on it" (98). Human identity is necessarily regional, Austin reasons, because "there is no sort of experience that works so constantly and subtly on man as his regional environment" (97). Austin was convinced that the natural environment exerted a significant influence both on the shape of individual lives and on the collective makeup of society.

Her belief that human identity to a large extent is environmentally determined can be traced to her earliest publications. "Not the law, but the land sets the limit," the narrator of *The Land of Little Rain* (1903) declares categorically (3). "For law runs with the boundary, not beyond it," the narrator of *Lost Borders* (1909) specifies in explaining the name of her region (2). Since human existence in the arid regions depends on the population's ability to adapt to the land, regional ways of life develop in response to environmental conditions. Grounded in their environment, they cannot be comprehended apart from their nonhuman matrix. As the narrator points out: "To understand the fashion of any life, one must know the land it is lived in and the procession of the year" (*LLR* 164).

Austin further elaborated the argument in later works such as *The American Rhythm* (1923, 1930) and in the numerous regionalist essays she published in the twenties and thirties. In her article "Regional Culture in the Southwest" (1929), she gives the following definition of regional identity: "A regional culture is the sum, expressed in ways of living and thinking, of the mutual adaptations of a land and a *people:* In the long run, the land wins" (474). While the development of regional cultures is said to involve a reciprocal relationship between the human population and its natural environment, the basic character of these "mutual adaptations" is determined by the land. Considered from a long-term perspective, the environment is seen to control the outcome of the adaptive process. "In the long run, the land wins."

Since the land manifests "immutable forces" (*LB* 80) that remain unaffected by human presence, human survival depends on competent adjustment to environmental conditions. The fatal consequences of a refusal to acquire the necessary environmental knowledge are dramatized in many of Austin's stories. Men go astray and die of thirst in the desert, and towns are destroyed by floods. A population reluctant to "adapt itself willingly and efficiently" is doomed, Austin prophesizes in "Regional Culture in the Southwest" (475). The "land destroys it and makes room for another tribe." Intent on provoking her predominantly white readership into reimagining the relation between their culture and its land base, Austin applies the trope of the vanishing American to European American settlers. In her work the land defines the limits of human existence. The environment determines the possibilities of regional development and by extension also the future of the nation.

REGIONAL IDENTITY FORMATION

How does Austin conceive of this process of geographical determination, of "the mutual adaptations of a land and a people"? Through which acts and responses is human identity environmentally determined? In "Regionalism in American Fiction" Austin describes the process through which people are molded by their environment as a transformation that involves all aspects of their lives. For any person, Austin tells us, the regional environment "is the thing always before his eye, always at his ear, always underfoot. Slowly or sharply it forces upon him behavior patterns such as earliest become the habit of his blood, the unconscious factor of adjustment in all his mechanisms. Of all the responses of his psyche, none pass so soon and surely into the field of consciousness from which all invention and creative effort of every sort proceed" (97). In Austin's account, our natural surroundings profoundly affect our sense of identity and agency in the world. Through our corporeal experience of our environment, we acquire behavioral patterns and bodily habits that govern both our inner processes and outer actions. Even if we are not consciously aware of this interaction, our response to the land and "the particular region called home" (98) is the component that coordinates the biological and social dimensions of our existence.

A similar analysis of the relation of self and world is developed by John Dewey in *Art as Experience* (1934). Dewey points out that our ties to our surroundings provide us with the sense that our inner lives and outer world cohere. "Whenever the bond that binds the living creature to his environment is broken, there is nothing that holds together the various factors and phases of the self. Thought, emotions, sense, purpose, impulsion fall apart. . . . For their unity is found in the coöperative rôles they play in active and receptive relations to the environment" (252). In order to integrate the different aspects of our existence, we need to acknowledge that our individual lives evolve out of and into our human surroundings and the natural world at large. In a way, our mental stability and our ability to act purposefully depend on a relational and reciprocal mode of being—and so does our culture. As Dewey reminds us, "culture is the product not of efforts of men put forth in a void or just upon themselves, but of prolonged and culmulative interaction with environment" (28).

The understanding that nature and culture constitute interrelated rather than mutually exclusive spheres also provides Austin with the basis for developing her theory and practice of regionalism. Her regionalist project is not an attempt to conceptualize and formulate a new synthesis of human and nonhuman, of environment and society, of self and other, then; rather, it is an effort to demonstrate that these elements are already interwoven on the level of lived experience. Austin's regionalist texts repudiate dualistic preconceptions, reminding the readers that nature and culture overlap in significant ways.[2]

Austin's and Dewey's argument that our interactions with the environment play a significant role in the ongoing formation of our sense of selfhood is supported both by phenomenological explanations of perception and by feminist concepts of relational identity. Both accounts of subjectivity assert that it is a basic human need to engage with a world outside ourselves. To conceptualize how our sense of identity depends on the physical experience of social and natural environments, it is helpful to think, as David Abram proposes, "of the sensing body as a kind of open circuit that completes itself only in things, and in the world."[3] The phenomenological understanding of human existence as fundamentally open to the world acknowledges that our senses cannot operate without a world surrounding us. It reminds us that our different senses converge in the perception of a world external to us. Hence, as Abram points out, it allows for the realization that "it is primarily through my engagement with what is *not* me that I effect the integration of my senses, and thereby experience my own unity and coherence" (125).

The phenomenological proposition that we do not live in a "night of identity"[4] explains on the sensory level of perception a phenomenon that also occurs on the psychological level, as feminist inquiries into the dynamics of subject formation have suggested. The experience of difference is integral to the development of identity. Feminist concepts of relational identity, such as the notion of ecological selfhood that Val Plumwood develops in *Feminism and the Mastery of Nature,* acknowledge that our psychological constitution requires us to encounter unmerged others in order to arrive at any sense of being a differentiated self. Plumwood explains, "The reciprocity and mutuality which form such a self are not only compatible with but actually *require* the existence of others who are distinct and not merged . . . union and contact [occur] in active exchange with an other who contributes enough difference to create a boundary to the self" (156). Unlike the stable, self-contained subject of Western Enlightenment discourse, the ecological self is seen as being shaped in dynamic relations of interdependence. Our sense of selfhood develops through the exchange with human and nonhuman others. The contact with whom and what we are not is integral to the development of our sense of self.

AUSTIN'S VISION OF ENVIRONMENTAL SELFHOOD IN *CACTUS THORN*

In her literary and critical writing, Austin argues that the development of individuals and their communities depends on their ongoing engagement with an environing world. Similar to the way in which firsthand experiences of place affect the personal sense of self, regional culture develops out of the collective encounter with the land. According to Austin, individual subject formation and cultural history always involve an interplay of social, cultural, biological, and geographical relations. Narrative dramatizations of this regionalist stance abound in Austin's work. A representative example is the rural heroine of Austin's novella *Cactus Thorn.*[5]

Dulcie Adelaid expresses the author's regionalist philosophy. She observes that her nonbuilt environment, the California desert, exists in its own right, while human survival depends on a successful adaptation to environmental conditions. Despite this apparent imbalance of power, Austin's protagonist regards the land and its human population not as antagonistic but as imbricated elements of a regional world. They are organized according to a common principle, which she indeterminately names "It." Convinced that human orientation is predicated on an embodied experience of place, Dulcie suggests that the development of regional culture should be directed toward realigning society with the organizational pattern of its environment. She explains the necessity of recognizing the nonhuman matrix of human life to her urban lover.

"It is something you learn in a place like this. There is something here." She waved her arm over the wild disorder of the ranges. "It goes on by itself, doing things that you don't see either the beginning of, or the end, except that It has very little to do with men. It can use men, It *will* use them, but It can get on without them. They have to make themselves worth using.

"You remember what happened when you went walking by yourself? You were just thinking and thinking, weren't you? And suddenly you were lost. That was because you got away from—It. And then you were scared. But if you had waited, just held still and waited, It would have come back. You would have found yourself."

"There were things like that in the city to me. The people had gone off by themselves, and they were beginning to run around and shout to one another that this was the way, and this. But if they would keep still, the way would have come forth like a wild thing and shown itself." (*CT* 47)

Because human life unfolds within a larger-than-human world, Austin's heroine explains, individual and collective self-definitions would benefit from a recognition of the nonhuman factors that enter into the formation of personal and collective identities. For Dulcie a culture that does not acknowledge its continuity with the natural environment is bound to remain confused about its place and purpose in the world. Blind to its nonhuman support system, it ignores an important condition of its existence. Having dissolved "the bond that binds the living creature to his environment," society resembles a terrified person who has lost his or her way. In Dulcie's eyes such a society is reduced to a hub of random motion and undirected activity. It makes its members run around without getting anywhere—except maybe farther away from one another.

Since Dulcie explains her regionalist ethic as the representative of western rural life to a visiting East Coast urbanite, it may seem as if she merely restates in regionalized terms the familiar opposition between wilderness appreciation and cosmopolitanism. The West is identified as the site of direct contact with wild nature, the East as the locus of urbanization and civilized culture. The West enables wholesome experiences of tranquility and a benignly ordered world; the East provokes confusion, self-aggrandizement, and senseless activity. Yet Dulcie neither returns with her argument to the wilderness cult prevalent at the turn of the nineteenth century nor does she advocate a nostalgia steeped version of regionalism.[6] She recommends neither a sojourn in the wilderness nor an antimodernist fantasy of a preindustrial golden age as an antidote to the complications of modern life. She acknowledges that the decidedly nonhuman appearance of her region's "wild disorder" is as alien to her visitor as the bustle of eastern urban life is to her. Comparing her friend's to her own regional experience, Dulcie asserts that cityscape and desertscape offer the same possibility for realigning human life with the environing world. The "way" is present in both desert and city.[7] Since "It" is the fundamental structure or pattern of the world, it can be perceived in all places—provided that one has acquired the necessary calmness, patience, and attentiveness.

Dulcie's argument that it is the manner of engaging with one's surroundings that makes the difference between being lost and finding oneself modifies the romantic belief in the integrative and healing function of encounters with the natural world. She extends it to include modern manmade environments. In this way her reasoning eschews the regressive tendencies that contemporaneous critics of regionalist literature found fault with. As Henry Nash Smith sums up in "The Feel of the Purposeful Earth" the critical climate at the time when Austin wrote *Cactus Thorn,* to "a New Humanist or to a Young Intellectual . . . talk of regional cultures sounds either Rousseauistic (and therefore evil) or naïve (and therefore ridiculous)" (31). What matters according to Austin's heroine are not the relative merits of different types of spaces but the particular mode of a person's or culture's engagement with place. Keeping with Austin's call for the development of plural regional cultures, Dulcie asserts the value of any sense of place, rural or urban, that involves the recognition that human life evolves out of and into a larger-than-human world.

CORPOREAL CONVERSATIONS

For Dulcie this realization is best facilitated by an embodied engagement with one's environment in a calm and alert state of mind. As she reminds her friend, human orientation is predicated on a somatic awareness of one's physical situation. He got lost on his walk, she says, because he was absorbed in his thoughts. Preoccupied with the workings of his mind, "just thinking and thinking, weren't you?" he isolated himself from the outside world. As a result, he "got away from—It" and lost his way. By valorizing the corporeal conversation between self and world, Dulcie affirms the environmental situatedness of human life.

In this respect Dulcie's account reads like a modern echo of Thoreauvian, rather than Emersonian, transcendentalism. Austin's words call up the epiphany that Henry David Thoreau describes in the "Monday" chapter of *A Week on the Concord and Merrimack Rivers* (1849). Sleeping in the open during a storm, his back pressed into the grass and attentively listening to the passing thunder, the speaker looks up at the night sky; he feels related to the stars and is elated by the feeling "that IT was well" (213). He is physically aware of a universal order, principle, or God operating in the natural world. "I see, smell, taste, hear, feel, that everlasting Something to which we are allied, at once our maker, our abode, our destiny, our very Selves; the one historic truth, the most remarkable fact which can become the distinct and uninvited subject of our thought, the actual glory of the universe; the only fact which a human being cannot avoid recognizing, or in some way forget or dispense with" (213). An effect of his embodied awareness of his surroundings, the epiphany itself is a somatic experience that involves all his senses.

Austin's and Thoreau's narratives suggest that the contemplation of human embodiedness provides an ideal starting point for reflections on the value of an environmentally grounded sense of identity. Inquiring what it means to be human in a larger-than-human world, both Austin and Thoreau focus on embodied experiences. The body indeed is an excellent case in point for assertions of the continuity of self and world. Our existence as bodies, who eat, breathe, grow, and decompose in social and natural environments, renders highly instable any dichotomy we may construct between nature and culture. Since bodies are to a certain extent pliable, they are shaped by and are shaping the matrix they live in, as feminist theorists such as Judith Butler, Elizabeth Grosz, and Donna Haraway recently have argued. The body always belongs to both realms, it is culturally molded and biologically given, and it acts in social contexts as well as in ecological systems. The transitions and overlaps between natural and cultural dimensions are an integral property of our bodies.

According to Austin, an embodied sense of place allows people to align the biological and cultural dimensions of their lives. It enables them to exchange a preoccupation with human concerns—the unproductive and hectic state of having "gone off by themselves" and the concept of culture, in Dewey's words, as something "men put forth in a void or just upon themselves"—for an attentive engagement with external realities that include but are not limited to human affairs. Paying attention to what lies outside the merely human ken, whether this is natural or supernatural, the encounter with what is other returns us to ourselves with a clearer sense of self. The "everlasting Something" now is recognized as "our very Selves." In other words, the experience of difference issues into an experience of continuity that deepens the understanding of our subjectivity. Dulcie describes to her friend this paradoxical movement in which the focus on the other leads to a heightened comprehension of the self. "But if you had waited, just held still and waited, It would have come back. You would have found yourself" (CT 47).

AUSTIN'S CONCEPT OF GEOGRAPHICAL DETERMINATION

Austin's idea of geographical determination has been admired as radical and utopian and dismissed as naïve and reactionary. B. A. Botkin attributed "cosmic grandeur" to her insights, whereas Mark Van Doren was more skeptical, finding that Austin's work "is impressive, and though it is not convincing it is great."[8] While most regionalists of Austin's time as well as contemporary bioregionalists and cultural geographers would agree with Austin's notion that cultural identity represents an interplay of social and geographical forces, the extent to which the nonhuman environment factors into the formation of regional culture was and still is open to debate. As Jared Diamond notes, "the notion that environmental geography and biogeography influenced societal development is an old idea. Nowadays, though, the view is not held in esteem by historians; it is considered wrong or simplistic, or it is caricatured as environmental determinism and dismissed. . . . Yet geography obviously has *some* effect on history; the open question concerns how much effect, and whether geography can account for history's broad pattern."[9]

The question to which degree place exerts an influence on the development of regional and by extension national society is central to Austin's work. Since many of her texts assert that nonhuman environmental conditions take precedence over human engineered factors—"not the law, but the land sets the limit"—it seems as if Austin advocated a strong form of geographical determination. Her narratives and essays frequently maintain that geography designs "history's broad pattern."

Yet while Austin was certainly convinced that the land should affect the pattern of regional cultures and that regional cultures in turn should determine the character of national culture, her texts also tend to acknowledge that regional identity formation is not a natural occurrence but requires directed effort and thus represents cultural work. As Austin contends in her lecture "What Is a Native Culture?" the colonization of the American continent demonstrates "that merely to be born in a given spot does not make a man native to that place" (1).[10] She argues that one becomes native to the place one inhabits solely by allowing one's natural and social environment to dominate one's habitus, outlook, and behavior. For Austin the determining factors are the climate and unbuilt environment; the mode of economy; and moral, religious, and philosophical values and systems of belief (1–2). Once these new influences are greater than the disposition acquired in previous environments, Austin concludes, "we have a native culture" (2).

Austin's inclusion of social processes, such as "the forming and reforming of new social patterns" and "the conflicts of racial temperaments," in her list of forces that direct the development of place-based cultures makes her concept of regionalism relevant to modern life in (post)industrialized Western societies, where the majority of the population leads urbanized lives in predominantly human built environments.[11] Austin's awareness of both social and natural influences is particularly important to note in light of the suspicions current critics have voiced, that regionalism represents just one more essentialism trap. While Austin's style, choice of words, and logic are bound to elicit nervous responses from contemporary readers, she usually does not present sociohistorical change as a natural process, directed entirely by nonhuman forces. She seeks not to exalt a preindustrial rural American nation but to conceptualize human identity and "the formation of a democratic society out of such diverse human materials as America has to work with" as bound to both a social and an environmental matrix.[12]

But if Austin did not regard the processes of adaptation an automated response to environmental factors, why did she routinely insist that human identity was geographically determined? Austin plausibly overstated her point for strategic reasons as she sought to convince her readers of the necessity of developing sustainable relations to their land base. For her it was a development into which a complicated web of human and nonhuman forces entered. If one wanted to expand on Austin's regionalist credo, one could say that the land sets the limit, but it does not dictate the process.

THE SIGNIFICANCE OF THE ENVIRONMENT IN DEFINITIONS OF AMERICAN IDENTITY

Austin's emphasis on the environment as a factor in the formation of cultural identity links her concept of regionalism to a long tradition of arguments about the nation's possibilities for developing a uniquely American culture. Since Americans tended to see the assimilation of new immigrants as dependent not only on their political allegiance to the republican ideology and on their acquisition of a common language but also on their contact with the land, the environment traditionally held a prominent place in definitions of American national characteristics. A famous expression of this position is Frederick Jackson Turner's essay "The Significance of the Frontier in American History" (1893), in which he argues that the development of American society could only be explained in terms of the westward movement of the settlements and the consequent colonization of the wilderness. Turner's dictum that the "frontier is the line of most rapid and effective Americanization" because the "wilderness masters the colonist" and forces him or her to either "accept the conditions which it furnishes, or perish" (3–4) testifies to the widespread belief in the assimilatory powers of the immigrant's encounter with the environment. While Austin did not subscribe to a Turnerian view of American history, her work echoes the established rhetoric that "the land will not be lived in except in its own fashion" (*LLR* 88) or that the "really astonishing thing would have been to find the American people as a whole resisting the influence of natural environment in favor of the lesser influences of a shared language and a common political arrangement" ("Regionalism in American Fiction" 98).

Generally speaking, the colonization of the American continent was envisioned as a process in which nature was transformed into culture, as

28

far as the agricultural development of the land was concerned, and in which culture was transformed into nature—in regard to the settlers. For the Americanization of the immigrant population was supposed to effect not only the cultural and social assimilation of the first generation into the American citizenry but also to culminate in the evolution of a new, distinctly American race. An exemplary description of this passage from a culturally to a biologically defined concept of national identity is offered by Hector Saint Jean de Crèvecoeur in his *Letters from an American Farmer* (1782): "He becomes an American by being received into the broad lap of our great *Alma Mater*. Here individuals of all nations are melted into a new race of men" (561). Although concepts of race changed considerably from Crèvecoeur's to Austin's times, a fundamental idea remained intact: Americanization involved a magical transformation of the newly acquired political, social, and geographical aspects of the immigrants' lives into biological reality.

This aspect is also present in Austin's work. In *The American Rhythm* (1923), Austin speculates on the influence of environmental factors on "the becoming race of Americans" (14). She describes the colonization of the American continent as an adaptive process that results in the physical transformation of the recently immigrated settlers. Austin's account lends a mythical quality to American history. "There was hunger in man for free flung mountain ridges, untrimmed forests, evidence of structure and growth. Life set itself to new processions of seed time and harvest, the skin newly tuned to seasonal variations, the very blood humming to new altitudes" (14).

Austin pictures the creation of the new "race of Americans" not as a singular event, however, but as an ongoing process that repeats itself with significant variations in each generation. In the course of our lives, Austin proposes, our experiential alignment with the rhythms of our natural surroundings becomes so ingrained that it begins to function analogous to our instincts. For Austin instinct is but another term for the "coördinations achieved as a result of habitual experiential adjustments to environment" (*AR* 149). Since our acquired regional identity is part of our physical makeup, Austin reasons, it can become hereditary. It can be passed on biologically "from the parent to the offspring," although, Austin kids, not as easily or intact as the family jewels (7, 150).

Since Austin embraces Lamarckian concepts of cultural evolution to predict the emergence of an American race in central works such as *The*

American Rhythm, it is helpful to briefly consider her logic in the context of nativist discourse. Historically, the Lamarckian belief that cultural components passed into the pool of transmittable biological traits had fostered a conceptualization of assimilation as a natural process that followed its own laws and did not have to be enforced. Since assimilation was supposed to occur regardless of the national origins of the immigrants, it might seem as if the idea of the geographical determination of American national character would posit a fundamental challenge to "the principle of racial consistency."[13] For if the contact with a common environment is seen to effect the evolution of a new race, the different races participating in this process cannot be defined as given immutable elements of identity. Yet, despite its stated universal applicability, the environmental definition of American nationality from its inception was a racialized concept since it excluded nonwhite people, in particular African Americans and Native Americans, on the basis of their racial identity.

Austin's argument, however, departs from this nativist logic. First, in her account, the process does apply to all races. Native Americans are presented to European Americans as role models in adaptation due to their longstanding experience and expertise in inhabiting American environments. Second, Austin argues that the process does not simply occur but requires cultural work and cross-cultural negotiations and the balancing of regional and national interests. Instead of making a nativist argument, then, Austin defines *ethnicity* as a positionality that shares with other components of human identity a genesis in sociocultural processes that are specifically concerned with relating the human to the nonhuman, with negotiating the conditions of human life within an ecological matrix. Both the social and environmental dimensions of human life thus become transparent; their interrelatedness, their continuities and discontinuities, are the subject of Austin's inquiry.

Austin's discussion of ethnicity as a factor in the formation of regional culture in her 1929 essay "Regional Culture in the Southwest" is a case in point. With the article Austin contributed to a symposium on the question of whether the Southwest could develop a unique culture "more satisfying and profound" than the imported dominant European American culture (474). In a familiar mode she argues that the region offers the environment and the Native American and Hispanic traditions to do so. She adds that the quality of a regional culture depends not only on the population's willingness to adapt but also on its racial profile. Only a "particularly good stock" will produce a "high" regional culture (475). Among the characteristics that determine the regional potential of a "stock," however, Austin enlists again the instinctual response to the environment that the process of experiential alignment with the environment facilitates. The "White elements," she concludes, still have not committed themselves sufficiently to a local way of life. Lacking the "cultural disposition . . . to understand and develop the country upon which it lives," the European American population is bent on "imposing its derived notions" on the environment (475).

Closing the circle by reasoning that regional identity is influenced by the ethnicity of the population engaged in the process of adaptation and that this ethnicity is not a naturally given component of identity but a result of the cultural practices that a group engages in as it tries to or refuses to adapt to its environment, Austin presents region and nation building as a response to biological and cultural as well as human and nonhuman conditions. Instead of naturalizing concepts of regional and national identity through a recourse to nativist views on the conditions and consequences of adaptation to the American continent, Austin's argument grounds biology in cultural work. When Austin asks, "[W]hat is race but a pattern of response common to a group of people who have lived together under a given environment long enough to take a recognizable pattern?" she suggests that race to a certain extent is a product of cultural practices and that cultural practices inflect human biology.[14]

The major achievement of Austin's theoretical regionalist writings, it seems to me, are those argumentative instances in which she elucidates the interrelatedness of the natural and cultural aspects of human identity and describes the perpetual transformation of one into the other, without reducing one to the other. Austin's cross-translation neither relegates all of biology to the cultural realm nor does it completely naturalize the cultural. It amounts to an argument that human identity is both culturally conditioned and naturally given. For Austin regional and ethnic identities are neither entirely determined by the nonhuman environment nor are they an entirely intrahuman concern.

In sum, Austin contended that the regional encounter with the land constituted the native origin of national character. For her, "the processes of regional culture" were the source "from which the only sound patriotism springs" ("Regionalism in American Fiction" 104). In shifting the balance of power from nation to region, Austin's argument exhibits one of the prime characteristics of the American regionalism of the twenties and thirties. As Robert L. Dorman demonstrates in his seminal study *Revolt of the Provinces*, the regionalists of the interwar years routinely questioned national self-definitions to dissolve centripetal distributions of power. Donald Davidson, for instance, proposes in his essay "Regionalism and Nationalism in American Literature" that "Regionalism is a name for a condition under which the national American literature exists as a literature: that is, its constant tendency to decentralize rather than to centralize; or to correct overcentralization by conscious decentralization" (53). By defining regional culture and diversity as the ground for the development of national identity, Austin can argue that the leveling of regional difference impoverishes national culture while the flourishing of a multiplicity of regional cultures contributes to the nation's prosperity and progress. Her assertion that regional interests serve national interests since regional identity fortifies national identity allows Austin to counter contemporaneous critiques of the regionalist project as a post–Civil War retrieval of agrarian sectionalism and lends authority to her rejection of a homogenized national culture. Austin can now legitimately criticize the "vast, pale figure of America" and call for the acknowledgement of "several Americas, in many subtle and significant characterizations."[15]

Regionalist Literature: The Relations among Environments, Writers, Readers, and Texts

Austin conceived of regionalism, as we have seen, as a place-based mode of identity formation and cultural development that followed an environmentalist and pluralist agenda and aimed at the reimagination of regional and national society. This section asks how Austin's sociopolitical stance informed her concept and practice of regionalist literature. How can we conceive of literature as a response to experiences of place and as an expression of cultural practices grounded in specific geographies? What exactly is regional literature?

AUSTIN'S DEPARTURE FROM LOCAL COLOR AESTHETICS

In the essay "Regionalism in American Fiction" Austin argues that an American literary masterpiece has to "come up through the land, shaped by the author's own adjustments to it" (101). She emphasizes that it is only through firsthand experience that authors can acquire a solid understanding of the region they are writing about. "The regionally interpretive book must not only be about the country, it must be of it" (106).[16] This requirement may seem so obvious as to be redundant; yet it is a crucial criterion that helps to differentiate Austin's concept of regionalist literature from other forms of regional writing. When we think, for instance, of a certain kind of local color fiction—fiction written about a region by outsiders for the amusement of an outside audience—the requirement may seem less superfluous.[17]

Austin repeatedly sought to distinguish her version of regionalism from local color literature, which she thought offered merely "an automobile eye view" of a particular region, "something slithered and blurred, nothing so sharply discriminated that it arrests the speed-numbed mind to understand" ("Regionalism in American Fiction" 107). The distinction informs her early collections, including *The Land of Little Rain* and *Lost Borders,* whose narrators over and again distance themselves from local color fiction. They mock the local color tradition in stories such as "Jimville—A Bret Harte Town," identifying it as a male-dominated field of literary production, written by short-term visitors to a region for the amusement of a disaffected readership.[18]

The suggestion that the perspectives and objectives of local color and regionalist writers are incompatible also provides a fitting conclusion for the *Lost Borders* story "The Last Antelope."[19] The story addresses the environmental degradation of California's arid regions by describing the death of the region's last wild antelope. The animal dies at the hands of a European American settler, who epitomizes the destructive "love of mastery, which for the most part moves men into new lands" (74). At the end of the emblematic story about the death of the last antelope, the narrator contrasts her understanding of regional reality with the perceptions of a local color writer. "There was a man once who skidded through Lost Borders in an automobile with a balloon silk tent and a folding tin bath-tub, who wrote some cheerful tales about that country, mostly untrue, about rattlesnakes coiling under men's blankets at night, to afford heroic occasions in the morning, of which circumstance seventeen years' residence failed to furnish a single instance" (80).

The nonresident writer, unwilling to adapt to local customs, is trapped in his romantic preconceptions of western life and gains only superficial impressions of the places he visits. Cut off from the physical and emotional experience of the region by a buffer of modern comforts, his insight into local ways of life remains as shallow as his engagement with the fundamental questions that his stories potentially could raise. Unable to "slough off and swallow [his] acquired prejudices as a lizard does his skin" (*LLR* 113), he writes "cheerful tales" that contrast sharply with the narrator's sad story about the environmental degradation of her region. As a resident writer, the narrator defines her responsibilities primarily in regard to her local community. She is more concerned with the preservation of her environment than with the entertainment of an outside readership. Her regional sense of identity allows her to explore the political, emotional, and spiritual significance of the events she reimagines, in contrast to the local color writer whose limited imagination adheres to preestablished story patterns. The text thus presents the narrator's experiential engagement with place as a source of environmental and communal ethics as well as the basis of original rather than imitative art.

AUSTIN'S EXPERIENTIAL CONCEPT OF REALIST LITERATURE

Austin's experiential concept of literary and critical practice distinguishes her regionalist version of realism not only from local color writing but also from the Howellsian tradition of realism. Austin contended that William Dean Howells initiated "the thinning out of American fiction by a deliberate choice of the most usual, the most widely distributed of American story incidents, rather than the most intensively experienced."[20] She considered Howells and Sinclair Lewis representative of a trend among American novelists to eschew regional subject matter and to withdraw "from the soil, undertaken on the part of Howells in a devout pilgrim spirit, bent on the exploration of the social expression of democracy, and on the part of Lewis with a fine scorn and a hurt indignation for the poor simp."[21] As an advocate of regional diversity and an experiential concept of culture, Austin suspected that certain forms of realism served to homogenize the American literary imagination. She saw them as offering generalized, ready-made images of American realities rather than inviting readers to participate in the creation of detailed, regionally specific fictional worlds. Therefore, Austin argued, they could not involve their readers in an imaginative process that would heighten their awareness of their present living conditions and expand their understanding of other parts of the country. Austin blamed both realist writers and the reading public for this situation. For her, the "insistence on fiction shallow enough to be common to all regions, so that no special knowledge of other environments than one's own is necessary to appreciation of it, has pulled down the whole level of American fiction" ("Regionalism in American Fiction" 99). In her work Austin sought to develop a regionalist form of realist writing that on one hand would allow her to describe in a spirit of detached sympathy and personal involvement the specifics of everyday life in the arid regions and that on the other hand would encourage her readers to reflect self-critically on their own ways of living in place.

A fuller portrait of the experiential concept of literature at the core of Austin's regionalist aesthetic emerges in *The Land of Little Rain*. Its self-referential narrator realizes Austin's ideal of a regionally committed writer. The narrator is cast as a long-term resident of the region of which she writes. She considers it her task to represent regional realities accurately, "to keep faith with the land" (ix). For Austin, to render the land faithfully does not mean to practice a form of mimetic realism, however, as the formulation may suggest. Austin's narrator makes no pretensions of offering an exhaustive objective description of the desert and its climate, flora, and fauna. Instead, she reflects on the basis and context of her observations and comments on the psychological, sociopolitical, and ecological implications of her narrative practices. She regularly addresses her readers to remind them that their perceptions and representations of the natural world are subjective and culturally mediated.

The preface to *The Land of Little Rain* offers a representative example of Austin's regionalist realism. In it the narrator discusses the options she has for selecting or inventing appropriate names for the places she describes. She prefers Native American to English place names because she considers the supposedly "Indian fashion of name-giving" to have the greater propensity for capturing regional particularities (vii). She uses names such as Oppapago, "The Weeper," for a mountain with "streams that run down from it continually like tears," while she dismisses established geographical names that fail to provide adequate characterizations of the land.[22] To qualify her preference she contrasts European American and Native American customs of naming. "For if I love a lake known by the name of the man who discovered it, which endears itself by reason of the close-locked pines it nourishes about its borders, you may look in my account to find it so described. But if the Indians have been there before me, you shall have their name, which is always beautifully fit and does not originate in the poor human desire for perpetuity" (vii–viii).[23]

The narrator thinks that her European American cultural heritage interferes with her attempt to give a personal and specific account of the land. She seeks to render the land in a way which would express her personal relation to the region—the lake, after all, is said to "endear itself" and she renames it to express her impression of the lakeshore's vegetation—without erasing the features of the land that caused her to respond. She adopts a flexible practice of naming in recognition of "a fluid world where identities are relational and communal rather than tied to a single fixed image."[24]

As an environmentally committed regionalist writer, the narrator is wary of literary conventions that would foster in her readers a disaffected stance toward the natural world. She directly addresses her audience: "And I am in no mind to direct you to delectable places toward which you will hold yourself less tenderly than I. So by this fashion of naming I keep faith with the land" (*LLR* ix). The narrator asks her readers to engage as she does in an environmental learning process. On this condition, they "shall have such news of the land, of its trails and what is astir in them, as one lover of it can give to another" (xi). The narrator's self-reflexive comments thus draw the reader's attention to the ongoing negotiations between self and world in which any writer would have to engage to fulfill the "two indispensable conditions" that Austin identifies in "Regionalism in American Fiction" as the prerequisites for regional writing. "The environment entering constructively into the story, and the story reflecting in some fashion the essential qualities of the land" (106).

THE RELATIONS AMONG ENVIRONMENT, AUTHOR, AND TEXT

But how can the biophysical environment enter a text? And how can a text reflect an unconstructed reality? At least in the contemporary critical climate, attempts to establish causal relations between the environment and literary practice as well as assertions that there may be such a thing as unbuilt reality tend to trigger the objections of poststructurally inclined critics. They ask, for instance, as does Peter Quigley in his essay "Rethinking Resistance," "If our 'reading' of the world is thoroughly constructed and if reference to a base is illusory, then what is it that we could possibly be faithful to, and how would we measure such faithfulness?" (304). The inquiry certainly is relevant for both Austin's theory and practice of regionalism and for ecocritical approaches to literary studies. This becomes even clearer when we consider the recent remarks of another irritated critic, Dana Phillips, which seem diametrically opposed to Austin's understanding of literature. "Poetry is not a 'manifestation' of anything, apart from the conscious decisions and unconscious motivations of poets, and the structural and aesthetic effects of the genres and languages in which they write. To suppose otherwise is occult" (581). Yet the concept of textuality that underlies this statement is not as incompatible with the idea of geographical influence as the exasperated tone would suggest. One could, for instance, rephrase the initial questions as follows: How does the experience of place enter into "the conscious decisions and unconscious motivations of poets"? How does it affect their textual practice and thus eventually enter the text? Rather than posit any direct or organic relation between text and environment, I propose with Austin that we produce our "thoroughly constructed" readings of the world in response to both sociocultural and environmental realities. Since the subjective, embodied experience of our environments is an integral element of our lives, it can also inflect our critical and literary practice.

"To keep faith with the land," in this sense, means to keep faith with our culturally and personally mediated experiences or embodied readings of the land. The base of reference shifts from the nonhuman environment to our experience of our surroundings; this experience, however—and this is the crux—is not an entirely human affair but a conversation between ourselves and the world that transforms and to a certain extent thus also produces self and other. As SueEllen Campbell reasons in "The Land and Language of Desire," our choices "depend on the shape of our lives—where we live, how we spend our days, how we've been taught—and especially on the role the land itself has played in what we might call the writing of our textuality" (209). To conceive of human identity and agency as an interplay of social and environmental factors allows us to reject the limited either/or logic of the determinism versus constructionism debates. Literature and criticism are neither organic manifestations of natural forces nor disembodied effects of cultural dynamics.

What assumptions, then, does Austin's regionalist aesthetic make about the relation between the environment, its perception and investment with meaning by human subjects, and the literary communication of these conceptualizations of the natural world? Austin was convinced that prediscursive, nonhuman systems of meaning existed—ecological and spiritual principles of organization, for example, that would function independent of human readers. The guiding universal principle or "way" that underlies the regionalist ethic of *Cactus Thorn*, as examined in the introduction to this study, is a representative instance of this perspective. Yet although Austin believed in a nonhuman world of consequence and significance, her theoretical proposition on the intersections of environment and text in regionalist literature—the "environment entering constructively into the story, and the story reflecting in some fashion the essential qualities of the land"—is misleading. For the assertion that the text needs to reflect an apparently already existing and essential reality suggests that Austin naïvely conceives of language as an instrument to mirror a prediscursive world and that she reduces the author to a passive recipient of sensory data, to a portal through which the environment can enter the narrative. Although Austin certainly was not an early believer in what we today would call radical constructionism, she also did not think of the author as a mere medium through which impressions of the object world passed unaltered into the realm of textuality. Instead, as the above discussion of the preface to *The Land of Little Rain* as regionalist realist writing demonstrates, Austin was keenly aware of the conceptual and textual conventions that come into play when literary attempts are made to communicate the mediated experience of being, or imagining oneself to be, out in nature.

Convinced that our human, sociocultural, and personal perspectives enable and delimit our access to the natural world, Austin insisted that nature writers had to include their personal response to the environment in their accounts. In *Earth Horizon* she states provocatively, "It is time somebody gave a true report. All the public expects of the experiences of practicing Naturists is the appearance, the habits, the incidents of the wild; when the Naturist reports upon himself, it is mistaken for poeticizing" (188). Since the personal experiences and sociohistorical situation of writers inevitably inform their descriptions, Austin reasons, the writer's subjectivity and his or her relation to the place under consideration should be recognized as an essential component of nature writing. Given the situatedness of our perceptions, a "true report" for Austin has to be self-reflexive; it has to strike "the authentic note of confession" (188). If an account limits itself to the presentation of factual information and does not comment on the conditions under which the presented knowledge was acquired, the observations are falsified and the report in its entirety cannot be considered accurate.

Accordingly, Austin includes in her natural history writing meta-narrative comments and self-critically reflects on her textual practice. Through the persona of the narrator, she offers us, for instance in *The Land of Little Rain,* both a fictional record of regional identity formation and a discussion of how the experience of a particular place can be communicated in writing. Although the narrator wishes to present herself as a "mere recorder" of regional life and reality (*LLR* 112), she is aware that her experiences are subjective. Therefore, she encourages her readers to "blow out this bubble from your own breath" (113). Instead of making claims to neutral observation, she marks in her account the experiential basis for her writing. She interpolates her descriptions of the desert ecosystem and its inhabitants with general discussions of the relations between language, self, other, and world.

In this way Austin attributes in her stories and essays a fundamentally reciprocal character to the relations between regionalist authors, including nature writers, and their environments. She suggests that the world inscribes itself in the subject while the subject inscribes itself in the world and that both are changed through their interaction. Thus Austin defines the authors' experiential negotiations between their sense of self and sense of place as the basis of environmental literature.

THE AESTHETIC EXPERIENCE OF
ENVIRONMENTAL RESISTANCE

Austin's regionalist aesthetic and her experiential concept of literature at times seem to anticipate the theory of art that John Dewey developed in *Art as Experience.* Austin shared with Dewey the conviction that the innovative force of a work of art rested on its aptitude to express the rhythms of the embodied conversation between self and world. In *Art as Experience* Dewey describes experience as a process of communication between self and environment in which the subject is neither entirely distinct from nor completely merged with but participant in the world. As Dewey puts it, "Experience is the result, the sign, and the reward of that interaction of organism and environment which, when it is carried to the full, is a transformation of interaction into participation and communication" (22). Both quotidian experiences and their intensified aesthetic renderings—art in Dewey's sense as "the clarified and intensified development of traits that belong to every normally complete experience" (46)—represent the result of ongoing exchanges with and readjustments to the world. For Dewey an experience always entails that self and world, step-by-step, are bound together as shapeshifting yet nonidentical entities. Therefore, Dewey points out, the "factor of resistance is worth especial notice at this point. Without internal tension there would be a fluid rush to a straightaway mark; there would be nothing that could be called development and fulfillment" (138).

Dewey's notion that participatory experience represents a cumulative response to resisting environmental forces reminds us that self and world, as well as the inner and outer realities of our lives, are mutually constitutive, interconnected, and yet disparate modes of reality. We create our experiences in a reciprocal process that originates in our encounter with forces that invite yet resist us and that builds in dialogue with these forces as we try to synchronize them with our way of being. "In an experience," Dewey explains, "things and events belonging to the world, physical and social, are transformed through the human context they enter, while the live creature is changed and developed through its intercourse with things previously external to it" (246). In other words, experiences can be considered relational processes into which the person enters not as a self-contained agent or "carrier of an experience" but as a communicating agency, as "a factor absorbed in what is produced" (250). Dewey's notion of environmental resistance, aesthetic tension, and experience as cumulative process can help us understand how the relations between embodied subjects and their surroundings give rise to experiences that reveal and express the continuity of self and world without denying that the encountered others also have an existence outside the formed relations.

Austin gives a representative account of this process in her portrait of her first encounter with southern California. "There was something else there besides what you find in the books" (*EH* 187), Austin writes of her initial impressions of the San Joaquin Valley, through which she traveled with her family on their way from Los Angeles to their new homestead in Tejon country in 1888.[25] In the unfamiliar landscape, Austin perceives a quality that arrests her attention. She phenomenologically describes it as "a lurking, evasive Something, wistful, cruel, ardent; something that rustled and ran, that hung half-remotely, insistent on being noticed, fled from pursuit, and when you turned from it, leaped suddenly and fastened on your vitals" (187). It is a presence that escapes her intellectual awareness but that encroaches upon her when she diverts her conscious attention. It provokes an "insistent experiential pang" and a desire to capture the sensation in language (187). Yet this "Beauty-in-the wild, yearning to be made human" resists easy acquaintance (187). Although Austin perceives it as inviting her to transform it into something human, her experience of this dimension of the landscape first requires her to change in response to her environment. The success of her effort to observe and describe the "evasive Something" is predicated, she feels, on her capacity to give "herself up wholly to the mystery of the arroyos" and to "be alone with it for uninterrupted occasions, in which they might come to terms" (187). In other words, as Austin physically experiences and perceptually makes sense of her surroundings, she changes in relation to the world while she also transforms the reality that she encounters. She seeks to understand and describe that which is not her, which is not human, and which she cannot readily assimilate by reconfiguring her subjective world. This process includes a negotiation of self and world, a mutual coming to terms, that is not innately harmonious but also marked by tensions. Despite her "kindred yearning," the "wistful, cruel, ardent" land escapes her grasp (187). To bring her fleeting sensations and her response to what she perceives as the spirit of the place, its genius loci, into concrete verbal form, she first has to adopt a flexible sense of self that allows her to continually realign herself in relation to her environment. In Austin's words, she has "to wrestle with the Spirit of the Arroyos" (188).

AUSTIN'S AESTHETICS, ECOCRITICAL PRACTICE, AND ENVIRONMENTAL ETHICS

Austin insisted that human perceptions of the natural world are situated and that the biophysical environment nonetheless should not be subsumed under the human world of linguistically mediated reality. Her ideas predate current ecological thought and ecocritical approaches to literary studies. Since "we do not create the land itself or its other inhabitants," as SueEllen Campbell writes ("The Land and Language of Desire" 205), the land matters beyond our readings of it. For an ecological understanding of reality the ability to distinguish, for instance, between a specific river as a thing in itself and the human construction of particular images of this river is pertinent. From an ecological perspective the respective components are both separate and converging. They are interrelated, Holmes Rolston points out in *Philosophy Gone Wild*, in that for "every landscape, there is an inscape; mental and environmental horizons reciprocate" (24). In studying the relations between literary, cultural, and social practices and the environment, ecocritics, therefore, tend to think of categories such as perception and representation or empirical reality and social construction as polarities in a continuum of interrelated processes rather than as mutually exclusive spheres. They draw on a concept of textuality that grants that reality is intersubjectively produced but also insists there are nonhuman texts that are not dependent on human readers. Lawrence Buell, for instance, argues in *The Environmental Imagination* "that reported contacts with particular settings are intertextually, intersocially constructed" and "that the nonbuilt environment is one of the variables that influence culture, text, and personality" (13). This understanding, Buell points out, avoids "reductionism at the level of formal representation, such as to compel us to believe either that the text replicates the object-world or that it creates an entirely distinct linguistic world" (13). Instead of following such a dichotomizing logic, an ecocritical reading, as delineated above, can interpret literary renderings of nature as aesthetic enactments of imaginary and actual encounters with the natural world within both a social and an ecological context.

For a brief illustration of an ecocritical perspective on the relations among the object world, human mindscapes, and their literary renderings—a perspective that helps to understand the implications of Austin's regionalist aesthetic—I return to the example of the river. The empirical reality of the river and the human inscapes and representations of it can be considered separate, because the particular river exists whether we look at it or ignore it, name it "river" or "ditch," or write about it as part of a watershed or a recreational area or as a local symbol for the Acheron. In short, the river exists within its own environmental context and natural history. It evolved at some point out of geological changes, and it has since changed its course, meandering, eroding the banks, and providing a habitat for an also changing vegetation and wildlife. Just as clearly, however, the components are not separate but interrelated both on a pragmatic and a conceptual level. First of all, it is likely that human history and river history have mutually influenced each other. On one hand, the river course may have been altered by human intervention or the water and the riverbed may be polluted; on the other hand, the river may have entered human history by providing fishing grounds or a trade route—any port city is evidence of this. But even if the river and its banks were a wilderness uninhabited by humans and unaffected by human-induced changes in other regions, when we speak of human contact with the natural world, it is difficult to disentangle nonhuman nature as such from the human perception of it. Our vision and experiences are mediated through multiple filters, including our sense of selfhood, prior experiences, preceding encounters with the nonhuman world, intentions, and the linguistic organization of our patterns of thought. The river has a different meaning for and plausibly looks different to a farmer on the neighboring fields, for a commuter driving by on the freeway, and for an ecologist studying the impact of the freeway on the river's wildlife habitats. Also, identifying the stretch of water that we may see from the riverbank as part of the larger entity "river" already constitutes an act of interpretation. Our general concept of "riverness" and its distinction from other bodies of water and entities come to bear on our experience, as does our acquaintance with symbolical readings of rivers and water, in which they may denote life or, conversely, the transitoriness of existence.

While many ecologically minded critics would agree with poststructural theorists that reality is intertextually constructed, their concepts of intertextuality diverge when applied to the relations between humans and nonhuman nature. While ecocritics tend to acknowledge that our readings inevitably produce culturally mediated environmental "texts," they also will maintain that the world cannot be reduced to these human-authored texts.[26] As SueEllen Campbell convincingly argues in "The Land and Language of Desire," poststructuralists have extended Ferdinand de Saussure's analysis of the relational and arbitrary character of linguistic signs to a conceptualization both of language and of empirical reality as a network of intertexts dependent on human readers, while ecologists have emphasized that the nonhuman world also has an existence apart from human signifying systems. Environmentally committed critics tend to insist, as Austin did, that human nonhuman interactions are reciprocal and that the nonhuman environment not only invites and provokes human readings but also escapes, resists, and exceeds the comprehension of human readers. As Donna J. Haraway points out in *Simians, Cyborgs, and Women*, "Accounts of a 'real' world do not, then, depend on a logic of 'discovery,' but on a power-charged social relation of 'conversation.' The world neither speaks itself nor disappears in favor of a master decoder. The codes of the world are not still, waiting only to be read. The world is not raw material for humanization" (198). While we may know and speak of the nonhuman only from a human perspective, this perspective is defined in relation to what we are not; it cannot claim to encompass a natural world that extends beyond the human, including our interpretations of it.

The articulation of this critical position is often motivated by environmentalist concerns. In contrast to the poststructuralist valorization that our readings of reality are situated and that we "always change what we study," environmentalists tend to perceive this complicity "not as liberating but as a call to caution," SueEllen Campbell explains (205). "A 'misread' text and a depleted acquifer present quite different practical problems and raise quite different moral and ethical questions" (206). Ecocritics frequently assert that in order to realign human life with its nonhuman matrix, in order to turn from viewing nature as a resource infinitely available for human use and consumption, we have to recognize its self-organizing existence. The acknowledgement that the nonhuman exists in its own right and on its own terms while it also influences human history is meant to facilitate a more acute comprehension of the limits that natural systems impose on human agency.

This understanding provides a possible basis for environmental ethics—as the concept of regionalist nature writing exemplifies that Austin develops in the previously quoted account of her first journey through southern California. Austin presents environmental literature as the product of an interaction between self and world, as an expression of a writer's subjective encounter with the natural world that is informed by the author's sense of self, by her mode of engagement with the environment, by the natural features and processes that attract her attention, and by the degree of resistance that the environment offers to human observation and participation. Austin reveals and emphasizes the environmentalist motivation of her critical stance by ending her autobiographical portrait of "the way a Naturist is taken with the land, with the spirit trying to be evoked out of it" with an expression of the "frustration" and "deep resentment" she feels in light of the environmental degradation of southern California (*EH* 188). Austin's attempts to experience and describe its *genius loci* have remained an "incomplete adventure," she asserts, because human development has severely altered if not destroyed the regional environment (188). The "place of the mystery was eaten up, it was made into building lots, cannery sites; it receded before the preëmptions of rock crushers and city dumps" (187–88). By contrasting her initial enchantment with her later aversion to southern California, Austin uses her autobiographical recollections for environmentalist purposes. She ends her discussion of the necessary psychological and physical adjustment of regionalist writers to the place they wish to describe with a blend of mysticism and environmental advocacy. She insists on the self-organizing existence of the nonhuman and indicts dominant society for the region's environmental degradation. In a place "slavered over with the impudicity of a purely material culture," Austin's "Spirit of the Arroyos" remains "wistful with long refusals" (189).

Austin's theoretical and literary explorations of the options writers have for keeping "faith with the land" thus seem to have anticipated the current ecocritical inquiry whether and to which extent reality can be perceived and rendered in human language from a nonanthropocentric perspective. In thinking about the factors that enter into the production and reception of regional and environmental literature, Austin persistently asked which possibilities textual practices have to mark the intersections between unconstructed reality and mediated human experiences of it. For her the question of how the environment could enter literary texts allowed for polemics but not for easy answers. Instead, it provoked a "yearning" (*EH* 187) and a narrative practice that suggests the porousness and mutability of categories such as subject and object, self and other, and environment and identity.

To return to her earlier definition of regionalist literature, Austin may have realized that the land's prediscursive "essential qualities" could only be experienced subjectively and rendered discursively. Yet she insisted that environmental writing has to alert its readers to the inevitable mismatch between human readings and environmental actualities through metanarrative comments, because paradoxically this self-referentiality—through its explication of what the text is and its simultaneous reference to what it cannot be—provides a way for the author to remain faithful to both the phenomenological reality of human encounters with the nonhuman world as an unmerged other and to the self-organizing existence of natural systems. Austin recognized the importance that our conversations with the nonhuman world hold for our sanity and survival. Hence, she simultaneously could consider it the writer's task to "give in human terms the meaning of that country in which the action of the story takes place" ("Regionalism in American Fiction" 105) and define the author's obligation in environmentalist terms as an accountability to nonhuman others.

THE SPIRITUAL AND DEMOCRATIC FUNCTION
OF LITERATURE

Literary, epistemological, and sociopolitical (environmentalist, feminist, and pluralist) concerns converge in Austin's regionalist work, as we have seen. The different aspects of her regionalist aesthetic cohere because they derive from one common source. They result from Austin's conviction that it should be the primary function of art to help people integrate the intellectual, emotional, corporeal, and spiritual dimensions of their lives and to align themselves with their community, environment, and the universal "Something" present in all of these. Literature, Austin believed, has to be environmentally grounded and has to validate the ordinary processes of life because these qualities make it most affective on a personal, social, and spiritual level.

Austin's most extensive comment on the social and religious purpose of art is "The American Rhythm," the introductory essay to her poetry collection of the same title, *The American Rhythm*.[27] In the essay she seeks to develop a place-based, democratic, and spiritual poetics out of her study of the aesthetic, ritual, and social functions of Native American oral traditions. According to Austin, poetry is an essentially rhythmic and somatic form of aesthetic expression, and as such it is prone to be affected by the factors that enter into the human experience of rhythm, namely the rhythms of our bodies— heartbeat, breath, biochemical, neurological, and energetic changes (*AR* 5)—and the variations that these corporeal rhythms undergo as they are affected by environmental conditions and experiential knowledge (3), by emotional states (13), and by modes of work and transportation (12–13). Made of words but molded by experience, poetry in Austin's sense is not primarily concerned with language or ideas but with relating the poet and his or her audience to the social, ecological, and spiritual matrix of their lives. For Austin the source and objective of poetry are collective and religious (21–22). She cites Native American oral traditions and ritual practices as evidence that poetry originally served no "other purpose than that of producing and sustaining collective states" (23), "those happy states of reconciliation with the Allness through group communion" (54). In other words, what interests Austin most about poetry is its spiritual and democratic potential.[28]

Again, Austin's regionalist aesthetic brings Dewey's experiential concept of art to mind. Dewey argues in *Art as Experience* that aesthetic perception presents us with a heightened recognition of the embeddedness of our daily lives in a world that extends beyond the human. Because it facilitates experiences of the subject's wholeness and the interrelatedness of the different dimensions of our lives and the world at large, Dewey reasons, art serves both a psychologically sustaining and a cosmological function. Through aesthetic perception, accompanied at times by "religious feeling," we are

introduced into a world beyond this world which is nevertheless the deeper reality of the world in which we live in our ordinary experiences. We are carried out beyond ourselves to find ourselves. . . . art operates to deepen and to raise to great clarity that sense of an enveloping undefined whole that accompanies every normal experience. . . . Where egotism is not made the measure of reality and value, we are citizens of this vast world beyond ourselves, and any intense realization of its presence with and in us brings a peculiarly satisfying sense of unity in itself and with ourselves. (195)

Dewey describes the potential of art to spiritually intensify and clarify the reality of our daily lives. Similarly, Austin argues in her regionalist work for the fundamentally integrative nature of art and validates the ordinary processes of life as the basis for the creation of literature. In *The American Rhythm* she asserts, as said, that the objective of poetry is to make us simultaneously feel personally integrated, part of our community, and aligned with our environment and the universal principles inherent in all these aspects of the world.

Certainly the notion that art is a modern effort to achieve "reconciliation with the Allness," as Austin says, or a modern attempt to preserve an interpretation of the world as "an enveloping undefined whole," in Dewey's words, is not a new insight. The rise of landscape perception in the history of Western art, for instance, is generally seen as contingent on the modern decline of the *theoria,* the philosophical tradition of interpreting the natural world as an all-encompassing divine whole.[29] In Western history the cosmological conception of nature in the sense of the *theoria* was increasingly replaced by conceptualizations based on empirical and rationalist studies. Industrialization intensified the split between society and the environment, since the human dependence on the nonhuman world ceased to determine the collective experience to the extent it had in preindustrial agrarian societies.

The experience of the unity of humankind and nature was not fully suppressed, however, but remained accessible for individuals in the aesthetic perception of nature as landscape. In this sense the development of landscape perception can be considered a modern attempt to preserve an interpretation of the world as a harmoniously ordered cosmos. Since it presupposes a distanced attitude of the observer to the environment, the conceptualization of nature as landscape can only facilitate the aesthetic experience of nature in the sense of the *theoria* if the vision of the observing subject has been adequately conditioned. Only when the observer has learned to assemble and integrate the components of a particular section of the respective scenery into a unified and coherent image and to invest it with subjective meaning does a "landscape" come into existence. In other words, the landscape does not exist outside the culturally trained mind and imagination of the observer, but it constitutes a subjective prospect, composed by means of a discerning individual vision from a single viewpoint. The historical evolution of Western landscape perception and representation demonstrates that the subjective processes involved in mentally organizing our biochemical vision into coherent aesthetic images are in themselves results of sociocultural developments.

While this line of reasoning helps to remind us that our perception of the environment is a cultural artifact, it unfortunately also relegates holistic aesthetic experiences of the kind described by Austin and Dewey to an isolated field of art. Aesthetic experiences are seen to serve primarily to compensate the observer's culturally conditioned mind and imagination for the lack of integration prevalent in his or her daily life. Austin's and Dewey's experiential theories of art, by contrast, refuse to base modern aesthetics on a fundamentally distanced relation between observer and world and writer and environment. Instead, they focus on our elemental connectedness with the world around us, on the experiences we undergo as environmentally bound "live creatures," irrespective of whether we are aware of this level of our existence. As Dewey contends in *Art as Experience*, "the uniquely distinguishing feature of esthetic experience is exactly the fact that no such distinction of self and object exists in it, since it is esthetic in the degree in which the organism and environment cooperate to institute an experience in which the two are so fully integrated that each disappears" (249). Rather than emphasize the potential of aesthetic experience to overcome dualistic conceptions of nature and culture, subject and object, Dewey and Austin insist that these aspects of reality are always already fundamentally interrelated at the level of our lived experience and creative processes.

REGIONALIST LITERATURE AND NATIONAL CULTURE

On the basis of her experiential regionalist poetics, Austin argues in *The American Rhythm* that American poetry can be considered distinctly American to the degree that it represents an aesthetic response to the peculiar rhythms of American environments. She asserts, for instance, that it is the contact with the "new earth" and "a new experiential adaptation of social mechanisms" that makes European American poetry distinctly American (*AR* 9). In answer to her query, "How much of the character called national in any literature is owed to the influences taken in through the senses?" Austin grants a predominant influence to present living conditions rather than to cultural heritage.[30] She proposes that the encounter with particular places and ways of living may provoke similar responses from poets of different cultural backgrounds. For her, similarities between traditional indigenous and modern European American poetry prove that American culture to a significant extent is environmentally determined. "That scene is immensely more potent than race is testified by the independent emergence of similar verse patterns among the poets of the race amalgam, taking its name from the scene, called American" (AU 11). As the contact with a common environment can level the cultural difference among diverse groups inhabiting one region, Austin suggests, so the contact with one continent can unify the different segments of the American population.

Yet the American continent and American society are heterogeneous environments that can hardly be expected to provoke a singular response. How could such a kaleidoscope of diverse forms and processes issue into a single American rhythm, as the title of Austin's study suggests? Austin's simultaneous advocacy of regionalized, and thus plural, American cultures and of a singular national character seems contradictory.[31] Her attempt to extend her concept of geographical determination from the sphere of regional society to the plane of the nation renders her argument problematic. For Austin here posits not only that specific environments influence particular people but that the common quality supposedly shared by the variety of built and natural environments on the American continent shapes American history and the process of nation building.

Even if we would assume that a common regional orientation could unite an otherwise diverse group of people, it seems arbitrary to define the limits of such a union in national terms.

Austin's search for the common denominator of the various rhythms that she considered particular to American environments and cultures seems to have been motivated by a patriotic attachment to the idea of a unified American nation. Her interest "in an Americanization program" considerably weakens her argument, however, as Lewis Mumford observes in his review "The American Rhythm" (24). To prove her point that the diverse American rhythms issue into a single national rhythm, Austin deliberately conflates, for instance, the differences among poets such as Amy Lowell, Vachel Lindsay, Edgar Lee Masters, and Carl Sandburg as well as between their work and Native American poetry to prove a common environmental influence (*AR* 46).[32] Although Austin angrily rejected the suggestion that her argument had nationalistic tendencies, Mumford's comment is justified in so far as Austin argues in *The American Rhythm* not only that environmental rhythms exert an influence on the production and reception of art but also that the environmental and social conditions prevalent on the American continent result in a distinctly national literature.[33]

The larger project that Austin pursues in regionalist works such as *The American Rhythm,* through her theory of geographical determination and her presentation of Native American culture as a role model for European American acculturation, is the creation of a national myth of origin. The definition of a common national origin is key to Austin's argument since the assertion of a shared foundation lends coherence to the diverse indigenous, imported, and hybrid American cultures. Equally important, the supposition of new particularly American sources of experience, thought, and identity makes it possible to value American culture on its own terms—an established line of thought since the declarations of cultural independence that dominated the field of American literature during the mid-nineteenth century. As Austin reasons in "What Is a Native Culture?": "For i[f] we are only a lot of mongrelized Europeans in the western continent, we are n[o]thing, but as the American People we are of first rank" (AU 625, 3).

Austin seeks to contribute with her work to the creation of a national mythology that would help Americans home into their regional environments. From *The Land of Little Rain* to *The American Rhythm,* from

The Land of Journey's Ending to *One-Smoke Stories*, she casts the place-based southwestern cultures as the prototypes of an environmentally grounded, democratic future American society. For her, the Native American and Hispanic regional cultures anticipate the desired regionalization and democratization of dominant American society. Austin proposes that the "general adoption of native symbols for experiences intimate and peculiar to the land" will accelerate the cultural development of the nation because the "cultural evolution" of any society depends on its adaptation to its land base (*LJE* 440). Accordingly, Austin adopts narrative practices and concepts of authorship and democratic culture gleaned from Native American oral traditions and Hispanic and white folk cultures. Appealing to the self-interest of her predominantly white audience, she argues that the subjugation of Native Americans and Hispanics and the eradication of their cultural heritages not only has a devastating effect on their communities but also harms the development of dominant American society, as it slows down European American acculturation. In "Cults of the Pueblos," Austin warns her readers, for instance, "we cannot put our weight on the left hand of God and not ourselves go down with it" (35). For Austin the definition of national identity represents not a purely political enterprise but also a mythical and spiritual task.

Austin's contemporaries appreciated her speculative talent and her mythological project of nation building. "She has issued a challenge which will make every honest American poet stop to examine himself. And that is an excellent thing," reckoned Mark Van Doren ("The American Rhythm" 472). Austin's intentions were clearly discerned by Henry Nash Smith, who had profited as a young regionalist and editor of the *Southwest Review* from his elder's expertise. In "The Feel of the Purposeful Earth," Smith notes, "Mrs. Austin is trying to do for the American race what myths did for the Greeks and for other European peoples. Modern skepticism makes this task hard; she has explored the mythology and the folk-lore of the Indians and the early Spanish settlers, but she has been forced in the end to express her meaning in philosophical terms and through the traditional form of nature-writing. Of course she has not been able to create an American mythology—it takes generations to do that. But she has seen the problem, and made it clear" (30). While Smith regarded it as Austin's achievement that she managed to "impose upon Americans the task of becoming a tribe, of building a civilization" (32), other critics found the implied criticism of the status quo as objectionable as the idea of cross-cultural learning. Anglo-Saxonism and racial prejudice against Native Americans fueled opposition to Austin's ideal of an "Amerindian" society.[34]

From a contemporary perspective, Mary Austin's focus on the dynamics of intercultural communication and her emphasis on the social, ecological, and psychological benefits of a place-based culture seem innovative. In works such as *The American Rhythm* she takes up the challenge of her precursors to create a distinctly American culture and develops a poetics that can be understood as a regionalist update of their romantic utopia of cultural autonomy. The historical continuity is readily apparent, and Austin was not the first regionalist to take up the romantic lead.[35] She certainly agreed with Emerson's dictum that "America is a poem in our eyes; its ample geography dazzles the imagination, and it will not wait long for metres" ("The Poet" 997). For Austin, however, the American poets had already arrived and were flourishing both within and outside European American society. Further cultural development now depended, Austin proposed, on a cross-cultural dialogue on the diverse experiences of place. In formulating the ideal of a place-based democratic American society that would emerge out of cross-cultural negotiations and the sustainable inhabitation of the American continent, Austin went beyond the romantic conceptions of her predecessors.[36] Her environmentalist awareness and sensitivity to social imbalances of power—for instance, along the lines of regional and educational backgrounds and ethnic, class, and gender differences—allowed Austin to contribute an innovative regionalist vision to American literary history.

2

NATURE WRITING AS REGIONALIST PRACTICE

How to Author a Walk and Other Questions of Gender

For Mary Austin the interest in natural history involved a transgression of late nineteenth-century gender codes. For women, Austin notes in her autobiography, an "occasional light reference to [John] Burroughs was permissible, but not Thoreau" (*EH* 112). As a girl, Austin was taught by her mother that her fascination with the natural world was unfeminine. She was told, as we have seen, to narrow her environmental perception to "a ladylike appreciation of the surroundings," so that her male companion, "as the author of the walk, might feel himself complimented" by her appreciation of the scenery (112). Yet Austin chose to become an author herself. In her environmental writing she frequently addresses the question of how to author her walks, that is, how to explore, observe, and live in her environment, and how to communicate these experiences in writing. The attention to the conceptual, social, and literary frameworks of environmental perception and representation is a hallmark of her work.

THE PLACE OF FEMALE AUTHORS IN THE
NATURE WRITING TRADITION

Austin has to be considered a major author in the Thoreauvian tradition of nature writing. Her first book-length publication, *The Land of Little Rain* (1903), has become part of the canon of American environmental literature. In the established although not undisputed outline of the nature writing tradition, Austin's work provides the link between earlier authors such as Henry David Thoreau and John Muir and later writers such as Aldo Leopold and Edward Abbey.[1] Besides Austin, few other women writers are routinely included in this lineage. Currently, critical attention is devoted mostly to either Susan Fenimore Cooper, situated at the beginning of the tradition with *Rural Hours. By a Lady* (1850), or to contemporary writers, such as Annie Dillard and Terry Tempest Williams. This is a critical situation that has changed surprisingly little since Henry Chester Tracy published one of the first studies of the genre, *American Naturists,* in 1930. When sent a general outline of the study, Austin responded, "The first thing that occurs to me is that you mention only men in speaking of your book. It is one of the mistakes very frequently made that in this connection no attention is paid to the women who have, as you say, penetrated the American scene, or attempted to do so. There must be other women beside myself. I seem to recall several names, such as Olive Thorne Miller and Gene Stratton Porter."[2] Tracy, however, could not think of any other female nature writers who merited his attention. Still, he felt obliged to account for the circumstance that of the twenty-one authors presented in his study only two were women— Austin and Olive Thorne Miller (11). To prove that the selection did not reflect a "masculine bias" (13), Tracy pondered the question why women did not seem drawn to produce nature literature. His answer was simple. Out of a combination of "natural accidents and social causes" (13), most women did not care about the outdoors and nonhuman nature. "By long inheritance and habit a woman's interest is personal and indoor. It does not go out instinctively to an impersonal and a useless outdoor world. When she has become further emancipated, perhaps it will" (12). Because Tracy conceived of women as the main carriers of American culture, he proposed that American society as a whole would benefit from women's increased interest in natural history. Blaming the supposed unnaturalness and inertia of American culture on women's apparent lack of nature appreciation, Tracy reasoned that their increased participation in nature studies and outdoors adventure would invigorate American society. "Indeed it is hard to see how there can be any check to the growing artificiality of our American living until women, around whose interests it centers, reinterpret the nature world from their own point of view" (13).

The progressive intentions of its author notwithstanding, one of the first critical definitions of the nature writing genre thus relies on an environmentalist update of the central masculinist myth of American wilderness literature. From the suffocating grip of a degenerate feminized society, the male hero, as the embodiment of either archetypal masculinity or universal humanist values, escapes into the wild. There he undergoes a process of physical and emotional replenishment and eventually returns to civilization to reinvigorate his community.[3] Like this mythic hero, Tracy's naturist turns from the female induced "artificiality" of American culture to the worship and study of nature. An "ardent lover and observer of the life out-of-doors" (5), he returns from the field as the herald of fresh insight and ethical improvement. "It is not a matter of information," clarifies Tracy. "A naturist does not tell you *about* nature. He drives you to it or he remains a naturalist, and nothing more" (14). Subtly, the nature writer has become a manly figure initiated in the wilderness.

Accordingly, Tracy clothed his analysis of Austin's and Miller's achievement in gendered terms. He saw Miller's accomplishment, for instance, as resulting from her ability to perceive and describe the minutest natural details—a capacity that "no male observer could possibly have" (119). The author herself would not have objected to this appraisal. Miller considered her area of interest, birding, "particularly suited to woman with her great patience and quiet manners."[4] From its beginnings, then, the critical reception of the American nature writing tradition, much like the study of natural history, was caught up in gendered concepts of identity, authority, and authorship.

How did female authors respond to and interact with this gendered tradition of European American nature writing? Contemporary critics have argued that women nature writers indeed wrote differently from their male contemporaries, either because they identified with the prevalent gender codes of European American society, as Olive Thorne Miller's comment suggests, or because their marginalized position in the literary field led them to adopt alternative points of view and modes of writing.

In *Made from this Earth* Vera Norwood argues that the female natural history writers of the nineteenth and early twentieth century tended to reflect self-consciously on their role as women writers and frequently chose to represent the natural world in terms of metaphors gleaned from domestic work. They often imagined nature as part of an extended domestic sphere.[5] Thus women writers from Susan Cooper to later authors such as Mary Treat, Olive Thorne Miller, and Florence Merriam infused their conservationist work with a decidedly feminine note (41–48). Reflecting the Victorian ideal of white middle-class womanhood, their writing shares an "appeal to women's special responsibility as wives, mothers, and teachers of the moral lessons derived from the domestic round" (52). Like the female authors of the frontier narratives that Annette Kolodny examines in *The Land Before Her,* these women nature writers often focused on the home and its vicinity and mythologized the domestic sphere rather than the wilderness.

Whether they wholeheartedly believed in the ideology of domesticity or only adopted its rhetoric for strategic reasons, the appeal to women's special roles as guardians of the home, caretakers of the young, and custodians of the family's and by extension the nation's future served generations of women to legitimize their work on behalf of the natural world. In Austin's time women involved in the Progressive Conservation movement, for instance, employed the concept of municipal housekeeping to justify their advance into the field of public policy.[6] While the rhetoric of domesticity initially helped women to obtain public authority and secured them a prominent place in the conservation movement and the nature writing tradition, its strategic potential was severely limited, since it relied on the ideology of separate spheres to define women's political work. Identified with the domestic sphere, women were excluded from public forums and institutions, such as the national Conservation Congresses and scientific journals, when the conservation movement underwent a period of professionalization at the beginning of the twentieth century.[7]

Women's influence on public policy further decreased when the professionalization of the sciences combined with the effects of another attempt to conserve the ideal of masculinity that the advent of the New Woman threatened—the wilderness cult of the Progressive Era. The privileged status that the conservation movement began to accord to scientific training as a source of environmental knowledge and to masculinist outdoor adventure as a means to recuperate individual and national character worked to exclude women from environmentalist discourse, as Norwood explains in *Made from this Earth* (48). We have seen this mechanism at work in the argument that Tracy develops in *American Naturists*. The cumulative effect of these sociocultural developments thus was also felt by female nature writers, who had become a major force in the nature writing tradition by the end of the nineteenth century.[8] They lost their prominent position when the canon solidified under the twin pressures of professionalization and the wilderness cult at the beginning of the twentieth century. Yet, although the processes of canon formation obliterated their work, women did continue to write natural history essays and environmental literature.

"VOICING ANOTHER NATURE"? THE RELATION OF GENDER AND GENRE

Because of their marginal status within the tradition, female authors recently have been reclaimed by critics engaged in a critique of the canon formation currently under way in the field of nature writing. Patrick D. Murphy, for instance, has suggested in *Literature, Nature, and Other* that women writers frequently have been "Voicing Another Nature" (31–46). Murphy sees the genre, as exemplified by the *Norton Book of Nature Writing,* as grounded in "colonialism, industrialization, and the growth of an urban leisure class" (32). He proposes that several generic conventions combine to codify within the tradition a Cartesian view of nature (33). As a result, Murphy argues, the nature writing canon excludes authors committed to relational ethics, biocentric concepts of self, and a dialogical approach to literary practice, for instance, feminist writers such as Austin and Susan Griffin (38, 40, 43) and certain Native American authors (32, 44).

Yet as tempting as it is to think of noncanonical female authors as writing from an alternative perspective outside the mainstream, the relation between narrative practices and gender politics often is elusive. The degree to which gender informs the conscious choices and unconscious attitudes of authors and critics largely depends on the sociocultural contexts of their readings and writings. Gender may be paramount to a writer's or critic's sense of self and concept of authorship, or other aspects of his or her identity may take precedence. Chances are that the stronger the literary field is structured along gender lines, the more the production and reception of literary works are influenced by gender politics— if only for strategic reasons.

The gender of the author, then, certainly may influence but need not dictate which conceptual frameworks are adopted, which stylistic devices are used, and to which end, if any, the author writes. It does not necessarily follow from the historical association of the constructs "woman" and "nature," for instance, that white middle-class women identify with the natural world or with anything or anyone else cast as Other.[9] The proposition that women nature writers generally have been and should be "voicing another nature" is problematic because it lends itself to essentialist conflations of specific women writers with the construct "woman."[10] As Stacy Alaimo points out in "The Undomesticated Nature of Feminism," "one cannot assume that women represent nature more propitiously. The female conservationists of Austin's time, for example, espoused a utilitarian view of nature, whereas male environmentalists like John Muir denounced utilitarianism" (75). It makes sense to assume that both female writers and male writers adopt their particular stances as a result of conscious deliberations and strategic choices rather than as a natural consequence of their gender or ethnic identity.[11]

Our present notions of femininity and masculinity obviously always influence our understanding of the historical realities that informed the work and reception of earlier writers. Yet the line of influence extends in both directions. In constructing gender-specific literary traditions, we sometimes follow the logic of our precursors and, as a result, remain stuck in the ideology of separate spheres. Consider, for instance, the association of biocentric nature writing with a female tradition and women's sup-posedly different voice.[12] Made explicit, the argument runs something like this: Women are socialized to develop a relational rather than a compet-itive sense of self; as relationally oriented persons, women are inclined to perceive their environment nonhierarchically; therefore, they fre-quently regard not only fellow humans but also the natural world with empathy and are likely to substitute a biocentric (that is, a relational, egal-itarian) point of view for an anthropocentric (that is, a hierarchical, hegemonic) framework. When we base our constructions of female na-ture writing traditions on such a concept of female subjectivity, do we re-main attached to Victorian notions of womanhood? Do we impose on women writers the obligation to turn from "angels in the house" into "an-gels in the ecosystem," as Val Plumwood quips in *Feminism and the Mas-tery of Nature* (9)? Or do our observations accurately reflect the concern of earlier readers and writers with appropriately gendered voices in nat-ural history writing?

An attempt to do the latter is undertaken by Vera Norwood and Lawrence Buell, who explain the affinity for a biocentric perspective that many female nature writers seem to have had in the context of contem-poraneous gender expectations. In *The Environmental Imagination* Buell identifies as a central characteristic of the female nature writing tradition an "aesthetics of relinquishment," a repudiation of egotism on the writer's part "to the point of feeling the environment to be at least as worthy of attention as oneself" (178). According to Buell, women writers from Susan Cooper to Sarah Orne Jewett, Celia Thaxter, Willa Cather, and Mary

Austin were either brought up to believe in the virtue of female selfless-
ness or they complied for strategic reasons with gendered literary conventions, including the expectation that women would not write ego-
centered narratives but realistic studies *en miniature* (177). In this sense,
Buell argues, their socialization as women endowed the female authors
with a certain advantage over their male peers. They "managed to cultivate a nonegoistic, ecocentric sensibility toward which Thoreau had to
grope his way laboriously" (177).

Yet even if we grant that these women writers either were apt at unfolding biocentric environmental narratives because of their gender socialization or that they felt obliged to adopt a nonegoistic narrative voice
because of their audience's gender-linked expectations, how can we rec-
oncile these arguments with the widely accepted critical proposition that
just such an "ecocentric sensibility" has always constituted one of the
defining characteristics of the nature writing tradition? From Henry
Chester Tracy to Lawrence Buell, critics have defined a nonanthropocentric orientation as an integral element of the genre. Are there two distinct,
gender-specific ways of writing from a biocentric point of view? Do separate female and male nature writing traditions exist that overlap in their
common biocentric emphasis? Or did earlier female authors write in biocentric fashion before the nature writing canon was established and
women were excluded from the illustrious ranks, as Buell suggests in *The
Environmental Imagination* (25)? I think it is best to resist answering these
questions in general. There are plausibly as many ways to write from a
biocentric point of view as there are natures and cultures. Buell concedes,
for instance, that a comparative look at male and female environmental
writers may well effect "that distinctions start to seem porous" (49).[13]

Still, despite this opacity of gendered difference in environmental literature, a critical relinquishment of the category of gender also is coun-
terproductive. There are authors who deliberately employ a clearly
gendered voice, often for political reasons, such as woman-identified or
feminist writers such as Susan Cooper and Terry Tempest Williams or
masculinist writers such as Theodore Roosevelt and Edward Abbey. Also,
claims to universality frequently have served exclusionary ends. Consider
Tracy's argument, for example, or take the sexist foreword that Abbey
wrote for the 1988 Penguin edition of Austin's *The Land of Little Rain*. In
his introduction Abbey espouses a universalist aesthetics that effectively
serves to disown his precursor of her achievement. Rather than ac-

knowledge Austin's expertise and talent or the debt that he owes her as a desert writer, Abbey presents Austin's accomplishment as an impersonal effect of the overpowering desert environment. "The subject matter looms above and burns through the lacy veil of words, as a worthy subject will, and soon takes precedence over the author's efforts to show herself an author" (xii). The universal voice that Abbey aspires to and that he finds in Austin's work despite her style and intentions is obviously masculinist if not misogynist.[14]

In light of the puzzling interrelations of gender and genre in the American nature writing tradition a dual task emerges as a central critical challenge: to conceive of the nature writing genre without polarizing the tradition along gender lines, while recognizing that the texts were and are written and read within a literary field and sociocultural context that, among other forces, has been organized according to gender codes and gendered dynamics of power. Such a critical stance will contribute greatly to an understanding of the work of environmental writers such as Austin who wrote in defiance of but not only in response to gendered conventions. Austin was not only engaged in a critique of certain gendered concepts of subjectivity, authorship, scientific practice, and nature but used the combined forces of these critiques to unsettle the underlying dualistic paradigm.

AUSTIN AS A WOMAN WRITER

Austin was aware of the exclusionary effects that gender politics could have on women writers. She self-consciously identified as a female author and, as a result, was wary of the reception of her work within a male-dominated field of literary criticism and public discourse. She once defined her position and her attendant apprehensions as follows:

I express myself as freely and as definitely in my literary medium, as I do in my social life, as a woman. I have always believed that there is a distinctly feminine approach to intellectual problems, and its recognition is indispensible [sic] to intellectual wholeness. All that I have ever, as a feminist, protest[ed] against, is the prevailing notion that the feminine is necessarily an inferior approach. . . . I feel that we ought to find somehow a medium for general truth which will be neither feminine nor masculine. Lately, however, I have begun to think that my special function may be to continue writing with the feminine approach and to insist, as I am doing here[,] that the reviewer should take account of and do justice to that element of my work.[15]

Opinionated as she was, Austin never seems to have formed a definite opinion on the question to which extent gender-specific modes of argumentation and writing were the result of biological and sociocultural forces. From a contemporary perspective, however, Austin's feminist stance cannot be considered an unmediated effect of her sex or gender. Instead, it appears as if she had deliberately adopted her feminist position to unsettle the concepts of human identity and of human and nonhuman relations implied in both the dominant gender code and gendered discourses on nature.[16]

Therefore, it proves misleading to designate Austin's work a "woman's text," as Marjorie Pryse does in her insightful introduction to *Stories from the Country of Lost Borders:* "Austin's mode of narration defines the book as a woman's text. What matters to her is the land, not the defeat of the land; relationships between human beings—including Indians and Spanish-speaking people—not their victories over each other; and the insights that lead to vision, rather than the organization of a tightly woven plot" (xxi). Pryse implicitly differentiates male and female literary traditions by defining women's writing as relational, empathetic, and nonaggressive. This critical procedure has the disadvantage that it does not allow Pryse to consider the intersections between the two lineages to which she links Austin's work—the male-dominated tradition of nature writing (xiv) and the female-dominated tradition of regionalist writing (xv–xvi).

In this respect Pryse's approach stands representative for an unfortunate trend in the Austin criticism of recent decades. In Austin's case the critical interest in gender-specific literary traditions frequently has worked to obscure one of the author's major achievements: her ability to reflect on and dramatize in her narratives the intersections of social and ecological concerns. Rediscovered either as a nature writer or a feminist author, Austin emerges in contemporary literary criticism all too often divested of her trademark awareness of the ways in which concepts of culture and nature inflect one another. Hardly any critical attention has been paid, for instance, to the interplay of regionalist and nature writing traditions in Austin's work. Yet to overemphasize either strand—her concern with sociocultural questions that initially seem to have little to do with the environment, such as gender or race issues, or her concern with human and nonhuman relations and definitions of the natural—is to miss a rewarding quality of Austin's writing. Her larger project is a regionalist attempt to disclose how our notions of the natural and cultural overlap. In this sense we might reappreciate Tracy's dictum, "No naturist has done finer work from a human point of view" than Austin (*American Naturists* 15).

Austin's Regionalist Narratives of Environmental Learning and the Thoreauvian Tradition of Nature Writing

Austin's nature writing and critical essays on the cultural ramifications of scientific methodology reflect her interest in the interplay of social and ecological issues. This section examines how she describes the dynamics of environmental perception and representation in her environmental narratives, particularly in her descriptions of desert ecosystems. It inquires which concepts of subjectivity and which models of literary and scientific practice her accounts of the natural world generate. In response to the ongoing canon debate, the chapter explores the functions that regionalist perspectives perform in environmental literature through a combined reading of Austin's critically most-acclaimed environmental work, *The Land of Little Rain,* and the natural history essays of Thoreau, the writer often considered the progenitor of the nature writing genre.[17]

THE DESERT ECOSYSTEM IN *THE LAND OF LITTLE RAIN*

The Land of Little Rain is a collection of essays, sketches, and stories about the Californian desert and its human and nonhuman inhabitants that seeks to reimagine the relation of American society to its land base. "The desert floras shame us with their cheerful adaptations to the seasonal limitations. . . . One hopes that the land may breed like qualities in her human offspring, not tritely to 'try,' but to do so" (7). In *The Land of Little Rain* Austin describes the adaptation of the vegetation and wildlife to the environmental conditions of the desert and the accommodation of the Native American, Hispanic, and European American populations to the region. The book's structure reflects the ecological organization of the desert as an interplay of factors such as geology, climate, flora, and fauna. It is segmented into chapters that present different aspects of the environment as examples of the "economy of nature" (60).[18] These samples include the dependence of animals on water holes and their interrelated drinking habits in "Water Trails of the Ceriso," the food chain in "The Scavengers," the altitude-defined vegetation zones of the Sierra Nevada in "The Streets of the Mountains," the plant distribution according to the desert's "Water Borders," and the weather's influence on the seasonal changes of the biota in "Nurslings of the Sky." Although the chapters are organized around distinct sets of ecological interrelations, the emphasis of the descriptions customarily move among various aspects of the environment. *The Land of Little Rain* thus creates a portrait of the desert as an intricate ecological network of interconnected parts.

Concerned that "we never fully credit the interdependence of wild creatures, and their cognizance of the affairs of their own kind," the narrator serves as a translator of the "voiceless" land for the readers (55, 10). She describes the "orderly arrangement" of the environment and interprets the meaning that natural "signs" carry within their ecological context (29). She explains that animal tracks point the way to water holes in arid regions (28–29). Vegetation zones and plant distribution are presented as indicators of the approximate elevation of the respective area, its average amount of yearly precipitation and range of temperature, the soil series, the direction of the slope, and the proximity of surface water. Plants thus appear as "the best index the voiceless land can give the traveler of his whereabouts" (10).[19]

Setting out to describe the desert as an ecosystem that functions independent of human observers, Austin's narrator tackles a dual task: she tries to give factually accurate accounts of the region, and she examines which ideas and habits might help her and her readers to become knowledgeable of the places they inhabit. To balance her subjective needs with her demand that the environment be perceived as a self-regulating ecosystem, the narrator continually changes her viewpoint and the focus of her attention during her excursions. She develops, for instance, an aesthetics of botany that allows for an impressive scope of responses to the regional environment, while it acknowledges that the desert's vegetation exists in its own right.

THE AESTHETICS OF BOTANY

A desire for aesthetically pleasing sights informs the narrator's perception of the desert's flora in *The Land of Little Rain*. Like Austin, she is convinced that aesthetic appreciation provides an antidote to the disaffected attitude that she associates with botanical classification. While "the life of the flower escapes between the presses of the herbalist" (*AR* 41), it is accessible for aesthetically and imaginatively involved observers. Like the narrator, they may discern in the seasonal changes of a meadow, for instance, "a succession of color schemes more admirably managed than the transformation scene at the theatre" (*LLR* 136).[20]

The narrator articulates her subjective response to the different plant species that she encounters on her excursions, without compromising her assertion that the desert's vegetation carries significance and value apart from the contemplations of human observers. She praises not only the beauty of the plants but also their sustenance (211) and ecological performance. Although she enjoys, for instance, lupine washes for their "display of color," she begins her precise description of the flowers by noting their habitat and botanical name. She depicts "a lupin wash somewhere on the mesa trail,—a broad, shallow, cobble-paved sink of vanished waters, where the hummocks of *Lupinus ornatus* run a delicate gamut from silvery green of spring to silvery white of winter foliage" (147). As the narrator continues her description, she centers her attention on the appearance of single plants, rendering them in detail and outlining their seasonal changes. Here the "tug of eco-consciousness" functions "as a corrective to ego-consciousness," to use Glen A. Love's words ("Revaluing Nature" 209). The narrator describes the growth, pollination, and decay of the plants, before she increases her vision's depth of focus again to finally present her view of the lupine wash in bloom. She notes that "every terminal whorl of the lupin sends up its blossom stalk, not holding any constant blue, but paling and purpling to guide the friendly bee to virginal honey sips, or away from the perfected and depleted flower. The length of the blossom stalk conforms to the rounded contour of the plant, and of these there will be a million moving indescribably in the airy current that flows down the swale of the wash" (*LLR* 148).

The narrator's appreciation of botanical details and ecological interrelations clearly enhances her enjoyment of the color play and shape of the plants. She engages in a mode of perception that Austin treasured as a reliable means to access "the mysterious complex called Nature"—the "absorbed contemplation of the mere appearance of things for their own sake" (*EH* 78). Yet her description does not only yield information about the plants but also about their beholder. Since the narrator synthesizes in her account various observations that she gathered from different angles of vision and points of interest over the course of several seasons, her description also traces the visual and conceptual process that informed her botanical study of the lupines. As a result, her account balances botanical information with imaginative and emotional renderings of her impressions of the regional vegetation.

The diverging moods and foci of the narrator's depictions of the desert's vegetation suggest that the adoption of a biocentric perspective does not preclude subjective responses of the observer to the environment. Instead of conceptualizing the desert from a single viewpoint, the narrator continually changes her perspective to present observer and observed as separate yet related constituents of the recounted scene. This "diffusion of centers of consciousness," as Buell puts it (176), enables her to describe the vegetation in its self-organizing existence while acknowledging her observational biases. Hence, when the narrator states her aesthetic preferences and aversions, she increases rather than limits her options for a biocentric representation of the environment. Indeed, one of the most elaborate depictions of a plant in *The Land of Little Rain* features an herb, the false hellebore, which the narrator finds "offensive" (218). Her aversion neither results in disinterestedness nor impairs her aptitude for precise observation and description. The narrator presents the build and appearance of the herb in detail, noting, for instance, the "tall, branched candelabra of greenish bloom above the sessile, sheathing, boat-shaped leaves, semi-translucent in the sun" (218). The narrator's aesthetics of botany thus enable her to reflect on the conceptual and experiential basis of her observations and to describe her regional environment from a nonanthropocentric perspective.

REGIONALIST PERSPECTIVES IN THE THOREAUVIAN
TRADITION OF NATURE WRITING

Austin's environmental writing is not only concerned with naming and describing the animals and plants and the geographical and climatic features of the arid regions of the American West, then; it also investigates which conceptual and aesthetic paradigms may foster or prevent environmental bonding. In its ethical orientation, Austin's regionalist nature writing shows a remarkable affinity to Thoreau's naturalist work. Like Thoreau, Austin rejected purely utilitarian concepts of nature. She shared with her precursor an impatience with the materialistic inclinations of her contemporaries and a moral outrage at the environmental degradation of the regions she cherished. Due to this affinity, the following passage addressed to the reader could almost be attributed to either writer:

"But you, between the church and the police, whose every emanation of the soul is shred to tatters by the yammering of kin and neighbor," the narrator inquires provocatively, "what do you know of the great, silent spaces across which the voice of law and opinion reaches small as the rustle of blown sand?"[21] The last word, reading "sand" instead of, say, "leaves," gives us a sure indication of the author; it is Austin writing about the California desert rather than Thoreau addressing a Concord audience. The cranky note sounds familiar, as does the challenge—an Emersonian poet returns with fresh insight from his or her sojourn in nature to reform his or her private life and community. Yet there is another side to this critique that has received comparatively little critical attention—the inscription of regional learning processes into environmental narratives. In light of this situation it is worthwhile to consider from an ecocritical perspective the tendency of regional writers to invest "the powers of artist and audience in an ongoing and communal project" of social reinvention.[22]

The pedagogical intent to sharpen the reader's environmental sensibilities has been considered a defining characteristic of the nature writing genre since Tracy's pioneering study, *American Naturists*. According to Tracy, the nature writer's moral orientation distinguishes the genre from other forms of nature literature. Instead of aiming solely to convey scientific knowledge (4, 7), the nature writer seeks to promote the environmentalist cause by refining the reader's environmental perception and imagination. From "Bartram to Beebe the books act as stimuli and as lures. By reading them you clarify your own seeing and quicken your senses" (14). Tracy thus attributes a pedagogical function to the genre. It is a tradition carried on by writers who entertain a "warm and generous" attitude toward the natural world, reject "all forms of ruthless exploitation" (10), and seek to instill the same environmental ethic in their readers.

While critical attention frequently has focused on the moral motivation and political implications of the nature writing tradition, the role that the regional orientation of the narrative plays in these processes, particularly in the communication between authors and readers, has attracted scant comment. Yet it is central to the work of environmental writers such as Austin and Thoreau who engage and educate their readers by confronting them with place-centered, ecologically informed redefinitions of human identity and of cultural practices such as nature writing and scientific inquiry. The appeal to place-based experiential knowledges serves in both Austin's and Thoreau's environmental narra-

tives to draw the readers in. Their texts invite us to refine our environmental sensibilities by offering us factual information about the particular regions that the authors knew and imagined and by providing us
with a model for the conscious reengagement with the built and nonbuilt
environments in which we live our daily lives.

Thoreau includes in his natural history essays, for instance, musings
on the possibilities of inventing a localized language that could capture
his regional experience and knowledge. In "Wild Apples" (1862), he unfolds a humorous taxonomy of apples, listing sorts such as "the Apple
which grows in Dells in the Woods (sylvestrivallis)," "December-Eating,"
"the Concord Apple, possibly the same with the *Musketaquidensis*," and
"pedestrium solatium."[23] Thoreau's amusing list obviously functions as a
critique of scientific discourses divorced from immediate regional experience. In "Autumnal Tints" (1862), he likewise calls for a "chromatic
nomenclature" that would reflect local realities.[24] He asks, "Shall we so
often, when describing to our neighbors the color of something we have
seen, refer them, not to some natural object in our neighborhood," but to
"ores and oxides which few ever see" or to "obscure foreign localities, as
naples yellow, Prussian blue. . . . Have we not an *earth* under our feet,—
aye, and a sky over our heads?" (162). Thoreau probes the potential of language to describe environmental realities adequately in terms of personal
experiences of place. Due to his localized perspective, his essays yield such
an impressive amount of regional detail that one of his biographers remarked, "Henry talks about Nature . . . just as if she'd been born and
brought up in Concord."[25]

In a similar gesture, Austin privileges Native American and Hispanic
over English American place names in works such as *The Land of Little
Rain* and *The Land of Journey's Ending*. Her place-specific mode of naming is intended to give relational and precise accounts of the experienced
world. It should express "the various natures that inhabit in us" and the
"sweet, separate intimacy" that the land is said to offer to its individual
human residents (*LLR* viii). Austin elaborates on her place-centered practice of naming in the preface to her 1924 *The Land of Journey's Ending*, her
biocultural history of the Southwest. "Anybody can write fact about a
country, but nobody can write truth who does not take into account the
sounds and swings of its native nomenclature."[26] Accordingly, Austin
makes extensive use of Native American and Spanish terms in *The Land
of Journey's Ending*.

—

As a regionalist, Austin considers native names superior to imported English names, because the former record the long-term interactions of local communities with their land base, whereas the latter project ideas and images onto the environment that derive from other social and geographical contexts. She contends that there "is no use trying to improve on Indian names, really" (*LJE* 421), because "the native phrase-makers . . . have had several centuries more than I have for making them both apt and interpretative" (47). While the native names result from an attentive engagement with the tribal land, Austin asserts, the English names impose a preestablished order onto the environment. They are "silly names cut out of a mythological dictionary and shaken in a hat before they were applied" (421).

The pedagogical impetus behind Austin's use of regional nomenclature becomes readily apparent when she mockingly addresses her European American readers. "A *barranca* is terrifyingly more than an English bank on which the wild thyme grows; an *arroyo* resembles a gully only in being likewise a water gouge in the earth's surface, and we have no word at all for *cañada,* half-way between an *arroyo* and a *cañon,* which—though, naturally, you have been accenting the syllable that best expresses the trail of the white man across the Southwest—is really pronounced can-*yon*" (*LJE* viii). Austin does not adopt Native American and Spanish names, then, to furnish her account with an attractive exotic veneer. Instead, in the context of the Southwest's accelerating development in the early twentieth century, she seeks to counteract the erasure of the region's ethnic and cultural diversity through an increasingly homogeneous, place-unconscious, and ecologically illiterate American culture. Works such as *The Land of Little Rain* and *The Land of Journey's Ending* invite readers to engage in a cross-cultural conversation on sense of place. They confront us with a literary rendering of the Southwest that does not report in a detached manner on the region's multicultural social fabric but that enacts its diversity in the form of a multilingual narrative. Thus Austin's regionalist texts encourage readers to shed their role of nonparticipant observers and to assume, at least for the time of their reading, the position of intercultural students, who attentively take note of and seek to comprehend other cultures and their modes of inhabiting American environments.

Both Austin and Thoreau incorporate meta-narrative elements into their nature writing to comment on the relation between their perception of their regional environments and literary, scientific, and social conventions. Their self-reflexive mode of narration draws the reader's attention to the negotiations between self and world that are involved in developing and expressing a regional sense of place. In "Autumnal Tints," Thoreau discusses and dramatizes the "different intentions of the eye and the mind" required by "different departments of knowledge" (174). In describing how the attitude and mental focus of the narrator influences what he sees, the text asks us to participate imaginatively in his regional learning process. Rather than confront us primarily with "the scientific account of the matter,—only a reassertion of the fact" (138), the essay traces the narrator's explorations of the autumnal landscape. The account offers a multitude of views of the woods, including intricate descriptions of the color, shape, scent, and even taste of trees and leaves, which give us a sense of the intensity of the narrator's engagement with the forest.[27]

The strategy of engaging and refining our environmental sensibilities by offering us a narrative proliferation of complementary perspectives that reflect the narrator's regional learning process also pervades Austin's *The Land of Little Rain*. As the narrative unfolds, the narrator's ecological literacy and her ability to respond appropriately to her surroundings increase. This development is inscribed into the text and thus rendered palpable for the readers by recurrent changes from anthropocentric to biocentric descriptions of the same natural phenomenon. The initially noted "babble of the watercourse [that] always approaches articulation but never quite achieves it," for instance, is transformed into "the most meaningful of wood notes" (235, 254). While the sound of the current fails to communicate any message to the uninitiated, the narrator's increased attentiveness to detail allows her to correctly interpret the "changing of the stream-tone following tardily the changes of the sun on melting snows" (254) as an announcement of impeding major snow falls. Aware of this warning, she can react appropriately and seek out protective surroundings—as do the animals withdrawing into their burrows or descending from higher regions to the valley. Correspondingly, observers unfamiliar with the desert's small mammals may perceive them as menacing, "strange, furry, tricksy things" (13), whereas the narrator feels reassured by the presence of these animals. Experienced in desert traveling, she perceives them not as alien objects but as reliable guides to water sources. Therefore, she admonishes her readers, "no matter what the maps say, or your memory, trust them, they *know*" (29).

In their environmental narratives, Austin and Thoreau present human perception and representation of the environment as mediated and limited in character. In "Autumnal Tints" Thoreau may unfold an extraordinary fantasy about creating a complete, exact, and permanent naturalist record of the autumnal turning of leaves (139). Yet the essay makes no pretensions at offering such an authoritative account of the phenomenon. On the contrary, readers are explicitly advised to regard the descriptions as a subjective although exemplary and instructive response to the seasonal changes of the woods. "If, about the last of October, you ascend any hill in the outskirts of our town, and probably of yours, and look over the forest, you may see—well, what I have endeavored to describe. All this you surely *will* see, and much more, if you are prepared to see it,— if you *look* for it" (173). Similarly, in the preface to *The Land of Little Rain* Austin's narrator appeals to the readers to pay attention to both the cultural conditioning of their environmental perception and to the fact that her literary renderings of the desert can never fully capture the regional reality. "Guided by these you may reach my country and find or not find, according as it lieth in you, much that is set down here. And more" (viii). Given the subjective nature of perception, the narrator considers unqualified claims to expertise a hoax.[28] Accordingly, Austin's narrative interpolates general discussions of textual politics—of the relation between language and world, fantasy and fact, and literature and society—with comments on the communication situation between narrator and readers.

In addition, Austin's narrators routinely remind their readers that they can only develop an adequate understanding of their natural surroundings if they are willing to become ecologically literate. They have to be able to interpret the discernible features of their natural environment as indicators of ecological relations that cannot be directly perceived. As the narrators of *The Land of Little Rain* and *The Land of Journey's Ending* never tire to explain, the desert only appears to be a region of purposeless desolation to observers who are unfamiliar with the particular organization of arid environments. They do not know that there "is neither poverty of soil nor species to account for the sparseness of desert growth, but simply that each plant requires more room. So much earth must be preëmpted to extract so much moisture" (*LLR* 12). Since the "real struggle for existence, the real brain of the plant, is underground" (12), viewers interested in developing an ample understanding of their region need to integrate their observations according to a conceptual framework adequate to the ecosystem. The narrator of *The Land of Journey's Ending* gives an example. "To appreciate a creosote plantation, one must be able to think of the individual shrub as having its tail waving about in the sun and wind, and its intelligence underground. Then the wide spacing of the growing crowns is explained by the necessary horizontal spread of the root system in search of the thin envelope of moisture around the loose particles of the gravelly soil" (137).

Like her narrators, Austin thought of landscapes as composites of visible and invisible parts. The invisible dimension of the land—the roots of plants, hidden from her view, or ecological relations that she could deduce but not touch—fascinated her. To her, the plants' alterior forms of existence were deliberate achievements, true vegetable art. In one of her natural history notes, Austin records her sense of wonder. "To me the life of the plant is always underground, working in secret as all great forces do, groping, grovelling among common things. And these structures that they raise, these delicate mechanisms of flower and leaf, and the height and mystery of trees, these are their works of art, their lyrics, epics, sculptures, their pyramids and Panthenons. And how patient they are and how imperturbable, dissolving the complexities of quartz mountains to their elemental needs, and always to produce and reproduce, to grow and spread by means of being beautiful and fit. And always in the dark!" (AU 363). Intrigued by the alterity of nonhuman forms of life, Austin integrated into her writing her sense of marvel at those aspects of her environment that felt alien to her. In her descriptions of the natural world Austin continually points to the limits of her understanding. Thus she reminds her readers that we live within and move through environments that extend beyond the human sphere.

ANIMAL VISION

Since Austin was fascinated with the experience of the nonhuman as a radically different yet also strangely familiar world, she sought to mark in her nature writing the discontinuities between the unbuilt environment and her observations and interpretations of it. In *The Land of Little Rain* she oscillates, for instance, among predominantly factual accounts of ecological interrelations, an extensive use of personification in descriptions of natural phenomena, and self-referential comments on her role as observer and writer to point out that her readings of the natural world can probe but never fully encompass nonhuman realities.

A passage from the chapter "Water Trails of the Ceriso" illustrates this pattern. In giving an account of the region's coyotes, the narrator presents herself as a trained naturalist and regional insider, yet she routinely digresses from her descriptions to comment on her observational biases and restricted knowledge. She begins her description by situating the coyotes in their environmental context. Adopting the role of competent observer, she explains that the appearance of birds of prey indicates the presence of the animals they feed on. "It is a sign when there begin to be hawks skimming above the sage that the little people are going about their business" (LLR 29). Correspondingly, to the coyote that she trails "some slant-winged scavenger hanging in the air signaled prospect of dinner" (31). The congruence of the narrator's and the coyote's "reading" of the appearance of the birds of prey attests to the ecological awareness of the narrator, while her substitution of the euphemisms "little people" and "dinner" for the word *prey* works to domesticate the wild animals. By presenting the narrator as a competent reader of the ecological text and by casting the animals as human-like interpreters of their surroundings, the passage asserts a continuity between observer and observed. The narrator's extended comparison of the coyote to a man reinforces this effect: "I have trailed a coyote often . . . and found his track such as a man, a very intelligent man accustomed to a hill country, and a little cautious, would make to the same point. Here a detour to avoid a stretch of too little cover, there a pause on the rim of a gully to pick the better way,—and it is usually the best way,—and making his point with the greatest economy of effort" (31). The narrator gives an appreciative account of the coyote's gate and way of tracking. Comparing the animal to a skilled and experienced man, she presents the animal's movements as deliberate and motivated actions. Her personification of the coyote thus works to portray the animal as a self-determined agent.

In addition, the narrator brackets her description of the coyote's route across the valley and mesa with self-referential comments that contrast the prevalent scientific view of "nightprowlers" as predominantly instinct driven with a description of the specialized senses and learning processes of the animals. The narrator dismisses the "careless" mechanistic view of the animals as "bound by some such limitation as hampers clock-work" (LLR 29). Instead of subscribing to a reductive view of the animals, she stresses their ability to adapt to different circumstances, to process sensory information, and to apply the knowledge they have gained through prior experience. "They know well how to adjust themselves to conditions wherein food is more plentiful by day. And their accustomed performance is very much a matter of keen eye, keener scent, quick ear, and a better memory of sights and sounds than man dares boast" (30). As the narrator observes the desert's wildlife, she seeks to comprehend the reasons for the animals' behavior and the ecological significance of their actions. Concerned with presenting the animals as intentional agents, she acknowledges that they have an existence apart from her interpretations of their actions. Her ecological literacy notwithstanding, she customarily notes the limits of her knowledge. "Watch a coyote come out of his lair and cast about in his mind where he will go for his daily killing. You cannot very well tell what decides him, but very easily that he has decided" (30).

The narrator can seek to comprehend the natural phenomena and ecological relations she observes; their significance, however, is not determined by her readings of the land. Her access to the nonhuman reality of the place remains limited. Yet in speculating on the motivation of the animals and on the extent of consciousness involved in their interactions, the narrator has to move beyond assertions of difference between the animals' and her own way of existence. To conjecture the learning processes and viewpoints of the animals, she posits certain similarities. "What would be worth knowing is how much of their neighbor's affairs the new generations learn for themselves, and how much they are taught of their elders" (LLR 56). Austin personifies the desert animals in an effort to investigate the degree of conscious deliberation involved in their behavior and ecological interrelations.

THE LITERARY AND THE SCIENTIFIC IMAGINATION MEET: THE NATURE FAKER DEBATE

In presenting the desert animals in their ecological context, Austin's narratives depart from the conventions of wildlife descriptions prevalent in American nature writing at the turn of the twentieth century. In response to Charles Darwin's theory of evolution and scientific materialism, the demand for literature about animals had drastically increased. As Lisa Mighetto argues in "Science, Sentiment, and Anxiety," the evolutionary theories caused anxieties that the natural world, once stripped of its sacred character, is amoral, arbitrary, and cruel, and that humans are either brutes or "helpless, inconsequential creature[s], subject to the whim of natural forces" (35). While these possibilities became the subject of literary naturalists, nature writers attempted to ameliorate these fears by portraying nature as divine, benevolent, and innately moral (35). In particular, they sought to humanize humans' animal relatives. They stressed the individuality, nobility, sensitivity, and intelligence of their animal characters (36–39, 43–46). Their portraits focused on the cooperation and knowledge rather than on the competition and instincts of the animals. Mighetto explains, "Americans found the premise that the development of an animal or plant could be affected by externalities comforting; it provided the feeling that they were in control and could improve their lot" (40).[29]

The highly fictionalized accounts of animal reason and altruism resulted in a heated controversy about the so-called nature fakers, during the years 1903 to 1907. The debate revolved around the standards of accuracy in natural history writing, yet it attracted the interest not only of nature writers but of the general public. Eventually, it even involved the president, Theodore Roosevelt, himself an accomplished naturalist. Roosevelt sided with John Burroughs, preeminent nature writer of the time, and he called for "a real knowledge and appreciation of wild things, of trees, flowers, birds, and of the grim and crafty creatures of the wilderness" and demanded a ban on "deliberate or reckless untruth in this study."[30]

In *The Land of Little Rain* Austin takes up themes popular in the genre of nature writing at the turn of the twentieth century. She humanizes the wildlife, gives diminutive accounts of the food chain, and stresses the intelligence and learning of the animals.[31] Yet the objective of her descriptions is not to assuage fears about the animal side of human existence. On the contrary, her account is an imaginative exploration of the self-organizing existence of the desert's flora and fauna that probes the ecological and sociocultural conditions of environmental perception. Austin's self-reflexive and humorous nature writing differs in rhetoric and logic from that of her contemporaries. In contrast to most participants in the nature faker debate, who strictly distinguished between aesthetics and science, Austin perceived a continuum, not an abyss between subjective and objective modes of observation and representation.[32] Her environmental writing avoids the false choices offered by the nature faker debate between "real and sham natural history," as John Burroughs puts it in his essay, between a nature writing devoted either to scientific precision or to the aesthetic or moral imagination. Austin's descriptions of the natural world are imaginative explorations and aesthetic experiments that tend to be factually accurate. Her environmental writing is both appreciative and correct; it includes mimetic depictions and literary self-reflections, technical information and stylistic elaboration, factual observations and ethical and spiritual readings, and classifications and interpretations. In short, Austin fuses science and aesthetics in her nature writing.

Significantly, Austin's most extensive comment on the nature faker debate is not an essay but a short story, with a title that already addresses the question of representation, "Speaking of Bears" (1925). It is an entertaining story about several incidents of literary and literal nature faking that focuses on questions of intertextuality and authorship, authenticity and plagiarism. "Speaking of Bears" humorously presents the telling and sharing of stories as a process in which truths and falsehoods are collectively fabricated and disseminated, as a communal exercise that establishes its own standards of accuracy. It addresses the similarities of and tensions between factual and imaginative kinds of literature by discussing a spectrum of representational modes, comparing historiographic, journalistic, naturist, and fictional forms of writing.

The narrator of "Speaking of Bears" identifies herself as a fiction writer (oss 112).[33] Drawing on various informants and regional oral history, she tells the supposedly true story of how a famous, "most charming," but untrue animal story came into existence (110). She recounts how the tale was told and published in several versions, until it was reviewed and criticized by "the Most Distinguished Citizen" and finally earned its well-known author "the weasel words of 'nature faking'" (112, 113). Disentangled and chronologically ordered, "Speaking of Bears" tells us this story: As a publicity stunt, the journalist Kellerman is dispatched by his magazine to capture a grizzly cub. Hunting for the bear, "in the interest of natural history and increased circulation" (116), Kellerman joins a cowboy outfit. Finding good poker company there, he foregoes his expedition and, when his copy installments are due, writes fake accounts of stunning hunting adventures. In thinking up "his allotment of hairbreadth escapes and death struggles with bear" (123), Kellerman does not simply rely on his own imagination though. Instead, he uses the embellished versions of episodes that the cowboys tell him out of the biography of a bear trapper, which is supposedly historically accurate (128–29). To keep up the spirits of their affluent visitor, the cowboys moreover literally imprint the ground of the camp with fake bear tracks. "'Which goes to show,' Jerke concluded, 'that this here nature fakin' you read about ain't altogether a lit'rary game'" (128). On the verge of complete failure, Kellerman finally buys a tame bear and passes it off as the wild creature he was sent to capture. As planned, the bear is given to the city park, where he eventually attracts the attention of the nature writer Seaforth, who decides to write the animal's biography (117). In describing the bear's life, Seaforth in turn relies on the fake account of Kellerman, which he considers credible due to its parallels to "a book of unimpeachable veracity," probably the same trapper's biography the cowboys quoted to Kellerman (117). Seaforth also has Kellerman corroborate "his story of the story" and personally explores the region in which the bear was 'captured' (118). Things are complicated further, however, when Kellerman publishes his own story after listening to Seaforth's version. "Kellerman's version of his own version of Kellerman's original story" then earns Seaforth, unjustly, the charge of plagiarism and of nature faking (120). While the narrator sides with Seaforth, convinced of his integrity and good intentions albeit his naïvete (113), her first informant of the story's "germinating core" (110), the historian who authored the trapper biography, is appalled both by Seaforth's particular bear saga (129) and by the general demand of the literary market for "fictionized" accounts of wilderness adventure (112). The story's final ironic twist reconciles the historian "to the nature fak—fictionists," though. The debate over the grizzly biography generates enough public interest in the subject for the historian's book, the biography of the bear trapper, to be republished for the first time in fifty years (130).

In "Speaking of Bears" Austin humorously comments on the exuberant possibilities of intertextuality. She points to the interdependence of the various genres of environmental literature in the literary market place. She demonstrates that these different modes of writing are compatible for readers who are interested in a given subject rather than invested in a certain methodology, as is the historian, or in a certain aim, as is "the Most Distinguished Citizen," who clearly stands in for the big game hunter Roosevelt. "Besides the fact that I would rather hear a bear story from a man who has loved bears than from one who has merely killed them, I was on Seaforth's side," explains Austin's narrator. "His methods were precisely the same as any novelist pursues in search of the human story, skillfully compounded of observation and intuition, and in comparison with the amount of human nature faking which goes on in the monthly magazines—!" (*oss* 115). The layering of competing accounts and modes of narration in the narrative—from the dignified talk of the historian in his library to the funny vernacular tale of the cowboy in his outback—produces a high-spirited medley that joyfully proclaims the diversity of writing styles and motivations. Austin's narrative expresses an unconstrained enthusiasm over the processes of storytelling and collective myth making, which communicates itself to the readers, involving us with the narrator in the adventure of peeling away the story's "many layers" (110).

While Mary Austin agreed with Theodore Roosevelt and John Burroughs that a certain facticity in nature writing was desirable, she also recognized that standards of accuracy were conventions, not necessarily arbitrary but definitely subject to change. In "Science for the Unscientific" (1922), Austin asserts that fiction writers, poets, and scientists share "the same obligation of relating fact to truth" (563). According to Austin, science as a mere accumulation of facts is both impossible and irrelevant. The perspective of the scientist always influences his or her findings; yet even if considered objectively verifiable, factual information in and of itself was of little interest to Austin. Only when related to the larger questions—of what it means to be human in a world that extends beyond the human and of how to behave as part of this world—did the natural sciences gain significance for her. Then the observed "facts" became "truth" (*LJE* vii). Hence Austin's environmental writing recommends the study of botany, zoology, meteorology, and other areas of natural science to the general public, while it encourages scientists to complement their studies with a dose of outdoors experience, preferably of the aesthetic and spiritual kind. It urges lay and professional students of natural history to ask what relevance their research holds for the ordinary living processes of their communities. As Austin puts it in one of her natural history notes, "The scientific age begins not with scientific discovery . . . but with its being put to practical use, that is, to pattern changing effect" (AU 514).

SCIENCE MYSTIFIED

In her environmental narratives Austin probes the social and environmentalist implications of scientific practices. As Thoreau before her, Austin integrates the descriptions of regional ecologies with reflections on the assumptions and modes of observation that inform her natural history studies. Thoreau had ended, for instance, "The Succession of Forest Trees" (1860)—an essay on the environmental factors involved in the dispersion of tree seeds and on the related topic of scientific method—with an invocation of both the "mysterious" quality of nature and of the triteness of human culture.[34] Thoreau closed his lecture on a supposedly "purely scientific subject" (73) on a note of enchantment with the spiritual treasures that his environmental studies yielded to ensure that his audience would put the new knowledge not merely to the utilitarian use of forest management. By lending a magical quality to the natural processes that transform seeds into plants, he attends in his account to an aspect of forest succession that empirical or pragmatic studies ignored. A strong mystical element also runs through Austin's nature writing. In *The Land of Little Rain* entire chapters, such as "Nurslings of the Sky," are given over to the attempt to develop a synthesis of scientific and spiritual nature study. Like Thoreau, Austin frequently uses her knowledge of natural history to redefine the relations among science, imagination, and spirituality and to point to their relevance for her community's relation to its land base.

In "Nurslings of the Sky," the narrator gives a detailed account of the weather's influence on the seasonal changes of the desert environment, while she advances a spiritual view of the natural world.[35] For the narrator the contemplation of the formation and configuration of clouds inspires religious sentiments. "The first effect of cloud study is a sense of presence and intention in storm processes. Weather does not happen. It is the visible manifestation of the Spirit moving itself in the void" (*LLR* 246–47). As the narrator observes the clouds, she begins to conceive of the weather as a purposeful process. Her attempt to explain the origin and purpose of storms leads her to adopt a perspective that echoes nineteenth-century transcendentalism. Based on an intuitive understanding of the weather's properties, on her "sense of presence and intention," she interprets the weather as a manifestation of a higher spiritual reality.[36]

Initially, the narrator's belief that a divine force orchestrates the weather lets her disregard the natural causes of storms. The sky is reduced to an absence, a "void," which is animated by a divine principle. Accordingly, the narrator presents spiritual contemplation and empirical observation as irreconcilable approaches. She criticizes the "Weather Bureau," which she personifies as a man who "taps the record on his instruments and going out on the streets denies his God, not having gathered the sense of what he has seen" (*LLR* 247). For the narrator observations that are solely motivated by scientific or pragmatic interests result in an inaccurate understanding of the natural world because they ignore its spiritual dimension. "It is astonishing the trouble men will be at to find out when to plant potatoes, and gloze over the eternal meaning of the skies (261–62).

The narrator does not object to scientific studies in principle, however, but dismisses resource-oriented and rationalist conceptions of reality that cannot account for aesthetic, emotional, or spiritual responses to the environment. In her portrait of the weather as a directed and meaningful process, the narrator dissolves the posited dichotomy between her reverential view of nature's divine origins and empirical and scientific observations. She renders the clouds, for instance, as sociable and intentful agents and bases her humanizing account on meteorological explanations of weather processes: "They gather flock-wise, moving on the level currents that roll about the peaks, lock hands and settle with the cooler air, drawing a veil about those places where they do their work" (LLR 248). The narrator now presents the clouds as accumulating and moving in response to air currents and thermic and geological conditions rather than divine forces.[37]

The narrator's spirituality does not interfere with her close observation of her biophysical environment, then. On the contrary, the final passage of the essay indicates that it is her joyful attentiveness to detail that inspires the narrator to ponder the spiritual significance of the clouds. She identifies her viewpoint and describes the spatial distribution of the cloud configurations in a particular area, their different shapes, altitudes, and movements, before she alludes to the spiritual meaning they hold for her.

From Kearsarge, say, you look over at Inyo and find pink soft cloud masses asleep on the level desert air; south of you hurries a white troop late to some gathering of their kind at the back of Oppapago; nosing the foot of Waban, a woolly mist creeps south. In the clean, smooth paths of the middle sky and highest up in air, drift, unshepherded, small flocks ranging contrarily . . . the eternal meaning of the skies. You have to beat out for yourself many mornings on the windy headlands the sense of the fact that you get the same rainbow in the cloud drift over Waban and the spray of your garden hose. And not necessarily then do you live up to it. (LLR 261–62)

To the narrator the principle lesson of cloud study is an awareness of the fundamental unity of the world. Through close observation, combined with aesthetic and emotional involvement, she experiences the interrelatedness of natural phenomena and the continuities between the wild and the domestic, between matter and spirit, and between her moments of religious insight and everyday reality. For the narrator the experience of union is a challenge to reorient her daily life. Her account renders both scientific study and spiritual and aesthetic nature appreciation relevant to the ordinary processes of living in place.

NATURAL HISTORY AND DEMOCRACY

"Nurslings of the Sky" thus testifies to a conviction that Austin expressed throughout her life: scientific and literary practices had to be socially relevant. Research had to speak to the current concerns of the average citizen, according to Austin. Scientific findings should be presented in understandable terms to the general public. "People don't want a lot of scientific data jazzed; they want it put straight, handle end foremost so they can use it."[38] In presenting scientific information, popular science writers were to pay particular attention to the bearing that scientific discoveries had on the everyday life of the community. By appealing to the experiential knowledges of their readers, they were to convey the significance that the discussed scientific findings held for present circumstances of living. "What you want is to show people that Science *is* News. . . . Trees, for instance, don't just exist in space. They have points of contact with human life. What is the relation of trees to human life *just now*, well, tie your facts to that point of contact" (AU 1151). Such a contextual approach, Austin thought, would foster the interest of lay readers in scientific theories. It would also establish the necessary rapport between science writers and their audience that would allow the presentation of new discoveries to truly affect the reader's outlook on life. As Austin proposed in her essay "Science for the Unscientific," it was the task of popular science writing to contribute to the development of society by transmitting to the general public the challenges, the "explosion," that scientific advances posed to established modes of thinking, rather than aim at popularizing new findings by relating them to already accepted notions (563).[39]

On her methodology, Austin remarked, "If there is a way in which a scientific con[c]lusion can be stated in terms of common experience, I choose that way rather tha[n] the accepted scholarly way."[40] Although it was clearly a matter of personal preference that Austin wrote speculative nonfiction, such as *The American Rhythm*, rather than scholarly research papers, she promoted popular science writing not merely to rationalize her approach. She was convinced that only literature mindful of the reading public's general standards of knowledge and communication could keep science from relapsing into its medieval status as "the profession of a special intellectual caste" (AU 24). Austin wished to advance a concept of science that defined it as a democratic practice. Hence, she cautioned against an increasing elitism. In "Getting Science into the Thought

Stream," she identified "as one of the things standing in the way of humanizing science, an attitude that what goes on in John Dewey's head is thinking, but what goes on in John Doe's head is not thinking" (AU 204). The scientific community and society at large would benefit, Austin noted, if they would recognize the validity of the knowledge and firsthand experience of common people, especially of those groups traditionally excluded from scientific discourse, such as women (AU 204).[41]

For Austin the objective of science was not to satisfy the special interests of researchers, lobbyists, or an intellectual elite but to contribute to the overall development of society. "Science unassimilated into the average life is an explosive sort of baggage for any people to carry about with it," she warned in "The Need for a New Social Concept" (299). People needed to keep up with the scientific advances affecting their lives if they did not wish to waive their right to self-determination, she added in "Science for the Unscientific." "Clearly if modern man is to keep both science and self-government, he must develop a swift and continuous method of assimilating the one to the other" (562). To ensure that scientific advances would be put to responsible use, it was important, Austin reasoned, that scientific knowledge was presented in a way that made it readily accessible for the general public and that the common reader acquired the necessary sophistication to follow this kind of popular science writing.[42]

Austin certainly formulated high ideals for the production and reception of scientific knowledge. The idealistic streak of her argument may best be understood in the context of the professionalization of the natural sciences in America at the time. The dispute over the relation among scientific, literary, and social practices at the core of the nature faker debate, for instance, suggests that the process of standardization and professionalization underway in the academic disciplines sparked public debates on the social function of science. The relation among scientific research, popular science literature, and the common interest and standard of knowledge became an item of general interest.

At the beginning of the twentieth century Austin and other nature writers tended to conceive of their work as a service to the public. On both sides of the nature faker debate authors claimed, plausibly correctly, that their mode of writing promoted environmental bonding and thus furthered the conservationist cause.[43] To reach general readers they made an effort to write in the vernacular and to ground their narratives in experiential knowledges. "Science must come *out* of the writer, not as it goes through the mind of the scientist, but alive, organic, with members for the audience to lay hold off."[44] In this estimate, Austin agreed, for instance, with John Burroughs, who not only insisted on the factual accuracy of natural history writing but who also acknowledged, outside his contributions to the nature faker debate, that the subjective impressions and concerns of the observer had to enter into his account to make it a successful piece of natural history writing. According to Burroughs, the writer had to become personally involved in his nature studies. "To interpret Nature is not to improve upon her: it is to draw her out; it is to have an emotional intercourse with her, absorb her, and reproduce her tinged with the colors of the spirit." The observed phenomenon would only come alive for the reader, Burroughs argued, if the descriptions acknowledged the author's personal bias and the human and environmental context of the observed scene. If "I relate the bird in some way to human life, to my own life,—show what it is to me and what it is in the landscape and the season,—then do I give my reader a live bird and not a labeled specimen."[45] While Burroughs ultimately found it difficult to balance objective and subjective modes of natural history writing, in particular scientific and spiritual interpretations, as Buell notes in *The Environmental Imagination* (191), Austin's regionalist focus on experiential knowledges allowed her to effectively integrate these approaches in her nature writing.

AUSTIN'S NARRATIVES OF REGIONAL LEARNING AND ECOCRITICAL PRACTICE

From her early essays in *The Land of Little Rain* to her later *One-Smoke Stories,* Austin eschewed polarized concepts of scientific and aesthetic traditions. She wished for "the great treasures of science" to "become part of the language of literature."[46] Hence, it may seem to contemporary readers as if Austin's environmental writing encouraged what Ursula Heise outlines in "Science and Ecocriticism" as an ecocritical reading practice. Austin's work presents readers with a textual weave of aesthetic and scientific strands that confronts them with "the conflict between science's claim that it delivers descriptions of nature that are essentially value-neutral, and the tendency of cultural analysis to see research as framed by specific ideological, political, and economic interests. . . . The text thereby becomes a place where different visions of nature and varying images of science, each with their cultural and political implications, are played out, rather than simply a site of resistance against science and its claims to truth, or a construct in which science is called upon merely to confirm the inherent beauty of nature" (4).

By drawing attention to the fact that the reading and writing of nature is a situated activity in response to nonbuilt environments and sociocultural developments, Austin's work speaks to both contemporaneous debates on the relation between science and imagination, such as the nature faker debate, and to current ecocritical discussions of how to render the nonhuman in human language without lapsing into anthropocentrism. Austin's creative exploration of regionalist and ecological concepts of subjectivity and textuality anticipates the recent efforts of ecologically minded writers and critics to redress, in Glen Love's words, the "devaluing of the real and consequential" by adopting a biocentric perspective ("Et in Arcadia Ego" 197).

In a nutshell, the basic biocentric standpoint is that "systems of meaning that matter are eco-systems."[47] As discussed in the previous chapter, biocentric criticism proceeds from the assumption that ecological systems exist in their own right and that our responses to the particular realities of the nonhuman world constitute an integral element of our sense of self.[48] In search of sustainable cultural practices, ecocritical studies seek to incorporate an ecological understanding of human identity into literary and cultural studies. A biocentric frame of reference, it seems to me, may be most successfully applied to literary criticism when it aims to extricate concepts such as reality and text, perception and representation, subject and object, human and nonhuman from their polarized definitions within the nature/culture dualism. Rather than denounce any human perspective as anthropocentric, as some critics have done,[49] a biocentric criticism should uphold the difference between envisioning the world from a human perspective and asserting this perspective as the exclusive center of meaning and value. If a distinction between particular standpoints and their repressive potential could not be made, it would be impossible to develop nondualistic concepts of culture, in which human agency no longer is identified with domination over nature.[50]

Since environmental writers cannot adopt a biocentric perspective in regard to nonhuman nature without also reconceptualizing human identity in nonanthropocentric terms, ecocritical studies profit from a combined analysis of the representation of the natural world and human subjectivity in environmental literature. Reading Austin's and Thoreau's

---

environmental narratives with attention to the ways in which their descriptions and meta-narrative passages trace and inscribe bioregional learning processes allows us to participate in their project of redefining human relations to the environment.

Austin dramatizes her narrator's environmental learning process to probe the social and ecological ramifications of literary and scientific practices. She uses a self-reflexive narrative voice to comment on the relation among language, social practices, and biogeography, between her impressions and environmental actualities, and between her literary practice and other forms of narratives, such as orthodox Christian or scientific discourses. In addition, narrative shifts from predominantly anthropocentric to ecological renderings of the nonhuman inscribe the narrator's increasing ecological literacy into the texts. By offering a spectrum of perspectives that register the narrator's shifting focus of attention and interest, Austin's nature writing engages and refines the reader's environmental sensibilities. It portrays "the mutual interaction of epistemology, consciousness, and place" to suggest that humans, including our signifying systems and bodies, are accountable participants in ecological interrelations.[51]

Paying attention to narrative voice, then, can aid in the development of a better understanding of the confluence of scientific, psychological, and philosophical aspects in environmental writing. This is pertinent, since the triad of "natural history information, personal responses to nature, and philosophical interpretation of nature" frequently is considered the defining characteristic of the nature writing genre.[52] If we read the nature essays of authors such as Austin and Thoreau as narratives of environmental learning, we realize that it is the regional perspective of the narrators that brings poetics into reciprocal relations with science, experience, and (environmental) ethics. As Thoreau and Austin author their walks and communicate their regional knowledge, their lived experience of particular places converges with literary, epistemological, and political considerations. Their regional narratives suggest the possibility that an environmental learning process that self-critically seeks to keep track of its own assumptions can provide us with a basis for questioning literary conventions, conceptual frameworks, and social dynamics that aim to disconnect humans from the natural world. Thus Thoreau's and Austin's work demonstrates the aesthetically and politically significant contributions that a regional orientation can make to our readings and writings of nature.

3

SENSE OF PLACE

The Processual Experience of Place

In her literary works Mary Austin frequently creates narrators and characters whose sense of place and literary preferences exemplify the regionalization of identity and cultural practices that Austin advocated in her critical essays. Equipped with a self-critical regionalist consciousness, Austin's narrators describe their acculturation and discuss how their firsthand experience of place influences their representation of regional reality. Not native to but longtime residents of the places they portray, the narrators possess a relational sense of selfhood that allows them to live into their environments. As they learn lessons in adaptation from the animals and plants they observe, they slowly develop new conceptual frameworks appropriate to their present environments. Since Austin's narrators seek to participate in the biocultural life of their regions, they cannot rely on the knowledge they have acquired prior to their life in the arid West and Southwest. Instead, they continually have to test their convictions, values, and modes of perception against their experience of place. As the narrator of *The Land of Little Rain* formulates, they need to "slough off and swallow" their "acquired prejudices as a lizard does his skin" (113).

LIZARD LOGIC

Several significant Austin characters, among them the narrator of *The Land of Little Rain* and the female protagonist of *Cactus Thorn*, choose lizards as models for their regional learning process. They point out that these animals have adapted to the environment to the point of becoming almost indistinguishable from their surroundings. To the narrator of *The Land of Little Rain* the camouflaging effect of the color scheme and pattern of the lizard's skin is "pure witchcraft" (155). It allows the animal to merge visually with the ground. "Now and then a palm's breadth of the trail gathers itself together and scurries off with a little rustle under the brush, to resolve itself to sand again" (155).[1] The narrator is aware that her impression depends on a prereflexive, sensual mode of observation. She cautions that a closer inquiry of the phenomenon will dissolve the enchanting effect of the animal's perceptual fusion with its environment. "If you succeed in catching it in transit," she points out, "it loses its power and becomes a flat, horned, toadlike creature, horrid looking and harmless, of the color of the soil; and the curio dealer will give you two bits for it, to stuff" (155).

The contrast between the narrator's two ways of looking at the lizard indicates that our experience of place is not an unmediated response to environmental forces but represents a form of cultural work that is influenced by our conceptual frameworks and perceptual habits. The narrator's prereflexive responsiveness to her environment facilitates a joyful awareness of the magical fluidity of her perceptual field. It allows for a relational experience of the lizard's presence. In the narrator's phenomenological description, the animals can be said to appear "as styles of unfolding—not as finished chunks of matter given once and for all, but as dynamic ways of engaging the senses and modulating the body."[2] An objectifying gaze, by contrast, is shown to cut off the dialogue between body and world. It privileges the perceiving human subject over the object of its attention to the extent of denying any reciprocal relations between the observer and the observed. As a result, the perceptual world is severed into subject and object. Since the observer is considered the sole center of striving and value, the observed is devalued and becomes available as a resource. As Val Plumwood explains in *Feminism and the Mastery of Nature,* if we assume that the nonhuman world "lacks its own goals and direction, it can impose no constraints on our treatment of it; it can be seen as something utterly neutral on which humans can and even must impose their own goals, purposes and significance. It represents a teleological vacuum, into which human ends must enter" (110). Nature, conceived of as the Other of culture, has neither the capacity for nor the right to self-determination. As a resource, the natural world is valued only insofar as it satisfies human needs. The lizard on the mesa trail, for instance, will be killed, stuffed, and sold for profit.

In making the dynamics of environmental perception a prominent subject of her nature writing, Austin addresses far-reaching questions. How can we perceive and value the other's existence as it unfolds beyond the boundaries of our lives? What allows us to become aware of and represent the existence of others apart from the ways they enter into relations with us? Obviously, there are no easy answers to these questions. Still, the effort to acknowledge the nonhuman context of cultural identity that Austin undertakes in her regionalist writing is pertinent for any attempt to develop sustainable social and cultural practices.

DEWEY'S CONCEPT OF EXPERIENCE AS PARTICIPATORY PROCESS

Austin's regionalist narratives suggest that we need a nondualistic model of the ways in which we physically encounter and aesthetically make sense of our environments (including lizards), if we are to understand our place in a world that extends beyond the human. In this context a more thorough examination of Dewey's notion of participatory experience as a cumulative response to resisting environmental forces is helpful. Dewey's concept of aesthetic experience stresses that our participation in the world, our communication with what we are not, takes the form of a cumulative reciprocal process that depends on a relationship of tension between self and world. "Life grows when a temporary falling out is a transition to a more extensive balance of the energies of the organism with those of the conditions under which it lives" (*Art as Experience* 14). Self and world are interconnected, mutually constitutive yet nonidentical aspects of reality. Therefore, Dewey argues, we experience our environment to the degree that we integrate what is not us and what cannot readily be assimilated nonetheless into our worlds by adjusting ourselves and our relations to it. He explains, "For only when an organism shares in the ordered relations of its environment does it secure the stability essential to living. And when the participation comes after a phase of disruption and conflict, it bears within itself the germs of a consummation akin to the esthetic. The rhythm of loss of integration with environment and recovery of union not only persists in man but becomes conscious with him; its conditions are material out of which he forms purposes" (15). In our continually shifting relations with our environment, we seek to bring our daily lives into accord with our surroundings. We establish a temporary equilibrium between self and world, lose it again, and then proceed to build a new balance. In recurrent progressions we move from states of imbalance to states of balance, back to relations of tension and on to the consummation of our previous efforts. This movement is continuous; it absorbs and modulates our past into our present; it gathers what has gone before in a fresh figuration of world and self; it is directed toward the resolution of the experienced imbalance.

The existential "rhythm of loss of integration with environment and recovery of union," then, provides the model for Dewey's description of the creative processes through which we transform our experiences into art. Dewey discerns parallels between the dynamics of our interactions with our environment and the character of our aesthetic experiences. His argument for an experiential concept of art in *Art as Experience* rests on the very idea that experience, creative process, and "esthetic form" share such "characteristics as continuity, cumulation, conservation, tension, and anticipation" (138). He asserts that "accumulation" in a work of art is a gathering together, an issuing forth, and a withholding, because the cumulative effect of a work of art depends on a continuous progression and accumulation of experiences that "must be such as to create suspense and anticipation of resolution" (137). Accordingly, the reception of a work of art moves through "recurrent" moments of preliminary "consummation" toward its ultimate culmination (137). The relations of tension that ensure our ongoing engagement with the world around us and that cause our experiences to take the form of cumulative processes also characterize the internal structure of a work of art and our reception of it.

The resistance that the environment offers to our perception and creative efforts thus is a prerequisite for having an experience and creating an aesthetic object in Dewey's sense. Without this tension we would not engage in an experiential process. As he states, an "instantaneous experience is an impossibility, biologically and psychologically" (220). For Dewey an experience always is the "product" of a cumulative process (220).[3] It entails that the subject builds new relations with the environing world and is transformed through these. In Dewey's terms, the narrator's perceptual experience of the lizard's magic, for instance, cannot be considered a complete experience. Rather, it generates and partakes in one, since her perception adds to the sequential development of a larger experience, geared toward aligning the narrator with her environment. In this case the experience that the narrator has on the mesa trail is her ongoing and cumulative meditation on the ways in which her mode of observation influences her relationship to the desert and its wildlife.

Dewey's notion of environmental resistance, aesthetic tension, and cumulative experience allows us to conceive of subjectivity and art within an environmental matrix without asking us to reduce either human agency to an effect of environmental forces or the world to a product of the experiencing subject. Our experiential processes, Dewey argues, are shaped by the resistance that the independent existence of others poses for us. Thus our experiences follow a "rhythm of surrender and reflection" (144). In experiencing the world we are neither entirely active nor entirely passive. We cannot be reduced to either self or world but enter into their interplay as a "force, not a transparency" (246). As a participatory force, we produce our subjectivity in response to others. Through phases of tension, conflict, and reintegration, we create relations with them. Dewey's model of aesthetic experience and experiential art, then, offers an alternative to the either/or logic of both essentialist and radical constructionist explanations of the relations between subject and world. Dewey's argument eschews both a dualistic framework and the concept of a naturally given harmonious symbiosis between human and nonhuman forms of life.

THE EXPERIENCE OF ENVIRONMENTAL RHYTHMS
IN *THE LAND OF LITTLE RAIN*

Austin's representation of regional identity formation likewise signals that a relational sense of environmental selfhood does not entail a dissolution of the boundaries between self and other but necessitates ongoing refigurations of these polarities. The narrator of *The Land of Little Rain,* for instance, distances herself from a prospector, "The Pocket Hunter," who has become "saturated with the elements" to the point where he "takes no account of them" (70). The narrator holds that the prospector has dissolved the boundaries between himself and his environment to the extent that he cannot consciously experience the beauty of the desert or appreciate the companionship he finds in the desert's animals and plants. His lack of self-consciousness and his superstitions lead him to misapprehend his surroundings. He does not get "the truth about beasts in general" (77). The narrator, by contrast, recognizes her intimate ties to her surroundings but remains self-reflexive and responds deliberately to her environment.

An exemplary account in this respect is the narrator's twofold description of a summer rain in the chapter "Nurslings of the Sky." In a move that can be considered typical for Austin's regionalist nature writing, the narrator describes the phenomenon from different perspectives—a strategy that allows her to suggest that subjective and objective worlds

cohere, without forcing her to render the world as an effect of human sig-
nification and imagination.

The narrator begins her description of the summer rain, which interrupts one of her hikes, by stressing the advantages of her experiential
knowledge and ecological literacy. She encourages her readers to follow
her example by paying close attention to the vegetation of their surroundings, since it is indicative of the area's climatic conditions. "One who
goes often into a hill country learns not to say: What if it should rain? . . .
the unusual thing is that one should escape it. You might suppose that if
you took any account of plant contrivances to save their pollen powder
against showers. Note how many there are deep-throated and bell-flowered
like the pentstemons, how many have nodding pedicels as the columbine,
how many grow in copse shelters and grow only there" (*LLR* 249). The
narrator's attentiveness, botanical training, and long-standing familiarity with her environment let her find "keen delight" in the rain, "with the
added comfort, born of experience, of knowing that no harm comes of a
wetting at high altitudes" (249). Since the narrator's experience progresses
through her recurrent reflections on the relations of what she has learned,
received, and done before, her experience has "pattern and structure" in
Dewey's sense. "It is not just doing and undergoing in alternation, but
consists of them in relationship. . . . The action and its consequence [are]
joined in perception. This relationship is what gives meaning" (*Art as
Experience* 44).

The narrator's aesthetic representation of her experience, in other
words, follows the experiential rhythm of disintegration and reintegration,
of surrender and reflection. The narrative reinforces this aesthetic effect,
which Dewey considered integral to any work of art, through the combination of two different yet converging depictions of the rain. The first description receives its unity through the presence of the narrator, whose successive observations trace the effect of the rain from a change in the general
atmosphere of the day to the rain's animation of the plants and streams:
"The day is warm; a white cloud spies over the cañon wall, slips up behind the ridge to cross it by some windy pass, obscures your sun. Next
you hear the rain drum on the broad-leaved hellebore, and beat down the
mimulus beside the brook. You shelter on the lee of some strong pine with
shutwinged butterflies and merry, fiddling creatures of the wood. Runnels of rain water from the glacier-slips swirl through the pine needles
into rivulets, the streams froth and rise in their banks" (*LLR* 249–50). As

the narrator focuses her attention on her close surroundings and lowers her gaze steadily toward the level of the ground, the presence of the rain seems to increase. The last sentence, in particular, echoes the water's movement. It renders in language first the stretched-out meandering movement of the rivulets, then the contrasting choppy motion of the streams. "Runnels of rain water from the glacier-slips swirl through the pine needles into rivulets, the streams froth and rise in their banks" (250).

Although the second description follows immediately to conclude the paragraph, it differs markedly from the first. It adds a minimized and impersonal depiction of the rain's passing to the account. "The sky is white without cloud, the sky is gray; the sky is clear. The summer showers leave no wake" (*LLR* 250). The anaphora renders the process, which the narrator describes in detail in the previous passage, in instant moments and depicts the rainfall apart from its effect on the land and its inhabitants. In comparison to the force and time frame of the natural processes causing cloud formation, the emotional response and competent behavior of the narrator now are of little account. Still, the concluding statement refers back to the narrator's preceding portrait of the downpour as a harmless and delightful event. It implicitly attests to the adequacy of her perception by phrasing her experience in terms of a law that universally describes the impact of summer rains on the area. The narrator thus presents herself as part of her environment and as an experienced resident of the region. In contrast to the prospector, she prides herself in her ecological and experiential knowledge and presents her actions as the result of her conscious deliberations.

Austin's representation of the narrator's regional acculturation in *The Land of Little Rain* hence attests to the conviction she shared with Dewey that aesthetic perception and art should express the quotidian rhythms of our embodied experience of living in particular places. Her nature writing enacts the experiential processes that the narrator undergoes as she seeks to synchronize her outlook and behavior with her environment and its resistant forces. The text's oscillation between different perspectives and modes of observation traces the narrator's processual experience of place and marks the recurrent phases of tension and realignment that she undergoes as she experiences herself among others in place. The narrative thus delineates the dynamics of environmental perception and regional identity formation, without presuming to represent the essence of either subject or environing world. The composition of the narrative is geared toward alerting us to the ongoing communication between our-selves and our surroundings. It reminds us of our participation in the world, while allowing us also to recognize that the nonhuman world shape shifts only temporarily into human sight and life.

The Place of Humans in the Desert Ecosystem

Rather than propose that subject and environment enter into a form of undifferentiated union, Austin's regionalist narratives insist that human life is not only of the natural world but also discontinuous with its non-human dimension and thus to a certain extent nature's other. Since human life depends on natural resources, while the desert ecosystem, for instance, can function efficiently without human contribution, human survival in the arid region is shown to depend on the population's will-ingness to acquire environmental competence. As the narrator of *The Land of Little Rain* points out, only the accurately prepared can safely enter or live in the desert (8, 246). The uninitiated or environmentally illiterate, however, are doomed, as "that hapless party that gave Death Val-ley its forbidding name" (8).

AUSTIN'S REGIONALIST USE OF THE TRAGIC
DESERT CONVENTION

"And yet—and yet—is it not perhaps to satisfy expectation that one falls into the tragic key in writing of desertness?" (20), the narrator of *The Land of Little Rain* wonders. In her regionalist work, Austin indeed fre-quently draws on the established convention of casting the desert as a hos-tile if not lethal landscape. The narrator of *Lost Borders,* for instance, initially relates her unbearable boredom with the unchanging and unin-spiring view. Analogous to her sensation of being subjected to "the coil of a huge and senseless monotony" (4), she depicts the land as desolate and dreary. The alkali flats are "straight, white, blinding," the mesa is "for-saken," the shrubs are "skimpy," the hills are no more than "starved knees," and the mountains are "rubbishy" (4). Such descriptions of the desert as a desolate and dangerous terrain echo earlier representations of tragic desertscapes. Take, for instance, Charlotte Perkins Gilman's poem "A Nevada Desert," written in the early 1890s. Gilman depicts the desert as "an aching, blinding, barren, endless plain," which is "corpse-colored with white mounds of alkali."[4]

Yet Austin's routine comments on the dangers that the extreme desert environment poses for its human visitors and residents indicate not frustrated aesthetic preferences but a strategic choice. Austin casts the desert as a landscape of resistance to challenge "our American way to think of our newly acquired desert merely as a place to be crossed, and its aboriginal population, unfriendly to invasion, as creatures to be hunted" (*LJE* 225). In the context of her regionalist work Austin's recourse to the image of the desert as wasteland serves to underline her contention that the adequate perception and sustainable inhabitation of different environments require different conceptual frameworks that can only be derived from an attentive observation of and adaptation to the land and its already established regional cultures.

In early works, such as *The Land of Little Rain* and *Lost Borders,* the representation of the arid regions begins with but consequently moves away from descriptions based on anthropocentric conceptions of the desert as a deadly, purposeless, and unintelligible landscape. The insistence that the desert "supports no man" (*LLR* 3), because its "foolish wastes of sand and inextricable disordered ranges" exceed the human "limit of endurable existence" (*LB* 2), gives way to detailed and appreciative accounts of the regional environment and cultures. In later works, such as *California: The Land of the Sun* and *The Land of Journey's Ending,* the use of the trope of the deathly desertscape is reduced even further. Impressions of horrifying desolation are cited in passing, while a positive representation of the region prevails from the beginning.[5] Austin does not inadvertently comply with an established literary tradition, then, but employs a conventional trope to advance her regionalist argument. In specifying that the land poses a threat only to the incompetent and by juxtaposing their frustration and failure with the successful inhabitation of the region by Native American communities and by Hispanic and white newcomers willing to adapt, Austin puts the tragic desert convention to regionalist use.

Austin's routine remarks on the frailty of human life in the arid regions have solicited different critical readings. Sean P. O'Grady, for instance, proposes in *Pilgrims to the Wild* that Austin's portrait of inhospitable desertscapes differs notably from the benign wilderness representations of the nineteenth-century nature writers preceding her. He posits that in comparison to Austin's work, "Thoreau's 'excursions' were recreational; John Muir's meanderings were those of a privileged vagabond; and Clarence King's geological aestheticism was dilettantish. In their writings, these men usually confine themselves to what sarcastically might be called the holiday side of the wild. Mary Austin, on the other hand, is most profoundly aware of the 'shadow side' of the wild— its dark, brooding, and, indeed, threatening aspects, those that undermine the foundations of society and even the integrity of the individual self" (125). On the same count Lawrence Buell distinguishes in *The Environmental Imagination* Austin's *The Land of Little Rain* from the work of her contemporary, John Van Dyke, "whose *The Desert* [1901] is a more traditional gallery of picturesque scenes" (176). Franklin Walker, however, argues in the chapter "The Desert Grows Friendly" of his *Literary History of Southern California* that Van Dyke's *The Desert* was the first literary representation of the Mojave and Colorado deserts that departed from the established tradition of casting the land as a death trap (180–208). Instead of emphasizing "its treachery, its ugliness, and its formidable terrors" (183), Van Dyke drew attention to the aesthetic beauty of desertscapes. Within the regional literary field, then, Van Dyke's appreciative depiction of the desert was culturally innovative.

Since *The Land of Little Rain* was but the second major work that cast the California deserts in a positive light, it is appropriate to consider Austin's portrait of the violent forces of the desert environment as a self-conscious revision of the deathly desert landscape convention. Within the context of both Austin's work and the regional literary history of California, her early regionalist narratives serve to replace the traditional image of the desert as a wasteland, which needs to be either conquered or avoided, with a view of the desert environment and its regional cultures as a learning model for the development of American society. Austin's vision is original because she manages to describe and value the desert in both its beautiful and terrifying aspects without overemphasizing either characteristic. Her texts insist on the resistance that the desert environment offers to its human population in order to promote an understanding of the desert as a self-regulating ecosystem to which the residents need to accommodate themselves, if they intend to inhabit the region for an extensive period of time. While the depiction of the land's dangerous aspects reinforces Austin's regionalist imperative to adapt, the description of the physical, aesthetic, and spiritual "compensations" that the land is said to offer in return (*LLR* 21) is also intended to present the process of regional acculturation as a valuable and rewarding undertaking.

THE PLACE OF HUMANS IN THE FOOD CHAIN

By dramatizing the fragility of human existence in the desert environment, Austin's accounts of human and nonhuman relations continually remind readers that natural forces may assume a determining influence over human life. "Nothing as large as a man can move unspied upon in that country, and they [the birds of carrion] know well how the land deals with strangers. There are hints to be had here of the way in which the land forces new habits on its dwellers" (LLR 14). By stressing the human inferiority to overpowering natural forces, Austin's narratives seek to redefine humanity as part of the natural world. Rather than conceive of humans as the apex of either evolution or creation, Austin's texts dispense with the belief in any form of a Great Chain of Being and advance a biocentric understanding of the desert environment and of human and nonhuman relations in general.

Austin's account of the food chain in the chapter "The Scavengers" in *The Land of Little Rain* is exemplary in this respect. She describes the slow death of starving cattle to remind her readers that human life is embodied and that death will inevitably effect the body's assimilation into nonhuman nature. At first the narrator assumes a disinterested stance and reduces the cattle to a mere element of the food chain. She praises the gathering birds of carrion for the "nice discrimination" they display in determining "which of the basket-ribbed cattle is likest to afford the next meal" (49). In observing the cattle closely, however, in seeing them "stretch out their necks along the ground, and roll up their slow eyes at long intervals" (50), the narrator comes to perceive them as sentient and suffering beings. In empathy with the dying animals she changes her perspective. "It is doubtless the economy of nature to have the scavengers by to clean up the carrion, but a wolf at the throat would be a shorter agony than the long stalking and sometime perchings of these loathsome watchers" (50). The narrator's compassion alters her perception of the animals. Her sympathies shift from the consuming to the consumed party. Yet her commiseration with the cattle does not obscure her understanding of the ecological function that the scavengers perform. Instead, her description aims to secure our emotional involvement as readers. The narrator calls on us to imagine ourselves in place of the cattle. "Suppose now it were a man in this long-drawn, hungrily spied upon distress!" (50). To help us to think of ourselves as part of the food chain, the narrator di-

gresses from her description of the particular scene and relates two inci-
dences in which men are stalked by birds of prey. By presenting the men
and the cattle in analogous situations, she indicates that humans, even if
we temporarily assume the role of nonparticipant observers, ultimately
are part of the natural world. She portrays the common suffering of the
animals and the men to encourage us to comprehend ourselves as the
peers of the animals about which we read and to bond with them in "a
fellow feeling" (LLR 15).

In her search for continuities between nonhuman and human nature,
the narrator renders the desert animals as the enemies, allies, teachers,
and peers of the human residents and sojourners. She casts animals,
plants, and people in interchangeable roles: the observer is also observed,
the arbiter judged, and the eater in turn eaten. Animals, plants, and people
alike are presented as purposefully striving beings who have to adapt to
one another and the environment in order to survive. The desert's vegetation and wildlife have the advantage over the human newcomers that
they have already developed interrelated and self-sustaining ways of existence in response to environmental conditions. Yet, people can also establish a home in the desert. They can live in the region "with no peril,
and, according to our way of thought, no particular difficulty" (LLR 20)—
if they pay close attention to their new surroundings, increase their ecological literacy, learn from the desert's biota, and adjust their behavior. In
presenting herself and other residents of the area as engaging successfully
in a bioregional learning process, the narrator defines acculturation no
longer as the lesser of two evils, overdetermination in choice of extinction, but sees it as facilitating a life of "great zest" and "delicate joys" (20).

By describing regional acculturation as the result of the embodied experiential processes that we undergo in response to environmental factors, Austin's work suggests that we inhabit places not as self-contained
agents, not as "havers of experiences," but as perceiving and communicating agencies. Although Austin's narratives stress the need for factual
knowledge and self-conscious reflection, they also insist that, on a physical and psychological level, we are nourished, made, challenged, and
changed through the environmental matrix of our lives. Austin's regionalist texts, as exemplified by the account of the desert's food chain in "The
Scavengers," frequently describe how we, as embodied subjects, neighbor
on, communicate with, consume, and repel the other bodies we encounter. Her literary portraits of human and nonhuman relations are

grounded in an understanding of reciprocity that is best captured by Maurice Merleau-Ponty's statement that "the body stands before the world and the world upright before it, and between them there is a relation that is one of embrace. And between these two vertical beings, there is not a frontier, but a contact surface" (*The Visible and the Invisible* 271). This means that we do not wholly belong to ourselves but also to others. Paradoxical as it may sound, we are part of what we are not. In Austin's words, "Man is not himself only" (*LJE* 437). As her portrait of the scavengers is geared to remind us, we quite literally thrive on one another's difference in being this world.

Instances in which we see nonhuman others, such as the scavengers, react to us and perceive in their response a reflection of the otherness that we represent for them, as in their stalking of us as potential carrion, are experiences that may return us to ourselves with an altered sense of subjectivity. In such moments, "the wheel of perceiving," as Austin calls it in "A New Medium for Democratic Drama," can be imagined to revolve; as it traverses our vision, we cease to be its "realizing center" (*AU* 373). We discern, in other words, that our subjectivities and materialities intertwine since we live simultaneously as sensing individuals in biocultural worlds and exist anonymously among the things that are perceivable for others. We realize, for instance, that we are also a part of the food chain and the natural world at large. As a result, we may come to regard ourselves and the encountered others as neither entirely distinct from nor completely merged with but as participant in this world. As we insist, for instance, that we are more than potential carrion, we may begin to comprehend that we matter and unfold beyond the boundaries and services we offer to one another. In this way, the realization that we are also others for others may foster an awareness of the larger context of human existence and facilitate an environmentally grounded sense of self.

"You Walk a Stranger in a Vegetating World": Spiritual Experiences of Place

The paradoxical sense of being other, of not wholly belonging to the natural world while also being made of it, sustained and eventually reabsorbed by it, is a contradictory sense of selfhood that emerges in Austin's writing as the basis for spiritual experiences of place. Since Austin pays close attention to the experiential processes involved in religious responses to the natural world, her descriptions at times almost read like phenomenological reports of mystical experiences. This agrees well with Austin's dictum, "Mysticism is not in the least mysterious."[6]

An exemplary account of an epiphany, which beautifully details the human and nonhuman interrelations giving rise to a mystical experience, is offered in *The Land of Journey's Ending*. Austin's narrator describes how, on a walk through the desert, she finds the juniper trees arrest her attention. The trees engage her senses and consciousness in a way that makes her feel as if she entered into a conversation with them.

About this time [early spring], walking among the junipers, still sticky yellow and friable like discarded Christmas trimmings, first one and then another pricks itself on your attention. As if all the vitality of the tree, which during the winter had been withdrawn to the seat of the life processes underground, had run up and shouted, "Here I am." Not one of all the ways by which a tree strikes freshly on your observation,—with a greener flush, with stiffened needles, or slight alterations of the axis of the growing shoots, accounts for this flash of mutual awareness. You walk a stranger in a vegetating world; then with an inward click the shutter of some profounder level of consciousness uncloses and admits you to sentience of the mounting sap. (39–40)

The narrator first is aware of encountering in the trees a fundamentally "alien" form of life (40). Through a change in consciousness, however, she gains access to this other dimension of reality. As a "flash of mutual awareness" passes between the narrator and the tree, her observation of the concrete juniper issues into an epiphanic experience of the nonhuman other. As a result, she ceases to feel like an intruding "stranger." Significantly, her newfound understanding of the "vegetating world" is not transcendental in character. The narrator gains insight not into supreme religious matters but into the tree's basic mode of existence. She apprehends its treeness, so to speak, or as the narrator puts it, she becomes sentient of its "mounting sap." Still, the narrator experiences this as a spiritual revelation because it connects her with a previously unknown reality. Pan has touched her mind (40).[7]

Although the narrator suggests that an elusive quality rather than the particular observable features of the tree triggered her experience of contact with the tree's life processes, her description carefully links the epiphany to her embodied experience of place. The detailedness of the account reveals that the narrator's attentive perceptual engagement with her environment prepared her for the moment of revelation. Moreover, her careful observation of the tree's build—her alertness to botanical details, such as the "slight alterations of the axis of the growing shoots"—suggests that scientific training has expanded and sharpened her powers of observation. In addition, the subsequent paragraph ranks the physical location and the approach of the observer ("doing nothing and thinking very little") as equally important in bringing about such epiphanies (*LJE* 40). An advantageous visual point of view and an attitude of meditative calmness and emptiness of mind combine to admit the narrator to an understanding of the tree as a sentient being, who actively engages her senses, while pursuing its own purposes and processes.[8]

In its portrait of human and nonhuman relations, Austin's mystical encounter with the juniper tree brings to mind Thoreau's celebration of nature's radical otherness in "Ktaadn" (1848).[9] Revising pastoral and sublime conventions in the essay, Thoreau describes an epiphanic confrontation with nature as other that transforms his understanding of what it means to be human. Like Austin, Thoreau portrays the epiphany as an experience of contact with something radically different that nonetheless is not experienced as entirely discontinuous with the self. "Talk of mysteries! Think of our life in nature,—daily to be shown matter, to come in contact with it,—rocks, trees, wind on our cheeks! the *solid* earth! the *actual* world! the *common sense! Contact! Contact! Who* are we? *where* are we?" (95). His physical encounter with nature as other destabilizes his prior sense of reality and issues into an altered sense of identity as he realizes that his own body belongs to this "hard matter in its home" (95). Thoreau redefines his notion of the wild to include himself as an embodied being, a shift in consciousness that produces not only fear but awe and an overall exhilaration and excitement.

In Thoreau's and Austin's accounts, the experience of human and nonhuman anotherness thus allows for the epiphanic realization that the relations between subjectivity and materiality are instable and that, through their differences, human and nonhuman forms of life cohere.[10] In both cases the sudden recognition of the simultaneous continuity and difference among dissimilar life forms is shown to have the capacity to jolt us into a conscious awareness of our continual readjustments to a world that actively engages our senses. Our experience of "contact" returns us to our lives with a changed perspective of both the natural world and our own identity. Because such mystical experiences draw on encounters with the nonhuman, they may be felt to introduce an ulterior element into cultural identity and thus to provide a basis for questioning established concepts and practices. In this way Austin's and Thoreau's accounts suggest, the contact with what is other and the experience of oneself as other, the realization that we live as anothers in a unified world unfolding in differences, may combine to challenge prior senses of selfhood and to spawn cultural developments.

IN "THE STREETS OF THE MOUNTAINS": HIKING THROUGH SUBLIMITY

In Austin's work, spiritual experiences of place frequently further the acculturation of the characters because they help them to develop an embodied, environmentally responsive sense of self. "The Streets of the Mountains" provides an example. In this chapter of *The Land of Little Rain* the narrator links her discussion of the water ways, wildlife, and altitude-defined vegetation zones of the Sierra Nevada to a description of her quest for religious vision. The narrator conceives of her hike as a spiritual pilgrimage.[11] The sacred site she journeys to is the top of a mountain, which she designates in the first sentence as its stronghold and defining center. "All streets of the mountains lead to the citadel; steep or slow they go to the core of the hills" (183). In describing her pilgrimage the narrator draws on the established trope of mountaintops as the sacred abodes of gods and thus as sites of religious revelation. She experiences her surroundings as invested with divinity.[12] Yet her spiritual vision complements rather than dominates her environmental perception. She describes the mountains and the valleys east of the Sierra crest, for instance, as the result of a joint effort of geological processes and God. She notes, "one keeps this distinction in mind,—valleys are the sunken places of the earth, cañons are scored out by the glacier ploughs of God" (183). The natural history information embedded in her spiritual narrative is factually accurate.[13] The narrator's religious experiences on the mountain trails, then, round out her physical encounter with the wilderness. Unlike Petrarch's religious meditation on Mont Ventoux in 1336, the narrator's spiritual reading of her surroundings heightens her appreciation of her biophysical environment. Hence it is hardly surprising that she uses the remainder of the essay to develop a locally grounded environmental ethics by testing her spiritual experience of place against diverse traditions such as Western landscape perception and pantheism.

The narrator's first depiction of her panoramic view of the Sierra crest from the mountaintop self-consciously conforms to the tradition of the sublime.[14] As she travels above the mountain's timberline, she finds the view produces "great exhilaration" (186). She describes the scene in this way: "The shape of a new mountain is roughly pyramidal, running out into shark-finned ridges that interfere and merge with other thunder-splintered sierras. You get the saw-tooth effect from a distance, but the near-by granite bulk glitters with the terrible keen polish of old glacial ages. I say terrible; so it seems. When those glossy domes swim into the alpenglow, wet after rain, you conceive how long and imperturbable are the purposes of God" (186).

The depiction enlists all the characteristic features of a sublime landscape. According to the definition Edmund Burke established in his *A Philosophical Enquiry into the Origin of Our Ideas of the Sublime and Beautiful* (1757), the sublime effect is dependent on the vastness, extension, massiveness, ruggedness, and darkness of the contemplated scenery and on the observer's emotional reaction to the view with a sense of terror. The discovery of a sublime perspective in the eighteenth century coincided with the rise of landscape perception, which interpreted nature in relation to an observing subject as cosmos.[15] The sublime landscape was primarily associated with the view from mountaintops because it offered a seemingly boundaryless prospect of largely unmodified natural scenery and thus facilitated the observer's reconceptualization of the natural world as an all-encompassing divine whole.

The first sentence of the narrator's description already encodes her sense of sublime terror. The imagery and the omission of linguistic markers that would uphold the distinction between unconstructed reality and the observer's landscape perception indicate the intense emotional response of the narrator to the view. The crest is not said to resemble but to possess dangerous shark-fins; the weather's slow erosive impact on the rocks is rendered from the limited perspective of the human onlooker as an instant and violent event; the landscape is "thunder-splintered." The sequence of the images within the first sentence moves from a distanced and abstract view of the form of a single mountain to an imaginative and emotional perception of the rugged mountain crest. If translated into the successive glances of one observer, the narrator, the sequence of visual imagery indicates that the effect of the sublime depends on the spectator's adoption of a panoramic vision. The narrator comes to regard the mountains with a sense of horror as her view fans out, and she registers the vastness and extension of the Sierra. The depiction thus agrees with Burke's assertion that a seemingly boundaryless view can result in an impression of infinity that contributes to the observer's sense of terror. "Infinity has a tendency to fill the mind with that sort of delightful horror, which is the most genuine effect, and the truest test of the Sublime" (73).

The second sentence of the narrator's description of the Sierra crest repeats the pattern and also moves from an abstract and detached statement to the narrator's emotional yet unmarked perception of the landscape. The direction of the gaze is reversed, however; the depth of focus decreases. The narrator concentrates for the first time on her close surroundings—the granite rocks dominating the foreground. She states her sublime impression more explicitly and substantiates it by referring to the glacial evidence that indicates the age of the boulders. The narrator's contemplation of the overwhelming time span in which mountains are formed and transformed, that is, the diachronic extension of their natural history, substitutes for her view of the Sierra's spatial extension. On another plane, the narrator's sense of terror still rests on an effect of boundarylessness. From a human perspective the age of the granite rocks, formed 240 to 65 million years ago during the Mesozoic era, approaches infinity. The conceptualization of this time-bound infinity, however, depends more on the narrator's geological knowledge than on her vision.

In reiterating her sense of terror the narrator then draws attention to the constitutive role of both her culturally trained imagination and her visual perception. By means of a self-referential comment, she interrupts her representation of the Sierra and distances herself temporarily from her sentiments. "I say terrible; so it seems." The narrator's account thus points to another prerequisite of sublime landscape perception: in addition to the distanced attitude of the observer to the environment that common landscape perception presupposes, the perception of the sublime is dependent on the observer's ability to retain an inner distance to his or her sense of horror. The observer has to feel threatened, yet the perceived danger has to remain remote or imaginary, since it cannot be assimilated into the aesthetic enjoyment of the view if it puts the spectator emotionally or physically at an actual risk. Burke argued, "When danger or pain press too nearly, they are incapable of giving any delight, and are simply terrible; but at certain distances, and with certain modifications, they may be, and they are delightful" (40). Having distanced herself from her sense of terror, the narrator succeeds in assembling the previously described components of the landscape into a coherent and meaningful whole. In the final depiction of her view from the mountaintop, the narrator returns to a panoramic format. The shiny surface of the wet mountains in the middle ground and background now echoes the glitter of the granite rocks in the foreground. Again, she renders them as constituents of a dynamic landscape and refers to the time span the existence of the mountains manifests.

Her religious conception of the mountains as expressions of a divine ground plan transforms the scene. The bright and "keen" light mellows to a glowing color play; the rugged contours of the peaks are softened to domes; the crest becomes a harmoniously ordered chain of mountains, which do not collide or "interfere" with each other, but "swim" in unison through the air; the sky glazes them with rain instead of crashing them with thunder. The mood of the depiction changes markedly as the narrator strives to express her belief that the mountains are invested with divinity. She now interprets the natural world by means of an aesthetic landscape composition as a harmoniously ordered cosmos. The presence of other humans, the evidence of human impact on the region, the previously discussed "successive waves of occupation or discovery" are absent from this religious rendering of the Sierra (*LLR* 185). Reaching back to preindustrial time, the narrator's landscape perception works to remythify the mountains. Her first depiction of the Sierra in "The Streets of the Mountains" is a narrated landscape, then, that exemplifies the conventions of Western landscape perception.

In the account of her second ascent, the narrator further probes the potential of landscape perception to facilitate a religious communion with nature. The aesthetic retrieval of a cosmological understanding of nature is to complement the narrator's physical experience of her sojourn and her ecological readings of her environment. As the narrator ascends through the "corrective" woods (*LLR* 190) and the "country of the conebearers" (189) to the mountaintop, she integrates the pine trees in her vicinity with the panoramic vista of the desert extending below her. The natural boundary that the trees provide for her view of the desert valley accentuates the outlook. Therefore, she appreciates their presence. "For such pictures the pine branches make a noble frame" (190). Once the forest becomes denser, however, and the interstices between the trees become too narrow for her to catch "glimpses of the tawny valley" (190), the narrator's relation to her close surroundings changes. She now regards the trees as an obstruction, impeding her view of the landscape beyond the forest. "Presently, they close in wholly; they draw mysteriously near, covering your tracks, giving up the trail indifferently, or with a secret grudge. You get a kind of impatience with their locked ranks," the narrator notes (190). Her irritation at finding her view blocked distorts her perception of the forest. The narrator reverses the relation between herself and the rooted trees. Instead of presenting her movement along the path and her consequently changing view of the trail, the narrator portrays the trees as moving in relation to her viewpoint. She thus presents herself as the center of the scene, defining the value and meaning of its components.

The narrator's sense of union with her environment is not restored until she "come[s] out lastly on some high, windy dome and see[s] what they are about" (*LLR* 190). The panoramic view from the mountaintop and her physical distance from the forest allow the narrator to conceive of the pines not as her adversaries but as harmoniously interrelated constituents of the scene. Delighted with the mountaintop view, the narrator perceives the scenery as animated. The pine trees "troop," "swarm," "circle," "part," "meet," and "scale" in the direction of the narrator's distanced viewpoint (190–91). The narrator adopts a pantheistic perspective and personifies the trees as priests who journey up the mountain on a pilgrimage to the "door of the storm chambers" (191). Since the sacred site of these "tall priests to pray for rain" (191) is the peak that the narrator has climbed, the dynamic landscape receives its material and spiritual unity by the relation of its components to the narrator's standpoint. Reclaiming her role as nature's disciple in her pantheistic vision, the narrator reveres the imaginary pine-priests for their refined ceremonial practice and superior devotion. "No doubt they understand this work better than we; in fact they know no other. 'Come,' say the churches of the valleys, after a season of dry years, 'let us pray for rain'" (191).

The epiphany passes, however, and the narrator brings her pantheistic celebration of nature with a humorous twist back to secular reality. She phrases the lesson she has learned in her communion with nature—the reverence or respect that is due to the pine trees—in a deliberately plain manner. "They would do better to plant more trees" (*LLR* 191). The abrupt change in tone draws attention to the fact that the significance of the narrator's spiritual vision extends beyond the moment of revelation. Since her pantheistic communion with the mountain forests is motivated by her desire to experience the union of human and nonhuman nature, it is meant to inform her secular relation to her environment.

For the narrator, as an author, this responsibility also extends to the relation between her literary practice and the natural world. As she seeks to determine the relevance that her spiritual experience holds for her bonding to the environment, the narrator's account turns self-referential. She comments, "It is a pity we have let the gift of lyric improvisation die out. Sitting islanded on some gray peak above the encompassing wood, the soul is lifted up to sing the Iliad of the pines. They have no voice but the wind, and no sound of them rises up to the high places" (LLR 191–92). The narrator proposes that her attempt to describe and speak for the trees, "to sing the Iliad of the pines," is complicated by the literary conventions of her time and by the discontinuities between her culturally mediated response and the nonbuilt environment.[16] For one, the narrator deems as outmoded the lyric tone of her preceding pantheistic account. More important, she perceives the trees as sentient beings, speaking a language of their own that is incompatible with linguistic signifying systems. Since the "voice" of the pines is the "wind," it cannot easily be translated into a narrative poem. Yet the major difficulty of the narrator does not result from linguistic or literary conventions but from her sense of being separated from the scenery she observes. From her "islanded" viewpoint the narrator cannot hear the rustle of the pine trees and comes to regard the sacred "dome" of the mountain as a melancholic "gray peak." It is this sense of detachment that impels her to imagine the absent forest sounds. Her desire to "sing" the epic of the forest expresses her longing to join the protective or "encompassing" community of the trees. She hopes to reduce her feeling of isolation by imagining continuities between human and nonhuman nature.

The narrator's lament of the belatedness of her lyrical attempt, then, is based on her recognition that she cannot subliminally merge with nonhuman nature outside her moments of religious revelation. She knows that the relation she could establish by speaking for the trees is necessarily one-sided, the companionship imaginary.[17] As she seeks to formulate environmental ethics on the basis of her spiritual experience of place, her nature-based religiosity moves away from the tradition of Western landscape perception. Instead of limiting the experience of her embeddedness in nature to the field of aesthetics, the narrator tries to develop spiritual and literary practices that would allow her to experience herself as part of her environment. The difficulties she has to confront in the process illustrate her need to negotiate among her culturally trained modes of perception, her desires, and the biophysical reality of her environment as she physically experiences it.

MYSTICAL EXPERIENCES OF PLACE AND REGIONALIST ETHICS

The narrator's spiritual experiences of place thus are presented as part of her effort to develop a regional sense of selfhood. They "uncramp the soul" and are "corrective to the spirit" (*LLR* 144, 190). The basis for this personally and culturally transformative process is not "a conventional, pew-fed religion" (*LB* 134) but her mystical experiences of place. The attentive encounter with her natural environment provides the narrator with a spiritual, social, and ecological learning model. On a material plane she sees the animals and plants as adapting more easily to environmental conditions than does the region's human population. "Whether the wild things understand it or not they adapt themselves to its processes with greater ease" (*LLR* 200). On a spiritual plane she sees them as conforming more willingly to the divine design of the world. "They are not pushed out except by the exigencies of the nobler plan which they accept with a dignity the rest of us have not yet learned" (201). Testing her cultural heritage against the reality of her environment, the narrator comes to accept the elemental interconnectedness of human and nonhuman nature. As the narrator of *The Land of Journey's Ending* puts it, she returns from her spiritual experience "knowing that long before men set up an anthropocentric deity there was a state, easily met among mountains, called holy, being whole with the experienceable universe" (390).

The parallels to Austin's biographical accounts of her mystical experiences are readily apparent. Austin, to whom "God happened . . . under the walnut tree" at the age of five (*EH* 51), believed that a spiritual presence inhered in the natural world. She gives one of her most notable descriptions of her experiences of mystical union in *Experiences Facing Death* (1931). "There was a wild foxglove at the child's feet and a bee dozing about it, and to this day I can recall the swift, inclusive awareness of each for the whole—I in them and they in me, and all of us enclosed in a warm lucent bubble of livingness" (25). Later in life Austin combined her quest for mystical insight with an exploration of Native American systems

of belief. She embraced the spirituality to which the Paiutes first introduced her and consequently reconceived the God "under the walnut tree"
as "something, not a god, [but] a responsive activity in the world about
you," which she called "the Friend-of-the-Soul-of-Man" or "Wakonda"
(EH 276–77, 289).[18] Given Austin's regionalist agenda and adoption of Native American concepts of nature-based religiosity, it is hardly surprising that she put her mysticism in her literary work to environmentalist
use. Like Thoreau and Muir before her, Austin equated the extensive development and transformation of the land with the loss of a potential
source of personal and cultural regeneration.[19] Accordingly, the concept
of correspondence between the natural and spiritual order of the world
routinely serves in her regionalist writing to reinforce its environmental
imperative: people should respond to nonhuman nature with respect and
humbleness and reenvision themselves as embodied beings in and of particular environments. In Austin's work spiritual experiences of place have
environmentalist implications.

Austin's insistence on the embodiedness of human experience and on
the self-organizing yet related existence of nonhuman nature marks the
major point of departure of her nature-based religion from the otherwise
clearly echoed tradition of nineteenth-century transcendentalism. The
similarities between Austin's spiritual views and Emerson's conception of
Nature are obvious.[20] Both writers propose that people can only overcome
their separation from nonhuman nature, their inner selves, and the spiritual dimension of the world by realigning themselves with the natural
order of the world. And both ground their argument in the belief that material reality manifests an all-encompassing divine principle. Both posit
the matter-soul analogy as the basis for a learning process that is to result
in a personal relationship with and an appreciative attitude toward the
natural world. Both present awe and wonder as a more appropriate response to nature's splendor than mere scientific curiosity or orthodox
Christian interpretations of the world as the Creation. Both reason that
contact with nature engages the senses and mind of human observers,
teaches us moral laws and the necessity of action, and thus facilitates cultural innovation. Yet Austin does not share Emerson's belief that nature
reserves a privileged position for humans because the divine principle
manifests itself in the human mind in conscious form. She does not express the hope that we will transcend nature, in the long run, by means
of our intuition. Instead, Austin sees such notions as obstructing the de-

velopment of respectful and sustainable relations to the environment. For her, environmental competence, long-term regional experience, and adaptability are to remain cardinal virtues.

In contrast to Emerson, Austin was concerned that humanity might have "become the capitalist of mind-stuff" (*AR* 151). She believed that consciousness, in its different forms, pervaded the natural world. For her natural phenomena generally were sentient, animate, and interrelated. As a result of the fundamental unity of all forms of life, she reasoned, the boundaries between both the human and the nonhuman and between individual human minds and the universal consciousness manifested throughout nature were permeable. A striking expression of this idea is her proposition that if "our minds could be looked on from above they would be like sea anemones. [A]ll spread out at a distance from the front of consciousness with all sorts of things entangled in their arms."[21] Rather than lead her to privilege individual vision and insight, Austin's mystical orientation let her insist that human consciousness was enabled by its embeddedness in a world that extended beyond the human. She asked "whether there was, in the beginning, any such thing as an individual mind as we know it now; whether, in fact, there was anything but a delicate web of consciousness, sustained from point to point of individual existence" (*AR* 151). To Austin embodied spiritual experiences served as a reminder, then, that sentience and consciousness still were diffused "throughout animate nature, a subconscious memory of the web, and the slight differentiation between such points of contact as a bear and a man" (151).

THE DEATH AND TRANSFORMATION OF THE BODY

In Austin's regionalist writing embodied spirituality allows for the experience that significant overlaps and interdependencies exist between the natural and cultural aspects of identity. As the medium of contact with nonhuman nature, the body becomes the source of spiritual experiences of place that in turn result in a reconceptualization of human subjectivity as embedded within a larger environmental context. Mortality, death, and the consequent reentrance of the human body into the food chain lose their terrifying aspects once this process is considered part of the endless and well-ordered transformations of the natural world. As the narrator of *Lost Borders* formulates it, "To be snatched at the dramatic moment, to be reabsorbed in the vastness of space and the infinitude of silences, to return simply to the native essences—that is nothing to make moan about" (80).

From this perspective death does not appear as a terrifying moment of annihilation but as a necessary and therefore welcome aspect of human existence. It is seen as one of the ways in which humans participate in the world's manifold processes of growth and decay. This understanding of death, as Austin's narrator is quick to point out, conflicts with a Christian culture preoccupied with questions of redemption and the soul's after-life. She concedes, "but when I had once taken part in a proper Christian funeral, after fifteen years without witnessing one such, I was less sur-prised at it [the fear of death]" (*LB* 80–81). Austin's portrait of human life as embodied and as subject to the material transformations of the natu-ral world, of course, is not without precedent in American literary his-tory. Although Austin may have preferred the comparison with Emer-son for reasons of propriety, her descriptions recall Walt Whitman's celebration of leaves of grass as a token for the never ending metamor-phosis of life—"the smallest sprout shows there is really no death. . . . All goes onward and outward, nothing collapses, / And to die is different from what any one supposed, and luckier."[22]

Accordingly, the narrator of *The Land of Journey's Ending* may even conceive of her death as an opportunity to inscribe herself literally into the landscape. Since the ground will absorb her decomposing body, the narrator is confident that she will be transformed into another, now non-human expression of the spirit of the place in which she lived and was buried. As the narrator muses on a place she feels particularly drawn to, Inscription Rock, she imagines her life after death as another material-ized expression of its "undying quality," its genius loci.[23] "But if not to live, then, perhaps, equally to my purpose to be buried here; and from my dust would spring the crêpe-petaled argemone. . . . You, of a hundred years from now, if when you visit the Rock, you see the cupped silken wings of the argemone burst and float apart when there is no wind; or if, when all is still, a sudden stir in the short-leafed pines, or fresh eagle feathers blown upon the shrine, that will be I, making known in such fashion as I may the land's undying quality" (231). In imagining her narrator persona rein-carnated as flower, wind, or eagle feather, Austin selects objects and phe-nomena that are not only associated with beauty or transience but also often charged with religious significance in Native American iconography. Her description thus to a certain extent evades the realization of her earlier writing that if human subjectivity is predicated on corporeal existence, and if death effects the body's reabsorption into the natural world, then death also signifies the dissolution of individual consciousness. In other words, after death, there can be no more "I."

Instead of seeing Austin shy away from the implications of her convictions, however, one could also argue that she adopts a belief in the continued existence of the souls of the dead as spirits, as it is held in some Native American religions. The fantasy of Austin's narrator brings to mind, for instance, the worldview expressed in the autobiographical essay of one of Austin's contemporaries, Zitkala-Sä, which was published in the *Atlantic* in January 1900 and thus also may have come to Austin's attention. In the section "The Dead Man's Plum Bush," Zitkala-Sä recalls that she was admonished as a girl not to eat from a certain shrub because it grew out of the remains of a man buried at the site and was thought to rustle still with the "strange whistle of departed spirits."[24] The difference between these two readings of Austin's reincarnation fantasy notwithstanding, it is clear that the passage is geared to remind its readers, "You, of a hundred years from now," that human and nonhuman lives and deaths cohere because they are bound to a common environmental matrix. In this limited sense the narrator indeed may continue her regionalist mission after her death. She will be transformed from a relationally and regionally shaped person into some other form of local matter that also expresses and responds to environmental conditions.

For Mary Austin embodied experiences of mystical union entailed the obligation to form lasting relations to the places one inhabited and to complement the insights gained in moments of religious revelation with sustained efforts at becoming environmentally literate. In this sense her regionalist writing can be said to anticipate the project of contemporary ecofeminism "to dispel the notion that poetry and politics, spirituality and activism, scholarship and vision are to remain forever divided, either from each other or within the same person."[25] The residents of Austin's arid regions are to pay close attention to their surroundings and to integrate their spiritual experiences with their "creature instinct" (*LLR* 75). The relation between their religious and embodied experiences of place is defined as reciprocal. While the contact with the natural world may facilitate a character's mystical vision, the spiritual experience in turn influences his or her environmental perception and environmental ethics.

Grounded in the physical experience of predominantly unbuilt environ-ments, the epiphanic moments provide an ethical framework for human and nonhuman interactions. Thus they have concrete sociopolitical con-sequences. Austin's portraits of mystical experiences, then, underline the regionalist claim of her narratives that the willingness and capacity to adapt to environmental conditions provide a measure for human com-petence and integrity.

4

DESERTING THE MYTH OF THE WEST
The Gender of Nature and the Nature of Gender

In her regionalist writing Mary Austin asserts that human and nonhuman forms of life are interrelated, that they share a common environmental matrix. While in chapter 3 the experiential processes involved in regional identity formation are examined with a generalized notion of the human, it is now time to complicate matters by considering how the particulars of human identity, such as gender and race, influence the ways in which subjectivities, cultures, and environments intersect.

The use of blanket categories such as *human* in discussions of human and nonhuman relations can work to conceal the different extent to which particular societies, groups, and individuals participate in and benefit from the subjugation of the natural world and of those human groups associated with nature. Since we live in a world in which all people do not have the same rights or the same chances to thrive and survive, it is important for democratic projects, such as Austin's regionalism, to emphasize that humans share certain characteristics—for instance, our dependence as embodied subjects on sustaining environmental conditions—while also recognizing that there are significant differences, which frequently are distorted or even created by political and cultural dynamics. Our bodies have different shapes, sizes, colors, ages, and sexes, after all, and these and other factors all too often influence who is allowed to move how and where, who gets to eat what, who can keep warm or cool, and who can grow old. We are kept from participating in the world equally, and until we change these dynamics of power we should be concerned with the social, political, and economic differences that inform our lives, including the ways we live in place.

How do Austin's regionalist narratives, then, render these differences?

The Association of Woman and Nature

"THE AMAZONS WERE NOT BORN BREASTLESS"

As a cultural feminist, Austin thought that human alienation from nature as well as most other fundamental problems of modern society were caused by the marginalization of women and the life-affirming attributes traditionally associated with the feminine. Environmental degradation, war, sexism, racism, classism, all these problems were results of "masculinity run amuck," Austin maintained.[1] In "Sex Emancipation through War" (1918), an essay on the feminist possibilities opened by the social reconstruction of American society during World War I, Austin contends:

The world is really a very feminine place, a mother's place, conceptive, brooding, nourishing; a place of infinite patience and infinite elusiveness. It needs to be lived in more or less femininely, and the chief reason why we have never succeeded in being quite at home in it is that our method has been almost exclusively masculine. We have assaulted the earth, ripped out the treasure of its mines, cut down its forests, deflowered its fields and left them sterile for a thousand years. We have lived precisely on the same terms with our fellows, combatively, competitively, egocentrically. Nations have not struggled to make the world a better place, but only to make a more advantageous place in it for themselves. Man invented the State in the key of maleness, with combat for its major occupation, profit the spur and power the prize. This is the pattern of our politics, our economic and our international life, a pattern built not on common *human* traits of human kind, but on dominant sex traits of the male half of society. (610)

Austin's concept of womanhood situates her within the discourse of cultural feminism, which asserted that there are essential differences between men and women and that women embody admirable traits such as nurturance, generosity, and community-mindedness. Austin agreed with her feminist nineteenth-century precursors and contemporaries that women are "maternal, cooperative, altruistic, and life-affirmative."[2]

Convinced that women's contribution to society lay in their personification of these beneficial qualities, cultural feminists often argued for the development of a separate "women's culture," which would provide women with the opportunity to unfold their feminine potential and that would thus constitute an important motor of social reform. Austin shared this belief. In "American Women and the Intellectual Life" (1921), she welcomes the creation of "a genuine woman culture, based upon generic differences in the woman approach," which she defines as a concern with communication, community building, and experiential knowledges in contradistinction to the self-absorption, arrogance, elitist jargon, and "pooh-Bah tradition of learning among men" (485). Austin thought that women are socialized to acquire cooperative modes of behavior that enable them to make significant contributions to the democratization and regionalization of American society. In a press release advertising *The Young Woman Citizen* (1918), her book on the opportunities and obligations that the vote created for women, she articulates her idea as follows: "What the woman must bring to civilization through her gift of citizenship is that woman-experience of making people at home in their environment, adjusting the members one to another. Woman had always been the centre of a group, not to dominate but to bring out the best in everyone of us, thus making it possible for all to work together" (AU box 128). In other words, "the Amazons were not born breastless," as Austin tells us in *The Young Woman Citizen* (42).

By affirming the identification of the feminine with a just and benevolent natural order and by associating all women with this ideal, Austin endorses essentialist notions of gender identity. Still, her aim is to disclose the social fabrication of unequal and destructive relations. She applies a feminist perspective to regionalist and environmental politics to disclose that the adoption of a place-based sense of identity entails different kinds of negotiations for women and for men of different ethnicities and classes. Her writing demonstrates that the regionalist project is implicated in gender, race, and class politics because it hinges on the affirmation of qualities, such as corporeality, reciprocity, and human and nonhuman interdependence, that have been used to define and hierarchically rank positionalities within dominant American society.

ASSOCIATED WITH NATURE, CAST AS OTHER

Historically, to be associated with nature in Western culture has meant to be marginalized within dominant society, because nature has been defined as the absence or negation of civilization. In *Feminism and the Mastery of Nature,* Val Plumwood notes the extent to which rationalist culture has disassociated itself from its "natural" others: "Nature as the excluded and devalued contrast of reason, includes the emotions, the body, the passions, animality, the primitive or uncivilised, the non-human world, matter, physicality and sense experience, as well as the sphere of irrationality, of faith and of madness" (19–20). Nature, in other words, has come to stand for everything that has to be avoided, controlled, or eliminated within rationalist culture. To be identified with nature in this context, Plumwood explains, "is to be defined as passive, as non-agent and non-subject . . . . It means being seen as part of a sharply separate, even alien lower realm, whose domination is simply 'natural,' flowing from nature itself and the nature(s) of things" (4).

Hence, the subordination of women has been legitimized through a recourse to naturalizing concepts of femininity that claim that anatomy is female destiny.[3] Woman, defined in terms of her biology as the Other of culture, is thought to be bound by necessity. Her existence is seen as conditioned by the laws of physicality rather than purposeful striving. She lacks reason and volition; the reproductive functions of her body are taken to be her defining characteristic. Thus the patriarchal association of femininity with nature has served to relegate women to the sphere of biological and social reproduction, that is, to the performance of those tasks that would betray the "master subject's" (Haraway 177) denial that it too depends as an embodied being on the natural world. To justify their subservience as part of a natural hierarchy of being, women are to personify the qualities attributed to nature as the devalued Other of reason—the unconscious, emotionality, and irrationality. Hence, Ynestra King explains in "Toward an Ecological Feminism and a Feminist Ecology" that the "building of Western industrial civilization in opposition to nature interacts dialectically with and reinforces the subjugation of women because women are believed to be closer to nature in this culture against nature" (119). Similarly, other groups have been cast as naturalized Others to legitimize their subjugation. Within societies dominated by whites, people of color frequently have been identified with physicality and animality.

Since their association with materiality, necessity, and nature has served to keep women, nonwhite people, workers, and other groups defined as Other in a subordinate position, the recovery of embodiedness and interdependence as positive values presupposes that these aspects are redefined outside a dualistic framework. Since terms such as *nature* and *body* are constituents of dualistic paradigms, efforts to recover these categories without considering how the claimed positionalities relate to and depend on others run the risk of reinforcing imbalances of power. Under the pressure of sexual and racial politics, the valorization, for instance, of corporeality by a subjugated group can be co-opted to justify its continued marginalization as naturalized Other—unless the affirmation is linked to a rejection of conceptualizations of the body as the antithesis of mind, volition, and reason. It should be stressed that the association with nature can unfold its oppressive potential only as long as nature is considered the opposite of the qualities that dominant culture is thought to represent. In order to conceptualize humans in regionalist terms as part of their environment, then, we have to value the material aspects of human life; yet we cannot meaningfully assert our embodiedness without understanding which cultural constructs and political dynamics have kept us so far from affirming our continuity with nature.

Gender, Race, and Place: Austin's Regionalist Case Studies

A common subject of Austin's regionalist stories are the psychological and social processes involved in a character's adaptation to a regional environment and culture. A cursory reading of Austin's work reveals that she portrays both men and women of different ethnic backgrounds as experienced inhabitants of the desert. Austin often contrasts the competence of her exemplary regional characters with the detached and ignorant attitude toward the natural world that she associates with dominant society. Accordingly, her narrators frequently recommend their fellow residents as learning models to the readers. While uninitiated travelers have "lost their lives proving where it is not safe to go," the narrator of *Lost Borders* maintains, the "best part" of the desert is known "to some far-straying Indian, sheepherder, or pocket hunter, whose account of it does not get into the reports of the Geological Survey" (9). In Austin's stories, characters who have gained their knowledge through their physical and emotional engagement with their natural surroundings—such as the French shepherd Little Pete, the Anglo-American Pocket Hunter, the Paiute basket maker Seyavi, and the European American transient called the Walking Woman—are cast as the most reliable source of information about the regional environment.

A comparative look at Austin's "folk-legendary biographies"[4] shows, however, that despite these commonalities, her female and her male characters frequently sojourn in the wild reaches of their region for fundamentally different reasons. They also adapt to their land base and local communities in disparate ways and with distinct social consequences.

LITTLE PETE AND THE POCKET HUNTER

Little Pete and the Pocket Hunter appear in several of Austin's essays and stories.[5] Both characters have developed lasting relations to their regional environment through long-term sojourns in its unsettled parts. This bonding is presented to the readers as a psychological necessity. The attachment of Little Pete to his flock, the desert, its wildlife and vegetation is defined as imperative for his emotional survival. "Well—what would you? a man must have fellowship in some sort" (*LB* 66). Likewise, we are told that the Pocket Hunter "depended for the necessary sense of home and companionship on the beast and trees" (*LLR* 74). The narratives initially suggest that the men form close relations to their environment either by humanizing nonhuman nature or by becoming animalized themselves. "Whoso goes a-shepherding in the desert hills comes to be at one with his companions, growing brutish or converting them" (*LB* 66). At first the shepherd and the prospector seem to represent these two mutually exclusive options. Little Pete conceives of the animals as fellow beings, the Pocket Hunter is assimilated into the environment. While the shepherd "loved his dogs as brothers" and "humanized his sheep" (*LB* 66), the prospector looks "as if he had the faculty of small hunted things of taking on the protective color of his surroundings" (*LLR* 64). To him "all places were equally happy so long as they were out of doors" (*LLR* 70).[6]

The further characterization of the figures, however, dissolves the posited opposition. We are told that the outward appearance of Little Pete is "of rather less account than his own dogs" (*LB* 66). Not only is he undersized, hairy, and washes himself "only once a year at the shearing as the sheep were washed" (66), he wears moreover a sheep skin with the wool outward as clothing and a wreath of leaves instead of a hat. In contrast to the animal-like shepherd who is said to humanize his sheep, the major ambition of the animalized Pocket Hunter is to "set himself up among the eminently bourgeois of London" (*LLR* 79). Austin thus casts the shepherd and the prospector as exemplary regional characters who strike a dynamic balance between their identity as members of society and as part of their natural environment. Their sense of selfhood is alternately determined by the cultural and natural components of their physical and mental makeup.

Austin's portrait of her male model characters thus defies dualistic notions of mind and body and of nature and culture. As the shepherd and the prospector come to regard the desert's biota as their fellow "folks" (*LLR* 28), they begin to perceive themselves as the fellow animals of the desert's wildlife. In the portraits of her female model characters, Austin likewise presents the acculturation to the desert as a transformative process. Yet significant differences emerge concerning the motivation, behavior, and social reputation of the characters.

THE BASKET MAKER

In "The Basket Maker," the narrator of *The Land of Little Rain* retells the life story of Seyavi, who lives in a "campoodie" near the narrator's home-town, Independence (139). The narrator refers to Seyavi in several essays as one of her primary sources of information about the precolonial history of the region (*LLR* 31, 139, 145). In her portrait of the older woman, the narrator explores the significance that the gender and race identity of the Paiute basket maker holds for her adaptation to the desert.[7]

As a member of Paiute culture, Seyavi was brought up to consider herself and her community part of the desert environment. She was trained in the "art" of living off the land (*LLR* 166). She learned which plants yield edible seeds, nuts, and roots and how to fish and hunt. The narrator points out that the Paiutes generally consider their local environment and not their particular settlement their home. "Not the wattled hut is his home, but the land, the winds, the hill front, the stream" (173). In light of the brutal relocation policy of the Bureau of Indian Affairs, the land-based character of tribal culture acquires political significance. The narrator explains to her European American readership. "So you see how it is that the homesickness of an Indian is often unto death" (174). Like the other members of her tribe, Seyavi has been forced by European American society into "the deplorable condition of hangers-on" yet successfully continues to resist the order to move to a northern reservation (174). Her life is characterized by an integration of the natural and cultural aspects of her identity and by a long-standing engagement with her environment.

In this respect, it resembles the lives of the narrator and her male European American model characters, the Pocket Hunter and Little Pete. Yet Seyavi acquired her regional knowledge not to sustain herself on voluntary sojourns in the wilderness but because the survival of herself and her family depended on her environmental competence. She neither explored the remote areas of the desert to test her sense of selfhood against her natural surroundings, like the narrator, nor did she prefer solitary retreats in the wilderness to a life in society, like Little Pete. It was not "destiny," as with the Pocket Hunter (*LLR* 80), that led Seyavi to live in the wilderness but the near genocide of her people by the European American invaders. She survived the war in which her husband and almost her entire band were killed by hiding with her young son in the mountains (*LLR* 163).[8]

The narrator seeks to invest Seyavi's ordeal during the war with meaning by pointing out that the Paiute woman developed a strong sense of self-reliance because she single-handedly ensured the survival of herself and her son. Seyavi is convinced that a "woman who has a child will do very well" on her own, whereas men depend for their survival on women (*LLR* 163). The narrator posits that Seyavi learned in the wilderness "the sufficiency of mother wit, and how much more easily one can do without a man than might at first be supposed" (164).[9] Clearly, the narrator aims at presenting Seyavi as a self-determined woman. Yet her racial prejudices initially interfere with this objective.

As the narrator tries to imagine the hardships and terror that Seyavi had to confront during the war, she describes the Paiute woman as an animal. She conjectures that Seyavi might have felt on her excursions to secure food for herself and her son like the "she dog, stray or outcast" that the narrator once observed in Antelope Valley. She explains her comparison by pointing out that the dog "had a litter in some forsaken lair, and ranged and foraged for them, slinking savage and afraid, remembering and mistrusting humankind, wistful, lean and sufficient for her young" (*LLR* 166). Although the narrator also compares her European American male model characters to animals, her comparison of Seyavi to a dog is problematic in at least two respects: the use of the blanket category *humankind* renders the European American invaders invisible, while the likening of Seyavi's emotions and behavior, her fear, endurance, and sustenance, to those of a "savage" dog caters to racist prejudices about the supposed barbarity of Native Americans.[10] The comparison screens out the fact that Seyavi was neither "stray" nor "outcast" by her community but forced at the threat of her life to take refuge from the European American colonizers in the mountains.

The narrative thus offers a naturalized version of California history. Although the narrator mentions in passing that the war was caused by an "influx of overlording whites" (*LLR* 166), she does not hold the European American soldiers and settlers accountable for their actions. Instead, she describes the war in historical hindsight as an inevitable sequence of events. Even when she reflects on the particular threat of rape that Seyavi had to face, she presents this danger as a natural and quasi-prehistoric eventuality. "You can surmise also, for it was a crude time and the land was raw, that the women became in turn the game of the conquerors" (166).[11] In her euphemistic depiction of the war, the narrator accords the responsibility for the violence not to white racism or American imperialism but to the impersonal categories of time and place.

Yet her romanticized portrait of the war and Seyavi's survival in the wilderness also reflects a desire to represent the Paiutes not as victims but as self-determined people who deserve the respect rather than the patronizing pity of the readers. For the narrator explicitly urges her white readership to regard Seyavi and the other female Paiute elders as learning models for "our kind of society" (*LLR* 167). Their way of life, their sustenance and self-determination, is to teach the readers to value embodied experience, especially sexual desire, to accept physical ailments and death, and to realize the spiritual dimension of their daily lives. As a regionalist writer, the narrator is particularly interested in the traditional stories that the Paiute women tell. She has a "keen hunger" for "bits of lore" (172) and treasures the women's stories and "gossip" (177) as a storehouse of their individual and collective experiences. Therefore, she advises her readers to seek contact with Native American women and their culture. "Then, if they have your speech or you theirs . . . there are things to be learned of life not set down in any books, folk tales, famine tales, love and long-suffering and desire, but no whimpering" (177, 178).[12]

By presenting the Native American women as the teachers of the narrator and her white readership and by reflecting on the conditions of intercultural communication, Austin's portrait eventually moves away from its tendency to colonize the Basket Maker and her culture. Although the story "The Basket Maker" offers a naturalized account of the racist politics that govern the relations between Paiute and dominant European American society, it pays attention to the specifics of Paiute culture. It casts Seyavi and the other Paiute elders as regional model characters who possess an alternative wisdom and exemplary self-determination that they have acquired through their engagement with their environment and through their communal land-based culture.

THE WALKING WOMAN

Another female regional model character is the Walking Woman, the protagonist of the concluding story of *Lost Borders*. "The Walking Woman" is the collection's singular portrait of a European American woman who chooses to live in the wilderness. Like Seyavi, the Walking Woman seeks refuge from dominant society in the wilderness and grows self-confident through her experience. Like the Basket Maker, she comes to discard those aspects of her gender identity that conflict with her newly developed sense of self-reliance. Yet the motivation of this European American woman for becoming an "outlier" (LB 208) differs considerably from Seyavi's. The Walking Woman lives in the desert because she prefers a self-determined life in the wilderness to an existence governed by the ideology of True Womanhood.[13]

Before the Walking Woman became a resident of the desert, she led the self-sacrificial life thought appropriate for a True Woman at the end of the nineteenth century. She took care of an "invalid" and the exhaustion of her longtime service left her "at last broken in body" (LB 199). When the invalid died, she plausibly had no financial means to support herself. The narrator comments, she had "no recourse but her own feet to carry her out of that predicament" (199).[14] Thus the Walking Woman began to walk and kept on walking in the wilderness. The narrator holds that she "had begun by walking off an illness" and finally "walked off all sense of society-made values" (199, 208). Liberated from social and cultural constraints, she underwent a healing process and began "to find herself" (202). She is "sobered and healed at last by the large soundness of nature" (199).[15]

In "The Walking Woman," as in "The Basket Maker," it is the resistance and opposition of the wilderness to dominant society that endow the desert with redemptive qualities for the female protagonist. While Seyavi seeks to escape the violent effects of American racial politics, the Walking Woman searches for a way of life that is not determined by Victorian gender politics. For this reason she decides to live permanently in the wilderness—quite unlike the famous male walkers of the romantic period, Jean-Jacques Rousseau, Friedrich Schiller, and Henry David Thoreau. Through her contact with the desert the Walking Woman undergoes a fundamental inner transformation. She sheds her cultural identity, symbolized by the loss of her name. Like the Pocket Hunter, the Walking Woman is identified with her primary activity in the wilderness.

The narrator seeks out the acquaintance with the Walking Woman because she is fascinated that the woman manages to live in the wild and to associate with men without being molested. She travels "alone in a country where the number of women is one in fifteen" and passes "unarmed and unoffended" (*LB* 197). The narrator supposes that the men share her surprise about their casual acceptance of the woman. She humorously reasons that "they talked of it because they were so much surprised at it. It was not, on the whole, what they expected of themselves" (197). The Walking Woman thus personifies for the narrator the promise that traditional gender roles may begin to crumble in the arid West. She hopes that more egalitarian gender relations will emerge within her regional culture and posits that a change is already underway. The locals, for instance, do not respect "a frame of behavior called ladylike" (198), because the rules of social conduct established in urban Victorian society are inapplicable to the relations between the sexes in the western desert settlements. As the narrator points out, "conduct which affords protection in Mayfair gets you no consideration in Maverick" (198). Since gender roles function only within their specific social contexts, the social standing of the Walking Woman can only be explained in reference to local standards. "What this really means is that you get no affront so long as your behavior in the estimate of the particular audience invites none" (198).

Yet the narrator's claim that her regional culture involves an alternative concept of gender identity is belied by the negative reaction of the community to the unconventional life of the Walking Woman. Although the locals "respectfully" call her "to her face Mrs. Walker" (*LB* 196), her lifestyle conflicts with the etiquette of regional society. The local community holds that on "the mere evidence of her way of life she was cracked; not quite broken but unserviceable" (198–99). As with Little Pete (*LB* 67), people doubt her sanity. Their perception of this possibly "comely" woman becomes increasingly distorted. "She had a twist to her face, some said; a hitch to one shoulder; they averred she limped as she walked" (*LB* 198). The gossip suggests that the community interprets the unusual behavior of the woman not merely as an individual eccentricity but as a deviation from the established standard of femininity. Just as they would expect a True Woman to personify the feminine ideal, so they expect a woman who defies this norm to embody deviance. They assume that the Walking Woman's departure from social norms will inscribe itself in her body and read her nonconformity as a physical "deformity" (198).

As a local resident, the narrator also oscillates between respecting and rejecting the Walking Woman. Like the rest of her community, she admires the environmental knowledge of the Walking Woman, which is "as reliable as an Indian's" (*LB* 199), but is irritated at her unfeminine apparel. She finds fault with the evidence of the Walking Woman's physical adaptation to the desert, contrary to her acceptance of Little Pete and the Pocket Hunter on the same count. The narrator contends that "*though she wore short hair and man's boots, and had a fine down over all her face from exposure to the weather, she was perfectly sweet and sane*" (199, emphasis added). When she finally meets the Walking Woman on her home-ground, in the wilderness of Antelope Valley "off a mile from the main trail" (200), the narrator is surprised to find that they share similar values. Both women have given birth and regard motherhood as one of the most precious "perquisites" of life (201). This discovery provides the starting point for an intimate conversation.

The Walking Woman tells the narrator that she considers motherhood, the romantic relationship with a man, and the collaborative work with him the most important aspects of life (*LB* 204). She learned this one summer when she helped a shepherd to bring his flock safely through a major sand-storm. Through their collaboration she recognized for the first time her own strength and competence. During the storm the Walking Woman had to trust in her own powers and thus overcame the insecurities she was trained to have as a member of the "weaker sex." "I worked with a man, without excusing, without any burden on me of looking and seeming. Not fiddling or fumbling as women work, and hoping it will all turn out for the best" (204). Her perspective certainly resembles Seyavi's. Like Seyavi, the Walking Woman derives self-confidence from her sustenance. Like Seyavi, she takes pride in her achievement. "And my work was good. We held the flock" (204). Unlike Seyavi, though, the Walking Woman believes that men and women can be of "one sort and one mind" and that they unfold their fullest potential in an egalitarian partnership (206). For her, the love between a man and a woman who come to respect each other as they work together is an essential of life. Again, the narrator admits her astonishment "that one who had the courage to be the Walking Woman would have cared!" (204–5).

The Walking Woman's philosophy of life is a tribute neither to traditional romance nor to marriage arrangements that would relegate women to a subordinate position. The narrator directly addresses her readers to emphasize that the Walking Woman's ideal defies social conventions. "But look you: it was the naked thing the Walking Woman grasped, not dressed and tricked out, for instance, by prejudices in favor of certain occupations; and love, man love, taken as it came, not picked over and rejected if it carried no obligation of permanency; and a child; *any* way you get it, a child is good to have, say nature and the Walking Woman" (*LB* 208–9).[16] The narrator admires the self-determination and unconditional love of the Walking Woman. She agrees with her that the value of her experience was not diminished either by the fact that she had to return to the settlements to give birth and never saw the shepherd again or by the death of the infant (207–8). Like Seyavi, who accepts the hardships of her life without "whimpering" (*LLR* 178), the Walking Woman talks of her loss without self-pity. The narrator esteems the Walking Woman, as she does Seyavi, for her rejection of conventions, especially the aspects of the female gender role that contradict her new sense of self-reliance. She backgrounds the emotional strain that the loss of her child and lover and her social ostracization might have put on the Walking Woman to emphasize her strength and her ability to understand "the naked thing" (*LB* 209).[17]

The similarities between the Walking Woman and the women of Seyavi's land-based culture are striking. The Paiute women also are said to "have the wit to win sustenance from the raw material of life without intervention, but they have not the sleek look of the women whom the social organization conspires to nourish" (*LLR* 176). While the narrator of *The Land of Little Rain* welcomes this immediate mode of existence for the Paiutes, the narrator of *Lost Borders* finds it difficult to accept a European American woman who resembles these Native American women. Although she has the "fullest understanding" for the Walking Woman's trinity of work, love, and child (*LB* 207), her radical break with social conventions complicates their bonding. Since the narrator lives in the desert settlements, she cannot easily apply the insights of the Walking Woman to her own way of life. As she watches her walk away into the wilderness "with her blanket and black bag over her shoulder" (209), the narrator concludes that their outlook and attitude must be incompatible. She reasons, at "least one of us is wrong. To work and to love and to bear children. *That* sounds easy enough. But the way we live establishes so many things of much more importance" (209). As a member of the local community, the narrator disregards the way in which the Walking Woman integrates the natural and cultural aspects of her life. From a distance, it seems to her "as if in fact she had a twist all through her" (209).

Yet the self-determination of the woman continues to fascinate her. Respectfully, the narrator tests her assumption against the evidence of the Walking Woman's footprints. "There in the bare, hot sand the track of her two feet bore evenly and white" (*LB* 209). With this final image, which concludes both the story "The Walking Woman" and the *Lost Borders* story cycle, the narrative moves beyond the narrator's conflicted stance to an affirmation of the woman's unconventional example. The straight tracks that the Walking Woman leaves in "the untrammeled space" (*LB* 196) now appear as one of the precious, so-called naked things, as part of the elemental wisdom that may be experienced outside the desert settlements and their restrictive social order.

To summarize, the portraits of Little Pete; the Pocket Hunter; Seyavi, the basket maker; and the Walking Woman focus on different aspects of the processes of regional identity formation and community building: The descriptions of the male characters stress their relational and environmental sense of selfhood and foreground the environmental matrix and animal side of human life. The portraits of the Basket Maker and the Walking Woman also emphasize the embeddedness of the characters within their regional environment. Yet, as these narratives ask whether the alignment with the desert provides the protagonists with a basis for resisting social pressures, they moreover confront the political implications of the traditional association of nonwhite people and women with nature. As a result, the texts encode and challenge the symbolic inscription of the female and/or ethnically marked body as the Other of rational culture.

In "The Basket Maker," the narrator is concerned with the problem of telling the story of Seyavi and her tribe without victimizing her. She strives to value the environmentally grounded culture of the Paiutes and presents the Native American women as regionalist teachers to the presumably white readers. Yet Austin's account alternates between affirming and challenging the distortions of ethnic and sex differences that the prevalent race and gender stereotypes of her time effected. The self-contradictory composition of "The Basket Maker" indicates that Austin's attempt to render her Native American female model character as a self-reliant woman who is a member of Paiute culture and part of the natural environment she inhabits can only succeed if she confronts the aspects of her own cultural heritage that interfere with her narrative objective—if she takes into account, for instance, that their association with nature traditionally has served to legitimize the subjugation of Native Americans and women. In "The Walking Woman" Austin reflects on the social construction of gender roles within her own culture. She explores whether European American women can develop greater self-determination on the basis of their embodied experience, particularly of motherhood, sexual desire, and work. Renegotiating her concept of femininity, Austin's narrator presents the Walking Woman as a self-reliant woman who defies the conventions of both regional and national society.

Austin thus seeks to portray her characters as learning models in matters of environmental adaptation and regional acculturation. Although their worldview and ways of life differ to a significant degree, they share a recognition of the interconnectedness of nature and culture, corporeality and subjectivity, and the human and the nonhuman. Literally living on the margins of society, these characters represent regional alternatives to dominant culture. Read as fictional case studies, Austin's regionalist stories testify to her belief that the contact with the unbuilt environment might serve as a source of cultural regeneration. Yet they do not naïvely render the encounter with the land as an escape to a terrain beyond the influence of social power dynamics. Instead, Austin's narratives persistently note the cultural context of environmental perception and indicate the need to confront the gender and race politics of regional and dominant society.

"If the Desert Were a Woman": *Lost Borders*

Austin was one of the first American authors who explored from a feminist and environmentalist perspective the association of woman and nature. She asked how current ideas about the nature of gender intersected with established notions about the gender of nature. In many of her essays, stories, and novels she renders women as representatives of the regional environment and probes the implications of feminized images of the land. Thus she appropriates for feminist and regionalist purposes the land-as-woman trope—a metaphoric figure that has been an integral part of the literary imagination of the American continent since the sixteenth century, as Annette Kolodny documents in her classic study *The Lay of the Land.*

THE FEMINIZATION OF NATURE

Representative for Austin's regionalist revision of the land-as-woman trope is her allegorical tale "Lone Tree." "Lone Tree" tells of the fatal consequences of environmental degradation, sanctioned by the feminization of nature. A prospector who is impatient with his present situation because he dreams of striking it rich elsewhere vents his anger at "the only sizable, living thing on the horizon" and uproots an "old-maidish" tree (oss 26). What he has failed to notice in his greed and machismo attitude is that the tree's roots stabilize the rock opening of the area's only spring and thus also secure the survival of human life in the vicinity. "Times when he came back to camp, heat-crazed and thirsting at every pore of his big body, Hogan could have slapped the little tree for the way it balanced and fluttered in the desert blast, offering its old-maidish, insufficient shade. It had a very woman's trick of spreading its roots about the ledge from under which the water seeped, as though its frail fibers were all that held Dripping Rock in place, and a woman's air of dispensing the spring, which was the only water in a half-day's journey, with hospitality" (26). The prospector simply cannot imagine that the meager-looking tree may have other functions besides offering him shade. He thinks of it "as inconsequential and as unrelated to the vast empty land as a woman would have been" (25). Since Hogan considers the unsettled reaches of the desert an exclusively male territory, he is appalled to find that the slender tree reminds him of domesticity and the qualities associated with this traditionally female sphere, such as hospitality, nurturance, intricate design, and delicacy. He "hated the Lone Tree in the same way and for much the same reasons that men occasionally hate their wives" (25).[18] Hence, when Hogan moves camp, he uproots the tree, without considering the consequences of his actions. He leaves it behind "like a woman fainting" (27). When he returns years later during a sandstorm, he finds neither the anticipated refuge nor water but a dead tree and a clogged spring. Left to his own devices, he dies, and eventually, the tale's last sentence tells us, "the bones of Hogan mixed with its stark branches" (27).[19]

In its portrait of the greedy, selfish, masculinist prospector, Austin's story demonstrates that an unqualified resource mentality may effectively combine with an androcentric bias to motivate environmentally destructive behavior. By consistently drawing parallels between the prospector's abusive stance toward the tree and the patriarchal subordination of women, Austin's tale illustrates that the domination of nature can be facilitated and legitimized by its feminization. Since the feminine traditionally has been perceived as inferior to the masculine and the attributes associated with rationalist culture, the feminization of nonhuman nature intensifies its devaluation. Hence, within the dualistic framework of Western culture, feminized images of nature, such as "old-maidish" trees or so-called virgin forests serve to perpetuate the illusion that there are no limits to the exploitation of the natural world—unless the master subject chooses to impose them. On one hand, "Lone Tree" suggests, feminized images of the nonhuman can serve to justify the instrumentalization of the natural world as a resource. On the other hand, they can also serve to romanticize nature as a nurturing mother or grateful lover in an effort to evade the troublesome aspects of human and nonhuman relations, such as the economic reasons for environmental degradation. By exaggerating or denying the differences between the human and the nonhuman, feminized conceptions of nature frequently preclude the recognition that nonhuman nature is organized in its own ways and exists on its own terms. Thus, Austin's story "Lone Tree" cautions, they interfere with the development of informed and sustainable relations to the natural world.[20]

While Austin made the intersections between the marginalization of woman as the naturalized Other and of nature as the feminized Other of rationalist culture a subject of her work, the feminist ecological impetus of her regionalism often has been lost on her critics, who have preferred to categorize her as either a nature writer or as a feminist author in the tradition of nineteenth-century women's regionalism. The frequent images of the desert as woman and of woman as desert in her work indeed seem to invite the question whether Austin primarily wrote about human and nonhuman relations and merely used gender imagery to make an environmentalist point or whether her main concern were gender politics and she employed nature imagery to make a feminist argument. As long as we are used to thinking of our cultural identity apart from the natural world, it may be difficult to recognize that Austin's feminist and environmentalist objectives constitute equally important and interrelated aspects of her regionalist work. Yet her ability to disclose and dramatize how our notions of the natural and the cultural overlap constitutes one of the most original and rewarding qualities of Austin's writing.

THE DESERT AS WOMAN

Austin develops her most striking vision of the desert as woman in *Lost Borders*. In this collection of regionalist stories Austin imagines the desert as an alluring, passionate, fertile, generous, and self-reliant woman. She unfolds a vision of the land that contrasts notably with the established feminized images of the American wilderness as either an "all-nurturing mother" or an "all-passive bride."[21] Austin's narrator muses, "If the desert were a woman, I know well what like she would be" (*LB* 10). With the use of the subjunctive she marks the subsequent image as an enabling fantasy. Conceived of as female, the desert would be "deep-breasted, broad in the hips, tawny, with tawny hair, great masses of it lying smooth along her perfect curves, full lipped like a sphinx, but not heavy-lidded like one, eyes sane and steady as the polished jewels of her skies, such a countenance as should make men serve without desiring her, such a largeness to her mind as should make their sins of no account, passionate, but not necessitous, patient—and you could not move her, no, not if you had all the earth to give, so much as one tawny hair's-breadth beyond her own desires" (10–11). In her version of the land-as-woman metaphor Austin stresses qualities such as fertility, sensuality, beauty, mental integrity, forgiveness, strength, and assertiveness. She confidently reconfigures established feminized images of the land to attribute sentience and self-sufficiency to the desert and sensual self-determination to the women who share the described characteristics.[22]

By gendering the land Austin gives a feminist spin to her regionalist contention that our cultural identity should develop in response to the places we inhabit. While the desert environment is seen to exert power over all its inhabitants, it is said to prove fatal to those who fail to adapt. By linking the image of the desert as woman to a regionalist ethic, Austin is free to reverse the traditional wilderness quest plot pattern. She describes the sojourns of her male characters in the wilderness not as heroic adventures but as abductions. In Austin's revision the male characters who set out to conquer a "virgin land" (*LB* 32) are possessed of a greed, self-inflation, and "love of mastery" (74) that makes it impossible for them to behave adequately in their environment. Thus they fall victim to the alluring but dangerous land. As the narrator notes with glee, "Out there beyond the towns the long Wilderness lies brooding, imperturbable; she

puts out to adventurous minds glittering fragments of fortune or romance, like the lures men use to catch antelopes—clip! and she has them"
(54). In Austin's revision of the traditional pattern of the male quest into
the wilderness and its violent eroticism, the desert turns into a dangerous
seductress, capturing and occasionally killing the men.

Austin parodies the masculinist "psychosexual drama" of conquering
the land and "possessing a virgin continent" that Kolodny describes in
The Lay of the Land (xiii).[23] The self-reliant heroine of her story is the
desert; the conquered are the male adventurers. Thus *Lost Borders* meets
in an original manner Austin's demand that the land be featured as a
major character in regionalist literature, which she formulated toward the
end of her career. In "Regionalism in American Fiction" she lists as one
fundamental criterion of regionalist writing "that the region must enter
constructively into the story, as another character, as the instigator of
plot" (105).[24]

Through her revisionist move Austin puts the essentializing identification of woman and nature to subversive uses, while she discloses "the
gendered semiotic practices that have been used to mask and excuse destructive behavior."[25] Taking a stance against social and cultural conventions that interfere with the adaptation of the frontier community to its
environment, *Lost Borders* ridicules the mythologization of American pioneer heritage in masculinist terms and rejects utilitarian concepts of the
natural world as merely a resource. By refuting the dominant gender
codes Austin's text mocks the masculinist "wilderness cult" of the Progressive Era, which sought to recuperate a masculine sense of selfhood
modeled on the presumed virility, strength, and self-determination of the
pioneers.[26] Writing at a time when the redemption of masculinity through
encounters with the wild was a popular concept, Austin imagined the
desert as a man-abducting woman to engage for feminist and environmentalist purposes in the battle of the sexes, which Sandra M. Gilbert and
Susan Gubar in *No Man's Land* have identified as a primary cultural force
in the formation of modernism. In *Lost Borders* Austin presents the feminized desert literally as a "No Man's Land." She thus revises the image of
the West championed in the works of some of her male contemporaries.[27]

On one hand, Austin sextypes the desert as female, then, to point to
the fatal consequences of the belief that humans could exert unlimited
control over the natural world. On the other hand, her revision serves to
challenge the gender politics of European American society at the turn of

the twentieth century. She presents the desert as an overpowering woman to substantiate her claim that the survival of the settlers depends on their ability to fundamentally reorient their attitudes, convictions, and behavior. They need to acknowledge that their lives are intimately linked to an environmental matrix. As the narrator observes, the wilderness "has its own exigencies and occasions, and will not be lived in except upon its own conditions" (LB 25). The borderers have to develop an informed understanding of their environment and a mode of behavior adequate to their surroundings.

GENDER-SPECIFIC RESPONSES TO THE DESERT AND FRONTIER LIFE

The gendered construct of the desert as "woman" (10) and undefeated "sphinx" (11) that Austin employs in the *Lost Borders* stories allows her to explore the different relations that the male and the female residents develop to their environment.[28] At first glance Austin's descriptions of the gender-specific responses of the settlers to the desert replicate the gender stereotypes of traditional frontier narratives. The men actively seek out encounters with the wilderness, whereas the women stay behind in the settlements. The men enter the unsettled territories of the desert to escape their social and familial obligations. They "love it past all reasonableness, slack their ambitions, cast off old usages, neglect their families" (10). Contrarily, the women detest the harsh living conditions. They "hate with implicitness the life like the land" (10). While the men choose to move west, the women often experience their western relocation as a rupture in their lives.

Austin's portrait of Mrs. McKenna in "The Hoodoo of the Minnietta" is exemplary in this respect. Married to a silver mine owner, Mrs. McKenna lives as the only woman in a mining camp. Her husband has "no screen to his commonness" (LB 20). He is a fraud, and his sole obsession is to strike it rich. As the narrator puts it, the desert "had him, catlike, between her paws" (18). The narrator points out why Mrs. McKenna wishes to return to the "cover" of town life. "In the second year Mrs. McKenna had a child, and it died. Did I say somewhere that women mostly hate the desert?" (19). Unlike the men, the women perceive the altered living conditions not as a liberation from social conventions but as a menace. In the unrefined desert settlements or solitary mining camps, their lives, households, families, and marriages threaten to disintegrate.

As the narrator explains, "through the thin web of their lives moves the vast impersonal rivalry of desertness" (41).[29]

The response of the female settlers to the desert is an effect of the gender role they adopted before they moved west. In dominant European American society, Austin's narrator argues, women derive their self-esteem from their domestic roles as mothers and wives. In accordance with the already outmoded ideology of True Womanhood, they idealize their position and perceive themselves as the carriers of culture, possessing the "four cardinal virtues—piety, purity, submissiveness and domesticity."[30] Relegated to the private sphere and dependent on the income of their husbands, they compensate for their lack of political and economic power by defining themselves as authorities in matters of morality and social conduct. In short, they identify with "all the traditions of niceness and denial and abnegation which men demand of the women they expect to marry" (*LB* 102). To obtain the position of an "angel in the house," they have to conform to the Victorian concept of femininity and other "social observances" (19). The narrator posits "that the sense of personal virtue comes to most women through an intervening medium of sedulous social guardianship" (121). Because they have not learned to lead self-determined lives, their move to less cultivated parts of the country and the consequent loss of social amenities either "shocks them into disorder" (19) or results in a "detached helplessness" (121).[31]

The male settlers, by contrast, consider themselves courageous and self-reliant adventurers. They move west and relocate their families in hope of a better life. In times of the West's increasing industrialization, after the official close of the frontier, they still seek to realize its mythic promise—the discovery of another paradise. Yet in Austin's version of the myth, the men enter the wilderness "fearlessly and unguarded" (*LB* 47) only to find themselves in peril. Unfamiliar with the land and too sure of themselves, the newcomers underestimate the force of nature and fall prey to the desert.

By casting the men as ignorant and incompetent victims, Austin obliterates the central myth of the frontier. Instead of presenting the male settlers as the masculine colonizers of a feminized land available for usurpation, Austin casts the desert as the dominant agent who determines the fate of the male residents. In the programmatically titled story "The Ploughed Lands," for instance, the European American grubstaker Curly Gavin is deceived by the beauty of the desert in bloom and sets out on his first trip with only one day's ration of water (*LB* 43). He gets lost and would have died of dehydration if the Shoshones had not accidentally found him and saved his life (44). The narrator contends that Gavin's incompetent behavior was prompted by his masculine sense of selfhood. Since "the concurrence of death and beauty" generally exceeds the comprehension of "man-mind" (10), he did not realize the danger of his undertaking. The narrator reasons that it is as difficult "to believe that such a land could neglect men to their death, as for man to believe that a lovely woman can be unkind" (43). The narrator thus envisions the desert as a woman to dispute the conflicting desires of the male settlers to colonize the wilderness and to realize "the myth of the renewal of life in a virgin embrace" (32).

In reversing the mythic power relation between the land and its male inhabitants, the narrator underlines her claim that the settlers should conform to their regional environment. They are to reject the social and cultural conventions that interfere with their deliberate adaptation to the regional environment. Within a largely unbuilt environment, the narrator clarifies, "the only unforgivable offense is incompetence" (*LB* 25). The *Lost Borders* stories thus develop a feminized image of the desert to present the wilderness in its self-sustaining existence and to criticize the gender and race politics of European American society. Austin's revision seeks to convey to the readers the necessity of developing alternative modes of social interaction and human and nonhuman relations.

THE COMPLICATIONS OF THE DESERT-AS-WOMAN TROPE

Austin's conceptualization of the desert as woman becomes problematic, however, when her characterization of the male sojourners as victims serves to naturalize social power relations. By rendering the land as the primary determinant of human life, the *Lost Borders* narratives run the risk of according the responsibility for the men's actions to environmental conditions. Gavin, for instance, is said to have "the mark of the desert" on him (*LB* 11). He is eventually led back to the ploughed lands by Tiawa, a Shoshone woman. While Tiawa loves him, Gavin is said to be "in the grip of another mistress," the desert as woman, "who might or might not loose his bonds" (45). Upon return to the settlements, Gavin deserts Tiawa. She is surprised to find "that a white man could take service from such as we and not requite it" (46). Although the narrator emphasizes the egotism, inconsiderateness, and greed of the European American grubstaker throughout the story, she does not hold him accountable for his behavior. She concludes her tale with the contention that "in encounter with the primal forces woman gets the worst of it except now and then, when there are children in question, she becomes a primal force herself" (50–51). Stressing the overdetermination of the male protagonists by the "wanton" desert (63), or, conversely, by the "austerely virgin" land (28), the narrator explains social dynamics as the result of a supposedly natural order. Such naturalizing accounts of gender and race relations conflict with Austin's intention to elucidate the social construction of gender roles and the sociohistorical situatedness of our concepts of human and non-human nature. As the narrator of "A Case of Conscience," another *Lost Borders* story that revolves around the issue of miscegenation, reminds the readers, "If this, which appears to have rooted about the time the foundations of the earth were laid, is proved amenable to the lack of shade, scarcity of vegetation, and great spaces disinterested of men—not these of course, but the Power moving nakedly in the room of these things—it only goes to show that the relation is more incidental than we are disposed to think it" (40).

THE FEMINIST POTENTIAL OF THE DESERT-AS-WOMAN TROPE

Austin employs the abduction plot in her stories to imagine for her female protagonists new modes of relating to the regional environment. A case in point is the humorous story, "The Return of Mr. Wills," which prominently features the image of the desert as rival woman to present the wilderness as a counterforce to the social conventions that restrict the lives of the female settlers. For the narrator, Mr. Wills is an exemplary newcomer to the West. He is a conformist, a "cask" held "in serviceable shape" by conventions (*LB* 53).[32] The narrator comments, "Back East I suppose they breed such men because they need them, but they ought to really keep them there" (52). Due to his lack of competence, Mr. Wills is easy prey for the desert. When he resigns his position as a clerk to search for lost mines, "the hoops" come "off the cask," and his mind fades "out at the edges like the desert horizon" (58). Since the story focuses on the consequences of the man's behavior for his wife, the narrator holds Mr. Wills accountable for his desertion of his family. Instead of presenting his three-year search for the fabled mines as a machination of the desert as woman, she points out that it is motivated by his wish to evade his familial responsibilities. His futile undertaking is "the baldest of excuses merely to be out and away from everything that savored of definiteness and responsibility" (58).

For Mrs. Wills, the long period of her husband's absence proves to be the best time of her married life. Left to her own devices, she hesitantly moves away from her prior way of life. She begins to question the traditional gender roles, especially "the tradition that a husband is the natural provider" (*LB* 59), and takes on paid work. Although her work and income increase her self-confidence, she initially cannot cope with her "new sense of independence and power" and retains "an ache of forlornness and neglect" (59). Thus it seems "as if the desert had overshot him and struck at Mrs. Wills" and her four children (57). In this context the narrator proposes that the order of the natural world lends itself in particular to women as a learning model for alternative forms of social organization. Again, it is their familial function as mothers that is to provide women with a basis for defying the female gender role. The narrator asserts that Mrs. Wills unnecessarily prolongs her agony. She propounds, "wild folk of every sort could have taught her that nature never makes the mistake of neglecting to make the child-bearer competent to provide" (59).[33] Yet, even without "studying life in the lairs" (59), Mrs. Wills eventually comes to value her self-reliance, like the Walking Woman and Seyavi. Her independence revitalizes her. She improves her garden, renovates her house, regains her premarriage beauty, and hopes that the desert will keep her husband for good. Consequently, it is "a stroke of desolation" to Mrs. Wills when her husband returns (61).

The narrator offers an ambivalent account of the return of Mr. Wills. On one hand, she is appalled by his self-congratulatory manners and in her role as neighbor notes that he settles "on his family like a blight" (*LB* 62). She holds him responsible for the renewed despair of Mrs. Wills and the disintegration of the family. On the other hand, she presents him as a pawn in the desert's game. "It was not only as if the desert had sucked the life out of him and cast him back, but as if it would have Mrs. Wills in his room" (62). Correspondingly, Mrs. Wills has to resist both the demands of her husband and the "power of the wilderness" that "lay like a wasting sickness on the home" (63). She seeks to get a divorce. Her church opposes her plans, however, since the minister, who has recently moved west, does "not understand that the desert is to be dealt with as a woman and a wanton" and thinks "of it as a place on the map" (63). He cannot grant a divorce on the count of a man's excessive indulgence in or illicit affair with the myth of the West, as the narrator suggests. Faced with a marriage and an institution that are not of "the slightest use" to her but insist on subjugating her, on "commanding her behavior," Mrs. Wills finally comes to envision the desert as woman as her ally (63). Whenever there is a hint that her husband's interest in mining rekindles, she looks out to the "inscrutable, grim spaces, not with the hate you might suppose, but with something like hope" (64).

Austin's revisionary portrait of the "psychosexual dynamics" that feminized images of the land may express and engender thus has notably different implications than the traditional quest for "a virginal paradise" that symbolically dispossessed women of an access to Eden.[34] The *Lost Borders* stories propose that the altered living conditions in the West can have a liberating effect for women. Mrs. Wills, at least, will seize the next opportunity, that is, the next abduction of her husband by the desert, to get divorced. "And this time, if I know Mrs. Wills, he will not come back" (*LB* 64). Analogous to the sojourns of the male miners and explorers, the lives of the women on the settled fringes of the desert can become "a sort of chemist's cup for resolving obligations" (51). Even if they do not take refuge from social constraints in the wilderness as does the Walking Woman but remain within the towns and mining camps, they can expand the scope of their experience. They can learn to rely on their own strength; and with increasing self-confidence, they can change their living situations. As the women realize how restricted their lives are, their attitude toward the wilderness changes. They still perceive their harsh environment as a threat to conventional ways of life concurrent with the ideology of True Womanhood. But once they come to view traditional notions of femininity as oppressive, the incongruence between their prior conception of a cultivated life and the actuality of their surroundings loses its menacing aspect. They now perceive the resistance of the desert to its colonialization by society as a promise.

Austin renders the desert in the character of a woman to challenge the established narratives of a masculine subjugation and feminine fear of the wilderness. She seeks to undermine both the myth of a virgin land waiting to be conquered by masculine heroes and the myth of a howling wilderness endangering women as the representatives of domesticity. By stressing the possible alliances that women who strive to liberate themselves from the ideology of True Womanhood can form with the desert, the *Lost Borders* stories depict the contact with the unbuilt environment as an alternative source of gender identity. By rendering the desert as a woman, Austin can present the regional environment "as a place of possibility, a space of disidentification from rigidly gendered cultural scripts."[35] She develops a feminized vision of the desert to expose the detrimental effect that the ideology of separate spheres has on men, women and their natural environment. The contact with the wilderness is shown to offer to both the male and the female borderers new models of domestic life and human and nonhuman relations—provided that they are willing to discard stereotypical gendered responses to their environment, acquire the necessary competence, and adapt.

Gender Wars and the Search for a Land-Based Culture: *Cactus Thorn*

In her novella *Cactus Thorn* Austin radicalizes her portrait of the possible implications of woman's traditional association with nature and of the deliberate identification of particular women, the female settlers, with their regional environment. As in *Lost Borders,* Austin casts in *Cactus Thorn* the struggle for nondualistic views of nature and culture and for sustainable modes of inhabitation as a gender war. Again, she aims "to 'disidentify' women from domestic ideologies with the help of nature, and to release nature from the grip of utilitarianism . . . by envisioning it as an unruly woman," as Stacy Alaimo describes Austin's strategy in "The Undomesticated Nature of Feminism" (80). Yet in this revision of the andropocentric myth of the West, Austin focuses on the identification of women with the landscape rather than on the identification of the land with the feminine.

Cactus Thorn offers a fictional scenario that dramatizes from a feminist and environmentalist perspective the disruptive potential that a regional sense of place can hold for American politics. Its battle of the sexes takes place between a progressive East Coast politician, Grant Arliss, and a woman, Dulcie Adelaid, whom he considers a personification of the desert—and who, in fact, is named after the place of her birth, Agua Dulce (45). Arliss meets Dulcie, this "girl of the wilderness" (40), when he sojourns in the California desert. He has headed out west to recuperate from the strain of his work as a politician and his urban lifestyle. Enchanted by Dulcie's "gentle wildness" (45), he falls in love with her. Their affair comes to an abrupt end, however, when Arliss returns to his political work in New York City. When he deserts Dulcie to marry another woman more opportune to his career, Dulcie responds violently. She seeks out Arliss in New York City and kills him, stabbing him with her thorn-shaped dagger—the title's cactus thorn.[36]

Its portrait of the battle of the sexes places *Cactus Thorn* in the modernist tradition, as Gilbert and Gubar have outlined it in their study *No Man's Land*. Yet what is at stake in Austin's feminist rendering of this murder is more than the possibility of heterosexual love in a patriarchal society. The conflict between Arliss and Dulcie maps the tensions between male and female gender identities onto the relations between other binaries, such as city and country, East and West Coasts, public and private, politics and experience, and mind and body. Each of these oppositional pairs stands in turn for the overarching conflict between dominant society and regional culture. In Austin's novella the "war between men and women" (*CT* 98) represents a struggle between regional and national and between egalitarian and hegemonic forces. It is a gender war over definitions of the natural and the cultural, over the value of embodied experience, relational selfhood, and sense of place for American politics and the formation of national identity.

The narrative justifies Dulcie's murder of Arliss by invoking an ideal of political integrity that recognizes the embodied experience of quotidian life as the impetus and basis for social reform. In Dulcie's words, which prefigure the women's movement of the 1970s, "there wasn't to be any difference between what was social and what was personal" (*CT* 97).[37] Arliss's fatal mistake is that he, unlike Dulcie, does not consider the political significance of his private life. When he decides to marry another woman without consulting Dulcie, in her eyes he fails his progressive political agenda.[38] She can neither accept his patronizing attitude towards her nor his denial of the relevance that their lived experience holds for his political work. She concludes, "So I wasn't real to you, ever," before stabbing her dagger into Arliss's heart (98). In her motivation Austin's protagonist thus differs markedly from other more "premodern" heroines who also kill the men that violate their rights and feelings. In contrast to female victim-turns-murderer figures, such as the absent heroine of Susan Glaspell's "Jury of Her Peers," Dulcie's suffering and decision to retaliate depend on her initial belief in her partner as a progressive social force. The insistance on the alternative ethical framework, which she believed to share with her former lover (*CT* 39–40), enables her to perceive the murder as a cathartic resolution of the conflict that restores her to a plane of "real" existence (98).[39] The novella ends with the image of Dulcie as she escapes prosecution by returning to the West, "her face slowly setting into the torpor of relief after great shock and pain" (99).

Dulcie's ethics and political imperatives are based on the regional sense of selfhood that she has developed through the close observation of her environment and its nonhuman inhabitants.[40] Like the narrator of *The Land of Little Rain,* Dulcie suggests that human life should be integrated with its environment in the way that a lizard blends with the sand. The lizard, of course, has adapted to its surroundings to the point where the boundaries between its skin and the environing earth are only perceptible to an environmentally attuned observer. Detecting the presence of a lizard, Dulcie draws Arliss's attention to its distinct yet flexible identity. She intends to teach him what she considers an adequate sense of selfhood in place—a self shaped in dynamic relations of mutual interdependence. She points out that the lizards "take it all out in making themselves a part of the big pattern" (*CT* 11). This larger pattern of the land in response takes on the qualities of its weavers. It may "come forth like a wild thing" (47) and assert its presence.

By presenting us with two characters who hold diametrically opposed views on the place of humans in the natural world, *Cactus Thorn* dramatizes the ramifications of different concepts of nature. Specifically, it invites us to look at the dynamics involved in defining someone or something as natural. On one side stands Dulcie. For her the contact with the land is a source of alternative knowledge and values. It provides her with a ground on which to resist social restraints without forcing her to consider herself an outcast. She privileges a relational self that knows how "to begin where *It* is" (*CT* 12) over both a self that is entirely constituted or "made up" by sociocultural forces (46) and the nonconformist self-enclosed subjectivity that Arliss endorses, a self that opposes "the church, the state, the party" (46) in an Emersonian assertion of aboriginal individuality and autonomy. For Dulcie the desert represents a space outside social constraints in which she can pursue her desires as a relational self. She observes, for instance, that while people frequently suffer because their marriages are shaped by social rules and structures established apart from and thus interfering with their lived experience, the "wild creatures mating" are never "unhappy in it" (12). Hence, as long as Dulcie takes "*It*," the larger pattern that exceeds but is not discontinuous with herself, as her vantage point, she can pursue her affair with Arliss in the desert without fear of harm or punishment. The desert is presented as a catalyst of sexual desire (52).

Yet Dulcie's relationship with Arliss cannot flourish because he represents just the opposite of her. He divorces his sensual experience from his social obligations and identifies Dulcie with the desert first to consummate then to distance himself from the perceived trinity of woman-desert-desire. By confusing the promise of an affair with Dulcie with the mythic regenerative promise of a western landscape, Arliss persuades himself that he can embark on a "sex adventure" that will create no obligations for him (*CT* 19). He mistakenly believes that a "girl of the wilderness" (40) will satisfy his desires without asking anything in return.[41] Like a fertile but undeveloped stretch of land, Dulcie is supposed to possess a selfless givingness, a quality that Arliss missed in both the True Woman and free love advocates of the East Coast, who either demanded marriage or a recognition of their own potential. It is precisely from these "contingencies" that he has "fled westward" in search of "that elusive quality of self-inflation called inspiration. This was the commodity which women had traditionally supplied" (20).

Arliss conflates Dulcie's identity with the features of the land and detaches himself from this perceived unity in an effort to evade being held accountable for his actions. "He had accepted her as the perfect expression of the place and occasion. He had told himself the man's fairy tale in which loving exists for its own sake from moment to moment, equally detached from its source in experience and from all its consequences; clapped in and out by desire, like those tables spread by the Genii in *Arabian Nights*" (*CT* 67). The narrative stresses that Arliss's denial of responsibility hinges on his perception of Dulcie as a natural element of the landscape. His "idea of her as a creature of the desert" (74), despite their admittedly "domestic" arrangements (59), is shown to depersonalize and exoticize Dulcie and to polarize the differences between them. "And yet, for all the effect she had upon him, she might, like the horned lizard starting from under his foot, have assembled herself from the tawny earth and the hot sand, or at a word resolve herself into the local element" (4). In contrast to Dulcie Adelaid, Grant Arliss does not recognize the lizard as a purposefully striving fellow being. Whereas Dulcie models her notion of relational selfhood after the lizard's adaptation to its surroundings,

Arliss identifies Dulcie with elements of her surroundings to deny her intentional agency.

The layering of conflicting readings of the same natural particulars in the narrative dramatizes the different understandings of cultural identity that the story's lead protagonists espouse. Equally important, it alerts us to the difficulties inherent in Dulcie's attempt to valorize ecological prime notions as organizing principles for societal processes. It suggests that concepts such as the interrelatedness of all things in their diversity cannot be transferred from the natural to the social world without questioning which concepts of difference and continuity and of agency and receptivity currently influence our behavior and sense of self.

___

In view of the text's general concern with the oppressive effects of naturalizing concepts of femininity, it is surprising that *Cactus Thorn* exhibits at the same time a strong tendency to affirm women's historical association with nature to invert the social gender hierarchy. The "nature of women" is defined in comparison to the subjectivity of men "as closer always to the moulding realities of earth" (CT 42). While men "try to do all the learning in their heads," women derive their knowledge from their organic immersion in and "surrender to" the environment (41). Their receptivity and relational sense of selfhood is presented as imbuing them with "strange powers" (42). As a result, woman and nature are perceived as essentially superior to the oppositional pair of man and patriarchy. Women realize the regionalist ideal of developing their sense of self in response to the land.

The text thus seeks to construe women's ability to resort to gentle "primitiveness" (CT 41) as a cultural asset. As often in Austin's work, responsiveness to the environment is rendered as a quality that is meant to replenish dominant society and that may best be learned from land-based Native American cultures, particularly from what Austin considered their "women's culture." Dulcie remarks, for instance, that the "Indian women," whom she sometimes accompanies on their excursions, do not approach the natural world with the dominant resource mentality but develop their artistry on the basis of their embodied experience of place. She explains to Arliss that "it's not as if they learned about willows and grasses in order to make baskets, but as if they learned to make baskets by knowing willows" (41). The Native American women teach Dulcie "the things that make women wise" (41) and help her refine her sense of place. Dulcie, like Austin after her relocation to California, thrives on her contact with the regionally based native culture.[42] While in other works, such as *The Land of Little Rain* or *Lost Borders*, the politics of this cross-cultural learning process are complex and geared toward an avoidance of cultural appropriation and racial typecasting, the representation of Native American culture in *Cactus Thorn* does not move beyond racial stereotypes. The descriptions lack cultural specificity, since the narrative is not concerned with Native American culture itself. It ignores the contemporary circumstances in which the native women live to present them as primitive female archetypes.[43] In other words, Austin imagines a Native American "women's culture" to lend a mythic component to the characterization of Dulcie as the female and regional antagonist of Arliss and dominant European American society.

Austin's identification of her lead protagonist and her Native American consorts with the desert environment results in a naturalizing depiction of gender identities that turns both gender codes and race politics into ahistorical givens. It results in a romanticized and thus conciliatory view of social power relations. Not only is the mind/body dualism mapped onto the dichotomy between male and female by rendering women as pliable bodies of the earth and men as disembodied thinkers, the entire complex of gender and race politics is removed to a realm of mysterious biology. The "root of sex antagonism" now is to be found in men's "fear" of "the unknowable" that is at the core of female identity due to women's privileged access to nature (*CT* 42). Austin's reasoning here adheres to a mode of value-hierarchical thinking that can easily work to perpetuate a logic of domination, both in regard to human concerns and to human and nonhuman relations. Also, her strategy of reversal valorizes aspects of the traditional female gender role, such as receptivity and caring, without reimagining the relation between passivity and activity. Thus it exhibits strong parallels to the ideology of True Womanhood. As Plumwood comments on the pitfalls of strategies of reversal that reclaim previously devalued properties without disentangling them from their dualistic context, it merely replaces "the 'angel in the house' version of women by the 'angel in the ecosystem' version," ignoring that "these sterling qualities are formed by powerlessness and will fail to survive translation to a context of power" (9).

Still, despite her penchant for essentialist celebrations of women's privileged access to nature, Austin seeks to criticize such naturalizing definitions of the feminine in *Cactus Thorn*. By means of ironic overstatement Austin's text often reflects critically on Arliss's attempts to negate Dulcie's volition and self-determination and to evade his responsibility by appealing to the workings of a natural law. When, for instance, Dulcie offers her food to him on their first encounter, he concludes that "In a country in which the whole machinery of impulse and foresight is sucked out of man, it is natural that food should simply appear" (*CT* 8). The text emphasizes that Arliss's maneuver of casting Dulcie as purely natural serves to delimit the claims that she can make on him as a member of society. It enables Arliss to rely on Dulcie's services without having to acknowledge the dependency that his reliance on her active support creates. As he puts it, "She never cheapened the flame-like quality of her surrender by lighting the kitchen fire with it" (54). The narrative repeatedly renders Arliss's attempts to place Dulcie with nature and outside culture as veiled efforts to perpetuate the inferior status that dominant culture assigns to her as a woman.

Consistent with the story's feminist impetus, *Cactus Thorn* builds to and concludes with the drastic reinsertion of female self-determination into the social realm. In the violent culmination of the narrative the unresolved tensions between the several oppositional pairs that the narrative maps onto one another surface. The text thus allows diverging but overlapping readings of the fatal conflict and generates a continuum of meanings for Dulcie's murder of Arliss.

On one hand, Dulcie acts as an enraged modern woman who demands equal rights. When she decides that "the man needed killing" (*CT* 58), she rejects the differences in social power and privilege that sexual difference carries in her society. She rebels against the gender code of the American white middle class in the first decades of the twentieth century that allows Arliss to remain unmarked by their sexual encounter (or, if marked, to be applauded for his virility), while relegating her to the ostracized position of a "ruined" woman (40).[44] Seeking to return to the self-sufficiency that she possessed when she first met him (15), Dulcie determines for herself what it means to be a woman. Considered from this perspective she attacks not only Arliss but the doublebind of the female gender role that requires her to be both body and the safekeeper of morality and domesticity, to enact the paradox of "gentle wildness" (45).

On the other hand, Dulcie indeed feels like a "wounded wild creature" (*CT* 93) and acts as desert personified. But what kind of feminized land does she stand for? The fiercely codependent desert that Dulcie characterizes in her first encounter with Arliss as a woman who loves her man and child "to death" (9)? Or the feminized desert wilderness who will no longer present her "round-bosomed hills and the cradling dip of the land seaward" to men who consider it their task, as one of them stammers enthusiastically, "to conquer her . . . make her bear . . . great civilizations" (24)? In either case Dulcie's murder of Arliss signifies a rejection of the popular Progressive Era concept of wilderness as a space in which to recuperate a masculinist sense of selfhood. Dulcie's double personification of the rights of women and the land discloses that in the traditional American wilderness quest narratives both the society from which the masculine heroes flee and the wilderness that they seek to subdue are associated with the feminine.[45]

In her different roles, then, Dulcie kills the man who "exploited" her, (CT 98), "the author of her pain" (90), to assert the validity of relational and environmentally based concepts of cultural identity. By murdering the influential politician Arliss, she enters the political field of a society that denies the natural world both a legitimate existence inside and a purposeful being outside the cultural. Thus she disrupts the "reason/nature story" that devalues everything and anybody considered natural.[46] If we take the multiple positionalities of Dulcie and Arliss into account, it is the proliferation of complementary meanings that finally allows the narrative to unsettle dualistic paradigms and to move beyond the distortions of difference they effect. In the figures of Dulcie Adelaid and Grant Arliss, *Cactus Thorn* presents us with the kind of embodied subjects that dualistic concepts of nature and culture have rendered invisible. They appear as both natural and cultural agents who are shaped by and contribute to the ecological and social matrix they live in. *Cactus Thorn* thus encourages us to consider how our situatedness and participation in the natural world affects our corporeality and cultural agency. And it explores how the specificities of our bodies and their definition, for instance, in terms of sex or race, inform these interrelations.

Cactus Thorn can be considered a typical Mary Austin text, then. It presents the contact with the land as a potential source of ethics and sense of self that provide alternatives to the power dynamics, gender codes, and corporeal politics of American society, which the narrative indicts. In this respect the feminist regionalist vision of the desert that Austin develops in *Cactus Thorn* can be said to "succeed in breaking out of the destructive gender oppositions and imperialist nostalgia endemic to American pastoral traditions and find a way to project a more realistic and responsible sense of Americans in their land."[47] To fulfill this task *Cactus Thorn* does not merely offer a benign vision of ecological selfhood, as it may be derived from an encounter with a largely unbuilt environment. Instead, Austin's text explores the value that an embodied sense of place and environmentally based culture can hold for contemporary American politics. *Cactus Thorn* dramatizes the negotiations that become necessary as representatives of dominant and communal place-based cultures meet, envisioning a reciprocal learning process but ultimately siding with the marginalized position for which Dulcie stands. The novella renders sexual politics as the site in which the absurd and violent effects of gendered dualistic notions of nature and culture can be experienced and challenged—because, as Dulcie is designed to prove and the regionalist Austin never tired of emphasizing, every human life unfolds within both a social and an ecological matrix. *Cactus Thorn* therefore draws attention to the conceptual frameworks that influence how we respond to the natural world, including the natural dimension of our lives, and that inform the stories we tell ourselves about our place in a world that extends beyond the human. The violent denouement of the narrative's central conflict signals that the neglect of regionalist and feminist interests may wreak havoc, resulting in a fierce battle over the distribution of sociocultural and political power within American society. *Cactus Thorn* thus reflects Austin's conviction that the future development of American society depends on a fundamental regionalist and feminist reorientation.

5

WHO OWNS THE PLACE?

Regional Development and the Future of the Nation

Mary Austin considered regionalism an aesthetic and a political agenda. It included for her, as it did for many regionalists of the interwar years, not only literary and cultural traditions but also sociopolitical programs.[1] Austin's regionalist work concerns itself with fundamental questions, such as "Is there any best way of relating people to the land? Has the community been better served by communal or by private holdings? Are the evils of industrialism due to intrinsic defects in the system, or a bad way of handling a sound method?" (*The Young Woman Citizen* 35). In search of answers Austin frequently combined her analysis of the status quo with feminist, environmentalist, and mystical explorations of alternative views of self, community, and place. What hopes, then, did Austin articulate for the future of American society? This chapter takes a closer look at the utopia of a regionalized American democracy that Austin unfolded in her critical and creative work.

Indivisible Utilities and Communitarian Economies: Austin's Utopia

In numerous essays, short stories, and novels, Austin developed the utopian vision of a regionalized American society. She envisioned a decentralized federation of sustainable regional cultures that would evolve out of and consequently express their close relations to their natural environment. Heralding the emergence of "the *next* great and fructifying world culture" in the American Southwest (*LJE* 442), Austin promoted the development of egalitarian, multicultural regional societies that would practice a form of environmentalist communalism.

Specifically, this meant that these regional communities of the future would be structured according to a "utility type of communalism." That is, Austin explained explains in "The Indivisible Utility" (1925), they would be organized around the use of commodities or services whose production and use depended on a collective effort and that, therefore, represented "indivisible" communal property (303). Austin's prime example for such an "indivisible utility" was the water crop of the arid regions of the United States, particularly the traditional irrigation systems of southwestern native cultures. In the arid regions, Austin points out, farming and urban development alike depended on water resourcing that exceeded the planning capacities of individuals and the family unit and depended on either the efforts of a group of specialists, administrators, and entrepreneurs or on a sustained effort of the entire community. Austin perceived the Pueblo cultures as an example for the latter communal type of resource management and recommended them to her European American readers as "the most successful form of communism known" (305).[2] For her the southwestern Native American cultures theoretically, or, as she said, "on paper—would fill the self-constituted prophets of all Utopias with unmixed satisfaction" (304).

In delineating her utopian ground plan, Austin focused on the example of the southwestern mother ditch, because it represented the adaptive response of rural communities to environmental conditions. To her the *acequia madres* signified "the new pattern of group adjustment demanded by the western environment" (305).[3] Yet she also ensured that her concept of socioeconomic cooperation remained extendable to other parts of the country that were industrialized and urbanized to a greater extent. To this end, she lists as further examples of "The Indivisible Utility" information technologies, such as the telephone and telegraph; transportation systems, such as the railroad; and public utilities, such as water, light, and power (303).[4]

Austin's utopian vision valorizes economic cooperation and place-based cultures. It considers the environmental conditions under which a given community exists and establishes a dialogic relation among the experiential knowledges, socioeconomic practices, and ethical commitments of its members. In this way Austin's notion of indivisibility acknowledges that human life is situated in and continuous with the larger world. An "extension of environmental consciousness," as Austin calls it in "The Indivisible Utility" (327), is at the core of her political thinking. For her an ideal regional self-perception recognizes the embeddedness of local life within a larger environmental matrix. "The farmer in the Southwest can not think produce without thinking dams and reservoirs, cannot think dams without thinking power, cannot think of power without thinking of its points of application in mines and factories, cannot therefore think of his own eighty acres without thinking of the whole geographical range of which it is an item. Finally he cannot think constructively of his regional habitat without eventually stretching his thought to include the watershed, the mountain slopes and forests which compose it, not infrequently . . . several states distant from his home" (305). Austin realized that sustainable regional planning has to take into account the interrelated human and nonhuman factors that influence regional development. She ends her essay on a cautionary note. "The problem of forest cover and annual rainfall and run-off, alone, must be dealt with in terms of generations, and centuries" (327).

Although Austin based her "theory of native village socialism"[5] on an analysis of rural conditions and although the Southwest never underwent the bioregional development Austin envisioned, her utopian regionalism is relevant to our contemporary living conditions. A regional and relational sense of identity, extended to include a recognition of both the sustaining nonhuman context of human life and the future consequences of present courses of action, as Austin conceived of it, has the potential to overcome the dichotomies with which contemporary environmentalists and bioregionalists still struggle—the opposition of human and nonhuman, rural and urban, agricultural and industrial, regional and national.[6]

Austin accepted neither the cosmopolitan, anti-rural bias of modernism nor a regressive romantization of the countryside as a refuge from the pressures of society and history. In essays such as "The Indivisible Utility" she objects to the underlying "idea of a fundamental detachment" of the country from the city (305). Turning against the "illusion of separateness" (305), she rejects the pastoral notion that the country represents a haven untouched by the exigencies of modern life. Austin contends that rural space cannot offer an escape from the modern world for the simple reason that it does not exist outside society but is an integral part of it.[7] The city relies on the natural resources and agriculture of the rural areas while it offers cultural and economic resources to them. For Austin, city and country as well as region and nation are interdependent entities. She was convinced, as demonstrated in chapter 4, that dominant society impacts regional culture and that regional variations and deviations can transform national politics.

Regionalization, Austin maintains in "The Indivisible Utility," offers

American society the best opportunity for developing a genuinely democratic culture and economy. "If there is any hope that a superior type of civic attachment may be evolved on American soil," she reasons, "it can only be in those communities which cannot even come into existence except by a prearranged community of *interest,* patterned around the indivisible utility. That a superior type . . . has already appeared in the Southwest is not possible to deny" (303). Austin held that a regionalist turn toward communalism and sustainable development, as we would call it today, would enhance the social cohesion and environmental adaptation of the nation. The fusion of European American and Native American cultures, she thought, would create a beneficial balance of cultural and economic and spiritual and scientific interests. Therefore, she considered the transcultural regionalization of American society "the most interesting possibility of social evolution," and declared, "Here, and not in the cafés of Prague or the cellars of Leningrad, is the stilly turning wheel on which the fair new shape of society is moulded" (327).

Modeling her regionalist utopia on the environmental adaptation and economic cooperation of Pueblo culture, Austin abandoned the traditional image of a highly individualistic West and reconceptualized the Southwest as a region in which the integration of Native American, Hispanic, and European American cultures could produce a sustainable democratic American society. In this respect, Lois Rudnick points out, Austin shared the outlook of her New Mexican associates Mabel Dodge Luhan and Alice Corbin Henderson. These European American women, Rudnick explains in "Re-Naming the Land," "opposed the belief that the American West had shaped only an individualistic, self-reliant, and aggressive personality—the white, male, Protestant profile that was often used to delineate the national character. In its place, they held up the folkways of nonwhite, community-oriented peoples whose guardianship of the past and integration of land, work, play, worship, and art could teach modern Anglo-Americans how to overcome the psychological fragmentation and alienating isolation of their modern, industrial society" (19).[8] Austin routinely presented Native American cultures as learning models to her readers and advocated a regionalist cultural syncretism. She held that European Americans had to go beyond emulating the Native American example and engage in a cross-cultural learning process that would create new cultural practices and ways of inhabiting the land. She claimed, for instance, that the Pueblos had developed "a too perfect communal-

149

ism" that privileged the common good to such an extent as to stall individual initiative and sociocultural innovation. "As I know the Pueblos at first hand, their power of cooperation, their even-handed distribution of benefits, surpassing all our Utopian dreams, is equaled only by their intolerance of change" ("The Indivisible Utility" 306). In contradistinction Austin characterized her political agenda as process oriented, arguing that any political movement that aimed at creating a preconceived, fixed socioeconomic order, such as Marxism, inevitably would arrest social development. A political program designed to effect a fundamental transformation of society, Austin reasons in *The Young Woman Citizen*, had to allow for "form without fixity, the flowing shape of a fountain, an elm tree, infinitely variable and airy and recognizable" (70).

Since Austin's utopian regionalism cannot be understood apart from her notions of Native American cultures and her ideas on cross-cultural dialogue, then, the next section outlines and contextualizes her understanding of Native American society, before the following parts return to the issue of land use and analyze the dramatization of water rights conflicts in *The Land of Little Rain, Lost Borders,* and *The Ford.*

Cultural Pluralism and Regionalist Appropriations: Native American Cultures as Regionalist Learning Models

Austin rejected the racist preconceptions of many of her contemporaries, objected to the assimilationist politics of the Bureau of Indian Affairs, helped to establish the Spanish Colonial Arts Society and the Indian Arts Fund, and effectively intervened on behalf of Native Americans. "We are trying to work up Indian arts and crafts," she explained, "in order to thwart the effort to drive them off their lands by forcing them to work for wages outside the pubelos [*sic*]."[9] While Austin's regionalism continues a long tradition of environmental definitions of American nationality, as noted in chapter 1 of this study, its multicultural orientation runs counter to the established discourse. In promoting a cultural syncretism, Austin's utopia of a land-based American democracy disputes those racialized concepts of American nationality that traditionally excluded nonwhites, in particular blacks and Native Americans, from the national community.

Yet Austin also relied on an organicist concept of culture and, as a consequence, espoused naturalized accounts of human society and history that had potentially racist implications, as the previous readings of "The Basket Maker" and *Cactus Thorn* indicate. She speculated that "the Indians are us a long time ago . . . all folded up as it were, and we are them in process of unfolding."[10] Both Austin's efforts to engage her white readers in a cross-cultural regionalist learning process and her environmentalist attention to the intersections of human and nonhuman history are compromised at times by her primitivist view of Native American cultures and her racialized and evolutionary notions about the processes of cultural development.

RACIST ESSENTIALISM

To contextualize Austin's attempt to valorize Native American cultures as a model for the regionalization of American society, a brief look at the related historical conversations on racial consistency and social heredity will prove helpful, since essentialist definitions of race frequently have served to legitimize the disenfranchisement of those people considered racially inferior. Historically, in regard to Native Americans and African Americans, race has been considered the defining characteristic and cast as a category that is to remain fixed and not open to change. While this view of racial consistency was complicated in the eighteenth and nineteenth centuries by the Christian belief in the divine design of the natural world and the common ancestry of humankind, scientific racism succeeded by the second half of the nineteenth century in popularizing the idea that humankind "was permanently divided into distinct races, biologically separate from one another" (Handlin 82). In his study *Race and Nationality in American Life* (1948), Oscar Handlin explains that this shift occurred as a result of the unconditional commitment of the scientific community to the methodology of natural history. He argues that the belief in quantifiable observation and taxonomic categorization let the scientists become entangled in a racist Linnean web of their own weaving. Their faith that "classification was the first step toward knowledge" (91), because generalizations could be drawn from the classified data, motivated them to attempt a categorization of humans in terms of racial origins (73).

Charles Darwin's evolutionary theory later discredited "both the polygenists and the monogenists" (Gossett 145) and offered a scientific basis for arguments in favor of flexibility and change rather than essences and fixed design. Yet his work was often adapted to the study of humankind in an effort to replace the classification of people into distinct racial categories according to their unchanging essence with a categorization based on the "fitness" that they supposedly displayed in the dynamics of natural selection. Races were now believed to differentiate themselves during evolutionary processes according to "differences in the capacity to survive" (Handlin 87). Social Darwinist racism relied on a view of social groups or political entities, such as nations, as organisms that evolved naturally and under consistent natural laws. Spencer, for instance, grounded his argument in "the Lamarckian idea that acquired characteristics are inherited" (Gossett 152). This maneuver allowed Spencer to transform Darwin's thesis that accidental variations that prove to have survival value are passed to the next generation into the thesis that the culturally and socially acquired characteristics of people can also be passed to the next generation. The faith in this kind of "social heredity" (Harper 255) and a corresponding natural hierarchy of fitness among humans amounted, as Handlin points out, to a scientific system of caricatures (91). The scientists merely "endowed the races they created with fixed, determinate characteristics, unaware that they were only putting an order to their own preconceptions" (92).

In regard to the Native American population, Thomas F. Gossett notes in his study *Race*, anthropologists such as Samuel G. Morton and Josiah C. Nott formulated in the first half of the nineteenth century the theory that Native Americans were a distinct unchanging race that was in its essence savage and not civilizable (237). Identified as part of the realm of wilderness that needed to be conquered and transformed by the white pioneers, the extinction of the Native American population was considered inevitable or even desirable. The Native American "will not learn the arts of civilization, and he and his forest must perish together."[11] The popular appeal of this kind of racism is readily perceptible in the following remark Theodore Roosevelt made in the late nineteenth century: "I don't go so far as to think that the only good Indians are the dead Indians, but I believe nine out of every ten are, and I shouldn't inquire too closely into the case of the tenth. The most vicious cowboy has more moral principle than the average Indian."[12] Essentialist concepts of race thus served to justify the disenfranchisement of Native Americans. At the time Austin came into contact with indigenous cultures and took up the cause of Indian rights, Native Americans had no legal standing and official U.S. policy, between the passing of the Dawes Severalty Act in 1887 and the Indian Reorganization Act in 1934, aimed at forced assimilation through the dissolution of tribal cultures.

BETWEEN PRIMITIVISM AND PLURALISM: AUSTIN'S VIEW OF NATIVE AMERICANS

It is in this context, then, that Austin launches her regionalist project of valorizing American native cultures. In her studies of Native American cultural practices, she frequently addresses the "crass and inexcusable ignorance" and racist preconceptions of her contemporaries (*AR* 44). In *The American Rhythm* (1923), she observes, "But I have found intellectual Americans generally baulking at the idea that there could be any informative relation between their own present or future culture and the many thousand-year-old culture of the race that we displaced" (44). In presenting Native Americans as learning models for European American society, Austin's apparent intention is to counter racist stereotypes.

In her essay "Aboriginal Fiction" (1929), for instance, Austin argues that Native American literature offers a valuable model for environmentally based art to European Americans. She asserts that this cross-cultural learning process requires, on one hand, that European Americans transcend their racist prejudices and learn to read across racial differences and that it depends, on the other hand, on the attention that the collectors and publishers of the translated narratives pay to the aesthetics and social context of their production. According to Austin, the oral traditions hold the promise of contributing to American literature the "figures of speech which have in them principles of growth, which vibrate and burgeon, which glow and darkle and change color"; that is, they offer linguistic and literary qualities that have their source in "the continuing adventure which ties a people to the soil" (597).[13] The oral traditions, although considered primitive in character, are presented as part of flourishing contemporary cultures. Unlike specimens collected for taxonomic classification, Austin clarifies, they do not possess "some sort of static quality which enabled them to be classified" (598). This conceptualization of Native American literary traditions as part of a living and developing culture that is valuable itself and constitutes a powerful force that can make significant contributions to dominant culture attests to Austin's learning process.[14]

Yet despite her later insights into the obligations and opportunities that the continued presence of Native Americans posed for European

American society, Austin's work remains grounded in a primitivist perspective. Austin was convinced that studies of contemporary Native American cultures could yield insights into the evolution of culture and the human mind. In her critical essays she repeatedly asserts that Native American cultures offer "direct contact with typically prehistoric social conditions" ("Primitive Man" 744).

In "Primitive Man: Anarchist or Communist?" (1927), Austin elaborates her idea that the basic traits of human nature can be studied in Native Americans. In an article whose title can be read as a pun on the Red Scare and the consequent intensification of nativist conceptions of American identity, Austin's insistence on the ancient and universal appeal of communal modes of organization can be understood as a critical response to those of her contemporaries whose socialist convictions were compromised by their Anglo-Saxonism, to writers such as Jack London, for whom socialism was a white enterprise. "Socialism is not an ideal system, devised by man for the happiness of all life; nor for the happiness of all men; but it is divised for the happiness of certain kindred races. It is devised so as to give more strength to these certain kindred favored races so that they may survive and inherit the earth to the extinction of the lesser, weaker races. . . . It is the law."[15] Austin's numerous articles on Native American cultures usually avoid and indict such blatant racism. It is one of her achievements that she does not present another argument for the existence of fixed laws that justify social imbalances of power by defining social conditions as part of a natural order and thus as not open to political intervention and change.

Still, Austin's endorsement of "aboriginal communism" ("The Indivisible Utility" 306) frequently remains problematic because her primitivism often results in a paternalistic stance that does not allow her to move beyond racist stereotypes and naturalizing accounts of social power relations. In "Amerindian Folk Lore," for instance, Austin's attempt to describe the uniqueness and diversity of Native American oral traditions is undermined by her conception of Native Americans as childlike primitives who represent the collective past of human civilization. In this article, Austin echoes the theory of biogenetic recapitulation that was employed by prominent figures such as Spencer and the psychologist G. Stanley Hall "to explain the characteristics of races as well as those of children" (Gossett 154). Austin generalizes about the commonalities of the ways in "which child and aboriginal view the environment" ("Amerindian

Folk Lore" 344). She asserts that European American children are able to relate to Native American tales because of a "residuum of pure savagery at the bottom of the child mind" (344) and thus suggests that Native Americans live in a state of perceptual childhood. As with her precursor Hall, the notion that "the mind of a child recapitulates the history of the human race in its development from savagery to civilization" prompts Austin to advocate a paternalistic variant of cultural pluralism.[16]

Austin restates Hall's belief that Native Americans "were incapable of profiting from the white man's civilization and would be happier if permitted to live in their traditional ways," as Gossett summarizes Hall's position (*Race* 155), in a highly idiosyncratic mix of arguments in "Why Americanize the Indian?" (1929). In this article Austin formulates her cultural pluralism in response to the brutal policy of assimilation enforced by the Bureau of Indian Affairs. Summarizing the findings of the *Merriam Report* (1928) on the disastrous system of Native American boarding schools, Austin argues for the establishment of village schools, for the general abandonment of forced assimilation, and for the restoration of the rights of Native Americans to practice their traditional religion, culture, and modes of economic organization, such as collective land ownership.[17] Her article is a politically provocative indictment of European American racism and the economic motivations underlying forced assimilation. Yet her political analysis is tinged by an essentialist view of Native Americans as primitives. She frames the political problem in terms of the general question, "how a highly civilized people should deal with a small, backward people in its midst" (173).

While Austin's ahistorical endorsement of the primitive accords well with the cultural pluralism of her time, her essentialist pluralism is logically inconsistent with her simultaneous advocacy of a subdued version of the melting pot ideal. In this respect Austin can be considered a typical representative of the "liberal approach to Americanization" that became popular after the implementation of the national origins law in 1924 drastically reduced immigration, an approach "that encouraged immigrants to retain their distinctive cultures during a period of initial adjustment, but anticipated eventual assimilation and the emergence of cultural unity."[18] Austin seems to have been unaware that the contemporaneous discourse on Americanization could not be readily transferred to the situation of the indigenous population, since Native Americans were neither immigrants nor newcomers to the politics of colonialism.

Still, Austin argues in "Why Americanize the Indian?" that Native Americans are "a cultural asset" to American society (172) and should be granted the freedom to practice the "peculiar gifts of their own" (171). Because of the "primitive's" potential for replenishing dominant culture, Austin speculates that "he could pass into the American strain to our advantage, especially if he were mixed with Nordic stock rather than Latin" (170). This melting pot scenario "of ultimately absorbing our native tribes into the body of our national life" (172) is a long-term perspective, though. For the time being, Austin reminds the readers, European Americans should consider Native Americans along the lines of cultural pluralism as an essentially different and racially defined group. Austin asserts that the energy "devoted to cajoling and compelling our Indians to behave like white men, would, if rightly applied, have made of them the best of all aboriginals" (167).

Although cultural pluralism usually upholds the equal value of all cultures as one of its main principles, Austin's primitivist outlook translates her analysis of the contemporary dynamics of power, which relegate Native Americans to a position of relative powerlessness, into a paternalistic belief that it is a "hard sociological fact that the tribal mind . . . must be protected from its own inexperience" ("Why Americanize the Indian?" 171). Austin's pluralism thus results in a naturalized and racialized account of cultural diversity. In the article she expresses, for example, her conviction that math and geography generally are not part of "all that an Indian needs to know" (169). Moreover, since reading is not a part of oral traditions, she offers the "intellectual inexperience with written language" to her white readership as "just one instance of the natural limitations of the primitive mind" (170). In Austin's essentialist argument literacy ceases to be an individual educational achievement and becomes an effect of racial identity. The logic of her primitivist plea for cultural pluralism cannot be considered anything but inconsistent.

Yet it is also important to note that Austin constructs her essay as an attack on and alternative to the assimilationist racism that was used to justify the repression of Native American systems of belief and social practice. Similar to the arguments that the first proponent of cultural pluralism, Horace M. Kallen, put forth in *Culture and Democracy in the United States* (1924), Austin considers forced assimilation an undemocratic practice. Like Kallen, she suggests that cultural subgroups could coexist harmoniously without forced assimilation in a common economical and political national structure. Like Kallen, Austin also attributes "the distinctive characteristics of peoples to inborn racial qualities whose origin and nature were obscure" (Gleason 44). Yet Austin's pluralism is predicated on the idea that any Native American who may volunteer to adapt to dominant society or wish to pursue further practical or academic learning should be allowed to do so. In "Why Americanize the Indian?" she advises, "Open all the doors to civilized opportunity, just as we have to all other racial elements according to their capacity; but neither nag nor compel them to enter" (171). Austin's recognition of the right of Native Americans for self-determination does not neutralize her racist essentialism. But it may have offered a beginning at her time.[19]

In her article "Cults of the Pueblos" (1924), Austin comes closer to relating her general reflections on primitivism to a meditation on the possibilities for and limits of cross-cultural learning. She begins her essay on the different southwestern Native American ceremonies that she has observed or read about with a disclaimer. "I doubt if any white man ever completely knows an Indian" (28). According to Austin, the difficulties of cross-cultural learning stem both from essential racial differences and from culturally acquired preconceptions. The observer's investment in a particular worldview is shown to interfere with his or her comprehension of a culture that differs considerably in language, cultural practice, and social organization from his or her own. Both an abhorrence of and a sensationalist fascination with unfamiliar cultural practices can result in gross misrepresentations—as the rumors about Native American life sacrifices to giant snakes exemplify that circulate in the white community (31–32). For Austin the encounter with Native American cultures yields not only an access to an aboriginal state of mind but returns the observer to herself as other. She describes both the moments in which she felt that the Native American performers, the Koshare, "turn up the roots of the human mind with lumps of our common clay sticking to it" and the moments in which they reminded her of the "absurdities of white life" (33).

Unfortunately, the view of Native Americans as embodying the ancient past of human evolution often works to erase the careful attention Austin draws to the problems of cross-cultural learning. Enchanted with the experience of a different culture she claims an ahistorical access that erases all cultural specificity and thus also the necessity to pay attention to details. In her description of ritual dances she remarks that it is "the charm of bodies moving from centers of self-realization, the charm of color and symbolic design so intuitively harmonized with place and purpose that without knowing anything you know all that is necessary for that spiritual participation which it is the business of the dance to evoke" (34). The appeal to the commonalities of human experience is strong in Austin's essay. It culminates in her implicit generation of a new American genealogy in which Native Americans feature both as the contemporaries and the ancestors of modern European Americans. The Hopi, for instance, are described as "our ancients" (31).

Walter Benn Michaels contends in *Our America* that Austin's turn toward Native Americans in search of a new cultural heritage constitutes a move that seeks to achieve "the nativist goal of Americanizing the American" (155). His statement is oblivious to the fact that American identity historically never included Native Americans and that Austin goes beyond using Native American cultures as a conceptual resource to redefine American identity. As her essays on behalf of Native American rights demonstrate, Austin's advocacy of Native American cultures as a learning model for the development of a distinctly American culture is meant to have practical cultural, social, political, and economic implications. Austin's apparent intention is to alert her readers to the concrete effects of colonization and forced assimilation. She insists on the accountability of the state agencies and establishes obligations for all members of European American society. The politics that result in a subjugated Native American population, she argues, hurt not only the "Indian" who is "robbed of his land, wounded in his respect for himself" but also doom European American cultures. As Austin puts it at the end of "Cults of the Pueblos," "we cannot put our weight on the left hand of God and not ourselves go down with it" (35).

Austin's regionalist pluralism intersects in multiple ways with the contemporaneous discourses on Americanization, racial consistency, and environmental definitions of American identity. Her originality lies in her rejection of forced assimilation combined with environmentalist advocacy and a promotion of Native American cultures as learning models for European American society. A most troubling aspect of her theoretical writing, however, is her tendency to temporarily abandon her concern with the contemporary realities of Native American societies for a study of them as a relict from the "Neolithic" past. This imbalance places Native American cultures "in the museum of white discourse."[20] Austin's penchant for conflating the analysis of current conditions and politics with the study of Native American prehistory threatens to reduce the cultures to which she turns for inspiration to mere stepping stones in the cultural development of dominant society. In these instances her work serves to diminish rather than enhance the political power and cultural influence of Native Americans in a multiethnic American society. Moreover, the essentializing pluralism that Austin's primitivist view of Native American cultures engenders conflicts with her project of redefining European American identity in regionalist and environmentalist terms. Within a naturalized account of cultural identity that defines cultures primarily in racial and essentialist terms, the environment in its local particularities cannot factor to a significant extent into the development of society.

Regional Development in the Country of Lost Borders

While Austin often focused on cultural practices and cross-cultural conversations, she also routinely addressed the economic dynamics and legal issues structuring the use of natural and human resources. Beginning with her references to the racial and gender politics of regional water rights conflicts and environmental degradation in *The Land of Little Rain*, she extensively treated regional economics and politics in several works of fiction and nonfiction, including her novels *The Ford, No. 26 Jayne Street,* and *Starry Adventure;* her essay collection *The Flock;* and her feminist educational treatise *The Young Woman Citizen.* Taken together these works reflect the ambivalent stance that Austin retained throughout her life on the question to which extent regional environments should be developed and to which extent they should be preserved in a wild or predominantly unbuilt condition. While her general attitude can be characterized as conservationist, her stance shifted according to the context in which she commented on regional planning.[21] Sometimes, when she identified with the concerns of rural communities, she stressed agricultural interests and advocated the development of the land. Sometimes, when she was more concerned with the environmental costs of social and economic progress, she emphasized the dangers of environmental degradation and cautioned against the extensive resourcing of the land. Sometimes, when she wished to express the regenerative promise that the encounter with the natural world held for her, she presented the wilderness as a testing ground for culturally determined values and concepts of identity and consequently demanded the preservation of wilderness areas.

While Austin addressed the various economic, political, and philosophical aspects of regional development in her literary and critical work, she rarely formulated which concrete form her vision should assume. If one synthesized her regionalist, environmentalist, feminist and mystical perspectives into a coherent position, one could say that Austin promoted the formation of a regionalized multicultural American society that was committed to sustainable development and the preservation of select wilderness areas. This chapter turns now to some of Austin's literary explorations of regional economies and their social and environmental impact.

RESOURCES IN A LAND OF LITTLE RAIN

Within the context of a primarily profit-oriented, environmentally indifferent economy, Austin's regionalist demands for flourishing rural economies and intact ecosystems often proved irreconcilable. A tension between agricultural and ecological concerns already surfaces in her first book-length publication, *The Land of Little Rain* (1903). In view of the vulnerability of the desert ecosystem to human influences, particularly to the extensive mining and agricultural development of the land, the narrator calls for a reorientation of human behavior. She wishes to see her local community and American society as a whole adapt to the environmental conditions of its land base. The reasons for her environmental commitment are twofold. On one hand, she considers the desert and its biota an ecological system whose needs delimit the human use of the land. On the other hand, she is concerned with the environmental destruction of the region because it holds the promise of personal and cultural regeneration for her.

The Land of Little Rain refers to the major modes of resourcing the desert at the turn of the twentieth century. The narrator reports on gold, silver, and borax mining, on the use of the land as pasture, and on the agricultural reclamation of the region by irrigation. She objects to the overuse of the desert's natural resources and warns, for instance, against the overgrazing of the land. The utilization of the mesas and hills as pasture already has modified the plant distribution. Certain wild plant species have been "banished by human use" and the "devastating sheep" (*LLR* 131, 144–45). The "virtuous and likable" gentians, for instance, no longer grow "outside the forest reserve" (216). The narrator is enraged by the sight of "shorn shrubs and cropped blossom-tops" and worries about the consequent "loss of ground-inhabiting birds" (158). For her neither the prof-

its of a "pound of wool" nor the enchanting view of the fires of the shepherds at night, reminiscent of "Judæa and the Nativity," can compensate
for the destructive impact of the sheep herds on the desert's biota (158).

In *The Flock,* published three years after *The Land of Little Rain,*
Austin revises her portrait of shepherding, however, and identifies with
the demands of the rural farming community. Instead of concentrating
on the issue of overgrazing and taking up the cause of wilderness preservation, Austin acknowledges the local need for pasture lands and defends
the agricultural interests of the rural community against the recreational
demands of urban visitors.[22] As she describes the particulars of shepherding and sheep behavior in *The Flock,* Austin depicts the shepherds as
representatives of an ecologically sound method of resourcing the land.
While she notes the destructive impact of the flocks on the regional environment, she does not disqualify the flocks and herders in general.
Instead, she presents overgrazing as the result of the incompetent or careless behavior of individual herders and explains under which circumstances
shepherding can contribute to the flourishing of both the regional economy and the pasture lands without putting the desert ecosystem at risk.

Whether adopted by rural or urban folks, in *The Land of Little Rain*
the conception of the natural world as a mere resource is shown to result in a careless and destructive relation to the land. The narrator considers most residents and travelers "great blunderer[s]" (60), who disturb
the ecological balance of the regional environment. "That is the economy
of nature, but with it all there is not sufficient account taken of the works
of man. There is no scavenger that eats tin cans, and no wild thing leaves
a like disfigurement on the forest floor" (60). Accordingly, the narrator
develops a preference for plants and animals that resist their instrumentalization by humans. In an environmentalist update of the romantic
flower poem, the narrator classifies the pale iris, which is native to the
mesa meadows, "a poet's flower" because it is "not fit for gathering up,
and proving a nuisance in the pastures, therefore needing to be the more
loved" (238).[23]

Aware of the self-sustaining organization of the desert environment,
the narrator argues for a low impact use of the land, which will not disturb its ecological balance. In her portrait of her "Neighbor's Field," she
differentiates between a high and low impact use of the land as a natural
or recreational resource. She associates an alienated and destructive stance
toward the desert with her European American community and an inte-

grative and sustainable relation to the land base with the Native American cultures that the white settlements dislocated.

The narrator contends that her white neighbors generally adhere to an unrestrained resource mentality. They consider the field worthless and view it as a bothersome intrusion of the wild into the domesticated world of their gardens. "The field is not greatly esteemed of the town, not being put to the plough nor affording firewood, but breeding all manner of wild seeds that go down in the irrigation ditches to come up as weeds in the gardens and grass plots" (LLR 125–26). In contrast to her peers the narrator values the diversity of the field's wildlife, vegetation, and soil and builds a house beside it to observe "the maturing of wild fruit" (134). She phrases the difference between her stance and the attitude of the town toward the natural environment in a nutshell: "though I own I am not a close weeder" (133).

Accordingly, the narrator is relieved to find that the field has remained mostly unaffected by the development of the town, that "the human occupancy of greed and mischief [has] left no mark on the field" (LLR 128). Yet her account of the history of human residency in the area shows that her use of the blanket term *human occupancy* is misleading. It is the ownership of the European American settlers, of "Edswick, Roeder, Connor, and Ruffin" (126), to which the land has proved resistant. The Paiutes, who were dispossessed by the white settlers, have left traces of their residency behind. The shrubs they planted and objects such as arrow points and potsherds indicate the former site of their camp (128). Since the Paiutes have formed close ties to their land base, the narrator considers the signs of their inhabitation and the trail leading to their present settlement in the vicinity of the town an integral element of the field's makeup. It enhances rather than diminishes the place's diversity. She contends that the field is "busy, and admirably compounded for variety and pleasantness,—a little sand, a little loam, a grassy plot, a stony rise or two, a full brown stream, a little touch of humanness, a footpath trodden out by moccasins" (139). The narrator thus underscores her portrait of the Paiutes and the other Native American tribes inhabiting the area as regional model collectives that develop through their interaction with the desert environment.

Contrarily, the current European American owner of the field threatens its continued existence. He is exclusively interested in the market value of his real estate and intends to convert the field into profitable building lots. The narrator does not explicitly question the right of her neighbor to resource his property, yet the prospect of the future development of the field unsettles her. On her way to a meeting with Seyavi, whom we met in chapter 4 of this study, the narrator envisions the field as a sentient other. She conjectures, "though the field may serve a good turn in those days it will hardly be happier. No, certainly not happier" (*LLR* 139). By reiterating the imagined response of the field in her concluding remark, the narrator distances herself from the desire of the field's owner to make "his fortune" (139). She aligns herself with the considerate attitude that she finds characteristic of the relation of the Paiutes to the desert.[24] She implicitly proposes that an appropriate use of the natural world has to take its self-organizing existence into account.

FROM MOUNTAIN STREAMS TO IRRIGATION DITCHES

The indirect way in which the narrator of *The Land of Little Rain* presents her concern with the conservation of her neighbor's field also is indicative of the difficulties Austin had in envisioning an environmentally sustainable use of the land by European American society. Although Austin advocated an appreciative and ecologically informed relation to the land, she rarely defined which concrete form a low impact use of the desert should assume. Representative for the ambivalent stance informing her descriptions of rural development is her account of the region's natural and man-made watercourses in *The Land of Little Rain.*

As a local resident, the narrator proposes in "Other Water Borders" that the cultivation of the land does not interfere with the ecological balance of the desert. She is impressed with the efficiency with which the water is channeled and distributed over "the tillable lands" (*LLR* 225).[25] Asserting that it "is the proper destiny of every considerable stream in the west to become an irrigation ditch," she speculates that "the streams are willing" to irrigate the fields (225). Nevertheless, the narrator finds it "difficult to come into intimate relations with appropriated waters" (225). She suggests that in order to comprehend the nature of irrigation canals one needs to have a knowledge of both their natural and cultural history. A long-standing relation to the natural streams that feed into the ditches is to complement one's understanding of the local history of water rights conflicts ensuing over their ownership (225–26). In other words, the *pastoral paradox* at the core of regional development can only be solved by a deliberate integration of its past and present, built and unbuilt, human and nonhuman components.[26]

Therefore, the narrator explores the natural source of the irrigation canals, the mountain streams, in the chapter "Water Borders," before she proceeds to draw a portrait of the local water rights conflicts in the subsequent chapter "Other Water Borders." The tone of her account of the ranchers' violent struggle over water allocations in times of a "short water crop" (*LLR* 226) is consistently ironic. Parodying the mythologized Wild West, the narrator emphasizes the race and gender politics informing the water battles within her community. Her exemplary saga begins with Amos Judson, owner of one-half of Tule Creek, shooting and killing Jesus Montaña, owner of the other half, to secure all the water for his ranch. Although the narrator proposes that this happened in "the Homeric age of settlement" and therefore "passed into tradition" (227), she also mentions that "Judson had the racial advantage" over her Mexican-Californian martyr for equal water rights (226).[27] Accordingly, it does not "become classic" when the subsequent white owner of Montaña's ranch, Greenfields, shoots one of the Judsons. The jury finds him guilty of manslaughter (227). Amos and his Winchester uphold their illegitimate claim to the entire water of Tule Creek—until a woman appears on the scene. Mrs. Diedrick and her family move into Greenfields, which is "not so very green by now" (227). She puts an end to Amos's rule by sitting on the head gate of the canal, armed with a shovel and "knitting through the long sun" (228). While Amos reasons that "he was too much of a gentleman to fight a lady," the narrator points out that Mrs. Diedrick "was a very large lady, and a long-handled shovel is no mean weapon" (228). The persistence of the woman brings the story to a happy ending. In the next summer the ranchers install a "modern water gauge" and take the water "in equal inches" (228). The participation of the woman thus restores the male-dominated public life of the community to order and peace.

While the narrator ridicules the race and gender politics of her community, she casts no doubt on its right to resource the desert streams. The success of Mrs. Diedrick's entrance into public life consists in the modernization of the water distribution system and the resolution of long-term neighborly animosities. As a carrier of cultural innovation, she ends the community's violent reaction to water shortages. Her achievement is that she transforms the relations among the settlers. In regard to the community's relation to its environment, she instigates a change that furthers rather than delimits the communal resourcing of the "water crop."

"THE SLAUGHTER THAT DEFINES THE FRONTIER"

While the narrator of *The Land of Little Rain* welcomes the agricultural development of her region in her discussion of water rights and irrigation systems, the story "The Last Antelope" exposes the destructive impact of European American society on the desert environment. Since Austin republished the story several times throughout her career, a closer look at this fictional portrait of frontier life and the devastating consequences of an anthropocentric concept of regional development proves rewarding.[28] "The Last Antelope" is an exemplary tale about the limited options humans have for forming enduring alliances with the desert's wildlife in times of the increasing agricultural cultivation and industrialization of the West. It is a story about the close friendship between the antelope and the narrator's regional model character Little Pete; it is also a story about the rupture of their interconnected lives through the expansion of the "Ploughed lands" (*LB* 48).

As the title "The Last Antelope" indicates, the story is set at a time when the development of the region has already fundamentally affected the desert's biota: With the exception of one last buck, the antelopes have become extinct in the area. The narrator presents the devastation of the land and its wildlife as a violent but routine event that occurs with each move of the frontier and the expansion of the settlements. She asserts that the antelopes have "ceased before the keen edge of slaughter that defines the frontier of men" (*LB* 68). The European American usurpation of the land is shown to destabilize the ecological balance of the desert environment. The hunt of the last antelope by coyotes, which would have been a regular event in an intact desert ecosystem, now threatens to result in the final regional extinction of the species. The alliance that the antelope forms with Little Pete temporarily averts this danger. The antelope comes to trust the animalized shepherd, who looks and smells like his herd and "the unhandled earth" (70), and takes refuge from the coyotes among the sheep. They meet on the feeding ground of the Ceriso, a crater on the mesa, each summer and develop a "reciprocal friendliness" (70). They compensate for their lack of a common language by conferring "favors silently after the manner of those who understand one another" (70). Their friendship prolongs the life of the buck and intensifies Little Pete's relation to the environment. The shepherd's countenance develops an even "keener likeness to the weathered hills" (72).

Yet the seven-year "fellowship" (*LB* 73) between the antelope and the shepherd cannot redress the initial imbalance of the ecosystem or halt the progressing development of the region. When a homesteader builds the first cabin at the foot of the crater, the Ceriso ceases to be wild and becomes the "remotest edge of settlement" (74). In contrast to Little Pete who appreciates that his life is connected to the desert, the homesteader views his environment as a mere resource. While the shepherd conceives of the antelope as "the noblest thing he had ever loved" (76) and considers the only tree in the vicinity, a juniper, an "old acquaintance" (65), the homesteader has no qualms about killing the antelope and cutting down the juniper for firewood (78–79). To the narrator, the homesteader's destruction of the desert vegetation and wildlife stands representative for the conquest mentality of the frontier. She defines his motivation for hunting down the antelope as "the love of mastery, which for the most part moves men into new lands, whose creatures they conceive given over into their hands" (74).[29] The shepherd and the homesteader thus appear as representative characters who exemplify a low- and a high-impact use of the desert.

As the story confronts the environmental degradation that may accompany regional development and dramatizes its tragic consequences for the regional community and the desert's wildlife, it offers a paradoxical denouement of the story. First, the narrator proposes that "in fact" Little Pete "had come up against the inevitable. He had been breathed upon by that spirit which goes before cities like an exhalation and dries up the gossamer and the dew" (*LB* 78). In other words, the last antelope was bound to be killed by human hunters in an ecologically destructive society. The fatalism of this assertion, however, collides with the story's environmentalist imperative. Therefore, the narrator posits a second general rule. "The fact is only when men struggle with men do you get triumphs and rejoicings. In any conflict with the immutable forces the human is always the under dog" (80). Obviously, the narrator's two tenets are mutually exclusive in their formulation as absolute laws, and the second "fact" is belied by the story's ending. The homesteader as an anonymous stock character, who represents the "slaughter" of the frontier, may be morally the "under dog" but his devastating actions go unpunished. He rejoices in "the luck of that day's hunting"; and his conflict with Little Pete is limited to the "quarter of an hour" he spends after the kill "with a wild and loathly shepherd" (78).[30]

In writing about the threat of ecological destruction, Austin cannot help but diminish her rendering of the desert as the primary determinant of human life. Members of European American society like the homesteader simply refuse to accommodate their lives to the environment and not even the "tardy" laws passed for the protection of the desert's wildlife are strictly enforced (*LB* 69). In view of this situation, the exemplary tale of "The Last Antelope" can no more than warn about the disastrous long-term consequences of environmental degradation. The narrator's statement that ultimately, "when the struggle is sharp enough to be dramatic" (80), nonhuman nature will eliminate those who fail to adapt is intended to function as an incentive to live up to environmental responsibilities *now*.[31] The positing of an impervious law of the wilderness serves to substantiate the narrator's claim that in one way or another European American society will have to accept that there are environmental limits to its development. The longer it ignores this "fact," the more devastating the consequences will be for both humans and nonhuman nature.

Novel Regionalism: *The Ford*

In contrast to the story "The Last Antelope" and Austin's prophecies of doom in the wake of the water rights controversies over the Los Angeles Aqueduct and Boulder Dam, her novel *The Ford* (1917) insists on the possibility of a regional development that balances the needs of the rural population and its land base. *The Ford* explores the alliances and conflicts that may evolve between individual and collective, rural and urban interests over questions of land use and regional planning. The novel dramatizes the "struggle between capitalistic and communal control" over natural resources that Austin would later address in her article "The Indivisible Utility" (306).

The Ford can be read as a regionalist reimagination of the historical water rights conflicts between Los Angeles and Owens Valley. Austin had witnessed this battle as a member of the rural community that lost its hopes for agricultural development when the city gained control over its water.[32] Together with other residents she had fought in vain for the local control over the Owens River, and the "cruelty and deception" of the valley's sell-out (*EH* 308) caused her to resent southern Californian culture and the unchecked commercialism it represented to her. This disdain, as noted above, also motivated her later opposition to the Boulder Dam scheme when she served as a New Mexican representative to the Second Colorado River Conference in 1927. Austin's representation of the conflict in *The Ford* mostly remains true to the historical precedent, except that she substitutes San Francisco for Los Angeles as the urban center that threatens to manipulate the development of the rural area for its own ends; and, most important, that she lets the interests of the farming community triumph over the interests of the private developers and urban planers.[33] Austin's novel acknowledges that both agriculture and urban growth within the arid regions depend on large-scale irrigation projects. In light of the water supply's indivisibility, *The Ford* examines the extent to which regional planning could and should be brought under private or public, rural or urban control.

The Ford is set in Tierra Longa, an imaginary region that Austin modeled on Inyo and Kern Counties of California at the beginning of the twentieth century.[34] The novel describes the psychological and professional development of Kenneth Brent, a farm boy growing up in a modern western environment. While *The Ford* can be considered a *Bildungsroman*, its central plot progresses along the lines of the water rights conflicts. It depicts the effort of the siblings Kenneth and Anne Brent to expose and undermine the plan of the region's greatest land owner, Rickart, to buy land and the attendant riparian rights under false pretext from the farmers to profit from the city's increasing water demand. While Kenneth initially fails in his attempt to organize the rural community around their shared economic interests, he eventually manages to secure the river surplus for himself and the other farmers willing to join his development company. His success is predicated on the cunning interventions of his sister, Anne, a clear-sighted real estate agent.

By linking the representation of the region's economic development to the depiction of the divergent individuation of Kenneth, Anne, and their childhood friends,[35] Austin creates a portrait of regional life that is sympathetic to agricultural interests without offering a romanticized view of small town life. *The Ford* does not project an idealized view of a preindustrial rural community that threatens to fall victim to the evil plans of capitalist land barons and urban administrators. Instead, by tracing the inner and outer development of its main characters, the novel emphasizes the intersecting gender, class, and environmental aspects of Tierra Longa's past and present situation. It demonstrates that "different relations to landscape produce or enable differing configurations of social and economic power"[36] and that, conversely, different social positionalities and economic practices facilitate disparate relations to the land.

KENNETH'S AND ANNE'S RELATION TO THEIR REGIONAL ENVIRONMENT

The most effective narrative strategy that Austin employs to describe the intersecting cultural, political, and environmental aspects of regional development is her antithetical characterization of the siblings Kenneth and Anne. While Kenneth is emotional, self-centered, and enamored with a Jeffersonian yeoman ideal, Anne is intellectual, far-seeing, and interested in profiting financially from the development of her region.[37] Kenneth has "the feel of the purposeful earth" (F 92). The land evokes in him a "sense of home, of the continuity of existence" (165). Out of his experiences of "the essence of the Wild" as a child (88), Kenneth develops a spiritual sensibility.[38] His vision of the future is grounded in his appreciation for the land (91), and although he first makes an apprenticeship in Rickart's office, he considers it his calling "to live upon the earth and work it" (431). As a young man, Kenneth's relation to the farming community is informed by his nostalgic yearning for an idealized rural past. By becoming a farmer, he hopes to recover not only his personal bond to the land but also the secure social order he associates with pioneer society. He envisions himself "in his prophetic fantasy, as the hope and center of the harmonious group, the leading citizen, the head of the family" (F 302). Given to patriarchal fantasies about the mythic promise of the West, Kenneth ignores the modern exigencies of rural life in an increasingly industrialized and urbanized region. He believes that his "instinct" and "feeling for the land" (403) will enable him to resist the investors and administrators who plan to appropriate the region's natural resources for the benefit of the city. Although Kenneth aligns himself with Progressivism and is aware of "the need and power of working together" (436), his alliance with the rural community remains precarious, because he thinks "for the Tierra Longans" rather than seeks to understand their outlook (227).

While Kenneth follows in the footsteps of his father and dreams of developing the valley through a large-scale irrigation project cooperatively owned by the local landholders (F 294, 361), Anne has no personal stakes in the region's agriculture. Like her brother and father, she has strong ties to Tierra Longa "through the nurture of common experience"

(361); yet, she is not interested in cultivating the land herself. As a real estate agent, her professional ambition is to direct and profit from the region's development. Anne considers herself "an agent for the land" (200). Her self-defined task is to determine how and by whom the land may best be used (199, 234). In contrast to her dreamy brother, she remains emotionally detached. Anne pursues her goals on the basis of a precise, often scientifically based analysis of the situation and pragmatically balances her personal interests with the common good. Unlike Kenneth, she is financially and professionally very successful. She buys back the family farm, Palomitas, for her brother and her father, who had sold it during a drought.

Anne's analytic capability, large-mindedness, and pragmatic outlook enable her to contribute to her community's development and to influence regional politics. Her personal life, however, remains overshadowed by the tragic example of her mother (F 235). While the mother's dissatisfaction with the monotonous and unrefined life at the homestead has influenced both children (49, 431), Anne is traumatized by her mother's early death, resulting from an abortion (149). She leads a self-determined life, yet her wish for a satisfying romantic partnership remains unfulfilled. Like the strong rural women characters that Willa Cather and Ellen Glasgow created in O Pioneers! and Barren Ground, Anne stays single.[39] Objecting both to her brother's infatuation with frontier individualism and to her friend Virginia's notorious blaming "of Capital and the Established Order" (185), Anne insists on people's personal responsibility to get out of the "sort of mirage" that "Androcentric culture produced" (233).

Bringing a feminist perspective to her profession, Anne seeks to balance the private and public and the economic, social, and environmental aspects of regional planning. Thus she occupies an intermediary position between the extremes of her brother's nostalgic attachment to the land's pioneer past and the destructive resource mentality of Rickart and his son for whom the land is only a commodity, "one of the pieces of the game" (F 165). In her professional resourcefulness, ability to think and act strategically, and capacity for relating disparate facts to one another, Anne resembles Rickart (274). He is, in fact, the only man who appreciates both her professional competence and her femininity (426–27, 435). Yet, unlike Rickart (F 175–76), Anne considers not only the potential profit and legal underpinnings of her business propositions but also takes the consequences of her actions on other people and the regional environment into account. While Rickart is the "local octopus" (110), epitomizing "power ungoverned by sensibility" (145), Anne possesses a keen sense of empathy (273–74) and acknowledges the diverse human and nonhuman factors entering into a situation.

KENNETH'S MATURING AGRICULTURAL VISION

Kenneth initially objects to Anne's and Virginia's claim that there may be a "social problem" at the base of his personal situation as a farmer in Tierra Longa (F 364). He prefers to equate his return to Palomitas with a return to an authentic and agrarian mode of living that moves him outside the reach of the capitalist economy. He declares, "I am done with business. From now on, I'm a producer. . . . Maybe I shall produce an irrigation canal and a farming district, but the thing I feel I have talent for is mutton" (406). Infatuated with the myth of the frontier, Ken considers himself the "consort" of the "lady" river (428, 429). He thus continues the ineffectual hopeful thinking of his father, who, as a young farmer, had looked at "that almost untouched valley as a man might at his young wife, seeing her in his mind's eye in full matronly perfection with all her children about her" (35). Undeveloped as the valley is, the farmers suck at the land's "dry breast" (225).

Still, *The Ford* presents the arid region as suited for agricultural development. The problems stem less from the climatic conditions than from the incapacity of the farmers to coordinate their efforts. Tierra Longa, similar to *The Land of Little Rain,* seems to require its cultivation. Collectively, the valley's river could be effectively resourced: "It was a little river, but swift and full, beginning with the best intentions of turning mills or whirring dynamos, with the happiest possibilities of watering fields and nursing orchards, but, discouraged at last by the long neglect of man, becoming like all wasted things, a mere pest of mud and malaria" (F 34). The farmers are incapable of transforming the arid region into a middle landscape, because they hesitate to organize their irrigation communally and thus fail to achieve "the miracle of coöperation" (388). When Kenneth returns to Tierra Longa, he feels both the land's "invitation and the advertisement of man's inadequacy" (225). The main reason for Tierra Longa's crisis, then, is the incapacity of the farmers to respond adequately to the socioeconomic and environmental conditions of their region rather than the near criminal methods of Rickart and his associates (289). Although Kenneth articulates Austin's conviction that "the people them-

171

selves" should be in "control of the regions in which they reside" ("The Colorado River Project" 115), *The Ford* is less concerned with the motivation of private investors and urban planners to appropriate this control than with the reasons for the failure of the rural community to respond successfully to the challenge.

What are the limitations of the farmers, their "invincible rurality" (*F* 221, 432), that keeps them from asserting their control over their region's development? Kenneth observes that the homesteaders are defeated by the same quality that "made them good farmers, producers rather than players of the game" (289). Their individualistic orientation and their largely commercial interest in their land base circumscribe their ability to cooperate. "The solitary, rural habit which admitted them to a community of beguilement could not lift them to a community of enterprise" (381). Rather than develop a collective strategy, the farmers adhere to a self-defeating individualism (221). Their failure to understand the implications of the water supply's indivisibility puts them economically and politically at a disadvantage. Lacking communal cohesion, they can neither resource their land through profitable large-scale development projects nor can they rely on their collective strength to prevent outside forces from usurping local resources.

Faced with the reluctance of his neighbors to sign the "Land and Water Holders' Agreement" he proposes (*F* 410), Kenneth's idealistic "passion for togetherness" (388) receives a severe check. He distances himself from the other farmers, whom he considers "inferior stuff of the same pattern" as Rickart (403), and appropriates the river surplus single-handedly. Glorying in the sense that he, after all, will realize the mythic promise of the West (*F* 403), Kenneth is satisfied with the regenerative effect that his pioneer style return to the family farm has on him—until Anne convinces him that it does not suffice to "escape" into the pleasures of his private life (430).

ANNE'S FEMINIST PERSPECTIVE

While Kenneth's self-complacency indicates the limits of his yeoman ideal, Anne addresses the political and economic exigencies of regional planning in modern America. With feminist insight, she formulates "public remedies for private relations."[40] She explains to her brother that his personal life is informed by social forces and that he needs to comprehend the interrelations between private and public, rural and urban economies if he wishes to influence their impact on his personal affairs, his farm, and his region. To ignore the relations of social and economic power that inform his life or to think of them as part of a natural order is to follow the example of his neighbors, which will make him vulnerable to failure. Anne makes this argument from a decidedly feminist perspective. "It was a mistake, she said, that women had always made, thinking that, because they enjoyed being ordered about by their husbands and cuddling their babies, it was their God-appointed destiny and they were therefore excused from any further responsibilities. So that if it was a notion he had of being a Heaven-built farmer, he could be one. . . . He could homestead a hundred and sixty acres under his own canal and be happy in it until she or Rickart or somebody of the same stripe came along and took it away from him" (F 430–31).

Anne's feminism often confuses and irritates her brother. She hurts his pride and his sense of propriety with "rendings of the ceremonious garments of sex as left him gasping" (F 183). In these moments, he has misogynist fantasies of violent backlash: "A wave of his old fierce desire that Anne should have a husband, and that he should beat her, surged over Kenneth. It was intolerable that a woman should talk so about men" (254). Yet, eventually, her clearly articulated point of view helps him to define his own position. With the help of his sister, Kenneth realizes that although he may consider himself "married" to the river (428), he needs to invest capital and labor to make use of this "lady." He creates a development company, a plan that Anne has anticipated and approves (435).

By constantly juxtaposing Kenneth's and Anne's perspectives, Austin transforms the story of her male protagonist's socialization into a larger conversation on the processes of individual and collective identity formation. By linking the portrait of Kenneth's achievement to a feminist analysis of regionalist politics, she "subverts the bildungsroman's anthropocentric and androcentric conventions."[41] The asymmetrical relation between Anne and Kenneth in *The Ford* and between Dulcie and Arliss in *Cactus Thorn*, to name another example, reflects Austin's belief that women are largely responsible for realizing the ideal of a just social and economic order that the American constitution envisioned.[42]

THE FORD AS A REGIONALIST BILDUNGSROMAN

Given her feminist agenda, why did Austin choose to describe the diverse aspects of regional development in form of a novel that focuses on a boy's coming of age? The centering of masculine consciousness may seem an unlikely decision for an outspoken feminist author such as Austin, who had produced as her third novel, *A Woman of Genius* (1912), a feminist *Künstlerroman,* and who continued to write from a female identified point of view throughout her career. Yet Austin also repeatedly explored regional politics through the perspective of male protagonists. *The Ford* (1917), *Cactus Thorn* (1927), and her regionalist novel *Starry Adventure* (1931) are narrated mainly from the point of view of their male protagonists. While we can only speculate on Austin's motives, we can describe the effect to which *The Ford* chronicles the psychological and material processes involved in Kenneth's development. The novel departs from the conventions of nineteenth-century regionalism to revise the male dominated tradition of American frontier writing.

Taking up the genre of the *Bildungsroman, The Ford* breaks with the tradition of nineteenth-century regionalism—which privileged the sketch form rather than the novel, which focused on "narratives of community" rather than on stories of initiation,[43] which depicted the interactions between adult and often elderly characters rather than concern itself with the psychological development of children, and which frequently centered on female rather than male protagonists. Still, *The Ford* is a regionalist work of literature. It has the development of regional characters, communities, and economies as its subject. It portrays the processes that transform Kenneth into "Brent of Palomitas" (*F* 385, 404). While the novel's attention to questions of male individuation accords well with the conventions of American wilderness adventure stories, *The Ford* also reworks this tradition. It is set in predominantly cultivated and built environments and its ironic treatment and feminist critique of the protagonist's self-infatuation, sexist preconceptions, and political and economic naïveté undermines the traditional masculinist bias of American wilderness quest narratives.

The Ford's regionalist narrative thrives on the tension between the protagonist's limited perspective and the larger outlook that the text's ironies and juxtapositions produce. In this respect, *The Ford* anticipates *Cactus Thorn.* The sympathetic yet critical presentation of her protagonists allows Austin in both cases to enter the imaginative space of a mythic western landscape and to expose its masculinist and anthropocentric base of reference.[44] Through the thoughts and emotions of her male characters, she conveys the appeal of the fantasy that virility and authenticity may be redeemed through encounters with the wilderness. In *The Ford* the passages narrated from Kenneth's point of view transport the "inexplicable excitement of those born to wrestle with the earth and conquer it" (228)—an allure that remains "inexplicable . . . almost to the point of irritation" to his female counterpart Anne (414). Concerned with exploring "the rural mind" (384), the novel also elucidates the role that the West plays in the national imagination. It shows that the idealization of the West's pioneer past and yeoman promise plays a significant part in definitions of American identity that posit that the contact with the land will issue into an authentic, autonomous sense of self and a homogeneous national community.[45] Since the narrative continually reinserts Kenneth's escapist fantasies into a socioeconomic context, it exposes the political repercussions of his "sort of sublimated mudpie making" (414). The novel thus draws the reader's attention to the challenges posed by the increasing industrialization and urbanization of the West. Or, to formulate it in terms more appropriate to the novel's focus on Kenneth's individuation, *The Ford* asks Californian and American society to finally grow up.[46]

By relating Kenneth's maturation to the development of the region's culture and economy, Austin can elucidate the psychological and cultural as well as the economic and political factors involved in community building and regional planning. For Austin these components were intimately related. She "thought of the mastery of the material environment as the mode of the development of consciousness itself" ("The Need for a New Social Concept" 301). Accordingly, Austin inscribes into the story of Kenneth's development as a farmer a regionalist learning process that creates alternatives to the obsolete individualism, commercialism, and romantic idealizations of the West that previously determined Tierra Longa's development and, to a certain extent, also national history. As Kenneth matures, he learns to adopt a nonegotistical perspective that deepens his spiritual and sociopolitical understanding. As he gazes into the night sky, he wonders, for instance, "what could men do in a world in which lands, waters, the worth of women, had no measure but a man's personal reaction. It was a moment of deep but revealing humility" (*F* 373). Kenneth's emotional attachment to his farm and his reverence for the nonhuman, for an "ultimate reality, not realized or measured except as he felt it sustain him" (373), help him comprehend social and ecological interrelations.

By describing her protagonist's regionalist learning process from a sympathetic perspective, Austin suggests that Kenneth's and Anne's different perspectives may be compatible, after all. Although *The Ford* offers no fully developed synthesis of their standpoints, the narrative allows the sensibilities of Kenneth and Anne to coexist.[47] Instead of canceling each other out, the differing relations of the siblings to their social and natural environment illuminate the advantages and shortcomings of both positions.

THE FORD OF JABBOK

The Ford offers a hopeful resolution of the water rights conflicts. It describes the obstacles to economic and political cooperation but insists on the possibility of intervening on behalf of rural and environmental interests. The novel thus is also a tale about regional resistance and persistence. It is in this context that its title may best be understood. The title alludes to the ford of Jabbok, where Jacob fought with God and was blessed for his persistence. An excerpt of the Book of Genesis serves as prologue to the novel, and the narrative begins with a scene in which the children act out the biblical drama in the local creek. Kenneth plays Jacob, Virginia the angel (*F* 3–5).[48] If we follow the title's religious connotations and read Tierra Longa as Penuel, the struggle for the assertion of local control over the region appears not as a disaster that has to be endured but as a challenge that can and indeed must be met. Rather than accept either "Rickart and his kind of work as a work of nature, gigantic, inevitable" (245) or the limitations of the farmers as "forces within themselves which had the form and dignity of gods" (290), the novel proposes that these opposing forces can be wrestled with and defeated. Against the assumptions of naturalism, *The Ford* signals that these powers are not immutable (Raine 254). They are neither natural nor God-given but result from a certain socioeconomic context that can be changed. The struggle against overdetermination is the cultural work of regionalism, Austin maintains. She explains in "What Is a Native Culture?" that "For all culture, all art is no more than this, a pillar of stone s[e]t of as Jacob's pillar by the brook Jabock, a sign that God wrestled with us in this place" (AU 625).

In sum, in describing a boy's coming of age and a regional land use conflict, *The Ford* explores the intersections between the cultural, political, and economic aspects of the West's development at the beginning of the twentieth century. The novel focuses on three major issues of regional planning. First, *The Ford* describes the capitalist drive behind the development of the arid regions. As Anne Raine argues in "The Man at the Sources," it represents the rural topography as "a systematically surveyed terrain traversed by flows of information and capital as well as of natural resources" and demonstrates that "the landscape of modernity does not end at the city limits" (246, 250). *The Ford* addresses the financial and political imbalance of power between urban and rural interests and criticizes that urban planners and profit-oriented private investors fail to consider the consequences of their actions on the ecology and agriculture of the West. It is this aspect of Mary Austin's work that aligns her with regionalists such as Lewis Mumford. Almost ten years after the publication of *The Ford*, he asked in *The Golden Day,* "Will our daily activities center more completely in metropolises, for which the rest of the country serves merely as raw material, or will the politics and economics which produce this state give place to programs of regional development? What is the meaning of Lindsay and Sandburg and Mary Austin?" (273). Second, *The Ford* shows that the agricultural development of the region depends on an indivisible utility and asks why the rural community fails to form the necessary communal alliances.[49] The novel portrays the political inertia and lack of cooperation among the farmers as the major reason for their failure to profitably cultivate and effectively develop their region. Third, *The Ford* probes the American cultural imagination for romantic notions about the West that serve to solidify individualistic concepts of identity and that engender an ahistorical and naturalizing view of social developments. The novel employs a feminist perspective to expose the shortcomings of farmers, investors, and administrators and to present an argument for a communitarian regional economy. Rather than subscribe to predetermined capitalist or socialist solutions, *The Ford* offers a vision of regional planning that takes the specificities and history of the social and natural environment into account.

6

REGIONALIST CONVERSATIONS

In analyzing Mary Austin's concept and practice of regionalism, the previous chapters of this study have described regionalism as a literature of community and place. They have examined the impetus of Austin's work toward social integration, situatedness, and the recognition of difference, and they have engaged the current critical question to which extent regionalism represents an antimodernist nativism or a utopian mode of cultural pluralism. Given the ongoing critical debate on the sociopolitical merit of the regionalist project, it is helpful to ask how regionalist texts, in their dual emphasis on community and place, render the processes of regional and cross-regional communication. How do they compose place-based subjectivities and construct regional and nonregional communities? Which specific narrative means and strategies do regionalist texts employ to construe and mediate between regional and nonregional perspectives? How do their narrative perspectives, particularly the configuration of the relation among narrators, characters, and implied readers, reflect on the dynamics of inclusion and exclusion through which regional and national identities are defined? This chapter analyzes the regional conversations embedded in Austin's texts. Specifically, it examines which concepts of regionalist literature, folk culture, and national culture underlie the orchestration of regional and nonregional voices in Austin's narratives.

Regionalism as a Female Tradition

In portraying regional environments and cultures, Austin's texts, especially her earlier short fiction and nonfiction, frequently address the social and literary relations that exist among narrators, protagonists, and implied readers. The central role that communication processes assume in Austin's writing places her in the tradition of women's regionalism.

This has been argued, for instance, by the editors of the Norton anthology of *American Women Regionalists, 1850–1910*. In their introduction Judith Fetterley and Marjorie Pryse propose that Austin's regionalist stories belong to the nineteenth-century tradition of women's regionalism. According to Fetterley and Pryse, women writers such as Rose Terry Cooke, Kate Chopin, Alice Dunbar-Nelson, Mary Wilkins Freeman, Sarah Orne Jewett, Mary Noialles Murfree, Celia Thaxter, Sui Sin Far, and Mary Austin shared an empathetic stance toward their regional characters and subject matter. In contrast to the local colorists these women regionalists wrote "not to hold up regional characters to potential ridicule by eastern urban readers but rather to present regional experience from within, so as to engage the reader's sympathy and identification" (xii). The women regionalists presented a vision of American society that was grounded not only in the folk traditions and physical environments of particular identifiable regions but also in the domestic sphere of nineteenth-century "women's culture" (xiii, xix). Fundamental to their regionalist writing was the search for alternative concepts of communal and local identity and a consequent privileging of character over plot (xvi, xv). On a formal level this resulted in a preference for the sketch form (xv).[1]

One of Austin's stories that perfectly matches the female regionalist tradition as Fetterley and Pryse outline it, although it is not included in their anthology, is "The Woman at the Eighteen-Mile," which appears in *Lost Borders*. Like other Austin stories that focus on the interaction of female characters, such as "The Basket Maker" and "The Walking Woman," "The Woman at the Eighteen-Mile" presents storytelling as a dialogical process that facilitates female bonding. As Melody Graulich notes in *Western Trails*, "Austin develops her repeating theme about how two women come to understand and empathize with each other through sharing stories" (57). The empathetic bonding of female protagonists through storytelling has been identified as a major theme in women's regionalist writing (Fetterley and Pryse xv, xvi). In our context Austin's story is particularly noteworthy because it centers on the encounter between the narrator, who is introduced as a conceited author, and a female character whose life story changes the narrator's literary agenda. Austin's portrait of the narrator's conversion into an empathetic regionalist women writer turns "The Woman at the Eighteen-Mile" into an exemplary tale on the significant influence that an author's local loyalties, especially her regard

179

for the experiential knowledges of other women, can exert on the creation of regionalist literature.

The narrator of "The Woman at the Eighteen-Mile" introduces her story with a self-confident declaration of her literary ambitions. "I had long wished to write a story of Death Valley that should be its final word" (*LB* 94). She initially envisions her story as a classic Wild West tale. It is to illustrate the "magnetic will of a man making manifest through" the stock ingredients of mines, murder, and mystery (97). Her plans fall short, however, because "at last it appeared there was a woman in it" (97). The woman at the Eighteen-Mile rest house gives the narrator a firsthand account of the incidents and confronts her with a conflicting version of the story. The man that she intended to cast as the hero now appears to have gained his "reputation of almost supernatural penetration" (101) through the information and the "vital remedies and aids" that the woman supplied (102). Since the narrator as a regional writer cannot simply ignore the lived experience of the woman, she hesitantly revises her story. She concedes, "hers was the right, though she had no more pertinence to the plot than most women have to desert affairs" (98). The narrator's assertion that the woman is only of marginal "pertinence" obviously is belied by the title of the story that presents her as the lead protagonist.

As the narrator listens to the woman, her perspective gradually changes and she begins to see a different but equally appealing regional story mapped out in front of her. She reconceptualizes her would-be hero as villain and experiences "the full-throated satisfaction of old prospectors over the feel of pay dirt, rubbing it between thumb and palm, swearing over it softly below the breath. It was as good as that" (*LB* 103). Yet the narrator cannot capitalize on her find, since the woman makes her promise that she will not publish a story that would discredit the man she loved. Consequently, the narrator discards the tale altogether. "If it were not the biggest story of the desert ever written, I had no wish to write it. And there was the Woman. The story was all she had, absolutely all of heart-stretching, of enlargement and sustenance" (108). Deprived of telling a tale of heroic adventure the narrator centers her story on her conversation and emotional rapport with the woman. Keeping with the tradition of regionalism she shifts the center of attention in empathetic response to the woman and inserts the woman's story into her own narrative.[2] By encoding in her story the creative process of collecting, editing, and imagining local tales, Austin's narrator underlines the distinction between regionalist writing and other genres, such as the formulaic western, that disregard the quotidian realities of western life. The ethics informing the narrator's selection and narrative arrangement of regional story material in "The Woman at the Eighteen-Mile" clearly link her regionalist poetics to the "women's culture" of nineteenth-century America.

As in Austin's story "The Woman at the Eighteen-Mile," the conflicts among the characters of regionalist fiction often encode the negotiations that the authors had to undertake between the demands of the different social groups they portrayed and addressed. Numerous regionalist stories dramatize the power dynamics between dominant and marginalized perspectives. Consider, for instance, the conflict between Sylvie and the ornitologist in Jewett's "A White Heron" (1886); the contrast between the detached, objectifying gaze of the visiting upper-class hunter and the empathetic responsiveness of Celia in Murfree's "The Star in the Valley" (1878); the relation between the white painter and Evariste, his African American model, in Chopin's "A Gentleman of Bayou Têche" (1894); the patronizing stance of the European American journalist toward his trusting Chinese informant, Pan, in Sui Sin Far's "Its Wavering Image" (1912). Also, numerous stories dramatize the need for intraregional solidarity. Exemplary story lines include the clash between the critical standards of the college-educated minister and the social function of Betsey's poetry in Freeman's "A Poetess" (1891) or the relation between the unemployed violinist Fortier and the upper-class souvenir hunter in Dunbar-Nelson's "M'sieu Fortier's Violin" (1899).[3]

This enumeration demonstrates that the regional characters, besides being identified with a particular locale, frequently embody at least one other traditionally marginalized position, which often is defined in terms of gender, race, or class. In "A White Heron," "The Star in the Valley," and "Its Wavering Image," as well as in Austin's *Cactus Thorn*, the relation between region and nation, for instance, is imagined in terms of a frustrated romantic attraction between a young, poor, or inexperienced female character and a well-educated, rich, or powerful male character. Accordingly, Marjorie Pryse suggests that we read regionalism as a critique of any form of hierarchical organization between a whole and its parts, as a critique of the distortions of difference that unequal distributions of power effect. In "'Distilling Essences'" she asserts that "a critique of hierarchy based on geographical and ideological differences as well as on the confinements of 'Woman's sphere' emerges as regionalism's essence" (12).

THE AUTHORS, NARRATORS, AND READERS OF REGIONALIST LITERATURE

The merit of attempts to systematically distinguish between regionalists and local colorists on the basis of their identification with their regional subject matter and their criticism of the status quo is contested among literary critics.[4] Richard H. Brodhead, for instance, posits that regional writers did not write for the general readership of the regions they described but for a removed upper-class audience. In *Cultures of Letters* Brodhead proceeds from the assumption that the regional cultures of nineteenth-century America "were often nonliterate and always orally based" (122). Nancy Glazener, however, argues convincingly in "Regional Accents" that regionalist literature also had a rural readership.[5] In the case of Austin it is certain that she intended to reach both national and regional audiences. While she was interested in familiarizing an outside readership with the desert Southwest, she also wished to be read by western readers. She hoped to expand their knowledge about their natural environment and to reinforce their regional identity with works such as *The Land of Little Rain, The Flock, The Land of Journey's Ending*, and *The Children Sing in the Far West*. Yet as a western woman regionalist, Austin had problems successfully marketing her early regional books, as Karen Sally Langlois shows in her essay "Mary Austin and Houghton Mifflin Company" (32–35). In the first decade of the twentieth century Austin's first publishing house, Houghton Mifflin, had neither a book distribution system in the West nor did the company consider rural California a financially promising market. Therefore, they marketed Austin's books in expensive hardcover gift editions to genteel and affluent eastern urbanites.

Still, while Austin initially faced practical difficulties in trying to secure a regional readership for herself, she created narrators who wrote about a regional culture that was both oral and literary. In her stories regional characters are portrayed as the source, the subjects, and the readers of regionalist fiction. In other words, Austin capitalized on the tension among oral storytelling traditions, the narrative practices of regionalist writers, and the demands of the literary market by turning it into a subject of her regionalist writing. Given this strategy, it proves helpful to ask whether the distinction between regionalist and local color writing can be traced on the level of narrative perspective in Austin's texts. What is the attitude of the narrator (rather than the author) toward her regional subject matter?

In their role of regionalist writers Austin's narrators define their responsibilities primarily in regard to their local communities, while they are keenly aware that they address both a regional and a nonregional audience. They simultaneously speak within a regional context and present their stories to an outside readership.[6] As they relate their experiences and the response of other locals to the regional environment, they continually remind the readers of the aesthetic preferences and social biases that govern the communicative design of their stories.

The narrators of *The Land of Little Rain* and *Lost Borders*, for instance, tell stories that accurately portray life in the California desert towns at the turn of the twentieth century and challenge stereotypical views of the American West. To underline the authority of their informants, the intrahomodiegetic narrators of the stories, the narrators incorporate metafictive elements into their accounts. Their task as regionalist authors is to assemble and complement the stories of the long-term residents without backgrounding or overemphasizing their local particularities. This involves, as said, that they reflect on their role as mediators between the inhabitants of the region and their remote readership. Rather than act as a "mere recorder" (*LLR* 112), the narrators have to take into account their audience's limited knowledge of the desert and its regional culture and their literary expectations and explicate the stories of the locals accordingly. As the narrator of *Lost Borders* explains to the readers, "You are not to suppose that in my report of a Borderer I give you the words only, but the full meaning of speech. Very often the words are merely the punctuation of thought; rather, the crest of the long waves of intercommunicative silences" (201).

Austin's regionalist narrators employ primarily two narrative strategies to mark the mismatch between the stories that their peers tell them and their interpretations of these accounts. They either self-referentially comment on their role as translators between regional and dominant culture or humorously juxtapose the curt remarks of the locals with their embellished versions of their conversations. A representative example for the latter strategy is the following passage: "It was, went on the Pocket Hunter, after he had told me all that I have set down about the four men who made the story, about nine of the morning when he came to Dry Creek on the way to Jawbone Cañon, and the day was beginning to curl up and smoke along the edges with the heat, rocking with the motion of it, and water of mirage rolling like quicksilver in the hollows. What the Pocket Hunter said exactly was that it was a morning in May, but it comes to the same thing" (LB 140–41). Through her self-referential narrators Austin draws attention to the tenuous balance between insider and outsider perspectives that regionalist writers have to strike in relating the ordinary circumstances of living in a particular place to an audience unfamiliar with the environmental and cultural context of the related events or stories.[7] By confronting her readers continually with self-reflexive comments that rupture the narrative flow, she encourages them to reflect on their reading habits. Like the narrators, then, the readers are asked to participate consciously in the construction of the described regional world.

The composition of Austin's early short fiction thus suggests that regionalist writing is designed to solicit a participatory reading practice. The readers are to engage in an imaginative conversation with the text's narrators and characters. This dialogic form of narration and reading has been characterized by Elaine Sergent Apthorp as a significant aspect of the female regionalist tradition. "In place of the solitary ego of the poet, who by heroic acts of imagination might impose a human order and significance upon the flux of material life, they posited imaginative relations among artist, audience, and material that required mutual imaginative participation—the investment of the powers of artist and audience in an ongoing and communal project, the creation and exchange of meaning and feeling" (10). Apthorp's characterization of the participatory concept of literature that underlies women's regionalism clarifies the historical continuity of this literary tradition with the other prominent nineteenth-century tradition of women's writing, domestic sentimentalism. It helps to explain the impact of Victorian gender roles, especially of the values associated with women's domestic sphere, on Austin's feminist and regionalist convictions and narrative choices. The participatory orientation of the female regionalist tradition also has been noted by Fetterley and Pryse, who argue that the empathetic narrative construction of women's regionalist writing is supposed to provoke an equally empathetic reading practice. The empathetic narrators not only enact the ideal of an emotionally supportive regional community by offering an appreciative view of regional reality, they also invite the readers to share their identificatory stance (xvii). In other words, the readers are to read the text in the same way that the narrators read the reality that they encounter.

To this argument June Howard objects that empathetic style certainly may aim at a certain effect but need not succeed in inducing a sympathetic response in readers, as the negative critical reception of women's regionalist fiction in the second third of the twentieth century has amply demonstrated (Introduction 24–25). Howard's distinction between anticipated and actual reader response certainly is valid. It reminds us that a text's effect depends not only on the construction of the narrative—for instance, on the dramatization of values such as empathy and inclusivity through the interaction of a story's narrator and characters—but also on the attitudes that the readers bring to the reading of it. It is fair to assume that the heterogeneity of the literary field in which the texts were created and initially received and our historical distance to these circumstances renders the relation between narrative perspective and reader response more complicated than Fetterley and Pryse's argument suggests. The sociohistorical context of our present readings, for instance, can work to "intensify the nostalgic effect of regional fiction," as Stephanie Foote argues, "precisely because we are so much more innocent of the urgent material and social history that produced it, but so much more inundated with the effects of that material history" (59).

To neglect the sociohistorical situatedness of reader responses is to run the risk of asserting an ahistorical continuity between narrators and readers as members of a community of empathetic storytellers and listeners, if not even of a commonly shared "women's culture." Such critical reasoning can work to reinforce essentialist notions of gender identity, particularly if it accepts the logic of separate spheres.[8] The critical extension of the narratives' community of feeling to include present-day readers, for instance, can work to erase the historical specificity of the association of women with sentiment, domesticity, and communal bonds. In this case the feminist examination of the intersections of gender and genre results in an affirmation of traditional concepts of femininity without prompting a consideration of the sociopolitical context of their formation. It relies on an essentialist understanding of women's "different voice" and asserts a transhistorical and cross-cultural continuity of gender identities. Hence the critical argument either threatens to remain locked within the logic of separate spheres or it repeats the troublesome reversal maneuvers of cultural feminism with which regionalist writers such as Austin strove to subvert the concept of True Womanhood.

Still, the conversation between texts and readers to a certain extent is also two directional, if not dialogic. We bring our world to the text in our reading of it, and although the text need not answer our efforts, it always is one of the forces that structure our reading experience. A text need not provoke but can accommodate or resist certain readings. Therefore, the empathetic or condescending stance that a narrative develops toward its regional subjects is a criterion that can facilitate a critical differentiation among different kinds of regional literature. A text's degree of identification with the interests of the described regional community can serve as a critical litmus test to distinguish between regional and regionalist literature in Austin's sense. The former depicts regional subject matter, whereas the latter sides with the concerns of the portrayed regional characters and communities.

AUSTIN'S REGIONALIST VISION IN
THE LAND OF LITTLE RAIN

Austin delineates her ideal of regionalist literature in one of her early stories, "Jimville—A Bret Harte Town." "Bret Harte would have given you a tale," the narrator explains, only to contrast his local color approach to the West with her regionalist standpoint: "I know what is best for you; you shall blow out this bubble from your own breath" (*LLR* 112–13). The narrator directly addresses the readers to challenge the stereotypical notions they may entertain about the West. For her the Wild West tales she has heard about stagecoach robberies have the single benefit that they "comfort you when the driver stops to rummage for wire to mend a failing bolt" (107). She dismisses Harte's work because she sees it as advancing an idealized, static, and thus inadequate image of the region. She holds that he failed to confront the historical development of the rural West. When he found "his particular local color fading from the West, he did what he considered the only safe thing, and carried his young impression away to be worked out untroubled by any newer fact" (105).[9] Consequently, the narrator considers the stories she has collected during her long-term residency in the desert settlements the "better ones" (105).[10]

Nevertheless, the narrator initially caters to the expectations that the title of the story provokes. In Jimville she proposes, "You are respected in as much ground as you can shoot over, in as many pretensions as you can make good" (*LLR* 113–14). An "anticipation of Poker Flat" (113), however, proves to be as misguiding as the narrator's comparisons between her own and Harte's characters (114). Her protagonists, after all, have "walked out of Mr. Harte's demesne to Jimville" (117). In contrast to other "Western writers," who focus on the surface excitement of western life and "smack the savor of lawlessness too much upon their tongues," the narrator is primarily concerned with the regional sense of selfhood of the Jimvillers (121). She emphasizes their close relation to their environment (they "understand the language of the hills"), their spirituality (they have a "personal relation to the supernatural"), their humbleness, simplicity, and valuation of the physical aspects of human life (120). They perceive themselves as members of both the natural world and their local cultures.

The inhabitants of the narrator's second regional model community, "The Little Town of the Grape Vines," share these characteristics. In the remote Mexican-Californian town Las Uvas, simplicity, charity, and generosity prevail. Like the Jimvillers, the residents of Las Uvas value the material and spiritual side of life and have developed close ties to their environment. The narrator presents Las Uvas as another learning model for European American society. "We breed in an environment of asphalt pavements a body of people whose creeds are chiefly restrictions against other people's way of life . . . but at Las Uvas they go for pure worship. . . . Come away, you who are obsessed with your own importance in the scheme of things, and have got nothing you did not sweat for, come away by the brown valleys and full-bosomed hills to the even-breathing days, to the kindliness, earthiness, ease of El Pueblo de Las Uvas" (LLR 279–81). Significantly, Austin links the utopian vision of regional culture with which she concludes The Land of Little Rain to the female tradition of regionalism. While the narrator generally presents literary traditions and criticism as male-dominated fields and can easily be imagined to contest the "city-surfeited demand" of male English Professors and journalists (LB 109), she introduces the portrait of her model community with a reference to Jewett's story "A White Heron" (LLR 265). To the narrator, it seems, regionalist literature is the sole domain female authors have successfully entered. The legacy of her literary precursors helps her to imagine a utopian alternative to dominant society.

In "The Basket Maker" Austin likewise links her regionalist ideal to place-based female traditions, by presenting the domestic skills of her regional model artist, the Paiute basket maker Seyavi, as a cultural asset. Instead of subscribing to the ideology of separate spheres, however, Austin's narrative carefully notes that Seyavi's creative processes and artwork dissolve the mentioned dualisms alongside the opposition of high art and

folklore. The narrator points out that Seyavi's weaving is one of the domestic "housewifely crafts" of Paiute tribal tradition (*LLR* 168). Seyavi's
art draws on her cultural heritage, is rooted in her present life, and belongs to both the private and public sphere. Seyavi "made baskets for love
and sold them for money, in a generation that preferred iron pots for utility" (168). Seyavi's motivation is emotional and pragmatic. The weaving
satisfies her "desire" (171), and the baskets provide her with an income.
Correspondingly, Seyavi blends in her artwork a subconscious creative
process, she "sees, feels, creates, but does not philosophize," with artisan-
ship and "technical precision" (168–69). Moreover, her artwork is inextricably tied to the regional context of its production. The narrator explains, "The weaver and the warp lived next to the earth and were
saturated with the same elements" (169). Seyavi collects the raw material
for her baskets in places she knows intimately well. Also, the quail pattern
she weaves is designed after birds that live on tribal land (168). Seyavi har-
monizes her creative intentions with the natural properties of her weaving material. The narrator is most impressed with "the sense that warns
us of humanness in the way the design spreads into the flare of the bowl"
(169). Seyavi's basket making thus realizes the narrator's ideal of regionalist art. Her basket weaving is both personal and communal; it exemplifies the interrelatedness of mind and body, subject and object, and culture and nature; and it manifests the connectedness of the artist with her
environment.[11]

Through her cross-cultural contact with Seyavi and the other Paiute
elders, by observing their integrated way of life and their use of a domestic
craft to express their place-based identity, the narrator develops an alternative vision of both regional selfhood and domesticity. She redefines
her concept of home by imagining that the mountain ranges encircling
her valley are the "walls" and the desert's vegetation and climate the "fur-
nishings" of their houses (*LLR* 173). As the narrator of *Lost Borders* notes,
the Paiute women cannot "get any rational explanation of the effect of
their familiar clear space and desertness upon the white man adventur-
ing in it" (40). To them the disaffected, incompetent, and colonizing response of most European American settlers to the desert is highly ir-
rational. The conduct of the white newcomers defies their standard
of adequate and sane behavior. "It was as if you had discovered in your
parlor-furniture an inexplicable power of inciting your guest to strange
behavior" (40). Listening to the Paiute women the narrator comes to

reconceptualize both her social and her natural environment. Through the tuition of the Paiutes and the experience of her sojourns in the wild, the narrator learns to envision a home for herself in the West that allows for a communal life that is not structured according to the ideology of separate spheres and that facilitates integrating and sustainable relations to the land. In stories such as "The Basket Maker," "Jimville," and "The Little Town of the Grape Vines," Austin thus develops a concept of regionalist culture that links the possibility of aesthetic innovation and social transformation not only to a reconceptualization of "women's sphere" but also to the local alliances and sense of place of the writers, artists, and their communities.

Southwestern History and Myth Making: *The Land of Journey's Ending*

In her regionalist work Austin describes how sense of place defines human identity in reference to an environmental context—a process she considered regenerative and productive, as we have seen. Her narratives delineate how regional identities develop in response to the tangible and intangible elements of local environments; how they build on aesthetic impressions and the (sometimes epiphanic) encounter with certain sites, animals, and plants; and how they answer to the testimony of human presence in the land. "These things," the narrator of *The Land of Journey's Ending* notes, "are important; they come down with the river as the silt comes, and enrich the human history enacted there" (430).

The cultivation of a sense of place, then, for instance by means of individual explorations of the region or through the collective sharing of regional stories, becomes a central cultural practice. Because the experience of particular environments shapes the understanding of one's place in the world, the stories, whether historical or mythical, that communities tell about their locales and their journey through space and time provide a fertile basis for further cultural development. Biocultural knowledge emerges in Austin's work as a potent source of cultural renewal. The narrator of *The Land of Journey's Ending* even imagines it as a sort of cultural fertilizer. She proposes that the combined human and nonhuman history of her region offers "something as precious to the culture that arises there as the alluvium of the delta. Never to the deltas of the Nile or the Ganges, never to Tigris and Euphrates, came a richer residuum of the things that make great and powerful cultures. Powerful, I mean, in their capacity to affect the history of all culture" (431). Since regional knowledge is supposed to transform desert into delta, making the land arable, the study of regional history and lore becomes a viable means to ensure the survival and flourishing of a given culture.

BIOCULTURAL HISTORY AS PROPHECY

In *The Land of Journey's Ending* Austin heralds the emergence "of the *next* great and fructifying world culture" in the American Southwest (442). While the book represents Austin's most comprehensive attempt at writing a biocultural history of the Southwest, she begins her account of the past development and present condition of the region's culture and biota with the declaration that this is "a book of prophecy" (vii). The subject of Austin's divinations, not surprisingly, is "the progressive acculturation of the land's people" (viii).

How are we to read Austin's self-fashioning as a prophet in the "Author's Preface" to *The Land of Journey's Ending*? Are we to understand it as a result of her mystical inclinations or as the manifestation of an eccentric personality? Austin's self-declared prophethood certainly reflects her need to present herself as an oracular expert on things southwestern. She wished to be recognized as a key figure in the development of the region. Yet there is more to her reiterated claim that "plainly, my business is prophecy" (*LJE* 222). Austin assumes the role of prophet to signal that her study of the natural and human history of the Southwest is motivated by a desire to comprehend current social realities and the predictable parameters of the region's, and by extension also the nation's, future development. As she explains her interest in the texture and weave of history to her readers, "What I would know is the far journey's end of all these threads of human enterprise, and my sole purpose, besides the pleasure of playing with them, in showing you the many-colored skein of the past, limp in my hand, is that you may presently feel with me the pull of the shuttle that flies to the pattern's completion" (222). Austin was not interested in a retrospective view at the regional past for its own sake. Her biocultural history, diagnosis, and prediction are neither motivated by a backward longing for bygone, supposedly better times nor do they express a disdain for a supposedly bleak past and an unqualified belief in national progress—an ambivalent stance toward regional history that at times informed the work of earlier regional authors. Instead, Austin expects her readers to trace and "feel" the effect of historical developments on their lives. She urges them to become actively involved in her project and to contribute to the formation of an egalitarian, pluralist, and sustainable America.

Writing with a political agenda in mind Austin frequently couples her predictions about the region's future development to direct addresses of the readers that serve to remind that they are to put the provided information to cultural work. From the first she asks her readers to imagine themselves as part of the recounted scene. In the preface to *The Land of Journey's Ending* she tells her audience, "Also, if you find holes in my book that you could drive a car through, do not be too sure they were not left there for that express purpose" (ix). Accordingly, *The Land of Journey's Ending* concludes with the narrator's advice to the readers to travel to the Southwest, where they might witness "Art Becoming" and the emergence of a multiethnic American culture, "the pulse of race-beginning" (445). By lending a sociocultural, if not patriotic, dimension to the study of regional history and culture, Austin calls on her readers to consider themselves not merely spectators of but participants in the collective story told.

Austin employs prophecy in *The Land of Journey's Ending*, then, as a form of regionalist advocacy. For her the regionalist project represents a sociocultural agenda that extends beyond the field of literature and aesthetics into the arena of political action. She shares this approach with other regionalists of the interwar years such as B. A. Botkin, Donald Davidson, Lewis Mumford, and Howard Odum who, like Austin, cast regionalism as "a democratic civil religion, a utopian ideology, and a radical politics."[12] In *The Land of Journey's Ending* and other regionalist works Austin develops a cultural mythology and a sociopolitical ground plan for the cultural, economic, and political changes that the nation would have to undergo to transform itself into a regionalized, democratic, and multicultural society.

AUSTIN'S KALEIDOSCOPIC VIEW OF THE SOUTHWEST

The Land of Journey's Ending takes its readers on a historical, cultural, and ecological journey through the Southwest—here conceived as roughly the region between the Colorado River and the Rio Grande, comprising Arizona, most of New Mexico, the southwestern corner of Colorado, and reaching into northern Mexico. Austin's dual focus on the region's natural and social history and her intercultural approach to historiography render the essay collection a comprehensive study of the Southwest. *The Land of Journey's Ending* presents us with a kaleidoscopic view that synthesizes the manifold aspects of the region's human and nonhuman past into the vision of an ideal regional society whose integration with its environment is to serve as paragon for the nation's development.

The book assembles a diverse array of voices as Austin relies on multiple sources—the journals of the conquistadors and early Franciscan missionaries, the reports of American trappers and British surveyors, scientific research and Native American mythologies, and her own observations and experiences of place. In presenting the Southwest as a unified biocultural region Austin integrates several fields of knowledge, including biology, zoology, meteorology, geology, conservancy, geography, evolutionary theory, history, archeology, mythology, theology, ethnology, and folklore. Since each area of interest offers a different route through the territory and brings a distinct aspect of regional reality into focus, Austin's interdisciplinary narrative synthesizes not only diverse subject matters but also divergent modes of inquiry and perception.[13]

The book begins with a romanticizing account of the European conquest of the Southwest. The first chapter situates the "Journey's Beginning" within the Spanish and Portuguese past before the second chapter, "Wind's Trail: I Am Seeking!" describes the tree and plant distribution according to wind patterns, water sources, and altitude. The third and fourth chapters, "The Days of Our Ancients" and "Cities that Died," then, are given over to a discussion of Native American history in the Southwest, from prehistory to the late seventeenth century. The subsequent chapters alternate among accounts of contemporary Native American societies ("Papagueria" and "The Left Hand of God"); descriptions of the missionary past and of the present-day conditions of Hispanic life in the Southwest ("The Saints in New Mexico" and "The Trail of Blood"); and portraits of the region's flora and fauna, both wild and domesticated, that is, native and introduced ("Cactus Country," "Making the Sun Noise," and "Katchinas of the Orchard").

Some chapters present a truly kaleidoscopic view, touching on all mentioned subjects, while taking as their focal point one particular site or frame of reference. Successful examples include the portrait of Inscription Rock as "a symbolic focus" (*LJE* 218) in the chapter "Paso Por Aqui," which presents the monument as a site around which "the time-streams bend and swirl" (231); the description of the rivers as powerful agents in the natural and human history of the arid region in "Down the Rio Grande" and "Rio Colorado"; and the spiritual cartography developed in "Sacred Mountains."

The Land of Journey's Ending concludes with a chapter that contains Austin's regionalist manifesto and predictions, "Hasta Mañana." Given the first chapter's location of the journey's origins in the conquest of the region, we can regard as programmatic the last chapter's Spanish title. While Anglo-Americans are welcome to join, the prophesied future of the place and the potential it holds for the transformation of American society is grounded in the Spanish-speaking cultures of the Southwest, which for Austin included both Hispanic and Native American communities. As Austin reminds her readers, "Not all the fine and moving things in American history were done in English" (LJE 193).

Adding layer after layer of information about the human and natural history of the region, The Land of Journey's Ending portrays the Southwest from multiple perspectives. As we follow the narrative and the interspersed account of the narrator's firsthand experiences, complementary readings of the same historical instances and natural phenomena accumulate. We learn, for instance, that the Grand Canyon was created through the combined action of one lowering and one lifting force—personified as divine twins in Paiute cosmology (LJE 397–98) but described as the river's erosion against the "steady up-push of the land" in Western geology (418). The different but converging explanations offer us distinct trails through the terrain. They facilitate various kinds of understanding. The narrative thus not only describes the outer contours and ecological organization of the environment but also imbues the portrayed landscape with history, meaning, and emotions.

Since the landscape resonates with the preliminary endings of the diverse types of journeys that make up the human and natural history of the Southwest, the places described in Austin's account do not appear as a stable setting for the migration of animals and people. The Land of Journey's Ending represents the natural world not as a place outside history, an inert background created once and for all. Instead, the land is shown to materialize history, as the chapter "Cactus Country" exemplifies. "Cactus Country" chronicles the evolution of sundry species of cacti in the arid Southwest. The chapter begins and ends with the assertion that the cacti are a highly specialized form of vegetation that represents "the ultimate adaptations of vegetative life on its way up from its primordial home in the sea shallows, to the farthest, driest land" (*LJE* 119). Austin discusses the build, mode of propagation, typical habitat, and ecological interrelations of the many southwestern desert plants—of saguaros, prickly pear cacti, fishhook cacti, and barrel cacti, chollas and yuccas, creosote, palo verde trees, and agaves and ocotillos. She presents the cacti as the result of evolutionary processes that allowed plant life to "leave" the seas, to become earthbound, and, finally, judging from archeological evidence probably in the Pleistocene (136), to adapt to arid conditions. As Austin notes, in cholla groves, "in the choyital, we reach the full diapason of the adaptive rhythms of the spirit of vegetating life. If the word spirit has too much color for you, say the complex of energy" that has evolved from protoplasm to cholla cactus (133).

Austin devotes three pages to the exposition of this evolutionary journey, and then she explains her motivation. She points out that evolutionary biology provides the necessary context for an informed appreciation of the desert's vegetation. "It is only by keeping these things in mind that you will get anything more than a poet's or a painter's notion of plant life in the arid regions" (*LJE* 135). For Austin scientific knowledge is a necessary complement to aesthetic vision.[14] The realization that intricate evolutionary processes of adaptation occur within inconceivably long time spans is meant to alter our environmental perception. Looking at a particular plant with the knowledge of its evolutionary journey in mind, we may observe not an inert object but behold a historical vista. Contemplating the specimen, we may imagine the entire evolution from protoplasm to the present figuration of vegetal life in the shape of a cactus. We see the plant's long travel route unfold and note that evolutionary history ends right in front of us, "here in the great sahuaro [*sic*], the Vegetative Spirit comes to rest" (140).

REGIONAL MYTHOLOGIES: NATIVE AMERICAN
STORYTELLING AND REGIONALIST WRITING

To describe the land both in ecological and geographical detail and in its sacred dimension, Austin imbricates her chronicle of the region's biocultural history with references to Native American cosmology. We are told, for instance, that the "Douglas spruce, by whose root, according to the Tewas, the first men climbed up from the under-world, flourishes on these altitude islands, manured by the lasting snows" (*LJE* 35). In its movement between mythical and historical time frames *The Land of Journey's End-*

ing draws on Native American concepts of storytelling. It balances myth-ical and empirical accounts of reality to affirm the interdependence of culture and place. From a traditional Native American perspective, the biophysical reality of the tribal land base and its mythical representation constitute equally real components of place. The "First people are trans-formed into all the species of animals and plants which we know today— as well as heavenly bodies, mountains and rocks. . . . All bear the same names as before, and indeed cannot be differentiated from the First People."[15] By imbuing the environment with a mythological dimension, the traditional stories mediate between people and their land base. And by relating exemplary human and nonhuman interactions, they define the community's relation to its environment and the larger order of the world. The place-based stories and myths render the intersections of human and natural history palpable and help people to live in their en-vironment. "It is through these stories too that we are given the basic tools and ways of knowledge with which to survive in the world."[16]

In *The Land of Journey's Ending* Austin imitates Native American oral traditions and presents the myths as an integral dimension of regional re-ality. As in earlier works, such as *California: The Land of the Sun,* the "leg-end of ancient life" is considered as significant a property of the described places as "the succession of vegetal cover" (*LJE* 438).[17] Austin's descriptions of the desert's biota frequently associate the animals and plants inhabit-ing the region with their mythical counterparts in Native American cos-mology. Pumas, snakes, and coyotes, for instance, are related to their mythic siblings, mokiách, the Keresian puma hunting god (296–97), the plumed serpent, guardian of the water sources (304), and the trickster, "the Charley Chaplin of pueblo folklore" (303).[18] In this way the envi-ronment and the stories emerge as separate aspects of one fundamentally unified reality.

Austin adopts for her regionalist writing practice a Native American understanding of storytelling as an inherently spiritual and collective cul-tural practice. As Paula Gunn Allen points out, "oral storytellers work within a literary tradition that is at base connected to ritual and beyond that to tribal metaphysics or mysticism."[19] While the stories testify to shared values and beliefs and record tribal history, the act of telling sto-ries is in itself thought to contain the power to sustain individual and col-lective health and the order of the world. This concept of literature as both affective and effective becomes understandable once one considers sentience and change primary characteristics of the world. From a traditional Native American perspective the world generally consists of elements that are endowed with life and that, therefore, undergo changes. Because they are in perpetual flux they can be manipulated through rituals and ceremonies. Among the tools that allow individuals to access spiritual reality and to influence the course of things are ritualized forms of expression such as dances, songs, prayers, and stories. By telling stories the community collectively continues the work of creator figures such as Spider Woman—they create and protect themselves and their world.

Austin's account of human and nonhuman relations in *The Land of Journey's Ending* frequently relies on this concept of storytelling as a spiritual practice that is aimed at affecting the order of the world. Her discussion of the saguaro harvest of the Papagos is a representative example. Austin presents the accompanying ceremony as a "rain-invoking rite" (153), and then she adds, "Between the gods and men, each season has its own mediator. For the saguaro festival there is the night-singing mockingbird, which can be heard at all hours shattering the moonlight in round, mellow notes and scattering them like rain. In the towering white cumuli reaching from Papagueria to heaven, lives his prototype, the mystical godbird whom thus the Keeper of the Smoke invokes" (153). The text continues with Austin's version of a prayer directed toward this deity. The passage describes humans and animals alike as actively involved in the perpetual creation of the world. Both interact purposefully with environmental conditions and the spiritual dimension of the world. Austin clearly shares the Native American understanding of storytelling as a ritual that can influence the forces that shape the life of the individual and the community.

Native American storytelling, then, fulfills other functions besides being a means of education and a way to pass on an awareness of tribal history, traditions, and cosmology over the course of generations. The telling of stories also represents a cultural practice that allows people to redefine the present reality that they live in. Allen explains in "The Sacred Hoop" that it is the function of Native American oral traditions "to embody, articulate, and share reality, to bring the isolated private self into harmony and balance with this reality, to verbalize the sense of the majesty and reverent mystery of all things, and to actualize, in language, those truths that give to humanity its greatest significance and dignity. . . . [F]or through language one can share one's singular being with that of the community and know within oneself the communal knowledge of the tribe" (4). The telling of and the listening to stories are shared activities through which the speakers and their audience reimagine their environment and themselves in relation to it. The association of the current features of the landscape with sacred or mythic stories transforms the experience of place from a merely personal encounter with the environment into a technique for remembering, testing, and qualifying traditional values and beliefs. The general sense that the land still is populated by the contemporary siblings of sacred mythological creatures, for instance, may reinforce a respectful attitude toward these animals and the environment, while the individual encounters with particular animals may call up traditional stories that in turn may strengthen or challenge the person's place-based sense of cultural identity. The myths, therefore, are considered an integral part of personal development and collective history. The stories shape the present and future identity of the community.

Accordingly, in *The Land of Journey's Ending* it is frequently the act of storytelling that binds the different strands of Austin's biohistory together. Rather than adopt an impersonal narrative voice and omit subjective experiences of place in her biocultural account, Austin relates the narrator's multifaceted exploration of the Southwest and presents the episodes of her acculturation to the region as part of the larger history of the place. As we follow the narrator on her excursions through the region's history and geography, our knowledge increases and the vicarious experience of place that we share with the narrator adds depth to the literary landscape. This effect becomes most palpable when the text returns to an already recounted story or repeats a memorable image. Because the narrative account, legend, or image was carefully developed earlier, a cursory mention now suffices to call up a vivid scene in the reader's mind—which has the effect, as said, of lending historical, mythological, scientific, or sensual depth to the described landscape while also conveying to the reader a sense of how the local population may perceive the region. By gathering information about the region from the diverse sources that the narrative integrates, readers mentally undergo a learning process that is geared toward heightening their awareness of the interplay of sense of place, environmental perception, and sense of selfhood.

An example of the narrative's use of repetition is the incorporation of the already mentioned Paiute myth about the creation of the Grand Canyon. First told in detail (*LJE* 397–98), the story later is taken up in descriptions of the Colorado River (415) and thus remains present in the reader's mind. The repeated allusions to the myth are calculated to prompt readers to apply their newly won mythological knowledge in their reading of the text. Otherwise, they cannot fully comprehend descriptions such as the following: "Across Kanab range dark cedars, mountain mahogany and the tree that was the younger brother of Pamaquásh" (422). The description refers to the Paiute story told earlier and to make sense of it, the readers need to recall that when the twin brothers, who personify "the paired upbuilding and down-pulling forces of nature" (397), fought for domination over the world, the benevolent force, Pamaquásh, triumphed and changed his banished brother Hínuno, who had created the Grand Canyon in his rage, "into the piñon pine, making food and shelter in what had been a foodless, shadeless reach of desolation" (398).[20] The composition of the narrative invites the readers to imaginatively undergo, in the course of reading the text, a process of increased acculturation to the described biocultural region. If they mentally participate and make the effort of relating the world of the narrative to concepts and terms probably more familiar to them—translating in their reading, for instance, "the younger brother of Pamaquásh" with "pine tree"—they learn to imagine landscapes in new ways and experience the various perspectives that different senses of place yield.

Storytelling, Folk Culture, and Regionalist Literature

ONE-SMOKE STORIES: AUSTIN'S FOLKLORISTIC ADAPTATION OF ORAL TRADITIONS

The oral traditions offered Austin not only a wealth of place-based stories and genuinely southwestern imagery, then, but also provided her with a model for her concept and practice of regionalism. The arrangement of her last collection of southwestern stories, *One-Smoke Stories*, illustrates this. *One-Smoke Stories* contains original stories by Austin and her retellings of popular tales and Native American legends. Whether the material is original or adopted, Austin seeks to reproduce the style of oral storytelling throughout the collection. In combining her stories about the current life of the Native American, Hispanic, and European American populations of the Southwest with traditional myths, legends, parables, prayers, sayings, and humorous anecdotes, Austin presents her original work as part of a collective regional culture. The makeup of *One-Smoke Stories* can be said to imitate the organization of anthologies of "actual" folklore, which were popular in the thirties.[21]

While the intricate narrative design and the artful self-reflexive composition of some of the stories, such as the already discussed story "Speaking of Bears," clearly indicate Austin as the author, the reader frequently is left to speculate on the extent of the author's involvement. There are hardly any textual markers that would indicate the specific origins of the narratives or sayings. Without prior acquaintance with the stories or reference to other collections of folktales and Native American stories, the reader cannot determine whether Austin created these narratives or merely collected folk stories, as she claims in the introduction (oss xiv–xv). The deliberate imbrication of individual work and collective heritage and the dissolution or at least concealment of the boundaries between personal vision and communal traditions in *One-Smoke Stories* serve several purposes. By backgrounding the figure of herself as author, Austin can parade her vision of southwestern culture as accurate and authentic. Assuming the multiple voices of southwestern "folk," Austin also reproduces a concept of authorship typical of oral traditions—the communal context and the act of storytelling are foregrounded, the storyteller's personal situation and motivation are de-emphasized.[22] It is only appropriate, then, that *One-Smoke Stories* is dedicated "To 'The Tireless Hearers of All Sounds With Meaning' From Whom the Stories Came." Austin here quotes from the Zuni creation myth, as a more extensive excerpt in the section "Sayings of the Ancient Men" reveals (22). The dedication acknowledges her indebtedness to Native American oral traditions and produces a communal southwestern context for Austin's work.

In contrast to the Native American myths included in *The Land of Journey's Ending*, most of the stories collected in *One-Smoke Stories* are secular stories.[23] Still, they are part of place-based communal traditions and linked to spiritual practices. As Austin explains, the stories are told in the interstices of "the unending seasonal rituals that keep the Indian snug in his environment—sib to it, in the old sense of communicable, answering back again" (oss xii). For European American readers the tales thus may perform the "essential service" of suggesting what an environmentally responsive and spiritually attuned culture on the American continent could look like—provided that they are adequately translated rather than distorted to fit European models.[24]

199

Accordingly, Austin assumes the role of communal storyteller in *One-Smoke Stories* (xv). She integrates multiple locally and ethnically defined perspectives and dialects in her collection. As Dale Metcalfe notes in "Singing Like the Indians Do," "Daring finally to speak as the 'other,' in *One-Smoke Stories* (1932[*sic*]), her last 'Indian' work, Austin returns to the personal tale shared with listeners she had first heard in the Paiute campoodies" (83). While Metcalfe's observation is biographically accurate and Austin indeed considered the short short story format that she adopted in *One-Smoke Stories* "the true Indian *genre*,"[25] it is misguiding to designate her folkloristic collection of southwestern stories an "Indian" book. True, the regionalist vision that Austin develops in *One-Smoke Stories* may be called "Indian" in that it privileges Native American cultures as the most thoroughly established regional societies. The Southwest is cast as "Indian country," and Native American oral traditions are said to provide the model for other ethnic groups (xiv). Yet rather than merely attempt to write in a supposedly Native American manner, or "to speak as the 'other,'" Austin draws on several oral traditions to create the portrait of a multiethnic folk culture. In Austin's rendition of southwestern culture, the voices of Native Americans, Hispanics, European Americans, and Asian Americans intersect, without any one voice assuming a permanently dominant position.[26] The interplay of the plural regional cultures transforms each group entering into the exchange. Austin outlines the process in "The Folk Story in America." "Something of the Indian method has been taken over by the Spanish speaking population, just as something of the legendary lore of the Saints has been taken up from the Spanish by the Indians, something of the terseness and figurative quality has gone from the Indian to the cowboy and prospector" (18–19). The interactions produce new experiences and expressions, hybrid forms that cannot be classified as simply "Indian." Instead, a larger pluralistic cultural context emerges as the regionalist ideal underlying the design of *One-Smoke Stories*. In Austin's collection the diverse folk groups take turns in describing and thus in producing regional reality, as do storytellers gathered to exchange tales—when one speaker stops "another takes up the dropped stitch of narrative and weaves it into the pattern of the talk" (*oss* xiii). Grounded in diverse traditions the stories create a common cultural matrix for all participating speakers and listeners.

THE INTERSECTIONS OF FOLK, REGIONALIST, AND
NATIONAL CULTURE

As a result of her regionalist orientation, Austin was highly interested in folklore and worked to preserve local arts and crafts. She collected, for instance, European American folktales, Hispanic songs and artifacts, and Native American chants, myths, and poetry.[27] Austin was convinced that "no man has ever really entered into the heart of any country until he has adopted or made up myths about its familiar objects" (*LJE* 302). To her, mythologizing the ordinary was one way of homing in on a place. Therefore, she considered the creation of folklore and popular stories in response to still-unfamiliar phenomena—the invention of tall tales about pack-rats by newly arrived European Americans, for instance (302)—a seminal form of cultural work. By mediating between prior knowledges and recently confronted realities, such myth making was to render the unknown familiar and to provide a frame of reference appropriate to the new surroundings. In this way folk literature could contribute significantly to the environmental adaptation of emerging cultural practices.

Vice versa, the degree to which established forms of cultural expression were geographically localized constituted an index of their "folkness." In "American Folk," Austin reasons, "To be shaped in mind and social reaction, and to some extent in character, and so finally in expression, by one given environment, that is to be Folk" (287). In this sense, Austin maintained, *folk* was a term "that was originally meant to include all of us, and has come at last to refer only to those minority groups whose social expression is the measure of their rootage in a given environment" ("Folk Literature" 33). As a communal art derived from and in turn informing a group's experience of living in a particular place, folklore reflected the specifics of space and time. It perpetually transformed itself to express the changing worldview and place-based identity of a given group. In sum, Austin noted, folklore recorded "the wisdom, the hopes, the traditions, the moralities of the people, the imaginations of their hearts, the voice of their unimagined desires" ("Mexican Folklore" 23).

Since Austin was not a professional folklorist but a regionalist author, her apparent intention in writing about American folk culture was less to systematically study and describe it than to affirm features such as local rootedness, experiential aesthetics, and cultural pluralism. Faced with the mobility and increasing cultural homogeneity of modern America, Austin turned to place-based folk cultures as a source of cultural regeneration. She thought that American folklore was created outside the cultural mainstream and that it therefore opened up a space in which her regionalist project could flourish. For, as we have seen, Austin entertained few romanticized notions about "the people." In several of her regionalist works she portrayed the narrow-mindedness and stultifying pressure to conform that frequently characterized life in rural communities. She studied mass psychology and was particularly concerned with the difference between productive group and destructive mob behavior. Yet she hoped to claim folk culture as an alternative base of operation for her program of cultural regionalization.

For this reason Austin defined *folkness* in distinction to dominant definitions of *Americanness*. In her essay "Folk Literature" she suggests that American folk culture developed predominantly outside the cultural mainstream. First, it developed among groups that were denied access to American democratic culture, particularly Native Americans and African Americans (33–34). Second, it appeared under frontier conditions or other circumstances in which "economic security" was suspended while environmental conditions determined to a significant extent the daily life of the population, as "among the Creoles of the south, cowboys of the west, lumberjacks of the north," and particularly in the "Kentucky and Tennessee woodland" (34). Third, it ripened in geographically isolated areas where people adapted not only to the natural environment but also to indigenous cultures, as in the Southwest (34).

Austin thus tried to reclaim the democratic potential of folk culture for her regionalist project. She argued that folklore had been rejected as a valuable expression of Americanness merely because *folk* was misconceived as a designation for people unable to transcend the limitations of their given natural and social environment. In other words, "folk-ness stood in the American mind for invidious social distinctions such as the Republic was constituted to deny" ("Folk Literature" 33). America's democratic culture, Austin thought, traditionally had sought to promote civic equality by leveling social distinctions. The diversity of American culture had been erased by "that furious obsession of alikeness which has expressed itself . . . through the medium of the Lyceum, the Chataqua, and the Outline-Story" (34). As a result of its obsession with social cohesion and cultural unity, American society developed an "injuriously repressive" type of monoculture (34). Austin links her reappraisal of folk cul-

ture and oral traditions to a utopian vision of an egalitarian but pluralistic American society, then, to present the new regionalism as a viable
political and cultural means to redress this sociocultural development.
She explains to her readers that American culture currently witnesses "un-
mistakably a movement toward the localization of cultures . . . as an escape from the tyranny of dulness [*sic*]."[28]

The replenishment of American culture would occur not directly
through folklore, however, Austin reasoned, but through the recourse of
regionalist artists to folk expression. Pondering the question "whether folk
literature has been in every case produced by folk," Austin concludes without signs of regret that "Much of American folklore, at any rate, is not
given its final shaping by the folk that produced it" ("Folk Literature" 34).
According to Austin, regionalist folk writers have to strike a tenuous balance between regional affiliation and interregional communication. They
have to identify with the limited perspective of one segment of the population without losing sight of the existence of others. They have "to become folk, in the completest sense, of that larger environment which is
for Americans the matrix of so many local intimacies and masteries" (34).
In other words, they have to be capable of deliberately limiting their point
of view for the production of regional art, without reducing the overall
scope of their vision. They have to temporarily assume a limited outlook
without actually losing their knowledge of other positionalities and their
capacity to empathize with these. In distinction to folk artists, regional
folk writers practice "voluntary restraint" and do not share the limited
perspective of their narratives.[29]

HOW TO NARRATE LOST BORDERS

Exemplary in this respect are the negotiations among folk, regional, and
national culture—particularly between regionalist narrative practice and
the assumed expectations of nonregional readers—that the narrator of
Lost Borders undertakes. Introducing herself as a resident writer in the introductory sketch, "The Land," the narrator immediately addresses the
question of how to convey her regional knowledge and story material to
her readers. She tries to balance her roles of mystified sojourner off the
"known trails," who has "seen things happen that I do not believe myself"
(3), and of reliable guide to the region by directly addressing and challenging her readers. She proposes that in the desert "almost anything
might happen; does happen, in fact, though I shall have trouble making

you believe it" (3). To substantiate her claim she relates a local tale and concludes her account with the description of her futile attempt to retell it at a fancy dinner party. She contends that the disaffected audience, "the white, disdainful shoulders and politely incredulous faces," reduced her story to "a garish sound" (6). Consequently, the narrator casts herself as a depreciated storyteller who has no choice but to limit her selection of local tales to those that may seem credible to an outside readership. "That is why in all that follows I have set down what the Borderers thought and felt; for that you have a touchstone in your *own* heart, but I should get no credit with you if I were to tell you what really became of Loring . . ." (6).

In articulating the concessions that she has to make as she tries to mediate between folk and national culture, the narrator delineates Austin's concept of regionalism. In the guise of a resident chronicler of local life, Austin's narrator conveys to the readers how regional cultures constitute themselves. In one of her meta-stories about the relation between fiction and fact, the narrator recounts how she collaborated with her friend Dr. Woodin to make up a story about a gold-speckled potsherd that he had found.[30] Since the mere mention of gold is reason enough for the locals to believe a story (*LB* 6), their tale circulates widely. At last the narrator almost believes the story herself and publishes it in a local magazine "of the sort that gets taken in camps" (8). Instead of heightening her acclaim as a resident writer, however, the printed story gives rise to various complaints by the prospectors: her "version varied from the accepted one of the hills" (8). The narrator's anecdote, then, can be read as an exemplary story about the collective fabrication of myths, the relativity of truth, and the difference between oral and written literary traditions.

As such, it also clarifies the narrator's relation to her local community. For the episode is bracketed by additional self-referential comments of the narrator that present her as a self-determined reformer of regional culture and a storyteller of integrity. Her motivation for thinking up the story is her annoyance with the superstitions and racist prejudices circulating in her community. When her friend recommends that she "find" a story about the ancient sherd, she answers with a challenge to local lore. "I was sore then about not getting myself believed in some elementary matters, such as that horned toads are not poisonous, and that Indians really have the bowels of compassion. Said I: 'I will do better than that, I will *make* a story'" (*LB* 7).

The presentation of the narrator's dispute with the "body of desert myths" (*LB* 8) in the collection's introductory sketch serves a dual purpose. On one hand, it draws from the start the reader's attention to the layering of narrative levels that characterizes the composition of the *Lost Borders* stories. It distinguishes between the stories that the narrator tells as a resident regionalist writer and the tales that are circulating in her local community and that are told to her by her peers. By differentiating among folk, regional, and nonregional storytellers and audiences, the narrative comments on the difficulties of intraregional and interregional communication. It sets regionalist literature apart from folk literature while imagining as their common matrix the natural environment and national culture. Thus the narrative relates the individual creation of literature to the communal creation of folk culture and the collective construction of national culture. On the other hand, this self-reflexive presentation of the experiential and representational processes through which reality is created helps Austin to make the regionalist argument that our perception and understanding of the world are situated, that our access to realities other than our own is mediated and therefore bound to remain limited. Although the narrator holds that her story is as accurate and even "more interesting" than other local tales (8), she concludes her meta-narrative by admonishing the readers to reject any unqualified claims to knowledge about the desert: "First and last, accept no man's statement that he knows this Country of Lost Borders well" (8). The narrator asserts that even the residents' understanding of their environment remains partial. She points out that human access to the nonhuman is as limited as the comprehension that outside audiences have of regional reality.

Significantly, the potsherd story features the narrator's local peers and audience not as her informants but as the readers of her work. Thus the relation between the regionalist writer and her local community is imagined as a reciprocal conversation, which is mediated through the literary market. The pragmatic measure for the appropriateness of the conflicting visions of the desert and its regional culture that circulate within this field is the extent to which they further or interfere with the creation of a sustainable and egalitarian regionalized American society. As a meditation on the relation among regionalist literature, folk culture, and dominant society, the sketch "The Land" enacts Austin's ideal of a participatory democratic culture. It invites the reader's imaginative participation in the construction of regional reality while testifying to the narrator's and the local community's creative "power to make and do rather than merely to possess" (*EH* 368).

REGIONALISM AND THE DEMOCRATIZATION OF AMERICAN CULTURE

For Austin the innovative potential of a democratic culture depended on the extent to which it allowed for the active participation and creative contribution of all segments of the population. She argued that everyday culture should be comprehended and appreciated as a form of art— not only when it presented itself in exotic guises to the visitors of foreign locales but also as it unfolded in rural and urban America.[31] For Austin popular culture at its best neither was part of the homogenizing cultural forces within dominant American society nor did it represent a mode of cultural expression inferior to the cultural mainstream or what traditionally was treasured as "Art." She rejected both middle-class concepts of culture, as expressed in the Chautauqua approach to public education, and the elitism of certain definitions of high art. Cultural expression, she insisted, had to be a participatory experience that was relevant to the ordinary circumstances of living. Regional culture, even when not produced collectively by the folk but individually by sophisticated artists, had to contribute to the present-day life of the communities more than a decorative veneer or a vicarious link to so-called high culture. "Fiction, in order to be interesting, has to be written in the pattern of our experience."[32] Cautioning against reductive views of culture as a fixed body of customs and conventions, Austin called for "a creative type of culture" that facilitated community involvement ("The Town That Doesn't Want a Chautauqua" 196).

Folk-oriented regionalism emerges in Austin's work as the key to the development of a unique national culture—an American culture that derives its democratic character not from the erasure of difference but from the informed recognition of its regionally and ethnically defined cultures. Austin proposed that the regionalization of America would ensure the flourishing of cultural diversity, while a cross-regional exchange on the level of folk culture would secure the communication among the different parts and strata of national society. Thus she reconceptualized national identity in geographical and experiential terms. She rejected the prevalent "habit of thinking of countries as places on the map and nationality as a matter of political organization" and maintained that "for producing literature, Nationality is a matter of experience, and all the country has to do with it is to determine the nature of the experience."[33] In other words, Austin defined American culture as the sum of the conversations that the diverse sociocultural groups led about their experience of living in particular social and natural environments.

AUSTIN'S REGIONALIST CONVERSATIONS

While Austin adopted the role of folklorist in exploring regional arts and crafts and carefully recorded her findings, she did not contend herself with the role of home ethnologist and editor. As the author of regionalist fiction and nonfiction, she also assumed the position of a "mediator between the land, the folk, and art, between the primitive and the sophisticated."[34] Rather than limit herself to the publication of popular tales and stories, Austin processed the material she collected into carefully arranged stories and essays. In collections such as *The Land of Little Rain, Lost Borders, The Land of Journey's Ending,* and *One-Smoke Stories,* Austin creates accounts of western and southwestern reality that take as their subject matter not only the regional environment or the everyday life of the area's diverse ethnic groups but that also explore the dynamics of environmental perception, cross-cultural learning, and the production and reception of regional literature.

Chief among the narrative devices that Austin employs to direct the reader's attention to the ways in which her texts frame and create regional reality is the use of meta-narrative passages and of self-conscious narrator personae. The narrators of *The Land of Little Rain, Lost Borders,* and *The Land of Journey's Ending* are cast as self-critical mediators between the regional world and an outside readership. They identify as residents of the portrayed regions and count themselves members of the local communities, while they also retain a degree of critical distance and a sense of being different from other locals. Whether they are characterized as longtime residents of the described region, as are the narrators of *The Land of Little Rain* and *Lost Borders,* or as well-informed newcomers, as is the narrator of *The Land of Journey's Ending,* Austin's narrators belong yet stand out. This ambivalent stance toward regional society allows them to anticipate the expectations and attitude of the outside readers and to serve as their guides.

On the extradiegetic narrative level, then, Mary Austin's regional narrators address an outside audience rather than share stories with their immediate community, as Native American storytellers would and as the narrator of *One-Smoke Stories* at times does. Their self-declared function is to serve as the regionalist and environmentalist tutors of the readers whom they frequently envision not only as outsiders to the particular region but as generally alienated from the natural world. As the narrator of *The Land of Little Rain* puts it rather belligerently, "You of the house habit can hardly understand the sense of the hills. No doubt the labor of being comfortable gives you an exaggerated opinion of yourself, an exaggerated pain to be set aside" (200). Yet, while they are cast as belonging to different regions and cultures, the narrators and their readers also are understood to share a common matrix—the literary market place and national American society. As the readers read, they are expected to explore vicariously the unfamiliar environment and regional culture and to undergo a biocultural learning process. The objective of this exercise is to encourage the readers to value their own regional background and to advocate the democratization and ecological reorientation of American society. The sociopolitical impetus of Austin's regionalist texts depends on this implicit construction of the narrators and readers as fellow members of a multicultural national community.

CONCLUSION

Mary Austin's desire to ground her art in American folk culture reaches back to the beginning of her career. As a young writer, she notes in her essay "The Folk Story in America" (1933), she identified her interest in folk literature with Washington Irving but thought it in conflict with the 1890s vogue for local color writing. At the time that Austin turned to the study of western places and lore, regionalism had been reduced to formula writing. Regional literature had become commodified. Austin explains, "What the editors of that day wanted was 'reading matter, next to which' advertisements could expediently be placed, of which the salient ingredient was what went by the name of local color. The more highly colored the better, and you might take as much space as you wanted for elucidating that color and spread it on as thickly as you liked" (10). At the end of the nineteenth century local color literature primarily served a "memorial function" (Brodhead 120). As a "literature of memory," Eric J. Sundquist points out, it depicted "the rustic border world rendered exotic by industrialism but now made visible and nostalgically charged by the nation's inexorable drive toward cohesion and standardization" (508, 509). Local color literature imagined preindustrial rural enclaves to assuage fears about the increasing industrialization, urbanization, and homogenization of American society. It offered its readers the relief of a transparently ordered and intelligible fictional world.[1] Designed to provide the reading public with the possibility of a temporary escape from the exigencies of modern life, it rarely explicitly addressed the social, political, and economic implications of national developments. Since it did not seek to imagine viable alternatives, it not only recorded but also legitimized the disappearance of the premodern world it described. As Richard H. Brodhead contends in *Cultures of Letters,* regionalist writing endorsed the myth of a linear historical progression from rural communities to a capitalist industrial nation. It served "not just to mourn lost cultures but to purvey a certain story of contemporary cultures and of the relations among them: to tell local cultures into a history of their supersession by a modern order now risen to national dominance" (121).

In contrast to late nineteenth-century local color literature, Austin's regionalist writing promotes the concept of a participatory, environmentally grounded folk culture. Rather than depict rural regions as emblems of an irretrievably lost golden age, Austin's regionalist work presents them as harbingers of America's future. In her texts it is not only the past of the Southwest but also its unrealized potential of future development that provides the model for the nation's progress. In diverse works such as *The Land of Little Rain, The Ford, The Land of Journey's Ending,* and *One-Smoke Stories,* Austin reenvisions regional historical developments to demonstrate that regional culture offers the possibility of cultural regeneration, political intervention, and socioeconomic change. Not nostalgic diversion but the formation of a democratic culture and sustainable economy emerges as the promise of regionalism in Austin's writing. Her regionalist work follows moral and political imperatives, as Henry Nash Smith recognized. It is "ethical, and thus political. She is seeking not a retreat from men, cities, and society, but a real avenue of approach to them. . . . She is not trying to get away from any of the bewildering complexities of modern life" ("The Feel of the Purposeful Earth" 23).

Austin was convinced that literature fulfilled a sociocultural function. She believed that the reading of fiction served to educate as well as to entertain, and this contention motivated her regionalist work. She asked, "How otherwise except through a sincere exchange of experience through the medium of fiction, shall we learn to deal with things with dignity and beauty and success?"[2] Austin held that literature could contribute analytic insight and imaginative vision to the sociopolitical conversations of her time. Accordingly, in her descriptions of fictional and actual regions she examines gendered, racial, and economic imbalances of power and conjectures regionalist and feminist alternatives. She hopes that the production, absorption, and transformation of folk culture could help to democratize American cultural life. "That is why it is entirely right," she explains, that the writers "who draw their material from the sentiment and wisdom of the street, the factory and the shop, should be, even in our narrow sense, more popular than those who attempt the individualized problems of the intellectual few."[3] Austin's insistence on a democratic perspective and everyday subject matter provides a link between her regionalism and William Dean Howells's concept of realism. Austin thought, however, that the democratic voice of American literature had to be diverse, steeped in the social and environmental particulars of regional culture. Unlike Howells, Austin believed that realist literature had to acknowledge geographical differences and gender, race, and class divisions rather than strive for a unified and universal vision of American culture.[4]

The regionalist theory and practice that Austin developed in the course of her career expands the cultural and political agenda of regionalism. Austin began to write in response to the female regionalist tradition, but then she used the concept of participatory culture at the base of both nineteenth-century women's regionalism and Native American oral traditions to create a version of regionalism that aims at transforming American culture in pluralist, democratic, and environmentalist terms. Rather than cast her literary regions as utopian spaces or anachronistic pastoral havens untouched by the challenges and problems of contemporary American society, Austin presents them in their historical, social, and economic context. She deliberately describes the processes of inclusion and exclusion through which local, regional, and national communities constitute themselves. Extending the thematic scope and analytic concern of regionalist literature, Austin recognized that the "regions painted with 'local color' are traversed by the forgotten history of racial conflict with prior regional inhabitants, and are ultimately produced and engulfed by the centralized capitalist economy that generates the desire for retreat" (Kaplan 256). These "forgotten" aspects of the regional past and present are remembered and reimagined in Austin's work. In her stories, novels, and essays, she presents the Native American and Hispanic past of the arid regions, the place-based folk cultures of the present, and the promise of the Southwest's further development as the basis for national progress.

Regionalism and Identity Politics in Current Critical Conversations

While Austin's emphasis on the gender, race, and class dynamics of regional acculturation and national history seems to anticipate the analytic focus of the regionalism criticism of recent decades,[5] Austin's insistence on the land as a factor in identity formation and the development of regional and national cultures sets her apart from many contemporary literary critics. In current critical conversations the sociocultural construction of subjectivity, corporeality, history, and nature is stressed, whereas the impact of biology, place, and environmental conditions on human agency is de-emphasized. Although there is a growing interest in the relation between culture and environment among cultural anthropologists, cultural geographers, and ecocritics, many literary critics still imagine the relation between culture and nature as one directional. Culture is seen to generate form and meaning, using and transforming nature, without being significantly influenced in return. Thus the intersections between literature and the environment appear to be of little academic interest even to critics of regionalist literature.

As a result of the shift within cultural studies and the general critical concern with the triad of gender, race, and class, critics increasingly use the term *regionalism* in a systemic sense rather than as a signifier of geographical locations and place-based relations. This holds true for the literary criticism of regionalism, as exemplified by Marjorie Pryse's reading of regionalism as a metonymic critique of social imbalances of power, as well as for the field of American studies. Philip Fisher, for instance, has severed the meaning of *regionalism* from its geographical connotations. In "American Literary and Cultural Studies since the Civil War" he uses the term to denote any identity politics–oriented movement that strives to consolidate for some segment of the American population a separatist identity, which may be defined along the lines of gender, race, class, or sexual orientation (242). Thus Fisher can speak of "the unnegotiable regional essentialism of gender, race, and ethnicity" (243). This transfer of the concept of regionalism from "the geographic, or more precisely, the physiographic plane to that of systematics and sociopolitical philosophy" has been greeted by some literary critics as legitimate and innovative.[6] Lothar Hoennighausen, for instance, considers regionalism an apt metaphor "for the decentering and pluralism of ethnicity and gender" (7). He reasons that to refer to gender and race as regions grants them "a peculiar solidity, a holistic, homogeneous quality, and a gestalt that make their ideological dimensions stand out even more" (7). For Hoennighausen, objections to a nongeographical use of the term *regionalism* "would be both pedantic and obtuse" (6).

I would like to voice a few obtuse objections, then. In his metaphoric use of the term *regionalism,* Hoennighausen pairs concepts such as multiculturalism and globalization and such entities as region and ethnic identity (9). He uses *region* as a metonymy for the particular, the homogeneous, the stable, and so on. While his understanding accords well with Fisher's reconceptualization of the term, it does not agree with the utopian impetus of the American regionalist movement of the twenties and thirties, as we see it in Austin's work. For Austin, regions are the democratic and multicultural basis of American society. For her, regional subjectivities are neither necessarily stable nor homogeneous. They are provisional, reciprocal, and contextual; they develop as a result of place-based communal relations and respond to the forces of dominant society. For Austin the regionalization of America involves the negotiation of diverse social positionalities, including regional, national, ethnic, gender, and class identities. The objective of Austin's regionalist project, then, exceeds identity politics or the lobbying of particularized interests. In other words, Austin's regionalism is not regional in Fisher's separatist sense. Moreover, the regionalism that Austin promoted has not only an egalitarian impetus but also an environmentalist agenda. She conceived of regionalism as a form of cultural practice and social organization that would redefine American culture in relation to its land base. Austin propagated sense of place and the experiential knowledge of particular environments as a necessary ingredient of human identity. Adaptability and sustainability emerge as central values in her work. A metaphoric use of the term *regionalism* cannot account for this environmentalist dimension. Instead, critics often construe this usage as an escape route from issues that have become suspect because they have been associated with essentialism.

Faced with the charge of essentialism, critics have redefined the term *regionalism* to tilt the balance toward constructionism. Convinced that "geographical region" stands "in the same relation to 'regionalism' as 'female' stands to 'feminism,'" Pryse, for instance, argues that "'region' and 'female' are naturalizing terms" ("Distilling Essences" 9). To rescue the term for feminist purposes in the poststructuralist nineties, she reduces regionalism to a "rhetorical construct" and identifies as the achievement of the regionalists that they defined region in relation to "some larger hierarchy frequently also characterized by the gender, race, or class of the characters" of their texts in an effort to debunk this hierarchy (9). The regional identity of the characters indeed allowed the women regionalists to address and "critique other categories of difference," as Pryse asserts (9). Yet the relation of the characters not only to their human communities but also to the places they inhabit is an integral element of regionalist writing. Place is not just "a sign," and regionalism not just a "rhetorical construct," although both may also function on these levels. I am concerned that in response to previous polarizing and distorting accounts of the intersections of nature and culture, biology and subjectivity, place and history (including reversal strategies that seek to valorize women's historical association with physicality and materiality), we should once again become wholly preoccupied with the sociocultural dimension of our existence. To confine the regionalist project to the plane of sociopolitical theory is to obscure the reality that individual subjectivities and social developments unfold within a nonhuman environmental matrix.

In sum, a critical use of the term *regionalism* that erases its geographical connotations to extend the concept to any form of sectionalism, including social or political separatism, has significant drawbacks. Granted, the spatialized representation of aspects of subjectivity such as race and gender may have the advantage that it renders these categories and their ideological implications more tangible. This appeal probably also impels the metaphoric use of signifiers such as sites, zones, and borderlands and the current critical vogue for studying social relations in terms of topographies and carthographies. Still, when we erase the geographical connotations of the term *regionalism*, we empty of its meaning yet another term that denotes a concern with the environmental matrix of human life. As so often in critical theory, materiality and the natural world are backgrounded and cultural constructs and social dynamics foregrounded. In contrast to the current trends of critical thought, as represented by Fisher's approach, however, the biophysical environment matters in Austin's regionalism. Her work reminds us that we live in particular places and that these places inform who we are. Social systems do not exist in featureless space. In view of the current ecological crisis and the impoverishing if not lethal effects of a worldview entrenched in dualistic notions of nature and culture, it is legitimate to ask, Why obliterate yet one more time (if only in critical discourse) a concern with the imbricated environmental, corporeal, and communal conditions of human existence? Regionalism, at least in the way that Austin imagined and described it, represents one of the few Western cultural practices that seeks to remind us that we are cultural and natural subjects who live and die in a world that extends beyond the human. To ignore that we are sustained and transformed through places and nonhuman others is to subscribe to the conceptual framework that has legitimized the unprecedented environmental degradation we presently witness. Just as it seems unduly limiting to reduce regionalism to the form it took among female authors in nineteenth-century New England, it impoverishes the scope of the regionalist project to divorce it from a concern with actual places and the politics and philosophies informing our relations to our environments.

Regionalism: A Literature of Community and Place

This study takes up Austin's regionalist concept of literature, then, and conceives of regionalism as a literature of community and place—rather than as a literature of memory, "women's culture," or identity politics. Regionalism here is understood as the category that subsumes all forms of writing that describe the processes of identity formation and community building within their environmental contexts and that espouse place-centered concerns and regional standpoints. As a literature of community and place, regionalism is seen to be concerned with the cognitive, experiential, and communicative processes that contribute to the development of individual and collective regional identities and that are involved in the mediation between regional and nonregional interests.

Many of Austin's stories and essays revolve around experiences of place and trace their impact on personal and collective senses of identity. They represent processes of environmental learning—solitary moments of epiphany as well as the collective efforts of Native American, Hispanic, and European American communities to adapt to their land base. For unlike certain strands of nature writing, regionalist literature deals not only with personal reactions to nature but also with the collective responses of regional communities to their environments. Austin's regionalist texts do not simply recount regional history and lore or depict local flora and fauna. Instead, they present self-reflexive narratives that alert us to the conceptual frameworks and sociocultural dynamics that may inform both our experience of our environments and our reading practice.

In her environmental nonfiction Austin probes the social and ecological implications of aesthetic and scientific practices by dramatizing the narrator's bioregional acculturation. Like Thoreau before her, Austin incorporates meta-narrative elements into her environmental nonfiction to comment on the relation between literary conventions and social practices. Her precise descriptions of the desert ecosystem are imbricated with contemplations of the assumptions and social dynamics that inform her experience and representation of nature. Austin's environmental narratives aim at refining the environmental sensibilities of the readers and at promoting a conservationist ethic. Her work thus captures the historical development of American nature writing. "In the West, the nature essay also reflects the European and eastern newcomers' drive to be at home in a new land: first to explore it, to list its ingredients and learn its history, then to settle in it, finally to cherish and defend it."[7]

In dramatizing cognitive and communicative processes Austin's regionalist writing also continues and revises the female tradition of regionalism, as Judith Fetterley and Marjorie Pryse delineate it in *American Women Regionalists*. Like her nineteenth-century precursors, Austin frequently identifies an empathetic mode of observation, representation, and reception with regional characters and contrasts these with the objectifying view or condescending attitude of outsiders, who usually represent dominant society. Yet in contrast to her predecessors, Austin rarely endorses empathy as an end in itself. Instead, she presents it as one of the qualities necessarily involved in developing a relational sense of self and in forming regional alliances. Compassion and the recognition of difference, empathetic understanding and the awareness of the limits of one's comprehension appear equally important.

Austin held that democratic cultural practices best evolve out of experiential knowledges based on informed collaboration rather than on unqualified identification. Accordingly, she frequently integrates complementary perspectives and conflicting voices into her text. In *The Land of Little Rain* and *Lost Borders* the narrators side with the subjects of their stories without identifying with them. In *Cactus Thorn* and *The Ford* the perspectives of the lead protagonists are constantly juxtaposed to delineate the possibilities and limits of their environmental perception and their understanding of regional politics. In *The Land of Journey's Ending* and *One-Smoke Stories* a diverse array of regional voices, including the orchestrating voices of the narrators, interweave but do not merge as they generate a body of regional history and lore. Austin's regionalist characters and narrators speak as part of their communities and on the basis of their firsthand experiences of place, yet they do not naïvely claim to mirror regional reality without distortion. Instead, in narratives such as "Jimville—A Bret Harte Town," "The Land," and "Speaking of Bears,"

Austin's narrators proudly profess their narratives' realistic intertexts, thus complicating claims to authenticity. Repeatedly they address the question of which narrative strategies allow regionalist writing to accurately convey regional culture to both regional and national audiences.

In creating a regionalist literature of community and place, Austin fuses environmental, social, and literary concerns. Some of her critics, accustomed to conceive of cultural identity and literary traditions exclusively within a sociocultural context, may have difficulties recognizing the egalitarian ecological impetus of Austin's regionalist work. Yet she was one of the first writers to link environmental concerns with an exploration of the race, gender, and class politics informing the European American colonization of the land. Although Austin's notion of geographical determination at times prompted her to give naturalizing accounts of social relations and historical developments, and although her primitivist preconceptions led her to racially typecast Native Americans and Hispanics, her objective was not a return to glorified images of a preindustrial rural American nation or to essentialist discourses on human nature. Austin deliberately challenged the myth of the frontier and the enshrinement of America's pioneer heritage in pastoral quest narratives and wilderness adventure stories to imagine an American society defined by environmental responsiveness, an egalitarian social order, and a nonpatriarchal and ethnically diverse culture.

In her feminist revisions of feminized images of the land and naturalized concepts of gender, Austin explores the intersections between the human domination of nature and the subjugation of human groups associated with nature. In *Lost Borders* she joins an ironic critique of masculinist desires to colonize the wilderness with a refutation of the gender codes of California society at the turn of the twentieth century. She mocks masculinist fantasies of mastery of nature, while imagining new possibilities for women to feel at home in the West. In *Cactus Thorn* and *The Ford* Austin addresses the possibility that radical political thought may remain implicated in mythic notions about the West—a continuity that is shown to diminish its transformational potential. As a feminist regionalist author, Austin challenged the literary conventions prevalent at her historical moment. In her autobiography she notes, "There was a growing interest in the experiences of women, as women, and a marked disposition of men to determine what should and should not be written.... There was, of course, the difficulty that my books were always of the

West, which was little known; and always a little in advance of the current notion of it. They were never what is known as 'Westerns'" (*EH* 319–20). Although female authors such as Ina Coolbrith and Mary Hallock Foote had contributed to western American literary history before her, Austin's decision to write from the perspective of a western woman was still a dare. The praise of Foote for Austin's *The Land of Little Rain* indicates the difficulties western women had to confront when writing of their marginalized experiences. Foote admiringly commented on the work of her younger colleague, "how precious a testimony. . . . For I know no one who has done or is likely to do what you are doing, dear young lady."[8]

Although Austin defied literary conventions, challenged social proprieties, and in many respects was ahead of her time, her regionalist writing still continues an established line of thought that conceives of the American environment as a determining force in the formation of national culture. In American history the West traditionally has served as a crystallization point for the belief in the assimilatory power of the settlers' encounters with the land. To a certain extent, Austin's writing reflects the American pastoral paradox of equating the West with the possibility of discovering paradise and of creating a unique national culture only to be confronted with the disappointment of these hopes precisely because the settlements transform the land. Yet, because of her feminist biocentric vision, Austin managed to use the pastoral tradition as a vantage point for regionalist politics. Her recognition that ecological relations place constraints on the resourcing and development of the land moves her protest against the environmental degradation of the arid regions beyond antimodernist provincialism. Likewise, the bioregional commitment underlying her call for the development of sustainable economies moves her ideal of environmental communalism beyond mere golden-age nostalgia. While "Arcadia has no identity of its own," as Glen A. Love points out in "Revaluing Nature" (207), Austin's literary regions are based on identifiable western and southwestern environments. Her feminist place-centered vision distinguishes Austin from most of her contemporaries; it anticipates the recent efforts of ecocritics to develop and advance biocentric models of textual and cultural practice.

In arguing for the regionalization of American culture Austin neither idealized the wilderness as an unproblematic fountain of individual and national identity nor naïvely presented the natural world as part of an already established social realm, as the rhetoric of domesticity demanded.

Instead, Austin's texts frequently invite us to reconsider the politics involved in defining someone or something as natural. They show how the bonding with the nonbuilt environment can constitute a liberating source of alternative knowledge and how it can also work to reinforce a marginalized position if it places one with nature in a culture that conceives of nature as the absence of civilization. For Austin the encounter with nonhuman nature is neither a means to consolidate sociocultural conditions nor an escape route from society. Her work suggests that the movement from one realm to the other—with the help of the disruptions that the nonhuman causes, by resisting in its alterity easy accommodation and integration—renders the overlap between the cultural and natural spheres tangible and allows for a heightened perception of the continuities and discontinuities between the human and the nonhuman.

The Earth Horizon

In sum, Austin's regionalist work presents human identity and history as bound to both a social and an environmental matrix. Drawing on Native American concepts of storytelling, Austin argues that the cultural function of literature is to make its authors and readers simultaneously feel whole within themselves, part of the group with which they are associated, integrated with their environment, and aligned with the universal principles present in all these aspects of the world. Austin recapitulates her regionalist philosophy in the last sentences of her autobiography, *Earth Horizon:*

I have known to some extent what the Earth Horizon has been thinking about. Measurably, its people and its thoughts have come to me. I have seen that the American achievement is made up of two splendors: the splendor of individual relationships of power, the power to make and do rather than merely to possess, the aristocracy of creativeness; and that other splendor of realizing that in the deepest layers of ourselves we are incurably collective. At the core of our Amerindian life we are consummated in the dash and color of collectivity. It is not that we work upon the Cosmos, but it works in us. I suffer because I achieve so little in this relation, and rejoice that I have felt so much. As much as I am able, I celebrate the Earth Horizon. (368)

These concluding remarks weave together several strands of Austin's concept and practice of regionalism. They express Austin's view that the natural world is sentient, intelligent, active, and dynamic. They signal her belief that the nonhuman "to some extent" is accessible to humans, that, in other words, the other is partially knowable because there is a signifi-cant overlap and exchange between self and world. By stressing our em-beddedness in natural and social environments, the passage promotes a relational sense of selfhood. Characteristic for Austin's argumentative logic, the sequence of statements in part collapses, in part reverses the tra-ditional Western dichotomy of human subject and nonhuman object. Austin's "I" appears as both active and as acted upon; it is participant in as well as recipient of the perceptions and ideas of human and nonhu-man others. In the last instance, the human subject constitutes one way of the universe expressing itself. The assertion that the cosmos works in us grounds Austin's aesthetic and political vision of a regionalized America in her spiritual understanding of the world's fundamental unity. Her valorization of "the power to make and do rather than merely to pos-sess" reflects Austin's processual and experiential concept of creativity, which she shared with her contemporary John Dewey and that under-lies her understanding both of cultural dynamics and of political and eco-nomic relations. In its affirmation of the inevitability and "splendor" of collectivity, the passage expresses Austin's conviction that culture ought to be a democratic practice in both the sense that all members of society should have access to its resources and contribute to its development and that it should be one of the basic functions of art to further the cultural and societal cohesion of a fundamentally pluralistic America. In naming this unified American culture "Amerindian," Austin draws attention to the cross-cultural negotiations involved in the process and acknowledges her indebtedness to the Native American cultures that she turned to in her search for nondualistic systems of belief and for learning models in environmental adaptation.

Mary Austin's concept and practice of regionalist literature, then, is both aesthetically and politically motivated. It exemplifies her belief that the reading and writing of literature should be grounded in experiential regional knowledges and that the literary field should be democratically structured, that is, it should draw on and influence the processes of daily life rather than be "marked off from the folk use by selective experiences of caste and class" (*AR* 11). Austin's ideal regionalist author would write out an awareness of the situatedness of his or her life within both a so-cial environment and a larger world extending beyond the human. On the level of individual perception, regional culture would facilitate the experience of the interrelatedness of the quotidian, the aesthetically refined, and the spiritual, of individual and collective senses of identity, of the self and place, of the natural and the cultural, and of the human and the non-human. On the level of society, regionalism ideally would provide a common matrix to its members, fusing private and public spheres and leveling socioeconomic hierarchies, while integrating the collective with its land base. Hence, for Austin, regional literature and culture represent both the individual accomplishment of particular writers and artists and a communal exercise. Due to her integrative vision, Austin's regionalism offers to contemporary readers a "project which knows intimately, looks far, and feels profoundly" (*LJE* 429).

NOTES

List of Abbreviations

The titles of works by Mary Austin are abbreviated as follows:

AR   *The American Rhythm* (first edition, 1923)
AR 1930   *The American Rhythm* (revised edition)
CT   *Cactus Thorn*
EH   *Earth Horizon*
F   *The Ford*
LB   *Lost Borders*
LJE   *The Land of Journey's Ending*
LLR   *The Land of Little Rain*
OSS   *One-Smoke Stories*

A Note on the Mary Hunter Austin Collection

Material from the Mary Hunter Austin Collection is cited as AU, followed by the archival number of the respective item. If the Huntington Library did not include an item number, the box number is provided instead.

Introduction

1. Austin, natural history note AU 363.
2. Austin, *EH* 368.
3. Austin, "The Future of the Southwest" 186.
4. C. Van Doren, "Mary Austin" 23.
5. Dorman, *Revolt of the Provinces* xiii. Dorman offers an excellent historical analysis of the regionalist movement of the interwar years. My understanding of regionalism is indebted to his work.
6. Austin, "Regionalism in American Fiction" 98.
7. Rudnick, *Utopian Vistas* 8. Rudnick borrows the term *transcendental modernism* from the music historian Judith Tick.
8. Compare, for instance, the contexts in which Austin's work is placed in the Norton anthology *American Women Regionalists*, ed. Fetterley and Pryse, and in Scheese, *Nature Writing*.

9. Austin, "The Colorado River Project and the Culture of the Southwest" 112–13.

10. For the official Sierra Club population policy, see the Sierra Club citation in the bibliography. Currently three members of the Sierra Club's board of directors are supported by the Sierrans for U.S. Population Stabilization.

11. Cf. Hoennighausen, "The Old and the New Regionalism" 8–9.

12. Jordan, *Regionalism Reconsidered* xi; Miller, "Jewett's 'The Country of the Pointed Firs'" 7; Sundquist, "Realism and Regionalism" 508; Dorman, *Revolt of the Provinces* xiii.

13. For a reading of the regionalism of the interwar years as "a national culmination of antimodernist impulses," see Thomas, "The Uses of Catastrophism" 225. An influential discussion of nativism in the literature and culture of the twenties is Michaels, *Our America*. For the debate on the implication of regionalism in the processes of nation building, see Kaplan, "Nation, Region, and Empire."

14. See, for instance, the recent collections *Regionalism Reconsidered*, ed. Jordan, and *Breaking Boundaries*, ed. Inness and Royer. For a brief discussion of the revived interest in place-based politics and aesthetics in the disciplines of cultural geography and cultural anthropology, see Feld and Basso, *Senses of Place* 3–11. A helpful overview is also provided in Steiner and Mondale, *Region and Regionalism in the United States*.

15. The term *borderlands* was popularized by Gloria Anzaldúa. The linguistic term *contact zone* was appropriated by Mary Louise Pratt for postcolonial theory. Donna J. Haraway first formulated her politics of partial perspectives in the chapter "Situated Knowledges" in her *Simians, Cyborgs, and Women*. The regionalist orientation of the New West historians is readily perceptible in Patricia Nelson Limerick's work.

16. Although the first works of ecologically informed literary scholarship began to appear in the sixties and seventies, the practice of ecocriticism did not gain momentum until the nineties. While ecocriticism still is in the process of establishing itself as a distinct area of literary studies, it already has produced a diversified field of scholarly research on the relation of culture and environment. The articles collected, for instance, in *The Ecocriticism Reader*, ed. Glotfelty and Fromm, indicate the potential scope of the ecocritical project. Affinities to different branches of contemporary environmentalism, such as deep ecology, bioregionalism, ecofeminism, and social ecology, diversify the field, as do diverging critical preferences for poststructuralist, feminist, psychoanalytic, new historical, and other approaches to inquiry.

17. Miller, "Jewett's 'The Country of the Pointed Firs'" 3. See, for instance, the essays collected in *Regionalism and the Female Imagination*, ed. E. Toth.

18. Tichi, "Women Writers and the New Woman" 598.

19. Apthorp, "Sentiment, Naturalism, and the Female Regionalists" 6.

20. The shift in feminist regionalism criticism is best illustrated by the striking revisions to which some critics have subjected their earlier work. Compare, for instance, Ammons, *Conflicting Stories* and Zagarell, "Narrative of Community" with Ammons's and Zagarell's recent contributions to *New Essays on "The Country of the Pointed Firs*," ed. Howard.

21. The most comprehensive bibliography of Austin's published works is provided

in Wynn, "A Critical Study of the Writings of Mary Hunter Austin." Stineman, *Mary Austin: Song of a Maverick* is the most recent biography of Austin and offers a representative selection. Earlier biographical studies of Austin are Doyle, *Mary Austin: Woman of Genius;* Pearce, *The Beloved House* and *Mary Hunter Austin;* Fink, *I-Mary;* and Langlois, *A Search for Significance.* My brief portrait of Austin is based on these accounts.

22. Pryse, Introduction, *Stories from the Country of Lost Borders* xi.

23. O'Grady, *Pilgrims to the Wild* 126.

24. The autobiographical aspects of Austin's work notwithstanding, this study presents her regionalist fiction as portraying imaginary western places and communities. Although Austin's literary regions, such as the Country of Lost Borders, Tierra Longa, or the Land of Journey's Ending, are modeled on identifiable California and southwestern regions at the beginning of the twentieth century, I consider it more appropriate for an analysis of her narrative and rhetorical strategies to regard the texts as deliberately crafted narratives that respond to and create rather than simply record regional realities. For the same reason, in this study I consider the nameless narrators of Austin's nonfiction as skillfully devised personae and thus as nonidentical with the author Austin. In accordance with the fictional reality of the texts, however, I refer to the narrators as European American women and writers.

25. Botkin, "Mary Austin" 64; Wynn, "A Critical Study" 363.

26. Smith, "The Feel of the Purposeful Earth" 19; Warren, "Regionalism or the Coterie Manifesto" 8.

27. Mumford, "The American Rhythm" 23.

28. Smith, "The Feel of the Purposeful Earth" 19.

29. McKinney, "Mary Hunter Austin" 110.

30. Wynn, "A Critical Study" 363.

31. Recently literary critics have repeated the argument in an effort to determine the relevance that the study of regional literature holds for an understanding of American literary history. Inness and Royer in *Breaking Boundaries* argue that the significance of regional literature for contemporary readers lies in the opportunities it offers to witness the dynamics of nation building (1–2). See also A. Kaenel, "After the Cold War" 75. Contemporary critics tend to regard regions as merely the stage for the rehearsal of national identity. They view regional society as a stepping-stone rather than a model for national development, because regionalism, in contrast, for instance, to sectionalism, makes only limited claims to the region's political sovereignty and power. But although regions comprehend themselves as part of the nation and do not insist on their potential rise to nationhood, as sections would, it is more appropriate to consider the relation between region and nation a reciprocal one. Regions cannot constitute themselves as regions outside a national context and national developments also depend on the processes of regional societies. On the distinction between region and section, see Cox, "Regionalism." Cf. Hoennighausen, "The Old and the New Regionalism" 10.

32. Porter, Afterword, *A Woman of Genius* 307.

33. O'Brian, "Becoming Noncanonical" 250. In her introduction to *Exploring Lost*

Borders Graulich succinctly outlines the changing biases of Austin criticism throughout the twentieth century (xiii–xx).

1   "The Land Sets the Limit"

1. Williams, *A Novelette and Other Prose, 1921–31* (Toulon: To Publishers, 1931) 185, qtd. in Bracher, "California's Literary Regionalism" 276.

2. Dualism has been thoroughly critiqued by feminist theorists as the conceptual framework that "interlocking systems of domination" share (hooks, *Talking Black* 22). For a comprehensive definition of dualism, see Plumwood, *Feminism and the Mastery of Nature.* "A dualism is more than a relation of dichotomy, difference, or nonidentity, and more than a simple hierarchical relationship. . . . Dualism is a relation of separation and domination inscribed and naturalised in culture and characterised by radical exclusion, distancing and opposition between orders construed as systematically higher and lower, as inferior and superior, as ruler and ruled, which treats the division as part of the natures of beings construed not merely as different but as belonging to radically different orders or kinds, and hence as not open to change" (47–48). Dualistic paradigms, in other words, require and effect distortions of difference that serve to legitimize the colonization of human and nonhuman others by a "master subject"; see Haraway, *Simians, Cyborgs, and Women* 177.

3. Abram, *The Spell of the Sensuous* 125.

4. Merleau-Ponty, *The Visible and the Invisible* 58.

5. Although it was plausibly written in 1927, *Cactus Thorn* was not published until 1988, as a result of Graulich's research (Foreword, *CT* viii). The novella is also analyzed in chapter 4 of this study.

6. In the chapter "The Wilderness Cult" in his study *Wilderness and the American Mind,* Nash points out that increasing urbanization and industrialization resulted in a positive reevaluation of the concept of wilderness at the turn of the century (141–60). For a history of the idea of wilderness from prehistory to present times, see Oelschlaeger, *The Idea of Wilderness.* A recent anthology that offers a variety of revisionary perspectives on concepts of wilderness and preservation is *Uncommon Ground,* ed. Cronon. Austin's feminist revisions of the wilderness cult are examined in chapter 4 of this study.

7. While the choice of words suggests that Austin was conversant with Eastern religions, especially Taoism, I have found no evidence in her published or private writings that she ever undertook any extensive studies of Asian philosophy.

8. Botkin, "Mary Austin" 64; M. Van Doren, "The American Rhythm" 472. Austin did not appreciate general dismissals of her work, no matter how galantly presented. She wanted to be taken seriously and not merely flattered. For her, Mark Van Doren's review was "the usual New York thing. Extremely complimentary in a vague large way and more or less irritated by the necessity for admitting that anybody who lives outside of New York and does not admire it, can have anything really vital to say" (Letter to Daniel Trembly MacDougal, 12 Oct. 1923, AU 1192).

9. Diamond, *Guns, Germs, and Steel* 25–26; also qtd. in Love, "Ecocriticism and Science" 568.

10. AU 625. Her audience at times chose to ignore this point and misread her argument on behalf of a self-conscious regional inhabitation of the American continent as an unqualified assertion of patriotism. A reviewer of a lecture Austin delivered in Carmel on the topic reports her as having said that "the greatest human achievements" were "the national roots which bind us to our own native soil" and that the "most essential fact of life, says Mrs. Austin, is our feeling for the land where we were born" (A. Burroughs, "Mary Austin's Ideas of American Patterns" 6). However, Austin's regionalist texts define as essential not one's place of birth but one's mode of inhabiting the place one chooses to live in. For a recent collection of essays on "becoming native," see *At Home on the Earth*, ed. Barnhill.

11. Austin, "Artist Life in the United States" 151.

12. Austin, *The American Rhythm* (1923) 153.

13. Harper, *The Course of the Melting Pot Idea* 253–54. The faith that assimilation simply occurred is reflected in the title of William C. Smith's 1939 social science work, *Americans in the Making: The Natural History of the Assimilation of Immigrants*, qtd. in Gleason, "American Identity and Americanization" 47.

14. Austin, "Regionalism in American Fiction" 97. Austin's concept of race is further analyzed in chapter 5 of this study.

15. Austin, "Regionalism in American Fiction" 98. It is important to note that Austin promoted the development of plural regional cultures rather than privileged one particular regional identity over others. Although the potential links between regionalism and xenophobic or nativist attitudes merit discussion, it is reductionist to interpret any assertion of regional identity as a value-hierarchical statement. To consider a particular place home is not necessarily to deny that other places are home to other people, nor does it inevitably imply that one's home is better than others or that it is even exclusively one's own. It is plausibly apparent to most people who feel intimately connected with one particular place that this place does not exist in a vacuum but is situated in and continuous with the larger world. The general refutation of the regional environment as a positive source of identity is in itself problematic because it establishes a one-directional relation between our ethical commitments and our lives, reducing our lived experience to pliable raw material that is passively shaped by preestablished norms and exterior structures.

16. Austin saw this ideal realized, for instance, "in the way that *Huckleberry Finn* is of the great river, taking its movement and rhythm, its structure and intention, or lack of it, from the scene" ("Regionalism in American Fiction" 106). By contrast, Austin did not consider novels such as Stowe's *Uncle Tom's Cabin* (106) or Cather's *Death Comes for the Archbishop* regional literature, since these works did not represent the outlook of the regional population they described (105–6).

17. The distinction between local color and regionalist literature is discussed in more detail in chapter 6 of the study.

18. Significantly, the narrator of *The Land of Little Rain* for the first time identi-

NOTES TO CHAPTER 1

fies herself explicitly as a woman writer in her criticism of Bret Harte and local color fiction (113).

19. First published in 1903, "The Last Antelope" was reprinted in *Lost Borders* and also included in *One-Smoke Stories* (1934), the last collection of stories that Austin published. In the 1934 version, as in the original, the story ends with the tale of the last antelope, eliding the self-reflective passages. Austin plausibly edited the reprinted version to fit the short short story format of the anthology, which features, as its title indicates, mostly brief narratives that could be read within the duration of a single smoke.

20. Austin thought *Silas Lapham* Howells's best work because she considered it regional of Boston ("Regionalism in American Fiction" 101).

21. Austin, "Regionalism in American Fiction" 102. A convincing argument that the satiric form and social concern of Austin's work exerted a crucial influence on her friend Sinclair Lewis is developed in Witschi, "Sinclair Lewis, the Voice of Satire, and Mary Austin's Revolt from the Village."

22. Austin, LLR 194, 261; Austin, *The Basket Woman: A Book of Indian Tales for Children* 221. Oppapago lies in the vicinity of the highest mountain in the continental United States, Mount Whitney, which was named after Josiah D. Whitney, the leader of the California State Geological Survey. Frederick Turner points out in *Beyond Geography* that the European conquest of the Americas involved from its beginning the replacement of names attributed to the land by the native population with new names registering the cultural identity of the colonizers (131). A joke of the 1990s captures the relation between the naming and colonization of the "New World": "Why are the Indians called Indians? 'Cause a white man got lost."

23. In *The Land of Little Rain* Austin generally presents Native American cultures, especially Paiute culture, as a learning model for the European American development of a sustainable place-based society. While in this work she avoids for the most part stereotypical notions about "the Indian," she does fall into essentialist arguments at other times, especially in her critical essays. The complications of Austin's cross-cultural work are examined in chapter 5 of this study. See also Hoyer, *Dancing Ghosts*.

24. Bredahl, *New Ground* 54.

25. Austin also described this journey in "One Hundred Miles on Horseback," her first significant publication. Originally published in the journal of Austin's alma mater, *Blackburnian*, the essay was reprinted in *One Hundred Miles on Horseback*, ed. Ringler.

26. An "intertext" may well be nonhuman; see S. Campbell, "The Land and Language of Desire." "A deer, for instance, has no being apart from things like the presence or absence of wolves, the kind of forage in its environment, the temperature and snowfall of any given winter, the other animals competing for the available food, the number of hunters with licenses, the bacteria in its intestines that either keep it healthy or make it sick" (208).

27. Although the essay formally introduces the collection, it is an independent piece of speculative critical writing rather than a foreword (AR 3–65). Its status is already indicated by its length. The essay takes up almost half of the first edition of *The Ameri-*

228

can Rhythm. The other half of this 1923 edition consists of two sections of roughly equal length: The first presents Austin's "reëxpressions" of Native American poems under the title "Amerindian Songs," the second contains her own poems or "Songs in the American Manner." The second, 1930 edition of *The American Rhythm* substitutes for Austin's original poetry and for the poems that communicate her general understanding of Native American thought more translated material. With its two new sections on "Magic Formulas" and "Tribal Lays," the enlarged edition includes significantly more translations and reexpressions of Native American poetry and legends than the first edition.

Reëxpression is Austin's term for her method of cross-cultural composition. The process of re-expression entailed that, in a first step, Austin would either listen to Native American poems and stories as they were performed and translated for her or she would work with the material collected and translated by white ethnologists. Her subjective experience of the particular poem and of the respective Native American culture and its regional land base, then, would provide her with the inspiration to write a poem that she hoped would express the essential qualities of the original poem or chant (*AR* 38). To check the accuracy of her interpretation, she ideally would read her rendition back to a Native American storyteller (*AR* 55).

While Austin considered herself a weak poet, the reviewers of the first edition of *The American Rhythm* frequently praised Austin's poems while they criticized the argument of the introduction. "Mary Austin's poetry was better than her theories" is representative in this respect (Wynn, "A Critical Study" 235). Wynn offers a comparison of Austin's method of reexpression and the work of contemporaneous translators (383–90). Helpful recent analyses that situate Austin's poetry within the American literary field of the early twentieth century are Ruppert, "Discovering America"; and Metcalfe, "Singing Like the Indians Do." On Austin's view of Native American poetry, see also Castro, "Early Translators of American Poetry"; Drinnon, "The American Rhythm"; and Zolla, "Mary Austin, Essayist and Student of Rhythm."

28. Judging from the recorded observations of her contemporaries, Austin's lectures on poetic rhythm must have been vivid performances. Austin danced, chanted, and acted to illustrate her theories. She performed, for instance, a Greek dance accompanied by a tambourine while reciting Shelley's "Ode to a Skylark" to prove that the origins of English meter were Greek (Major, "Mary Austin in Fort Worth" 307). Audiences seem to have been particularly impressed by Austin's rendition of the "Gettysburg Address," which she recited while she mimed chopping wood to demonstrate its supposed underlying rhythm. One reviewer enthusiastically recalls the "dazzling splendor" of Austin's performance (Worthington, "American Patterns Skillfully Woven in Austin Lecture" 7); an anonymous reviewer is taken by the "utmost realism" of Austin's delivery ("Creative Worker in Literature Gave Interesting Lecture" 1). This account of Austin's "Aboriginal Poetry" talk at Mills College in February 1928 reveals more interesting details that are suggestive of the lecture hall atmosphere during Austin's readings. The writer reports: "The lecturer gave a very dramatic and tense rendition of an Indian prayer for rain accompanying herself on

the drum. She then requested President Reinhardt to help her, and Mrs. Austin beat the drum while the president read the poem . . . by Carl Sandburg, and a selection from Walt Whitman" ("Creative Worker" 4). While this scenario may seem bewildering to contemporary readers, the audience did not consider Austin's performance eccentric. At least the reviewer gained the general impression that Austin "speaks in a calm, unimpassioned tone of voice, and her lecture was delightfully punctuated with bits of dry humor" (4).

29. Studies that agree on this point include Tuan, *Topophilia;* Merchant, *The Death of Nature;* Jauß, "Aisthesis und Naturerfahrung"; Piepmeier, "Das Ende der ästhetischen Kategorie 'Landschaft'"; and Ritter, "Landschaft."

30. Austin, untitled draft version of "The American Rhythm" AU 11.

31. In a private letter to Arthur David Ficke, Austin concedes "that the book would have been more truly called 'American Rhythms'" and attributes the choice of title to her publisher (Letter to Ficke, 27 Mar. 1930, AU 1096).

32. Jones, "Indian Rhythms" 647. Cf. the criticism of Austin's argumentative inconsistencies in Wynn, "A Critical Study" 216. Austin overstates her case in *The American Rhythm* in several respects. She establishes simplistic connections between physical experience and aesthetic expression, claiming, for example, that she can determine the type of environment that a given poet inhabits by listening to his poetry, even when it is in Native American languages unknown to her (AR 19).

33. Austin certainly was aware that the formation of national culture was an ongoing process, involving an array of changing factors, that was too complex and extensive to make its course entirely controllable or predictable. In her refutation of Mumford's criticism, she points out, "the whole conclusion of my argument" is that these processes "*can not be controlled by program*" (AU 24, emphasis in original). Still, Austin was interested in the development of a distinct national identity. Her concern with the issue of Americanization was not chauvinistic, however, as implied by Mumford. Her use of the term *American* is variable. Sometimes it refers specifically to citizens of the United States, at other times to all inhabitants of the American continent. In the second edition of *The American Rhythm,* for instance, Austin recommends Mexican culture as a genuinely American role model to her European American readers, particularly to her critics (AR 1930, 84).

34. Mumford, for instance, proceeds in his review "The American Rhythm" from the assumption that "Mrs. Austin's latest work will not get the attention that it deserves" because the general reading public has "an a priori objection to the belief that a sophisticated culture can tie up with a primitive culture when it is planted in the same geographic environment" (23).

35. Sundquist notes, for instance, that Hamlin Garland's veritism follows Whitman's call for a democratic culture rooted in local realities ("Realism and Regionalism" 518).

36. Cf. Ruppert, "Mary Austin's Landscape Line in Native American Literature" 389–90; Ford, "*The American Rhythm*" 3.

2   Nature Writing as Regionalist Practice

1. For a representative account of the genre, see Scheese, *Nature Writing*. Other extensive surveys and studies of the genre include Lyon, *This Incomparable Lande;* Fritzell, *Nature Writing and America;* O'Grady, *Pilgrims to the Wild;* and Slovic, *Seeking Awareness in American Nature Writing*. For an entertaining and loving polemic against the genre's conventions, see Oates, "Against Nature."

2. Letter to Henry Chester Tracy, 24 July 1929, AU 1249. The most innovative aspects of Tracy's study, judged from a contemporary perspective, go back to suggestions that Austin made in their private correspondence. She urged him to include both "the Indian approach to nature" and women writers (AU 1249), or, if the latter were impossible, to discuss at least why there seemed to be no prominent women naturists (Letter to Henry Chester Tracy, 31 July 1929, AU 1250). Tracy addressed this question in the introductory "Of Women as Naturists" in *American Naturists*, (11–18), and he devoted a chapter to what he considered Native American nature literature, "Forest Man as Naturist" (264–82).

3. See Baym, "Melodramas of Beset Manhood" 72–73; Kolodny, *The Lay of the Land;* Westling, *The Green Breast of the New World*.

4. Miller, *In Nesting Time* (Boston: Houghton, 1888) 18, qtd. in Norwood, *Made from This Earth* 44. The characterization of Miller as "a worker in miniatures" in Tracy, *American Naturists* 116–17 immediately brings to mind the early critical response to women writers in the related genre of regionalist writing. Sarah Orne Jewett's work, for instance, was regarded as an assortment of delicious but inconsequential "trifles light as air" (Anon. Review, *Bookman* 5 [1897]: 80–81), qtd. in *New Essays on "The Country of the Pointed Firs,"* ed. Howard 2.

5. Norwood, *Made from This Earth* 38–39, 41–48. For an anthology of writings by women naturists from the late eighteenth century to present times, see *American Women Afield,* ed. Bonta.

6. The idea of municipal housekeeping, Stacy Alaimo explains in "The Undomesticated Nature of Feminism," "adhered to a utilitarian conception of nature and promoted women's domestic skills as their qualification for conservation work" (73). The rhetoric of progressive women conservationists frequently had classist and racist overtones as the women sought to conserve not only natural resources but also the privileges of white middle- and upperclass womanhood (77–80).

7. See Merchant, "Women of the Progressive Conservation Movement." Cf. Norwood, *Made from This Earth* 47; Alaimo, "The Undomesticated Nature of Feminism" 94.

8. Buell notes that about "half the nature essays contributed to the *Atlantic Monthly* during the late nineteenth century, the point when the nature essay became a recognized genre, were by female authors" (*The Environmental Imagination* 44–45).

9. In "Unraveling the Problems in Ecofeminism" Cuomo warns against such romanticizing notions, reminding us that women, "especially members of industrial and technological societies, have contributed to the oppression of the nonhuman world,

and must admit to this complicity so that they can create alternatives" (356). The woman nature association is further discussed in chapter 4 of this study.

10. A representative example is Toohey, "Mary Austin's *The Land of Little Rain.*" Toohey offers a convincing reading of Austin as an ecologically oriented, feminist writer. Still, I am uneasy about her attempt to turn Austin qua an appeal to her marginalized status as a woman writer into a spokesperson for "woman," subjugated ethnic groups, and nature, while she presents male writers generically as advocates of dualism, imperialism, and environmental despoliation. The link Toohey seeks to establish between the literary practice of Austin and her contemporaries and the gender of these authors runs the risk of reinforcing essentialist conceptions of femininity and masculinity and of female and male authorship. Unlike Toohey, I would not read a statement made in 1904 that the desert seems cursed, "weird and fantastic" as exemplifying "the androcentric discourse of colonization" (210), for instance, but regard such a comment as a tribute to the tragic desert convention, to the conceptualization of desertscapes as alien and dangerous places, which was current among both male and female writers at the time. Walker describes the convention in "The Desert Grows Friendly," *A Literary History of Southern California* 180–208. Cf. chapter 3 of this study.

11. Cf. Murphy's suggestion in *Literature, Nature, and Other* that feminist nature writers have developed a dissenting voice "as a result of self-conscious intent and out of the necessity of their subject positions within contemporary society" (34).

12. The influence of Gilligan's work *In a Different Voice: Psychological Theory and Women's Development* on such arguments is readily apparent. In her study Gilligan proposes that the gender socialization of boys and girls significantly affects their moral development and results in a different ethical orientation of men and women.

13. Likewise, Paul Brooks, the retired editor-in-chief of Houghton Mifflin, answered, when asked whether he could correctly identify the sex of the author of a given environmental text without relying on any outside clues, "I don't think the sense of gender comes in much at all. . . . No, probably not" ("Dialogue Four," *Writing Natural History,* ed. Lueders 115).

14. The current Penguin edition of *The Land of Little Rain* reflects a feminist change in critical climate and offers an appreciative foreword by Terry Tempest Williams. Cf. Murphy, *Literature, Nature, and Other* 37.

15. Austin, Reply to Lewis Mumford's review of *The American Rhythm,* summer 1923; AU 24. Austin's cultural feminism and her intersecting concepts of gender and nature are examined in chapter 4 of this study.

16. Cf. Alaimo, "The Undomesticated Nature of Feminism." Alaimo demonstrates that Austin employs in her fictional works nature imagery to counter the constructions of gender, particularly notions of domesticity and motherhood, dominant at the turn of the century, and that she feminizes the natural world to dismiss the utilitarian orientation of the Progressive Conservation movement. This argument also holds true for Austin's nature writing.

17. The nature writing tradition, of course, reaches back further than Thoreau's

work. As a literary and scientific tradition, it did not originate with any single writer but grew out of multiple sources, such as the study of natural history, travel writing, and the pastoral tradition. For an overview of the genre's origins, see Scheese, *Nature Writing* 1–38. Still, outlines of American nature writing frequently present Thoreau as the first major American proponent of the genre. The most extensive study of Thoreau's contribution to the development of American environmental literature is Buell, *The Environmental Imagination,* which includes a discussion of "The Canonization and Recanonization of the Green Thoreau" (339–69).

The environmental politics of Thoreau's work are the subject of an ongoing critical debate. While many readers of American nature writing have come to regard Thoreau as a patron of American environmentalism, critics only recently have begun again to focus on Thoreau's natural history essays and the extensive natural history notes contained in his journal. The image of the transcendentalist Thoreau following in Emerson's footsteps, then, has slowly given way to a complexer view of Thoreau, which takes seriously his interest in natural history and the natural sciences. Consider, for instance, the view of Thoreau as a naturalist that emerges in influential 1980s biographies such as Howarth, *The Book of Concord* and Richardson, *Henry David Thoreau.* Thoreau's shift from a transcendentalist preoccupation with the symbolic significance of Nature toward an increasingly scientific yet spiritually informed examination of natural phenomena and principles is the subject of *A Wider View of the Universe* by the environmental historian Robert Kuhn McGregor. Although McGregor's study would have benefited from a more sophisticated analysis of transcendental thought, his portrait of the naturalist Thoreau complements in significant ways earlier studies of Thoreau's intellectual development and contribution to environmental thought. For a contrasting feminist ecocritical critique of Thoreau that focuses on *Walden* rather than on his naturalist work, see Westling, *The Green Breast of the New World* 39–53.

18. *Oikos,* the Greek root of the term *ecology,* carries the double meaning of household and economy. The term *ecology* was coined by Ernst Haeckl in 1866 to express the idea that "the living organisms of the earth constitute a single economic unit resembling a household or family dwelling intimately together, in conflict as well as in mutual aid" (Worster, *Nature's Economy* 192).

19. Austin's narrative draws on the established trope of "the book of nature." For an ecocritical contemplation of the concept of nature as scripture and text, see Armand, "The Book of Nature and American Nature Writing."

20. The narrator's preoccupation with botanical observation agrees with the historical identification of botany as a field of nature study particularly suited for women, which developed during the nineteenth century. For a brief account that locates the sources of American women's nature studies in the accounts of English amateur naturalist travelers, sentimental flower books, and Victorian botanical textbooks, see Norwood, *Made from This Earth* 1–24.

21. Austin, *Lost Borders* 23. *Lost Borders,* a compilation of short stories about life in southern California desert settlements, can be read as a companion work to *The Land*

of Little Rain. In the two collections Austin creates out of her intimate knowledge of the California deserts an imaginary biocultural region that she names the "Country of Lost Borders" (*LLR* 3, *LB* 2). In geographical terms the Country of Lost Borders can be mapped as follows: It extends from the Sierra Nevada south of Yosemite in southeastern direction to the California deserts, continuing into Death Valley and the Mojave Desert. The core of Austin's country is Owens Valley. The valley lies at 4,000 feet above sea level on the eastern slope of the Sierra, between the highest point in California, Mount Whitney, and the lowest point in the United States, Badwater. It is a narrow yet spacious basin, measuring an average distance of ten miles between the Sierra and the eastern desert ranges and running more than one hundred miles from its well-watered north to its desert south (Walton, *Western Times and Water Wars* 3–5). Historically Austin's Country of Lost Borders belongs to the West at the beginning of the twentieth century: The frontier had officially been declared closed and California had gone through its first recession. As industrialization, urbanization, and commercial agriculture were on the rise in the West, the wilderness was rediscovered as a source of personal and cultural recuperation. The anxiety about Darwinian evolution theories gave way to a call for wilderness preservation. In Owens Valley the European American settlers had subjugated and dispossessed the native Paiutes. The white settlers had begun moving into the valley in 1861; at the turn of the century they still hoped to transform it into a fertile agricultural region. But when in 1906 Los Angeles secured the water rights of the Owens River for the urban water system, the region was reduced to an appendage of the city. Austin lived, with intermissions, in Owens Valley from 1892 to 1905. With her husband, Wallace, and her daughter, Ruth, Austin spent several years in the two towns that the narrators of *The Land of Little Rain* and *Lost Borders* call home—Independence and Lone Pine.

22. Apthorp, "Sentiment, Naturalism, and the Female Regionalists" 10.

23. Thoreau, "Wild Apples," *The Natural History Essays* 178–210, 204, 205. Austin owned a copy of "Wild Apples" (AU box 132).

24. Thoreau, "Autumnal Tints," *The Natural History Essays* 137–77, 162.

25. Franklin B. Sanborn, *Henry D. Thoreau* (Boston: Houghton, 1882); qtd. in Tracy, *American Naturists* 68.

26. Austin, *LJE* vii. Austin may have learned this early in her career from Charles Lummis (writer, editor, and cofounder of the Southwest Museum in Los Angeles), who admonished her: "If you are 'not in the least ashamed of your ignorance of Spanish derivations' then you ought to be. . . . When you use Spanish names, it is your business as a decent woman, and as a writer, to have them right" (Letter to Austin, 24 Nov. 1904, AU 3617). For an anthropological study of a Native American practice of place naming, see Basso, *Wisdom Sits in Places.*

27. On Thoreau's ambivalent attitude toward scientific research and methodology, see Walls, *Seeing New Worlds;* Richardson, "Thoreau and Science"; and Rossi, "Roots, Leaves, and Method."

28. They reveal the observer's lack of integrity. The narrator of *Lost Borders* cautions her readers: "But a boast of knowledge is likely to prove as hollow as the little

yellow gourds called apples of Death Valley" (9). Like her narrators, Austin detested claims to absolute knowledge. She admired environmental writers and scientists who revealed the subjective basis of their knowledge and opinion, as her following comment on Albert Einstein suggests: "His willingness to let it be seen that his notions of politics, war, and personal survival spring from his personal bias of temperament and training put to shame the intellectual pretensions of too many one-subject specialists" ("Mary Austin on Einstein" xlviii).

29. Conversely, moral values and social norms were presented as part of the benevolent natural order of things, as the title of one of Ernest Thompson Seton's articles signals, "The Natural History of the Ten Commandments," *Century* 75 (Nov. 1907): 24–33, qtd. in Mighetto, "Science, Sentiment, and Anxiety" 46. Seton, one of the most popular American writers of animal stories, is also included in Tracy's *American Naturists* (233–43), possibly at the suggestion of Austin (Letter to Henry Chester Tracy, 31 July 1929, AU 1250). Austin had met Seton during her early years in California and the two writers loosely kept in touch over the years (EH 296–97; Pearce, *Literary America* 226–27).

30. Roosevelt, "Nature Fakers" 427–30. See Lutts, *The Nature Fakers* for the most detailed account of the dispute to date.

31. On the point of the intelligence and learning of animals, Austin would have been considered a potential nature faker by John Burroughs, who was convinced that "there is nothing in the dealings of animals with their young that in the remotest way suggests human instruction and discipline. The young of all the wild creatures do instinctively what their parents do and did. They do not have to be taught; they are taught by nature from the start" ("Real and Sham Natural History" 305).

32. In his criticism of Seton's *Wild Animals I Have Known* (New York: Scribner's, 1898) and William J. Long's *School of the Woods: Some Life Studies of Animal Instincts and Animal Training* (Boston: Ginn & Co., 1903), John Burroughs maintained: "It is always an artist's privilege to heighten or deepen natural effects. He may paint us a more beautiful woman, or a more beautiful horse, or a more beautiful landscape, than we ever saw; we are not deceived even though he outdo nature. . . . [W]e know that this is the power of art. But when he paints a portrait, or an actual scene, or event, we expect him to be true to the facts of the case" ("Real and Sham Natural History" 303). While John Burroughs granted that even scientific writing might be "all the more true for the style" ("Real and Sham Natural History" 303), he still proposed that "only a person with a scientific habit of mind can be trusted to report things as they are" ("On Humanizing the Animals" 780, qtd. in Lutts, *The Nature Fakers* 85). Significantly, Austin seems to have appreciated exactly those qualities of Burroughs's writing that the author himself wished to de-emphasize. In one of her few remarks on the matter, she recommended him as a model to writers of popular science on account of his "style and clearness and the art of relating facts so that they create an atmosphere of charm" (Letter to Daniel Trembly MacDougal, 15 Feb. 1922, AU 1151).

While Long, a Congregationalist minister, heartily objected to John Burrough's point of view, he did agree with his opponent that the scientific examination and the aesthetic or moral contemplation of the natural world were irreconcilable fields of study that yielded different kinds of knowledge: "The study of Nature is a vastly different thing from the study of Science; they are no more alike than Psychology and History. Above and beyond the world of facts and law, with which alone Science concerns itself, is an immense and almost unknown world of suggestion and freedom and inspiration, in which the individual, whether animal or man, must struggle against fact or law to develop his individuality. It is a world of *appreciation* . . . rather than a world of *description*." Long continued his discourse by saying that "It is a world that must be interpreted rather than catalogued. . . . In a word, the difference between Nature and Science is the difference between . . . the woman who cherishes her old-fashioned flower-garden and the professor who lectures on Botany in a college classroom" ("The Modern School of Nature Writing and Its Critics" *North American Review* 176 [May 1903]: 687–98, qtd. in Lutts, *The Nature Fakers* 61). For a discussion of the divergent positions of Long, John Burroughs, and Austin, which stresses the environmental ethics involved, see also Toohey, "Mary Austin's *The Land of Little Rain*" 204–6.

33. First published in *Bookman* 62 (Dec. 1925): 440–47, "Speaking of Bears" was reprinted in Austin's last collection of stories, *One-Smoke Stories* (1934). To date, the story seems to have received no critical attention. In the story the sex of the narrator remains indeterminate. Yet the narrative voice and geographical setting of the story place it with Austin's other essays and stories about the Country of Lost Borders, her mythologized California region, whose narrators are female. Hence, the narrator of "Speaking of Bears" also is assumed to be female.

34. Thoreau, "The Succession of Forest Trees," *The Natural History Essays* 72–92, 91.

35. Significantly, Austin lifted the chapter title from a line of Shelley's poem "The Cloud:" "I am the daughter of Earth and Water, / And the nursling of the Sky." I thank Professor Peter Huehn at the University of Hamburg for alerting me to this intertextual aspect of Austin's writing. For another sample of Austin's observations on the formation and movement of clouds, see *The Land of Journey's Ending* 423–25. The extreme climatic conditions of the arid regions made the weather a popular subject of California storytelling. Carey McWilliams even included in his account *Southern California Country: An Island on the Land* (New York: Duell, Sloane & Pearce, 1946) a chapter on "The Folklore of Climatology" (Veysey, "Myth and Reality in Approaching American Regionalism" 40).

36. The narrator supports her critique by referring to John Muir, whom she presents as an authority on transcendental nature observation. She declares, "John Muir, who knows more of mountain storms than any other, is a devout man" (*LLR* 247). Like her narrator, Austin agreed with Muir's spiritual readings of nature (*EH* 298). She objected, however, to his personification of "the spirits of the wild" as angels, because it reminded her of her Methodist upbringing which she came to abhor—"the pietistic characteristics of the angels she had heard of prevented such identification" (*EH* 188).

37. Again, the narrator reflects Austin's approach to nature study. In her autobiography Austin comments on her need to acquire ecological literacy and to engage in mystical communion with nature: "But the fact is Mary was consumed with interest

as with enchantment. . . . For Mary is one of those people plagued with an anxiety to know. Other people, satisfied by the mere delight of seeing, think they pay her a compliment when they speak of her 'intuition' about things of the wild, or that they let her down a deserved notch or two by referring to her fortunate guesses" (*EH* 194–95).

38. Austin, Letter to Daniel Trembly MacDougal, 15 Feb. 1922, AU 1151.

39. There is an obvious parallel between Austin's concept of scientific writing for lay readers and the concept of poetry that she develops in *The American Rhythm*, as outlined in chapter 1 of this study. Both forms of literature are geared toward "affecting" the consciousness of the audience rather than toward "effecting" it through entertainment or manipulation. Compare, for instance, "Science for the Unscientific" 565 and *AR* 24.

40. Austin's reply to Mumford's review of *The American Rhythm* AU 24. Austin once evocatively described her motivation as a writer like this: "And what I am really interested in isn't the theory of rhythm, but being able to experience rhythm in all its varieties. I like to dive into a rhythmic stream like a fish into the gulf current and go where it takes me. I like to be a sun swinging through space with all my seven planets disposed about me, and I like to be the green flush that creeps up and dies rhythmically along the sides of Palo Corona." She continues, "Best of all I like to flash into the life rhythm of some other human being, and find myself suddenly knowing all about what it was, is now and will be. Then I like to repeat some of these experiences by writing books or poems about them" (Letter to Daniel Trembly MacDougal, 2 Jan. 1922, AU 1144). The suggestion Carl Van Doren voiced in "American Rhythm" that nature writing provided the best outlet for Austin's talent since it called for the integration of personal experience and technical knowledge seems to concur with this self-perception.

41. That Austin was sincerely interested in the matter is also indicated by the fact that she negotiated with Science Service for a position as "Editorial Advisor" in the spring 1922 (Letter to Edwin E. Slosson, AU 1242).

42. Austin repeatedly argued that the flourishing of American democracy depended on a more sophisticated public discourse that took as its base of reference the ordinary living circumstances of the majority of the population. She frequently distinguished her concept of adult education and democratic culture from "the Chautauqua approach," which she thought merely offered "learning, as an ornament, a flourish, a veneer, spread thin in order to be easily acquired" (Letter to Daniel Trembly MacDougal, 15 Feb. 1922, AU 1151). Cf. Austin's articles "Science for the Unscientific" (563) and "The Town That Doesn't Want a Chautauqua." See also chapter 6 of this study.

43. Cf. Mighetto, "Science, Sentiment, and Anxiety" 47–50; Brooks, *Speaking for Nature* 214.

44. Austin, Letter to Daniel Trembly MacDougal, 15 Feb. 1922, AU 1151.

45. J. Burroughs, *Wake Robin* (Boston: Houghton, 1904) xv–xvi, qtd. in Lutts, *The Nature Fakers* 9.

46. Austin, Letter to Arthur David Ficke, 27 March 1930, AU 1096. In "Science for

the Unscientific" Austin even goes so far as to argue that scientific findings could be communicated most efficiently to the general public by interested nonfiction writers rather than by the researchers themselves. She asserts, "science, on its way to modify the common consciousness, must travel the path trodden out by the poet and the novelist" (563). For a contemporaneous critique of this notion that defends the capacity of scientists to write readable prose, see Fishbein, "The Middleman in Science Literature." Fishbein's review must have piqued Austin, judging from her huffed response in her "Letter to the Editor."

47. S. Campbell, "The Land and Language of Desire" 209. In *Nature's Economy* Donald Worster defines the concept that humans are part of larger ecological communities as the central tenet of biocentrism; he discusses Darwin as its major early proponent (180–87).

48. Buell, *The Environmental Imagination* 13; S. Campbell, "The Land and Language of Desire" 209.

49. John Cooley, for instance, defines ecocriticism as a challenge "to recognize the primary role of biological systems, against which all anthropocentric activities and values, including the production of language and texts, play a minor and dependent role" (*Earthly Words* 253). Instead of challenging dualistic views of nature and culture, Cooley here accepts the either/or logic and simply inverts the hierarchy.

50. This distinction also applies to other positionalities and their repressive potential, such as between European and eurocentristic perspectives or between heterosexual and homophobic standpoints.

51. Kowalewski, "Bioregional Perspectives in American Literature" 37. Michael Kowalewski's statement that the "most compelling bioregional works attempt to establish imaginative title to specific American places" (43) reveals the proximity of current bioregional perspectives to Austin's point of view. Kowalewski almost paraphrases the assertion that Austin makes in the preface to *The Land of Little Rain:* "So by this fashion of naming I keep faith with the land and annex to my own estate a very great territory to which none has a surer title" (*LLR* ix).

52. Lyon, *This Incomparable Lande* 3.

3   Sense of Place

1. Similarly, lizards are described as "a part of the sun and shade-mottled sand" in *Cactus Thorn* (11). To the untrained eye of the urban sojourner Grant Arliss, the boundary between lizard and ground is not readily perceptible. He is amazed to see that "the greyish spot of earth . . . gathered itself together and scurried off toward the shelter of the cactus thorns" (11). Compare also *The American Rhythm* 31.

2. Abram, *The Spell of the Sensuous* 81.

3. Likewise, Austin contended in *The American Rhythm,* more than ten years before the publication of *Art as Experience,* that experiences, although frequently regarded as homogeneous units of human life, would best be conceived of as the sum of processual responses to environmental factors (*AR* 53–54).

4. Qtd. in Walker, *A Literary History of Southern California* 183.

5. The narrator of *California: The Land of the Sun* (1914) limits herself to the brief remark that "desperation is in every contorted stem of *mesquite* and *palo verde*" (7). The narrator of *The Land of Journey's Ending* likewise notes the "terror of desertness" (3) but immediately argues that this impression dissolves once one acquires an understanding of the region's geology (3–4). There is also something involuntarily comic about the narrator's comment that "much of this country, if it were marked truly on the maps, would be marked black, unexplored, perhaps unknowable" and about the fact that she derived from some of her excursions only a "sense of desolation on a scale of deific grandeur" (180), because *The Land of Journey's Ending*, after all, offers over four hundred pages of detailed and thoroughly researched description of the region.

6. Letter to Mr. Schroeder AU 1223. The correspondence Austin carried on with Schroeder in 1919 is a rich source of information on her spiritual practices and beliefs. Austin later drew on these letters when she worked on books particularly concerned with religious subject matter, such as *Can Prayer Be Answered?* (1934).

7. Interestingly, the human mind is depicted here as a mechanically functioning artifact. Like a camera, it has "shutters" that can open and close with a metallic click. The image indicates that something has to release in appropriate manner—shutters, after all, are devised to open and close—to enable an intensified experience of vital and productive processes of growth. The technological image combines well with the overall precision of the description to render the epiphany a concrete experience rather than a vague, inexplicable happening.

8. Austin was convinced that consciousness was not a human prerogative but distributed throughout the natural world. There was, therefore, "no good reason why a plant may not be, in its own degree, aware of man, as foot is aware of hand" (*LJE* 278–80).

9. Thoreau, "Ktaadn," *The Maine Woods* 1–111.

10. In *Literature, Nature, and Other* Murphy proposes that we reenvision self and other as anothers, as agents who are neither stable nor self-contained but shaped in dynamic relations of mutual interdependence. The self as another defines itself partially in relation to others and their potentially nonidentical needs and goals, "recognizing that we are not ever only one for ourselves but are also always another for others" (152).

11. Climbing the peaks of the Sierra Nevada in search for higher vision is a classic theme of California literature—see David Robertson's discussion of Clarence King's *Mountaineering in the Sierra Nevada* (1872), John Muir's *The Mountains of California* (1894), Jack Kerouac's *The Dharma Bums* (1958), and the poetry of Gary Snyder in his collection of essays and photographs *Real Matter* (1997).

12. In the chapter "Sacred Mountains" of *The Land of Journey's Ending*, Austin returns to this trope but employs Native American beliefs rather than Western aesthetics to explore the spiritual character of her region. Thus she includes in her account of her region's prominent mountains their Navajo names, their ceremonial names, and their English American names. Tsotsil, for instance, is Blue Turquoise Mountain is Mount Taylor (376). As the narrator describes the sacred mountains of the Nava-

jos, Zunis, Hopis, and Papagos, she notes that mountains have been considered sacred sites where "man felt God in the earth" (375) in diverse cultures throughout history. In an effort to explain why it seems an anthropological constant that people consider mountains holy, such as "Sinai and Olivet, Olympus and Ida and Pentelicus" (383), she lists several "rational" reasons before she affirms the divine immanence of mountains: The view from a mountaintop has the advantage that it allows for an overview over a vast territory and thus increases the spectator's spatial orientation (377) and sense of home (378–79); it also offers the possibility to study the geologic history of the world (383). Yet, the narrator concludes, "not the lift of mastery which comes with knowing the world you live in, nor yet the stretching of man's mind to take in distance and detail, neither the pure air nor the accelerated pulse of altitude not the quickened sense of beauty quite accounts to me for the universal habit of mankind of counting high places holy. Not unless we have gone completely astray on this business of holiness; not unless God *is* the mountain" (383).

13. Compare, for instance, the concurring outline that Schaffer gives of the geologic history of the Tahoe Sierra: "But somewhere around 3–4 million years ago the land to the east began to sink, and as it did, the sinking left a fault scarp whose apex was a Sierra crest. . . . The rising of the land in the Tahoe Sierra coupled with a worldwide cooling trend may have brought on glaciation as much as 3 million years ago. Nevertheless, the early glaciers were probably small and ineffective, and perhaps not until about one million years ago did major glaciers fill the canyons of our area" (*The Tahoe Sierra* 30). Austin's interest in geology was awakened by Hugh Miller's *Old Red Sandstone*, a geological textbook, which she read at the age of twelve in spite of her mother's objections (*EH* 103–4). The book, Austin writes in her autobiography, gave her a "sense of the unfolding earth" and "the feel of the purposeful earth" (104).

14. Van Dyke, who, as said, can be considered Austin's immediate literary precursor in regard to her writings of the California deserts, may have inspired her revival of the sublime landscape tradition. In *The Desert* Van Dyke proposes that no other region could equal the sublimity of the desert's "wide plains, its grim mountains, and its expanding canopy of sky" (qtd. in Walker, *A Literary History of Southern California* 186). Austin owned a copy of Van Dyke's *The Desert* (AU box 132). An ecocritical discussion of the environmental ethics of the aesthetic of sublimity is offered in Hitt, "Toward an Ecological Sublime."

15. Jauß, "Aisthesis und Naturerfahrung" 172, 175.

16. Positing analogies between California society and ancient Greek culture was a popular motif in the late nineteenth and early twentieth centuries. As Kevin Starr has shown, Mediterranean symbolism expressed the hopes that Californians set in their developing regional culture (*Americans and the California Dream* 365–414).

17. The narrator of *The Land of Journey's Ending* likewise is at a loss of words with which to describe her spiritual experience, the epiphanic "definite, memorable moments," as her use of ellipses and repetition signals: The mountain's color attains "the hue of the spirit's most poignant mystery . . . holy, holy, holy. . . . The moment comes and goes" (389). Again, the vision is accompanied by a sense of isolation, by a feeling

of "intolerable loneliness," which is associated specifically with the aesthetics of sublimity (391). For, as the narrator points out, landscapes of "terror" (391) possess a "beauty which man perceives without participating, beauty to which he feels himself a stranger" (389), whereas milder and more pleasing scenes (the "Beautiful" in Burke's terms) allow for "a joyous sense of well-being" (390).

There may be an autobiographical aspect to the frustration that Austin's narrators experience. In her "Tejon Journal," one of the notebooks she kept during her first years in California, Austin records that she found it difficult to retain the sense of communication and communion with the natural world that she experienced on her excursions. "I never forget the names of things and where I saw them but I forget what they make me feel and think. Also I forget the words that came with the first time the flower or the mountain speaks to me. It is like that—like someone speaking. I am starting a book for the words. I remember much better if I put them down as if I were to write them in a poem. [L]ike I used to" (AU 267, 22).

18. For the most extensive analysis of Austin's assimilation of Native American thought, beliefs, and cultural practices, see Hoyer, *Dancing Ghosts*.

19. In *The Land of Journey's Ending* she states explicitly that "the wildness of mountains serves us far more than their tameness" (*LJE* 393).

20. In her autobiography Austin maintains that Emerson was the only writer she read as a teenager who influenced her style (*EH* 165). While stylistic features seem the aspect of Emerson's work least echoed in Austin's writings, it is readily apparent that she was familiar with transcendentalist thought. Austin's interest in Emerson may have been awakened by her father, who was an avid reader of the British and American romantics (*EH* 34).

21. Austin, natural history note AU 363.

22. Whitman, "Song of Myself," *Leaves of Grass* 34.

23. In *The Practice of the Wild* Gary Snyder aptly defines genius loci as the "sum of a field's forces" (38). He elaborates, "To know the spirit of a place is to realize that you are a part of a part and that the whole is made of parts, each of which is whole. You start with the part you are whole in" (38).

24. Zitkala-Sä, "Impressions of an Indian Childhood" 543. Austin had a copy Zitkala-Sä's *American Indian Stories* in her library (AU box 132).

25. I. Diamond and Orenstein, *Reweaving the World* vii.

4   Deserting the Myth of the West

1. Austin, "Sex Emancipation through War" 610.

2. Donovan, *Feminist Theory* 54. Austin describes her affiliation with various feminist causes during her New York years in her autobiography (*EH* 325–29). For brief discussions of the difference among cultural, liberal, socialist and ecological feminism that pay particular attention to the divergent feminist responses to the association of woman and nature, see Plumwood, *Feminism and the Mastery of Nature* 19–40; Merchant, "Ecofeminism and Feminist Theory"; and King, "Healing the Wounds."

3. Therefore, liberal feminists have rejected the historical association of woman and nature and have proposed that women's exclusion from rationalist culture should be resolved by a full integration of women into the power structures of society. See, for instance, Ortner, "Is Female to Male as Nature Is to Culture?" Ecologically minded feminists have objected to this strategy, saying that it perpetuates dualistic notions of nature and culture that sanction environmental degradation. The ecofeminist objection in a nutshell: "What is the point of partaking equally in a system that is killing us all?" (King, "Healing the Wounds" 106).

4. Jaycox, "Regeneration through Liberation" 8.

5. The Pocket Hunter is featured in "The Pocket Hunter" in *The Land of Little Rain* and in "The Pocket-Hunter's Story" in *Lost Borders*. Little Pete is mentioned in *The Land of Little Rain*, a lead character in *The Flock*, and the major human protagonist of the *Lost Borders* story "The Last Antelope." He is modeled on a shepherd Austin knew while living in Owens Valley. She gives a short account of him in her autobiography (*EH* 288–89).

6. The Pocket Hunter here appears as the alter ego of Austin, who asserts in her autobiography that "to Mary all places were beautiful and interesting so long as they were outdoors" (*EH* 78).

7. A "campoodie" or campodee, as it now is commonly spelled, is a Native American settlement. After the European American settlers and military had destroyed their original villages, the Paiutes in Owens Valley established these camps, each comprising a number of families, on government land or unclaimed public land (Walton, *Western Times and Water Wars* 39–40). The largest of the Owens Valley campodees was located at Camp Independence—the home base of both the narrator and the author of *The Land of Little Rain*.

Since Seyavi is approximately sixty years old at the time the narrator tells the story (*LLR* 176), she must have been born circa 1840. The Spanish rule over California was transferred to Mexico in 1822. After the war between Mexico and the United States, 1846–1848, and the discovery of major gold deposits in 1848, the number of American traders, prospectors, and settlers increased rapidly. California came under United States control in 1846 and officially entered the Union as the thirty-first state in 1850. As to the regional history of Owens Valley: the first white settlers arrived in the late 1850s; the first silver and gold strikes affecting the region occurred in 1859; permanent white settlement of Owens Valley, however, did not commence until August 1861 (Walton, *Western Times and Water Wars* 12, 17).

8. Walton provides the following information on the Indian war that raged in Owens Valley intermittently from 1862 to 1865: Prior to white settlement, two thousand Paiutes, who lived in thirty permanent villages, made up the native population of Owens Valley. During the war at least two hundred Native Americans and thirty European Americans were killed. A significant number of Indian survivors relocated after the war. A late nineteenth-century census put the Native American population at half its prewar size (*Western Times and Water Wars* 14, 22, 50, 60–61). Of "the most conservatively estimated 100,000 Indians in California at the time of the Gold Rush . . .

some 70,000 were killed or exterminated by disease and starvation ten years later" (Drinnon, *Facing West* 502). For an extended study of the Native American cultures of California, see Heizer, *The Natural World of the Californian Indians.*

9. While Austin considered maternity a rewarding experience and generally thought of the reproduction and conservation of life as a predominantly feminine concern (attributing this to both sociocultural and biological causes), she usually rejected the idea that women should define themselves through their roles of mothers and wives. In "The Best Twenty Years: Growing Up and Growing On" (1928), Austin cites Native American cultures to underline her claim that womanhood possibly includes but certainly extends beyond motherhood (9).

10. In *Made from This Earth* Norwood notes that "Austin chose one of the most racist stereotypes that her own culture held about American Indian women to describe a 'new' way of interacting with nature" (322).

11. In contrast, Austin asserts in her autobiography that she became involved in the Indian rights movement because of the violence of European American settlers against Native American women that she witnessed while living in California. She points out that Native Americans were "the most conspicuously defeated and offended against group" in the region and describes several instances in which Indian women were molested, beaten, raped, and killed by white men (*EH* 266, 267). Austin was enraged and appalled by the "Christian pretense and democratic inadequacy" of her community, which let the perpetrators of these crimes go unpunished (267).

Because of "the potential she recognizes for alliance and sympathy between white women and Indian women," Pryse places Austin's work with Lydia Maria Child's *Hobomok* (1824) and Catharine Sedgewick's *Hope Leslie* (1827) (Introduction, *Stories from the Country of Lost Borders* xvi). Austin also takes up the work of late nineteenth-century social reformers who drew attention to the injustice and cruelty of the European American subjugation of the Native American population. Prominent among these is Helen Hunt Jackson's *A Century of Dishonor: A Sketch of the United States Government's Dealings with Some of the Indian Tribes* (1881).

12. Austin's turn toward Native American oral traditions as a model for regionalist literature is examined in chapter 6 of this study.

13. Like other characters in *The Land of Little Rain* and *Lost Borders,* the Walking Woman is modeled on a person Austin met while living in California. Austin describes the woman in her unpublished "Tejon Journal" as of indeterminate age, not very tall, with thick greyish hair, carrying a black bag on a stick over her shoulder (*AU* 267). She recounts: "She told one of the women at Tembler that her first name is Jenny, but she answers to Mrs. Walker." Austin also records the community's response to the extraordinary woman, noting that her mother "says she looks like a woman who has had a child," while the men "say she has just as good sense as anybody except that she is a little bit crazy" (21). Austin also refers to the Walking Woman in *Earth Horizon* (201, 311).

14. In this respect Austin's story echoes earlier regionalist stories about female characters who learn to rely on their own strength by enduring hardships. A case in point is Mary Wilkins Freeman's "A Church Mouse" (1889), which describes how an older

woman successfully deals with the loss of her home and income through the death of the person she has nursed. Out of sheer necessity the protagonist gathers her strength and, as she fights for her right to become her community's first female sexton, she experiences her capacity for self-determination.

15. Apparently, the illness of the Walking Woman is an allusion to the "hysterical" breakdowns, the neurasthenia, with which middle-class Victorian women often responded to the crippling constraints imposed on their lives. Ailment and "invalidism" were established "metaphors for the position of bourgeois women in women's texts of the era" (Jaycox, "Regeneration through Liberation" 9). Instead of submitting herself to the traditional remedy, a so-called rest cure, as administered and popularized by Dr. S. Weir Mitchell in the 1890s, the Walking Woman, however, does just the opposite and engages in strenuous physical activity. Austin herself suffered two nervous breakdowns during her college years (*EH* 151–53, 156–57; Stineman, *Mary Austin* 22–23).

16. Jaycox clarifies that the convictions of the Walking Woman "attack conventional femininity point by point. Hard and equal work was believed to dissipate the physically and morally frail female . . . free and equal sexuality without institutional restraints contradicted women's supposed moral superiority; and the bearing of a child without a name attacked patriarchy at its foundation" ("Regeneration through Liberation" 9).

17. In several of her poems, stories, and novels, Austin examined the dilemmas and "bitterness" (*LB* 177, 260; *AR* 111) that self-determined, professionally ambitious, and family oriented women of her generation experienced because the dominant gender code reduced women to the roles of submissive wife and nurturing mother. Although they desire both a fulfilling work and domestic life, several of Austin's protagonists are forced to choose between their professional calling and a satisfying love life— among them Olivia Lattimore, the heroine of *A Woman of Genius,* Austin's feminist *Künstlerroman* (1912); Anne Brent, the central character of the novel *The Ford* (1917); and the woman writer figure in the story "Frustrate" (1912). In her last regionalist novel, *Starry Adventure* (1931), then, Austin creates the portrait of a woman who manages with the help of an entirely rational and unromantic approach to marriage to form a lasting partnership with her husband without having to forsake her nondomestic ambitions. For an appreciative discussion that places Austin's feminist portraits of career-oriented women in the context of other new woman writers, see Porter, Afterword, *A Woman of Genius.*

18. And he assails the tree, one might add, in the same way that certain naturalist writers denounced the spinster figures of local color fiction and denigrated the supposedly effeminate concerns and "old-maidish" style of their regionalist and realist precursors. Donna Campbell describes the rise of naturalism as the development of "a gender-based countertradition not only to realism but to female-dominated local color writing" in *Resisting Regionalism* (5). Since Hogan certainly represents the naturalist preoccupation with excessive emotions, the doomed battle of man with the larger forces of his environment, and the idea that only the world of male activity mat-

ters, one could read "Lone Tree" with a slight stretch of the imagination as a regionalist parable on the limitations of the masculinist bias of naturalism.

19. Austin also takes up the trope of nature as woman in *The Land of Journey's Ending* to warn her readers that a thing's apparent frailty is no reliable index of its power. Lichen devour rocks, she notes, adding that the small plants, because of "their power of extracting sustenance from minerals, seem terrible in their frail prettiness, as to men must seem certain sorts of women" (*LJE* 392).

20. For a critical inquiry of feminized images of nature, see, for instance, Roach, "Loving Your Mother." A survey of feminized images of nature from ancient Greek to Renaissance art and science is in Merchant, *The Death of Nature* 1–41.

21. Baym, "Melodramas of Beset Manhood" 75.

22. Several critics have remarked that the desert as woman resembles in her physical attributes Austin. Pryse, for instance, understands the feminized image of the desert as "a mirror in which Austin explores 'her own desires'" (Introduction, *Stories from the Country of Lost Borders* xxix).

23. Intent on mocking the masculinist prejudices and preoccupations of her time, Austin realized that fiction rather than nonfiction offered her an outlet for her satiric perceptions, since the fictional treatment removed her criticism to a certain extent from the supposedly masculine sphere of politics and thus rendered it acceptable to her male editors and audiences. "Only women whose work on its way to the public has to pass through the hands of men, realize to what extent the ancient taboo against women laughing at men, is still in force. It can get by in fiction and drama . . . but in the form of a critically humorous treatment of politicism or of political figures, not at all" ("The Sense of Humor in Women" 12). Given these constraints, Austin's feminist appropriation of the land-as-woman trope proved a successful strategy to caricature masculinist politics and to undermine the anticipated editorial resistance, which one of her fictional women characters describes as follows: "Between you and your public there is a wall of men, a felted, almost sound-proof wall of male intelligence, male reporters, critics, managers, advertisers" (*No. 26 Jayne Street* 6).

24. Tim Poland has argued that western narratives generally display a tendency to invert the traditional relationship between character and setting, for the western landscapes are presented as imprinting their qualities on the human protagonists ("'A Relative to All That Is'" 197). In *West of Everything* Tompkins shows, however, that the choice of a particular region as setting is already informed by the gender codes of dominant society. Within the genre of the western, Tompkins argues, desert landscapes became the quintessential western setting because they were considered a "womanless milieu" (44). Although the qualities of the desert were transferred to the western heroes, this process was meant to reinforce masculinist conceptions of male identity. The perceived harshness, austerity, purity, and monumentality of the desert turned the land into an ideal testing ground for macho individualism, maintains Tompkins (69–88). The relation between character and setting thus was not inverted but only rendered in a more covert form. Although such narratives do not background the desert as a passive setting, then, the land is primarily represented for purposes of

characterization, symbolization, and the development of plot. In short, the land participates as a stock character in a preconceived plot in which the male heroes take center stage.

25. Westling, *The Green Breast of the New World* 169.

26. According to Nash, the shift from a perception of the wilderness as the antagonist of American civilization to a celebration of it as the last remainder of America's pioneer heritage occurred in the 1890s (*Wilderness and the American Mind* 141–60). With the 1890 census the frontier officially had been declared closed, and Frederick Jackson Turner used the report as a vantage point for his argument that the development of American society could only be explained in terms of the westward movement of the settlements and the consequent colonization of the wilderness. His reading of American history helped solidify the mythic conception of a national American character whose distinctive trait was the capacity to heroically transform the wilderness into a pastoral middle landscape. Turnerian interpretations of American history have shaped the image of the West and numerous revisions, most recently by the New West Historians, seem to have barely diminished the popular appeal of mythologized images of the frontier and pioneer experience. Nash argues that since the sense of American national identity was intimately bound up with the myth of the frontier, the close of the frontier caused anxieties that the end of the supposedly heroic conquest of the continent could effect a loss of what were considered "unique and desirable national characteristics" (145). Thus the preservation of wilderness areas, alongside their utilization for purposes of primitivist outdoors recreation, became a means to transport a preindustrial variant of American identity into the Progressive Era. Specifically, this meant, as can be inferred from Nash's argument, that the positive redefinition of the wilderness was an effort to preserve a masculinist sense of selfhood modeled on the mythologized power and vigor of the pioneers.

27. In this respect Owen Wister's novel *The Virginian* (1902) can be considered paradigmatic. It blends a tale about the regeneration of male virility in a yet partially wild country (which symbolizes the restoration of the American character to its mythic pioneer promise) with a tale about the recuperation of the supposedly natural patriarchal relations between the sexes. In light of the sociocultural context in which the novel was written and published, it is interesting to note how much care Wister took to dissemble the antifeminist undercurrent of his work by combining stock ingredients of western quest narrative with more innovative elements, such as allowing the schoolmarm in need of protection to rescue the hero, or focusing for extended passages on the adventures that the Virginian has in barns and ranch and town houses rather than in the wild.

28. The feminized image of the desert as woman and sphinx constitutes in itself such a response. The local poet Madge Morris writes in her late nineteenth-century poem "To the Colorado Desert" of the land as a "brown, bare-breasted, voiceless mystery," and she asks, "Hot sphinx of nature, cactus-crowned, what hast thou done?" (qtd. in Walker, *Literary History of Southern California* 184). Unlike Morris who concludes that "God must have made thee in His anger, and forgot," Austin takes obvious

delight in the resistance that the desert offers to the attempts of the settlers to extensively resource their environment.

29. The careful distinction that Austin makes in *Lost Borders* between the desert
and the female borderers, who adhere to a stereotypically feminine response to the
wilderness, is sometimes ignored by her critics. Wyatt, for instance, reads Austin's revision in terms of a Freudian sexual archetype. The stories, he says, "cohere into a
repetitive pattern characterized by a movement of penetration, embrace, and with-
drawal. The man is the thing that comes and goes, the desert—or the woman [Wyatt
refers here to the female protagonist]—what remains" (*The Fall into Eden* 90–91).
Such an interpretation reinscribes the very tradition that Austin seeks to defy—the
essentializing equation of woman and nature that renders both as passive objects that
invite their conquest through masculine actors.

30. Welter, "The Cult of True Womanhood" 152. Traditionally, European American
pioneering women have been conceived as the carriers of domestic values. As Deming posits, they "assumed a 'receptacle' function where the culture is concerned. Bearing the white civilization to the frontier, their main function was to preserve it" ("Miscegenation in Popular Western History and Fiction" 90). Recently, however, historians
have sought to revise the image that women were either reluctant pioneers and genteel civilizers or oppressed helpmates and passive companions of the male settlers.
Jameson and Harris, for instance, argue that these stereotypical concepts in themselves derive from the cult of True Womanhood, that they uphold the dichotomiza-
tion of the pioneer experience into public and private spheres, and that they interfere
with a recognition of the extent to which the female settlers initiated and participated
in community building at the frontier (Jameson, "Women as Workers"; Harris,
"Homesteading in Northeastern Colorado").

31. Accordingly, Austin asked her female readers in critical essays such as "Women
as Audience" to reject women's traditional position within "our androcentric culture"
as decorative and passive "spectator[s] to the male performance" (1) and challenged
them to exchange their "rôle of patrons of culture" (4) for an active and influential
participation in the development of American society.

32. In the introductory essay to *Lost Borders* the narrator introduces the barrel
image as a symbol for the other-directed self, which she associates with East Coast society and by extension national culture. Elaborating on her categorical distinction between "law" and "land," the narrator explains: "I am convinced that most men make
law for the comfortable feel of it, defining them to themselves. . . . They pinch themselves with regulations to make sure of being sentient, and organize within organi-
zations. Out there, then, where the law and the landmarks fail together, the souls of
little men fade out at the edges, leak from them as water from wooden pails warped
asunder" (2–3). By linking her dismissal of established social arrangements to an assertion of the land's primacy, the narrator stresses the inadequacy of a sense of selfhood that lacks inner-directedness and a responsiveness to natural environments. In
a region of *lost* borders that has "no use for the formal side of man's affairs" (*LB* 51),
adhering to a sense of identity grounded in restrictive social conventions is shown to

have psychologically devastating, if not deadly, consequences. For a discussion of the typical standards of behavior and forms of community organization that derive from frontier conditions, see, for instance, Barker, "The Influence of Frontier Environments on Behavior."

33. In *Made from This Earth* Norwood points out that the location of "human gender codes" in the breeding and nesting habits of animals belongs to the nineteenth-century tradition of women's nature essays. The "images of middle-class animal families" served as a "positive reinforcement of their domesticity" (51). Austin's reference to the matriarchal organization of wild animal families, then, functions as a positive reinforcement of her call for social reform.

34. Kolodny, *The Land Before Her* 3.

35. Alaimo, "The Undomesticated Nature of Feminism" 75. For a discussion of the attempts of male authors to revise concepts of masculinity by imagining encounters with wild places outside the social order, see Boone, "Male Independence and the American Quest Genre."

36. The editor of Houghton Mifflin who rejected the manuscript for publication, Ferris Greenslet, obviously took exception to this violent resolution of the conflict, arguing that "the hero's defection and his subsequent murder by the lady are not made absolutely convincing" (Letter to Austin, 25 July 1927, AU box 25, qtd. in Graulich, Afterword, *CT* 118.) Interestingly, Austin argued in an article published the same month in which *Cactus Thorn* was rejected for publication that the time of "sex antagonism" had passed ("The Forward Turn" 57). After women had won the right to vote, Austin maintained, feminism had entered a new phase and now was chiefly concerned with "the redistribution of sex emphasis," that is, with the dissolution of gender-specific separate spheres and the attendant gender codes (59).

37. Austin elaborates on this idea in *The Young Woman Citizen* (31–33, 177).

38. There is an autobiographical side to Austin's portrait of the figure of the male radical who betrays his political ideals in his treatment of the women who love him. Austin suffered severely when Lincoln Steffens, the muckraking journalist, broke off an affair with her for another woman. Subsequently, she created several fictional scenarios in which she explored the ethical implications of the situation she had experienced, among them the relations between the main protagonists of her novel *No. 26 Jayne Street* (1920). Cf. Graulich, Afterword to *Cactus Thorn* (114–15). Graulich sarcastically comments: "Had *Cactus Thorn* been published when it was written in 1927, Lincoln Steffens . . . might have spent the rest of his life looking over his shoulder" (112–13). The most extended account of Austin's relationship with Steffens and her traumatized response to the breakup is offered in Langlois, *A Search for Significance.*

39. Austin develops a similar fantasy of revenge in "The Medicine of Bow Returning," one of the *One-Smoke Stories*. In this story the male protagonist, Taku-Wakin, is punished directly by god, "the Sky-Walker" (134), for taking the love and support of his wife for granted. Again the man is disciplined for failing to live up to the teaching he is supposed to spread. In this case he betrays the insight he received on his vision quest that "man can hurt nothing without also hurting himself" due to the

world's fundamental unity (133). When Taku-Wakin leaves his family to instruct others in the teachings he has received, he finds that his powers fail him. Returning home he discovers that "his wife had died of grieving and his son had been given to another" (134). Inquiring of "the Sky-Walker" why he has to suffer even though he has lived according to his teaching and not harmed any man, animal, or thing, he receives a counterquestion as reply: "Did I not also make woman?" (135).

40. See also chapter 1 of this study for a discussion of Dulcie Adelaid's regionalist outlook.

41. Arliss's attitude toward Dulcie thus replicates the traditional masculinist stance toward a feminized landscape, customarily displayed by the protagonists of wilderness quest narratives. Baym, "Melodramas of Beset Manhood" notes that the "heroes of American myth turn to nature as sweetheart and nurture, anticipating the satisfaction of all desires through her and including among these the desires for mastery and power" (75).

42. The parallels between Austin and the lead protagonist of *Cactus Thorn* are manifold, including their common study and emulation of Native American cultural practices, particularly basket weaving (cf. AR 40, EH 247).

43. Austin's tendency to regard Native American cultures as relics from a common human prehistory is also discussed in chapter 5 of this study.

44. Tellingly, the woman Arliss intends to marry upon his return to New York is a conservatively raised upper-class woman who "simply existed in her admirable utility as daughter, wife, or woman; but she was to be had and used, this was obvious, only through marriage" (*CT* 22).

45. Cf. Baym, "Melodramas of Beset Manhood" 72.

46. *Reason/nature story* is Plumwood's term for the master narrative of western culture (*Feminism and the Mastery of Nature* 196).

47. Westling, *The Green Breast of the New World* 53.

5   Who Owns the Place?

1. See Dorman's, *Revolt of the Provinces*.

2. In *The Land of Journey's Ending* Austin explains that communism in this context signifies the "coöperative effort with psychological implications" with which the inhabitants of the arid regions responded to the extreme climatic conditions of their environment (89).

3. Schlenz points out that Austin's utopian ideas were prefigured by John Wesley Powell, then head of the U.S. Geological Survey, who had argued "for organizing municipalities in the new western states around the natural boundaries of hydrographic basins rather than by the orthogonal grid of the Jeffersonian land survey system" ("Waters of Paradise" 184). Differentiating among local, state, and federal administrative levels and granting to the local community the sovereignty over the natural resources of its hydrographic district, Powell had proposed in "Institutions for the Arid Lands" (1890): "Let such people organize, under national and State laws, a great irri-

gation district, including an entire hydrographic basin, and let them make their own laws for the division of the water, for the protection and use of the forests, for the protection of the pasturage on the hills, and for the use of the powers. This, then, is the proposition I make: that the entire arid region be organized into natural hydrographic districts, each one to be a commonwealth itself for the purpose of controlling and using the great values which have been pointed out" (47–48). Schlenz notes that Austin also shared Powell's preference for the established Spanish rather than the English water rights system. She "juxtaposed the English—or riparian—tradition of water law, which grants first privilege to owners of land adjoining a stream, with the Spanish tradition of 'beneficent use' or 'appropriative rights,' in which precedent use guarantees continued privilege to a stream's waters and protects users from subsequent diversions by upstream property owners" ("Waters of Paradise" 185). Cf. *EH* 206.

4. In the political sciences the study of new commons, such as the Internet or genetic pools, and of global commons, such as the atmosphere or oceans, increasingly complements the study of traditional common property resources, such as groundwater or fisheries.

5. Rudnick, "Re-Naming the Land" 21.

6. Critics agree that Austin's vision of community organization and inhabitation anticipates contemporary bioregionalism. Cf. Rudnick, "Re-Naming the Land" 26; Kowalewski, "Bioregional Perspectives in American Literature" 39; and Schlenz "Waters of Paradise" 184. Like some of their regionalist precursors, bioregionalists promote the formation of a network of decentralized cultures, all aligned with their regional ecologies. As Gary Snyder asserts, "Bioregional awareness teaches us in *specific* ways. It is not enough just to 'love nature' . . . . Our relation to the natural world takes place in a *place*, and it must be grounded in information and experience" (*The Practice of the Wild* 39). Bioregions usually are defined in terms of watersheds. For recent works that detail the diverse aspects of the bioregional movement, see McGinnis, *Bioregionalism;* Van Andruss, Plant, Plant, and Wright, *Home! A Bioregional Reader;* and Sale, *Dwellers in the Land.*

7. Austin thought that the new culture of the Southwest would be decentralized in itself, "diffused throughout the region named, rather than concentrated in one great city as it has been in the past, in Athens, in Rome or London or New York" ("Mary Austin Abroad" AU 341).

8. This perspective was also shared by some of their male contemporaries. Henry Nash Smith, for instance, regarded Native American culture as "a treasure house of realized understanding of the scene in which modern America must enact the drama of her national life" ("The American Rhythm" vi).

9. Letter to Daniel Trembly MacDougal, 25 May 1923, AU 1186. For discerning discussions of Austin's political and aesthetic work on behalf of Native Americans and the Native American arts revival, see Rudnick, "Re-Naming the Land" 24–25; and Lape, "'There Was a Part for Her in the Indian Life'" 132–33.

10. "Mary Austin Sways Hearers with Rhythm," Anon. Rev. of Austin Lecture, *Fort Worth Record Telegram* (3 Dec. 1927): AU box 127.

11. Parkman, *The Works of Francis Parkman,* vol. 14, ed. Frotenac (New York, 1915) 45–48, qtd. in Gossett, *Race* 244.

12. Roosevelt, *The Winning of the West,* Vol. I (New York, 1889–96) 334–35, qtd. in Gossett, *Race* 238.

13. Austin had already claimed in *The American Rhythm* that Indians were "an American race singing in tune with the beloved environment, to the measures of life-sustaining gestures, taking the material of their songs out of the common human occasions, out of the democratic experience and the profound desire of man to assimilate himself to the Allness as it is displayed to him in all the peacock splendor of the American continent" (AR 18–19). Although generalizations are tricky and much has been published recently to complicate the notion of the ecological Indian, such as in Shepard Kretch's study of the same title (1999), it still is true that the appreciation of their land base was an intrinsic part of the American Indian cultures that Austin turned to for inspiration. As Paula Gunn Allen writes, "We are the land. To the best of my understanding, that is the fundamental idea embedded in Native American life and culture in the Southwest" ("INYANI" 191; also qtd. in Rudnick, "Re-Naming the Land" 242). By presenting the Native American communities as learning models for the reorientation of "Western man's relationship to place and to the nature surrounding him and within" (Castro, *Interpreting the Indian* xviii), Austin anticipates one of the central themes of twentieth-century European American representations of Native American culture. Nature writing and bioregional writing and criticism often discuss or draw on Native American thought. Consider, for instance, the work of Barry Lopez or Gary Snyder.

14. The position Austin outlines in "Aboriginal Fiction" in 1929 contrasts markedly with the romantic racism she expounds, for instance, in one of her earlier regionalist essays, "Art Influence in the West" (1915). In this article her celebratory view of California's developing European American culture finds its expression in the familiar trope of the vanishing race of the noble savage.

15. London, Interview excerpt, qtd. in London, *Jack London and His Times;* also qtd. in Gossett, *Race* 206.

16. Gossett, *Race* 154. Austin wrote several children's books on Native American culture, such as *The Basket Woman* (1904) and *The Trail Book* (1918). These works, however, represent a sincere effort at multicultural education. Rather than infantilize Indians, these collections of interrelated stories are designed to teach European American children (and their parents) about the worldview, cultural heritage, and past and present living conditions of Native Americans and about the devastating consequences of racism.

17. Austin also addresses the erasure of southwestern Native American and Hispanic cultures through government policy and the interference of the white population in *The Land of Journey's Ending* (317, 339, 345). She criticizes the white residents and invasive tourists (320, 344, 364, 368) and advocates an intercultural conversation that seeks to comprehend the other's culture without reducing it to a spectacle (352–53). See also AR 1930, 83–84.

---

18. Gleason, "American Identity and Americanization" 45. Abandoning her usually pluralistic perspective, Austin even speculates in her lecture "What Is a Native Culture?" that miscegenation and the continued influence of a shared environment may erase racial particulars and create a unified American populace. "But in the end, by intermarriage and subjection to the common environment we all become of one general temperament" (AU 625).

19. Rudnick summarizes the positive results of the cross-cultural work that European American women such as Austin, Luhan, and Henderson undertook in the 1920s. They fought "alongside the Pueblos, one of the few successful battles to protect Indians rights in the 1920s, and to help lay the groundwork for John Collier's 'Indian New Deal' legislation in the 1930s. . . . Henderson, Luhan, and Austin also helped create a national audience for indigenous folk arts that had been neglected or ignored, particularly by museums and galleries" ("Re-Naming the Land" 25).

20. Nielsen, *Reading Race* 52. Austin creatively explored this fantasy in the framing narrative of her collection of children's stories *The Trail Book,* which describes the fantastic adventures of a boy and a girl for whom the specimen and artifacts exhibited at a Natural History Museum come alive. The interrelated tales always commence in the museum setting, where the children pass the time as they wait for their father, the janitor, to finish his work. As the children imaginatively enter the showcased past, the stories lead the readers into the reality of precolonial America. While *The Trail Book* is a work of fiction designed to enchant and teach children about the natural and multicultural history of North America, the objective of Austin's critical essays is not to conjecture "wonderland" (vi) but to promote the cause of Indian rights and regionalist reform.

21. For an outline of conservationist thought in Austin's time, see Hays, *Conservation and the Gospel of Efficiency.* On Austin's conservationist stance, see Blend, "Mary Austin and the Western Conservation Movement."

22. In her essay *"The Flock"* Nelson offers an excellent discussion of the different class perspectives and ecological standpoints that Austin's and Muir's writings on sheep and shepherding reveal. Nelson argues that Muir advocated wilderness preservation for recreational and scientific reasons, whereas Austin conceived of the land as a place to live and work. Considering agriculture more pertinent than tourism, Austin sided with the needs of the farmers against both the demands of urban centers and tourists (223). Nelson speculates that Muir may have written *My First Summer in the Sierra* (1911) in an effort to counter Austin's defense of shepherding in *The Flock* (225). A contemporaneous reviewer of *The Flock* recommended that the chapter "'The Sheep and the Reserves' should be read by our lawmakers, for its wisdom and intimate vision" (Rev. of *The Flock* AU box 125).

23. Once again there is an astonishing congruence between Austin's and Thoreau's perspectives. In "Autumnal Tints" Thoreau remarks on two kinds of grasses common to his area: "Perhaps I have more sympathy with them because they are despised by the farmer, and occupy sterile and neglected soil" (144).

24. A shared knowledge of the natural environment could provide the basis for in-

tercultural communication and learning, Austin proposed in *The American Rhythm*. She reports on her own experience: "Better than I knew any Indian, I knew the land they lived in. This I hold to be a prime requisite for understanding originals of whatever description. It was only by such familiarity with the condition under which a land permits itself to be lived with that I was able to overcome the difficulty of language" (AR 38–39).

25. Although the narrator refers to "tillable" lands, the irrigation ditch and not the plow seems the most appropriate symbol for a pastoral drama set in the desert, since the agricultural transformation of wild arid regions into middle landscapes depends foremost on water availability. The classic study of the pastoral tradition is Marx, *The Machine in the Garden;* for the middle landscape ideal and the middle state ethic, see in particular 73–144. Marx also offers a rereading of his earlier arguments in his essay "Pastoralism in America." Recently American pastoral criticism has moved from an understanding of the pastoral as primarily an ideological construct—which is defined as an antimodern desire to escape into an idealized rural landscape in Marx's work; as a psychosexual fantasy of masculinist conquest in Kolodny, *The Lay of the Land;* and as a motivating force behind the imperialist colonization of the continent in the works of New West historians—to an ecocritical reconceptualization of the pastoral as both an ideological construct and as a response to particular biophysical regions that can prove both potentially detrimental to and helpful for the development of sustainable cultures (Buell, *The Environmental Imagination* 33–36, 440–41; Love "Et in Arcadia Ego" 198–99).

26. In *The Lay of the Land* Kolodny defines the pastoral paradox as a situation that allows the settlers to "win mastery over the landscape, but only at the cost of emotional and psychological separation from it" (28).

27. Schlenz points out that "With the passing of Jesus Montaña—and the exoneration of his Anglo murderer—Austin symbolically acknowledges the passing of Spanish water-use traditions in the American West" ("Waters of Paradise" 194).

28. The story, as said, was published in the *Atlantic* in 1903, in *Lost Borders* in 1909, and in *One-Smoke Stories* in 1934. The additions to the *Lost Borders* version are discussed in chapter 1 of this study.

29. The leisure hunting and gratuitous killing of animals upset Austin throughout her life. In the unpublished "Tejon Journal," which she kept during her early years in California, she notes mournfully, "I wish the men had not shot so many ducks and geese and herons. We can not eat all of them—and I liked the herons [*sic*] wings better on the herons than tacked against the wall." (10). Austin apparently felt guilty about the unnecessary killings and identified with the suffering of the animals. Decades later she writes of one place in which such gratuitous violence occurred: "But sometimes I have dreamed of it, and in my dream the mountain has a face, and on that face a look of hurt, intolerably familiar" (LJE 388).

30. The religious overtones of the narrative reinforce the paradox. The number seven, which alludes to the psalm "He shall deliver thee in six troubles, yea, and in seven shall no evil touch thee" (LB 164), recurs throughout the story: At the beginning,

seven coyotes hunt the antelope, which leaps in "seven-leagued bounds" (*LB* 69). Likewise, Little Pete cuts seven notches into the juniper to mark the years of his friendship with the antelope (*LB* 65). Yet the higher forces do not interfere, as promised in the psalm, when the homesteader disrupts the balance of power among the coyotes and the antelope and Little Pete. Instead, the homesteader kills the antelope in the eighth year. Thus the numerical symbolism seems to imply that the collective impact of European American society on the region curbs the overpowering force that the desert is said to unfold "when it deals with men singly" (*LB* 25).

31. In the description of her reaction to Los Angeles' appropriation of the water of Owens Valley, where she lived, Austin employs the same strategy: "Mary did what she could and that was too little. . . . She walked in the field and considered what could be done. She called upon the Voice, and the Voice answered her—Nothing. She was told to go away. And suddenly there was an answer; a terrifying answer, pushed off, deferred, delayed; an answer impossible to be repeated; an answer still impending; which I might not live to see confirmed, but hangs suspended over the Southern country" (*EH* 308). The sense of impending disaster and the frustration over the refusal of the developers and administrators to consider the long-term consequences of their actions also informs Austin's account of the Second Colorado River Conference in 1927. Austin participated as a New Mexican representative in the conference, at which the water rights for seven states were decided. She eventually withdrew because she felt that "there is little one can say against an enterprise that will not come to the proof for perhaps fifty years. . . . None of us will live to see that *débâcle*" (*EH* 362–63). Austin articulates her objections to the Boulder Dam scheme also in "The Future of the Southwest," "The Colorado River Project and the Culture of the Southwest," "The Colorado River Controversy," and in her response to a reader criticism of this article, "To the Editor of the Nation." She warned that "if the city evaded the rights of the farmers, presently the land itself would speak. This is not poetry" ("The Future of the Southwest" 186).

32. In the first decade of the twentieth century Owens Valley, the region on which Austin modeled *The Land of Little Rain,* received nationwide attention because of the battle over its most precious resource—water. Beginning in 1904 a land company bought up the land along the Owens River to secure the attendant water rights. The land company represented Los Angeles and San Fernando Valley business interests. The residents realized too late that the water was not to be used for the irrigation project that the Bureau of Reclamation had begun to plan in 1903. Despite the massive protests of the local population, Congress passed the Los Angeles Bill in 1906. Two years later the construction of the Los Angeles Aqueduct began, and eventually the water of the single river running through Owens Valley was channeled off to the urban water system over two hundred miles southward. The desiccation of Owens Valley continued throughout the century—as did the local protest against it, including eleven bombings of the aqueduct between 1924 and 1931. By the 1970s, augmented by the city's additional ground water extraction, the water table had gone down, the frequency of dust storms had increased, and the vegetation and wildlife habitats had

been severely damaged, if not destroyed. The struggle over the dominion over the valley's natural resources is fully documented in Walton, *Western Times and Water Wars*. See also Kahrl, *Water and Power*; Starr, *Material Dreams* 1–64; Reiser, *Cadillac Desert*.

33. By selecting San Francisco, Austin connects her fictional scenario to a second historical water controversy—San Francisco's use of the Hetch Hetchy Valley as a reservoir. Following the lead of John Muir, preservationists had fought without success to prevent the flooding of the valley. In *The Ford* the urban planners turn to Hetch Hetchy when their original scheme to satisfy the city's water demand by appropriating the waters of Austin's fictional Tierra Longa threatens to fail (422). This twist puts a considerable damper on the optimistic note on which Austin's novel ends. The conflict between rural and urban interests is not resolved but only transferred to another region. On the Hetch Hetchy controversy, see Nash, *Wilderness and the American Mind* 161–81.

34. Walton, Foreword, *The Ford* xii.

35. These are Frank, the son of their neighbor Rickart, who is satisfied with his role of being heir to the "Old Man," and the daughter of Rickart's farm manager, Virginia, who takes up labor agitation and acting.

36. Raine, "'The Man at the Sources'" 247. My reading of the novel is indebted to Anne Raine's analysis of *The Ford*. Raine examines the novel in the context of the rural revitalization and conservationist movements and argues that its portrait of the conflict between agricultural and capitalist interests incorporates and finally rejects a naturalistic perspective. Given Austin's regionalist concept of literature and her novel's subject matter, it makes sense to read *The Ford* as a response to Frank Norris's *The Octopus* (1901), which also deals with historical events that occurred in Kern County. John Macy, a contemporaneous reviewer remarked on this connection: "The great social and commercial plot behind these children is strongly handled and conveys more than any other American fiction since Frank Norris of what Mrs. Austin calls 'the epic quality of the west'" ("Honest American Fiction" 112).

37. Brother and sister clearly reflect Austin's belief that men and women possess different capacities. Austin thought that women generally were more pragmatic and utilitarian than men (AR 1930, 71–72). Men distinguished themselves as individuals, whereas women achieved greatness through their service to the community ("Greatness in Women" 200).

38. He shares these traits with Gaard, the protagonist of Austin's other regionalist novel *Starry Adventure* (1931).

39. In representing a professionally successful but sexually frustrated woman, Anne is a typical Austin figure. She resembles, for instance, Olivia Lattimore and Neith Schuyler, the main protagonists of her feminist novels *A Woman of Genius* (1912) and *No. 26 Jayne Street* (1920).

40. Austin, "Woman Alone" 230.

41. Raine, "The Man at the Sources" 247. Raine points out that Anne can be considered *The Ford's* covert heroine (248), since Kenneth's successful resumption of the role of farmer does not resolve the central concern of the novel, which "continues

for sixty more pages of revelations, setbacks, resolutions, and deliberations, during which the female characters critique the way Kenneth's rural revitalization project is circumscribed by his relentless personal project of masculine identity formation" (255).

42. In one of her lectures, "Understanding America through Her Literature [II]: Fiction of Home and Business Life," Austin describes this civic work as women's founding experience in the American republic. "They had to produce a social democracy to fill out the raw framework of political democracy their men had just put together" (AU 8).

43. See Zagarell, "Narrative of Community" 504–5. The influence of the female regionalist tradition on Austin's work is discussed in chapter 6 of this study.

44. Austin also may have chosen male protagonists for strategic reasons. She anticipated editorial resistance to her work because female authors were not expected to make the traditionally male-dominated fields of economics and politics the subject of their fiction. In one of her lectures Austin formulated as her dilemma that "women who write of the man's world with a woman's approach are editorially nipped, when they write as men write they are not understood. Which leaves them the alternative of writing as men would like to have women write and remaining inconsiderable" ("American Literature as an Expression of American Experience: The American Pattern" AU 8).

45. Cf. Baym, "Melodramas of Beset Manhood" 71. Austin's most amusing ploy to represent the psychological and socioeconomic implications of mythic conceptions of the West in *The Ford* is her hyperbolic portrait of Virginia's brief career as the muse of a socialist playwright. Her representation of the movement of "Democratic Drama" (240) mocks both radical phraseology and romantic misconceptions of the West. In "The Battle," an agitprop play produced for the "Friends of Labor" (303), Virginia is to play "the Spirit of the West," which the playwright from Connecticut imagines along the lines of "Owen Wister and the Sunday Supplements" (242). The "Democratic Drama" episodes, similar to the characterization of Grant Arliss in *Cactus Thorn,* show that even radical thought may remain implicated in romanticized notions of the West that do not contribute to cultural innovation but stall further development.

46. In this context it is interesting to consider the following suggestion of the geographer Roger G. Barker: "Psychological environments on the frontier relative to those in settled regions have something in common with the environments of adolescents relative to those of adults. . . . [W]e have used terms commonly used in connection with adolescents in our consideration of pioneers in their new frontier environments: exploration, errors, false steps, radical moves, frustration. Indeed, adolescents and pioneers are both frontiersmen; they are both entering new territory" ("The Influence of Frontier Environments on Behavior" 84–85).

47. The possibility of such a synthesis is suggested in the character of Ellis Trudeau, who becomes Anne's assistant and Kenneth's fiancée. She combines the talents of the siblings and undergoes an exemplary process of regional acculturation, yet she is not a fully realized character.

48. A parallel between Kenneth's and Jacob's situation is also implied in the close of the novel, which describes Kenneth after "the angel of his struggle went from him" as "limp a little on the sinew of material success" (F 439), which recalls Jacob's limp after his struggle with God's angel.

49. It is hardly surprisingly, then, that Kenneth's plan is associated with the region's Native American past. He realizes the irrigation scheme of his father, who had planned to restore the "ancient dam known as 'Indian Gate'" (F 298). Although the novel leaves unexplained why the dam has fallen into disuse, Kenneth acknowledges his indebtedness to the Native Americans who, like the Paiutes of Owens Valley, built the region's first irrigation system. He names both the canal with which he appropriates the river surplus and his development company "Howkawanda," adopting the indigenous name for a rock formation that towers over the dam (411, 434). Subtly, *The Ford* thus affirms Austin's claim that Native American society provides a model for the regionalist development of the land and American culture.

6 Regionalist Conversations

1. Like Jewett's *The Country of the Pointed Firs* (1896), several of Austin's works are organized as a series of interrelated sketches, among them *The Land of Little Rain, The Basket Woman, The Flock, Lost Borders, California: The Land of the Sun,* and *The Land of Journey's Ending.* It should be stressed, however, that Austin also wrote a regionalist novella, *Cactus Thorn,* and published several regionalist novels, chief among them *The Ford* and *Starry Adventure.* Several other Austin novels deal at least in part with regional issues—such as the suffocating atmosphere of small town life in *A Woman of Genius,* Austin's feminist *Künstlerroman,* or the enchantment with the natural environment in *Outland,* a fantasy novel that offers a tripartite classification of the population into housefolk, outliers, and farfolk according to their mode of living and their relation to the land.

2. Fetterley and Pryse describe a "shift in perception" that renders a previously marginalized character central to a given story as one of the narrative means that regionalist woman writers employed to solicit the empathy of their readers (xvii–xviii).

3. All these stories are reprinted in the anthology *American Women Regionalists,* ed. Fetterley and Pryse.

4. Fetterley and Pryse concede that most women regionalists would not have made the distinction they suggest (xii). One of the few critics who likewise differentiates between local color and regionalism is Hobbs, "Harriette Arnow's Kentucky Novels" 83.

5. Unlike Kaplan and Brodhead, Glazener examines regionalism in the context not only of the elite urban-based readership of magazines such as the *Atlantic* but also of the populist rural audience of periodicals such as the *Arena.* Glazener points out that regionalism reached its peak popularity in the decades that the populist critique of the status quo gathered force, the 1880s and 1890s. Therefore, she reasons, "it seems likely that one of the most important ideological effects of the high-culture magazines' packaging of regionalism as nostalgia was precisely to cover over the political

force and vitality of what was often euphemized as 'rural discontent.' *The Arena,* in contrast, made it possible to read rural discontent, poverty, and isolation as indictments of the government's political and economic collaboration with industry" ("Regional Accents" 35).

6. The narrators of *The Land of Little Rain, Lost Borders,* and *The Land of Journey's Ending* function as extra-homodiegetic narrators, that is, as participating characters in the stories they tell. They address both extra-heterodiegetic and intra-homodiegetic narratees. The so-called narratees are classified as members of two distinct groups, whereas the narrators constantly oscillate between the different levels of narration. The extradiegetic narratees are identical with the implied readers. They are addressed as an anonymous "you" and are considered outsiders to the region and its culture by the extradiegetic narrators. To avoid unnecessary complication I will refer to this group as "readers." For the terminology used to distinguish between the narrative levels and their respective participants, see Rimmon-Kenan, *Narrative Fiction.*

7. Since Austin's narrators fulfill the strategic function of mediating among the heterogeneous audiences of regionalist literature, it is sometimes difficult to evaluate the attitude that they assume toward the other members of their local communities. This also holds true for the work of Austin's precursors. To take the most notorious precedent, Jewett's *The Country of the Pointed Firs,* it is plausible to argue that Jewett (unconsciously) expressed an ambivalent and partially elitist stance toward the rural population of New England by creating a narrator who expresses a patronizing attitude towards the locals and their "childish certainty of being the centre of civilization" (1). Yet it is just as plausible to regard the narrator as a strategic ploy that Jewett used to confront her implied urban-based readership with their assumed prejudices. This reading recognizes, on one hand, the significance that the propositions of the narrator carry, since she is the work's organizing center of consciousness and vision, and it acknowledges, on the other hand, that her perceptions and judgments are constantly challenged by the comments and self-perceptions of the locals, which in turn let the narrator appear conceited. In regard to Austin's early regionalist stories, one similarly can note an influx of racial and classist prejudices counteracted by a sincere attempt to learn across social and ethnic differences. In Austin's work the reciprocal character of these regional conversations is strengthened by her vision of cross-cultural communication as the basis and motor of social reform. Also, Austin's narrators, unlike Jewett's, are not visitors but residents of the regions they describe. They cultivate rather than merely resource local culture.

8. Cf. Brodhead, *Cultures of Letters* 144; Bell, "Gender and American Realism in 'The Country of the Pointed Firs'" 71; Gillman, "Regionalism and Nationalism in Jewett's *The Country of the Pointed Firs*" 103.

9. Like Harte, other writers of California's frontier period left for New York and Europe after 1869—among them Adah Menken, Joaquin Miller, Prentice Mulford, Charles Warren Stoddard, and Mark Twain (Egli, *No Rooms of Their Own* xxi, 216).

10. Sherwood Anderson congratulated Austin in a personal letter that she had "found and set down with such fine understanding" the aspects of the western envi-

ronment and life that "Twain and Harte missed" (qtd. in Pryse, Introduction, *Stories* xviii). Austin suggests in her autobiography that she derived her first notions about the West from dime novels and Harte's tales (*EH* 63, 97, 177). She later sought to revise these traditions in her work by emphasizing "the non-heroic aspects of the encounter with wilderness," a focus that Armitage considers characteristic for women's literature about the frontier experience ("Women's Literature and the American Frontier" 10).

11. The narrator here appears as the alter ego of Austin, who asserts in her autobiography that she learned to write creatively through her study of the art of the Paiute basket makers. "The Paiutes were basket-makers, the finest of their sort. What Mary drew from them was their naked craft, the subtle sympathies of twig and root and bark . . . the struggles of the individual soul with the Friend-of-the-Soul-of-Man. She learned what it meant; how to prevail; how to measure her strength against it. Learning that, she learned to write" (*EH* 289).

12. Dorman, *Revolt of the Provinces* xiii. While Botkin was convinced that "American culture and literature must remain in debt to and enriched by her regional theory and example" ("Mary Austin" 64), other early Austin critics were irked by her posing as a regionalist prophet. Wynn, for instance, declared "that Mary Austin's liking for the role of prophet, her unmanageable mysticism, her lack of logic and consistency and learning kept her from forming a philosophy of regionalism. She was temperamentally unfitted for any role except that of catalyst to set off enthusiasm" ("A Critical Study" 202).

13. It was certainly an ambitious task that Austin set for herself in writing such an inclusive biocultural history of the Southwest. The project nearly exhausted her. In a letter to Daniel Trembly MacDougal, a close friend who had inspired her to write the book, Austin vowed: "Never again will I undertake so tremendous an intellectual effort all at one swoop" (Letter to Daniel Trembly MacDougal, 2 July 1923 *AU* 1189). Lawrence Clark Powell concludes that the synthesis of "history, anthropology, mythology and religion, flora and fauna, the seasons and the weathers, in strong and poetic prose" renders *The Land of Journey's Ending* Austin's best book (*Southwest Classics* 95; also qtd. in Evers "Mary Austin and the Spirit of the Land" xxiv).

14. In comparison to Austin's earlier attempt at creating the portrait of a biocultural region in *The Land of Little Rain, The Land of Journey's Ending* devotes less space to the description of the desert ecosystem, however, and it concentrates more on the human history and folklore of the region. Still, Austin's descriptions of the desert's biota in *The Land of Journey's Ending* are detailed studies based on close observation and thorough scientific research. She clearly profited from the expertise of her close friend Daniel MacDougal, a southwestern botanist, to whom she dedicated the book. In recognition of MacDougal's contribution, Evers even calls *The Land of Journey's Ending* a "collaborative project" ("Mary Austin and the Spirit of the Land" xvi). For more biographical information on Austin's first trip to Arizona, her excursions with MacDougal, and the composition of *The Land of Journey's Ending,* see the firsthand reminiscences of Austin's one-time travel companion Ina Sizer Cassidy, "I-Mary and Me."

15. Bright, *A Coyote Reader* 20.

16. Beck, Walters, Francisco, *The Sacred* 57. My understanding of the intersections of literature and place is indebted to Basso's anthropological study of Apache place names, *Wisdom Sits in Places.*

17. *California: The Land of the Sun,* a collection of essays that Austin wrote to accompany a series of watercolor landscape paintings by Sutton Palmer, opens with the narrator's assertion that Native American creation stories present the most notable and concrete accounts of regional topographies. "For a graphic and memorable report of the contours of any country, see always the aboriginal account of its making. That will give you the lie of the land as no geographer could sketch it forth for you" (3). Accordingly, the chapter begins with the retelling of a Native American story about the making of California (3–5).

18. Mythic creatures, such as mokiách, also populate Austin's *The Trail Book* (1918).

19. Allen, *Spider Woman's Granddaughters* 4. This is particularly true for storytellers who work within tribal cultures that assume that acts of thinking and naming created the world. In the Laguna tradition that Allen works in, for instance, the creator of the world is thought of as Old-Woman-Spider, Ts'its'tsi'nako, who imagines the world into being and names all things (Allen, "The Sacred Hoop" 14; Boas, *Keresean Texts* 7). For a contemporary version of the myth, see the introductory poem to Leslie Marmon Silko's novel *Ceremony* (1977). The belief that the world originates in the imagination and words of the Spider Woman connects storytelling to religious practices that are geared toward aligning people with the other forces of creation. Since creation is made of words, language becomes a viable tool to access spiritual reality.

20. A longer version of the Paiute legend is included in the "Tribal Lays" section of the second edition of *The American Rhythm,* where it is attributed specifically to the Owens Valley Paiutes (AR 1930, 143–46).

21. Austin was familiar with such folklore collections. She reviewed, for instance, *El Folklore Literario de México,* an anthology of Mexican folklore, which comprised "riddles, anecdotes, songs, ballads, epigrams, fables, legends, pasquinades, dramas, hymns, prayers, and political bywords" (Austin, "Mexican Folklore" 23).

22. Austin, "The Folk Story in America" 16–17.

23. In "The Folk Story in America," Austin characterizes them as "short and explicit and packed with reality" (13). Austin was aware that many ceremonial stories were either not told to white outsiders and thus might perish under the continued pressure of forced assimilation or that they were passed on and recorded as secular tales (18).

24. Austin, "Folk Literature" 34.

25. Austin, "The Folk Story in America" 19.

26. It should be stressed that this is the ideal vision that Austin's creative work generates. Austin, as we have seen, was also concerned with the political power dynamics that structure intercultural communication within American society. Her notion of Native American cultures as learning models for European American society and the attendant questions of cultural appropriation is addressed in chapter 5 of this study.

27. Austin, as said, contributed significantly to the work of the Indian Arts Fund and the Spanish Colonial Arts Society. She also collaborated with the New Mexican

folklorist Arthur Leon Campa on collecting Spanish poetry, dramas, and songs. The Austin collection at the Huntington Library contains, for instance, a collection of 108 New Mexican songs, *Canciónes* (AU 59). Moreover, Austin was involved in the community theater movement in California, New York, and New Mexico, and she frequently lectured on American folk drama—for instance, at the Department of Drama at Yale University in 1930 (AU 294). Folk drama, for Austin, included a broad range of dramatic arts, reaching from Native American ceremonial dances to Hispanic and European American community plays (AU 467). Austin considered community theaters a European American variant of oral traditions and held that their revival signified "the rehabilitation of the spoken word as the medium of the People" ("Maverick and the Thespian Muse" AU 346).

28. Austin, "Folk Literature" 34. Wynn lists as signs of "a reviving sense of localism" in the 1920s the publication of journals such as "*Space* in Oklahoma, *The Southwest Review* in Texas, the activities of the Texas Folk-Lore Society under the leadership of J. Frank Dobie, *Frontier* in Montana, *Midland* in Nebraska, the spread of the Little Theater movement, the organization of folk festivals in numerous regions" ("A Critical Study" 192).

29. Austin, "Folk Literature" 34. Austin's argument in "Folk Literature" is inconsistent, however. Although Austin conceives of regionalist folk writers as mediators between regional folk culture and dominant culture, she maintains that their work only retains a folk character if it entirely limits itself to the perspective of a particular group, without considering its "larger environment," for instance, its reception by an outside audience (34). Given this criterion, Austin's work certainly would not qualify as folk, since she frequently creates narrators who converse both with their local peers and with an implied national readership.

30. Dr. Woodin was a friend of Austin's when she lived in Owens Valley (EH 243–45, 256). And, adding an intertextual dimensions to the anecdote, Austin wrote a short story that fits the description—"The Pot of Gold" (1901).

31. Austin, "Why the P.E.N. Is Having a Benefit of Abie's Irish Rose" (AU 640). Austin's promotion of folk culture at times reads like an early defense of popular culture. She recommended to her highbrow readers, for instance, comic strips "as a true expression of folk humor" (AU 640).

32. Austin, "American Literature as an Expression of American Experience: The American Pattern" AU 8.

33. Austin, "American Literature as an Expression of American Experience: The American Pattern" AU 8

34. Botkin, "Mary Austin" 64.

Conclusion

1. Donna Campbell notes that local color literature portrayed problems that were "not only recognizable on a human scale but amenable to human intervention" (*Resisting Regionalism* 23).

2. Austin, "Understanding America through Her Literature (II): Fiction of Home and Business Life" AU 8.

3. Austin, "Essay on Shakespeare" AU 142.

4. Cf. Jordan, *Regionalism Reconsidered* x–xi.

5. Melody Graulich notes that Austin "anticipates poststructuralist, feminist, environmentalist, and postcolonial theory" (*Exploring Lost Borders* xii).

6. Hoennighausen, "The Old and the New Regionalism" 6.

7. Lyon, "The Nature Essay in the West" 221.

8. Letter from Mary Hallock Foote to Mary Austin, 12 Oct. 1903, AU 2414.

BIBLIOGRAPHY

A Note on the Manuscript Source

The principle collection of Austin's manuscripts, drafts, documents, correspondence, journals, notes, and files is held by the Huntington Library, San Marino, California. Referenced material from the Mary Hunter Austin Collection is cited in the notes as AU; individual pieces are not listed in the bibliography. Material from the Mary Hunter Austin Collection is reproduced by permission of the Huntington Library.

A Selection of Published Works by Mary Austin

BOOKS

The American Rhythm. New York: Harcourt, Brace, 1923. *The American Rhythm: Studies and Reëxpressions of Amerindian Songs.* Rev. ed. Boston: Houghton, 1930.

The Arrow Maker. New York: Duffield, 1911. Rev. ed. Boston: Houghton, 1915.

The Basket Woman: A Book of Indian Tales for Children. Boston: Houghton, 1904.

Beyond Borders: The Selected Essays of Mary Austin. Ed. Reuben J. Ellis. Carbondale: Southern Illinois UP, 1996.

Cactus Thorn. Reno: U of Nevada P, 1988.

California: The Land of the Sun. London: Adam and Charles Black, 1914. Rev. ed. *The Lands of the Sun.* Boston: Houghton, 1927.

Can Prayer Be Answered? New York: Farrar, 1934.

The Children Sing in the Far West. Boston: Houghton, 1928.

Christ in Italy. New York: Duffield, 1912. Last chapter rpt. separately. *The Green Bough.* New York: Doubleday, 1913.

Earth Horizon: An Autobiography. Boston: Houghton, 1932.

Everyman's Genius. Indianapolis: Bobbs-Merrill, 1925.

Experiences Facing Death. Indianapolis: Bobbs-Merrill, 1931.

The Flock. Boston: Houghton, 1906.

The Ford. Boston: Houghton, 1917.

Indian Pottery of the Rio Grande. Pasadena: Esto, 1934.

Isidro. Boston: Houghton, 1905.

The Land of Journey's Ending. New York: Century, 1924.

The Land of Little Rain. Boston: Houghton, 1903.

Literary America 1903–1934: The Mary Austin Letters. Ed. T. M. Pearce. Westport: Greenwood, 1979.

Lost Borders. New York: Harper, 1909.

Love and the Soulmaker. New York: Appleton, 1914.

Lovely Lady. New York: Doubleday, 1913.

The Man Jesus. New York: Harper, 1915. Rev. ed. *A Small Town Man.* New York: Harper, 1925.

A Mary Austin Reader. Ed. Esther F. Lanigan. Tucson: U of Arizona P, 1996.

The Mother of Felipe and Other Early Stories. Ed. Franklin Walker. Los Angeles: Book Club of California, 1950.

No. 26 Jayne Street. Boston: Houghton, 1920.

One Hundred Miles on Horseback. 1889. Ed. Donald P. Ringler. Los Angeles: Dawson's, 1963.

One-Smoke Stories. Boston: Houghton, 1934.

Outland. London: Murray, 1910. New York: Boni, 1919.

Santa Lucia: A Common Story. New York: Harper, 1908.

Starry Adventure. Boston: Houghton, 1931.

Taos Pueblo. Text by Mary Austin. Photographed by Ansel Easton Adams. San Francisco: Grabhorn, 1930.

The Trail Book. Boston: Houghton, 1918.

Western Trails: A Collection of Short Stories by Mary Austin. Ed. Melody Graulich. Reno: U of Nevada P, 1987.

A Woman of Genius. New York: Doubleday, 1912. Rpt. Old Westbury: Feminist, 1985.

Writing the Western Landscape. Mary Austin and John Muir. Ed. Ann H. Zwinger. Boston: Beacon, 1994.

The Young Woman Citizen. New York: The Woman's Press, 1918.

CONTRIBUTIONS TO ANTHOLOGIES AND OTHER BOOK-LENGTH WORKS

"Aboriginal American Literature." *American Writers on American Literature.* Ed. John A. Macy. New York: Boni, 1931.

"American Literature Moves On." *Recent Gains in American Civilization.* Ed. Kirby Page. New York: Harcourt, 1928. 183–203.

"Amerindian Verse." *Braithwaite's Anthology of Magazine Verse for 1926.* Ed. William Stanley Braithwaite. Boston: Brimmer, 1926. 104–15.

"The 'Deep-Self' and the Part It Plays in Writing." *The Psychology of Writing Success.* Ed. George Frederick. New York: Buisness Bourse, 1933. 93–109.

"The Friend in the Wood." *Wind's Trail: The Early Life of Mary Austin.* By Peggy Pond Church. Ed. Shelly Armitage. Santa Fe: Museum of New Mexico P, 1990. 181–98.

Introduction. *Native Tales of New Mexico.* By Frank G. Applegate. Philadelphia: Winston, 1935. 5–8.

Introduction. *The Path on the Rainbow.* Ed. George W. Cronyn. New York: Boni, 1918. xv–xxxvii.

BIBLIOGRAPHY

Introduction. *Zuni Folk Tales.* Trans. and ed. Frank H. Cushing. New York: Knopf, 1931. vii–xxix.

"Modern Lore of the Pueblos." *They Know New Mexico: Intimate Sketches by Western Writers.* Passenger Department Atchison, Topeka & Santa Fe Railway. Black, 1928. 17–21.

"Non-English Writings: Aboriginal." *Cambridge History of American Literature.* Cambridge: Cambridge UP, 1933.

Austin, and Anne Martin. *Suffrage and Government: The Modern Idea of Government by Consent and Woman's Place in It, with Special Reference to Nevada and Other Western States.* New York: National American Woman Suffrage Association, 1914. 3–15.

Austin et al. *The Sturdy Oak. A Composite Novel of American Politics.* Ed. Elizabeth Jordan. New York: Holt, 1917. 286–311.

"The Temblor: A Personal Narrative." *The California Earthquake of 1906.* Ed. David Starr Jordan. San Francisco: Robertson, 1907. 341–60.

ESSAYS AND CRITICISM

"Aboriginal Fiction." *Saturday Review of Literature* 6 (28 Dec. 1929): 597–99.

"American Fiction and the Patterns of American Life." *Florida Forum News* 8 (1 Mar. 1931): 1–4.

"American Folk." *Folk-Say: A Regional Miscellany, 1930.* Ed. B. A. Botkin. Norman: U of Oklahoma P, 1930.

"The American Form of the Novel." *New Republic* 30 (12 Apr. 1922): 3–4.

"American Indian Dance Drama." *Yale Review* 19 (June 1930): 732–45.

"American Indian Murals." *American Magazine of Art* 26 (Aug. 1933): 380–84.

"Americans We Like." *Nation* 127 (28 Nov. 1928): 572–73.

"American Women and the Intellectual Life." *Bookman* 53 (Aug. 1921): 481–85.

"Amerindian Folk Lore." *Bookman* 56 (Nov. 1922): 343–45.

"Amorousness and Alcohol." *Nation* 122 (23 June 1926): 691–92.

"An Appreciation of H. G. Wells, Novelist." *American Magazine* 72 (Oct. 1911): 733–35.

"Arizona: The Land of Joyous Adventure." *Nation* 116 (4 Apr. 1923): 385–88.

"Art Influence in the West." *Century* 89 (Apr. 1915): 829–33.

"Artist Life in the United States." *Nation* 120 (11 Feb. 1925): 151–52.

"Automatism in Writing." *Unpartizan Review* 14 (Oct.–Dec. 1920): 336–47.

"The Best Twenty Years: Growing Up and Growing On." *Survey* 60 (1 Apr. 1928): 9–11, 70.

"Beyond the Hudson." *Saturday Review of Literature* 7 (6 Dec. 1930): 432, 444.

"Book Service to Main Street." *Bookman* 53 (Apr. 1921): 97–101.

"B'er Rabbit and the Tar Baby: A New Mexico Variant of the Most Popular American Folk Tale." *El Palacio* 6 (14 June 1919): 205–6.

"Cantu in Baja California." *Nation* 111 (14 Aug. 1920): 184.

"The Colorado River Controversy." *Nation* 125 (9 Nov. 1927): 510–12.

"The Colorado River Project and the Culture of the Southwest." *Southwest Review* 13 (Oct. 1927): 110–15.

"Community Make-Believe." *Good Housekeeping* 59 (Aug. 1914): 213–19.

"The Creative Process." *Southwest Review* 10 (Apr. 1925): 70–76.

"Cults of the Pueblos: An Interpretation of Some Native Ceremonials." *Century* 109 (Nov. 1924): 28–35.

"The Delight Makers." *Theatre Guild Magazine* (Mar. 1929): 23–25, 54.

"Do We Need a New Religion?" *Century* 106 (Sept. 1923): 756–64.

"A Drama Played on Horseback." *Mentor* 16 (Sept. 1928): 38–39.

"Education in New Mexico." *New Mexico Quarterly* 3 (Nov. 1933): 217–21.

"Folk Literature." *Saturday Review of Literature* 5 (11 Aug. 1928): 33–35.

"Folk Plays of the Southwest." *Theatre Arts Monthly* 17 (Aug. 1933): 599–610.

"The Folk Story in America." *South Atlantic Quarterly* 33 (Jan. 1933): 10–19.

"The Folly of the Officials." *Forum* 71 (Mar. 1924): 281–88.

"Food Conservation and the Women." *Unpopular Review* 9 (Apr.–June 1918): 373–84.

"The Forward Turn." *Nation* 125 (20 July 1927): 57–59.

"Frank Applegate." *New Mexico Quarterly* 2 (Aug. 1932): 213–18.

"The Future of the Southwest." *New Republic* 42 (8 Apr. 1925): 186.

"Genius, Talent, and Intelligence." *Forum* 80 (Aug. 1928): 178–86.

"Geographical Terms from the Spanish." *American Speech* 8 (Oct. 1933): 7–10.

"George Sterling at Carmel." *American Mercury* 11 (May 1927): 65–72.

"Greatness in Women." *North American Review* 217 (Feb. 1923): 197–203.

"A Historical Memorial." *Commonweal* 16 (5 Oct. 1932): 533.

"Hoover and Johnson: West Is West." *Nation* 110 (15 May 1920): 642–44.

"How I Found the Thing Worth Waiting For." *Survey* 61 (1 Jan. 1929): 434–38.

"How I Would Sell My Book, 'Rhythm.'" *Bookseller and Stationer* 39 (1 May 1923): 7.

"Indian Arts for the Indians." *Survey* 60 (1 July 1928): 361–88.

"An Indian Captive." *Saturday Review of Literature* (21 June 1930): 1150–51.

"Indian Detour." *Bookman* 68 (Feb. 1929): 653–58.

"Indian Poetry." *Exposition of Indian Tribal Arts* (1931): 3–5.

"The Indivisible Utility." *Survey* 55 (1 Dec. 1925): 301–6, 327.

"Keats and a Fellow Student." *Saturday Review of Literature* (21 Dec. 1929): 590.

"The Kitchen Complex." *Suffragist* (Oct. 1920): 238–40.

"Letter to the Editor." *Bookman* 58 (Sept. 1923): 103–4.

"Life at Santa Fe." *South Atlantic Quarterly* 31 (July 1932): 263–71.

"Mary Austin: Her Page." *The Independent Woman* (Mar. 1929): 7–8.

"Mary Austin on Einstein." *Forum* 84 (Dec. 1930): xlviii–xlix.

"Mary Austin on the Art of Writing: A Letter to Henry James Forman." Intro. James E. Phil[lips]. Los Angeles: The Friends of the UCLA Library, 1961.

"The Meter of Aztec Verse." *Southwest Review* 14 (Jan. 1929): 153–57.

"Mexican Folklore." *Nation* 131 (2 July 1930): 23.

"Mexicans and New Mexico." *Survey* 66 (1 May 1931): 141–44, 187–90.

"Mexico for the Mexicans." *World Outlook* 2 (Dec. 1916): 6–7.

"My Fabian Summer." *Bookman* 54 (Dec. 1921): 351–56.

"Native Drama in Our Southwest." *Nation* 124 (20 Apr. 1927): 437–40.

"The Need for a New Social Concept." *New Republic* 31 (9 Aug. 1922): 298–302.

BIBLIOGRAPHY

"A New Medium for Poetic Drama." *Theatre Arts Magazine* 1 (Feb. 1917): 62–66.
"New Mexican Spanish." *Saturday Review of Literature* 7 (27 June 1931): 930.
"New York: Dictator of American Criticism." *Nation* 106 (31 July 1920): 129–30.
"The Path on the Rainbow." *Dial* 66 (31 May 1919): 569–70.
"A Poet in Outland." *Overland Monthly* 85 (Nov. 1927): 331, 351.
"Poetry in the Education of Children." *Bookman* 68 (Nov. 1928): 270–75.
"Primitive Man: Anarchist or Communist?" *Forum* 78 (Nov. 1927): 744–52.
"Ramona." *New Mexico Quarterly* 2 (Nov. 1932): 345–46.
"Regional Culture in the Southwest." *Southwest Review* 14 (July 1929): 474–77.
"Regionalism in American Fiction." *English Journal* 21 (Feb. 1932): 97–107.
"Religion in the United States." *Century* 104 (Aug. 1922): 527–38.
"The Reorganization of the New Theatre." *American Magazine* 73 (Nov. 1911): 101–4.
"Rimas Infantiles of New Mexico." *Southwest Review* 16 (Oct. 1930): 60–64.
"The Road to the Spring." *Nation* 123 (13 Oct. 1926): 360–61.
"Science for the Unscientific." *Bookman* 55 (Aug. 1922): 561–66.
"The Sense of Humor in Women." *New Republic* 41 (26 Nov. 1924): 10–13.
"Sex Emancipation through War." *Forum* 59 (May 1918): 609–20.
"Sex in American Literature." *Bookman* 57 (June 1923): 385–93.
"The Sheep-Dog." *Harper's Monthly* 113 (Oct. 1906) 757–61.
"The Situation in Sonora." *Nation* 110 (22 May 1920): 680–81.
"Social and Economic Organization of the New Mexico Pueblo." *Progressive Education* 9 (Feb. 1932): 117–21.
"Sources of Poetic Influence in the Southwest." *Poetry* 43 (Dec. 1933): 152–63.
"Spanish Manuscripts in the Southwest." *Southwest Review* 19 (July 1934): 402–9.
"Supernaturals in Fiction." *Unpartizan Review* 13 (Mar. 1920): 236–45.
"The Town That Doesn't Want a Chautauqua." *New Republic* 47 (7 July 1926): 195–97.
"To the Editor of the Nation." *Nation* 125 (28 Dec. 1927): 737.
"Wanted: A New Method in Mexico." *Nation* 110 (21 Feb. 1920): 228–29.
"Where We Get Tammany Hall and Carnegie Libraries." *World Outlook* 4 (Jan. 1915): 4–5.
"Why Americanize the Indian?" *Forum* 82 (Sept. 1929): 167–73.
"Why I live in Santa Fe." *Golden Book Magazine* 16 (Oct. 1932): 306–7.
"Woman Alone." *Nation* 124 (2 Mar. 1927): 228–30.
"Woman and Her War Loot." *Sunset* 42 (Feb. 1919): 13–16.
"Woman Looks at Her World." *Pictorial Review* 26 (Nov. 1924): 8–9.
"Woman Sees Steel." *Bookman* 53 (Mar. 1921): 82–84.
"Woman's Prefered Candidate." *Collier's* 65 (29 May 1920): 7.
"Women as Audience." *Bookman* 55 (Mar.–Aug. 1922): 1–5.
"Women's Clubs To-Day and To-Morrow." *Ladies Home Journal* 39 (June 1922): 27.
"Zuni Folk Tales." *Dial* 71 (July 1921): 112–17.

SHORT STORIES AND PLAYS

"The Christmas Fiddle." *Century* 81 (Dec. 1910): 239–47.
"The Divorcing of Sina." *Sunset* 40 (June 1918): 26–29, 74–75.

"Fire: A Drama in Three Acts." *The Playbook* 2. Wisconsin Dramatic Society (Oct. 1914): 3–25; (Nov. 1914): 11–26; (Dec. 1914): 18–30.
"Frustrate." *Century* 83 (Jan. 1912): 467–71.
"The Kiss of Nino Dios." *Out West* 21 (Dec. 1904): 535–41.
"The Little Coyote." *Atlantic* 89 (Feb. 1902): 249–54.
"A Lost Dog." *Catholic World* 89 (Aug. 1909): 624–35.
"Mamichee." *Catholic World* 91 (May 1910): 183–97.
"The Pot of Gold." *Munsey's Magazine* 25 (July 1901): 491–95.
"Sekala Ka'ajma." *Theatre Arts Monthly* 13 (Apr. 1929): 265–76.
"A Shepherd of the Sierras." *Atlantic* 86 (July 1900): 54–58.
"The Song-Makers." *North American Review* 194 (Aug. 1911): 239–47.
"The Souls of Stitt." *Harper's Monthly* 142 (Dec. 1920): 71–74.
"Spring o' the Year." *Century* 75 (Apr. 1908): 923–28.
"The White Cockatoo." *Century* 83 (Feb. 1912): 549–60.
"The White Hour." *Munsey's Magazine* 29 (Apr. 1903): 88–92.
"The Wooing of the Senorita." *Overland Monthly* 29 (Mar. 1897): 258–63.

Secondary Works

Abram, David. *The Spell of the Sensuous: Perception and Language in a More-Than-Human World.* New York: Vintage, 1997.
Abbey, Edward. Introduction. *The Land of Little Rain.* By Mary Austin. New York: Penguin, 1988.
Alaimo, Stacy. "Cyborg and Ecofeminist Interventions: Challenges for an Environmental Feminism." *Feminist Studies* 20.1 (1994): 133–53.
———. "The Undomesticated Nature of Feminism: Mary Austin and the Progressive Women Conservationists." *Studies in American Literature* 26.1 (1998): 73–96.
Allen, Paula Gunn. "INYANI: It Goes This Way." *The Remembered Earth: An Anthology of Contemporary Native American Literature.* Ed. Geary Hobson. Albuquerque: U of New Mexico P, 1979. 191–93.
———. "The Sacred Hoop." Allen 3–22.
———, ed. *Spider Woman's Granddaughters: Traditional Tales and Contemporary Writing by Native American Women.* Boston: Beacon, 1989.
———, ed. *Studies in American Indian Literature: Critical Essays and Course Designs.* New York: MLA, 1983.
Ammons, Elizabeth. *Conflicting Stories: American Women Writers at the Turn into the Twentieth Century.* Oxford: Oxford UP, 1992.
———. "Material Culture, Empire, and Jewett's 'The Country of the Pointed Firs.'" Howard 81–99.
Anderson, Benedict. *Imagined Communities: Reflections on the Origin and Spread of Nationalism.* 1983. Rev. ed. New York: Verso, 1993.
Andruss, Van, Christopher Plant, Judith Plant, and Eleanor Wright, eds. *Home! A Bioregional Reader.* Philadelphia: New Society Publishers, 1990.

Anonymous. "Creative Worker in Literature Gave Interesting Lecture in Lisser Hall: Mary Austin Discussed Aboriginal Poetry before Mills Audience." *Mills College Weekly* 18 (22 Feb. 1928): 1, 4.

Anzaldúa, Gloria. *Borderlands/La Frontera: The New Mestiza.* San Francisco: Spinsters, 1987.

Apthorp, Elaine Sergent. "Sentiment, Naturalism, and the Female Regionalists." *Legacy* 7.1 (1990): 3–23.

Armand, Barton Levi Saint. "The Book of Nature and American Nature Writing: Codex, Index, Contexts, Prospects." *ISLE* 4.1 (1997): 29–42.

Armbruster, Karla, and Kathleen R. Wallace, eds. *Beyond Nature Writing: Expanding the Boundaries of Ecocriticism.* Charlottesville: UP of Virginia, 2001.

Armitage, Susan H. "Women's Literature and the American Frontier: A New Perspective on the Frontier Myth." *Women, Women Writers, and the West.* Ed. L. L. Lee and Merrill Lewis. Troy, NY: Whitston, 1980. 5–13.

Armitage, Susan, and Elizabeth Jameson, eds. *The Women's West.* Norman: U of Oklahoma P, 1987.

Ayers, Edward L., ed. et al. *All over the Map: Rethinking American Regions.* Baltimore: John Hopkins UP, 1996.

Babcock, Barbara A., and Nancy Parezo. *Daughters of the Desert: Women Anthropologists and the Native American Southwest.* Albuquerque: U of New Mexico P, 1988.

Ballard, Rae Galbraith. "Mary Austin's *Earth Horizon:* The Imperfect Circle." Diss. Claremont Graduate School, 1977.

Barker, Roger G. "The Influence of Frontier Environments on Behavior." Steffen 61–93.

Barnhill, David Landis, ed. *At Home on the Earth: Becoming Native to Our Place. A Multicultural Anthology.* Berkeley: U of California P, 1999.

Basso, Keith H. *Wisdom Sits in Places: Landscape and Language among the Western Apache.* Albuquerque: U of New Mexico P, 1996.

Baym, Nina. "Melodramas of Beset Manhood: How Theories of American Fiction Exclude Women Authors." *The New Feminist Criticism: Essays on Women, Literature, and Theory.* Ed. Elaine Showalter. London: Virago, 1986. 63–80.

Beck, Peggy V., Anna Lee Walters, and Nia Francisco. *The Sacred: Ways of Knowledge, Sources of Life.* Tsaile: Navajo Community College P, 1992.

Bell, Michael Davitt. "Gender and American Realism in 'The Country of the Pointed Firs.'" Howard 61–80.

Berry, Wilkes. "Characterization in Mary Austin's Southwest Works." *Southwestern American Literature* 2 (1972): 119–24.

———. "Mary Austin: Sibylic Gourmet of the Southwest." *Western Review* 9.2 (1972): 3–8.

Berthoff, Warner. *The Ferment of Realism: American Literature, 1884–1919.* Cambridge: Cambridge UP, 1965.

Blend, Benay. "Mary Austin and the Western Conservation Movement: 1990–1927." *Journal of the Southwest* 30 (1988): 12–34.

Boas, Franz, ed. *Keresean Texts.* 2 vols. *Publications of the American Ethnology Society* 8. New York: 1928.

Bonta, Marcia Myers, ed. *American Women Afield: Writing by Pioneering Women Naturalists.* College Station: Texas A&M UP, 1995.

Boone, Joseph A. "Male Independence and the American Quest Genre: Hidden Sexual Politics in the All-Male Worlds of Melville, Twain and London." *Feminisms: An Anthology of Literary Theory and Criticism.* Ed. Roby R. Warhol and Diane Price Herl. New Brunswick: Rutgers UP, 1991. 961–87.

Botkin, B. A. "The Folk in Literature: An Introduction to the New Regionalism." *Folk-Say: A Regional Miscellany.* Ed. Botkin. Norman: Oklahoma Folk-Lore Society, 1929. 9–20.

———. "Mary Austin." *Space* (Sept. 1934): 64.

———. "The New Mexico Round Table on Regionalism." *New Mexico Quarterly* 3 (Aug. 1933): 152–59.

———. "Regionalism and Culture." *The Writer in a Changing World.* Ed. Henry Hart. Equinox Cooperative P, 1937. 140–57.

Bracher, Frederick. "California's Literary Regionalism." *American Quarterly* 7.3 (1955): 275–84.

Bredahl, Carl A. *New Ground: Western American Narrative and the Literary Canon.* Chapel Hill: U of North Carolina P, 1989.

Bright, William. *A Coyote Reader.* Berkeley: U of California P, 1993.

Brodhead, Richard H. *Cultures of Letters: Scenes of Reading and Writing in Nineteenth-Century America.* Chicago: U of Chicago P, 1993.

Brooks, Paul. *Speaking for Nature: How Literary Naturalists from Henry Thoreau to Rachel Carson Have Shaped America.* Boston: Houghton, 1980.

Buell, Lawrence. *The Environmental Imagination: Thoreau, Nature Writing, and the Formation of American Culture.* Cambridge: Harvard UP, 1995.

Burke, Edmund. *A Philosophical Enquiry into the Origin of Our Ideas of the Sublime and Beautiful.* 1757. London: 1958.

Burroughs, Ann. "Mary Austin's Ideas of American Patterns." *Carmel Pine Cone* (17 Aug. 1922): 6.

Burroughs, John. "On Humanizing the Animals." *Century* 67 (Mar. 1904): 773–80.

———. "Real and Sham Natural History." *Atlantic* 91 (Mar. 1903): 298–309.

Butler, Judith. *Bodies That Matter: On the Discursive Limits of 'Sex.'* New York: Routledge, 1993.

Campbell, Donna. *Resisting Regionalism: Gender and Naturalism in American Fiction, 1885–1915.* Athens: Ohio UP, 1997.

Campbell, SueEllen. "The Land and Language of Desire: Where Deep Ecology and Post-Structuralism Meet." *Western American Literature* 24 (fall 1989): 199–211.

Canby, Henry Seidel. "Back to Nature." *Yale Review* 6 (July 1917): 755–67.

Cassidy, Ina Sizer. "I-Mary and Me: The Chronicle of a Friendship." *New Mexico Quarterly* 9 (Nov. 1939): 203–11.

Castro, Michael. "Early Translators of American Poetry." *Interpreting the Indian:*

Twentieth-Century Poets and the Native American. Albuquerque: U of New Mexico P, 1983. 3–42.

Columbia Literary History of the United States. Ed. Emory Elliott et al. New York: Columbia UP, 1988.

Comer, Krista. "Sidestepping Environmental Justice: 'Natural' Landscapes and the Wilderness Plot." Inness and Royer 216–36.

Cooley, John, ed. *Earthly Words: Essays on Contemporary American Nature and Environmental Writers.* Ann Arbor: U of Michigan P, 1994.

Coupe, Laurence, ed. London: *The Green Studies Reader: From Romanticism to Ecocriticism.* New York: Routledge, 2000.

Cox, James M. "Regionalism: A Diminished Thing." *Columbia Literary History* 761–84.

Crèvecoeur, Hector Saint Jean de. "Letter III: What is an American?" *Letters from an American Farmer.* 1782. *The Norton Anthology of Literature.* Ed. Nina Baym et al. 3rd ed. Vol. 1. New York: Norton, 1989. 558–68. 2 vols.

Cronon, William, ed. *Uncommon Ground: Rethinking the Human Place in Nature.* New York: Norton, 1995.

Cuomo, Christine. "Unraveling the Problems in Ecofeminism." *Environmental Ethics* 14 (winter 1992): 351–63.

Davidson, Donald. "'I'll Take My Stand': A History." *American Review* 5 (1935): 301–21.

———. "Regionalism and Nationalism in American Literature." *American Review* 5 (Apr. 1935): 48–61.

Deming, Caren J. "Miscegenation in Popular Western History and Fiction." *Women and Western American Literature.* Ed. Helen Winter Stauffer and Susan J. Rosowski. Troy, NY: Whitston, 1982. 90–99.

Devine, Maureen. *Woman and Nature: Literary Reconceptualizations.* Metuchen: Scarecrow, 1992.

Dewey, John. *Art as Experience.* 1934. New York: Perigee Books, 1980.

D'haen, Theo, and Hans Bertens, eds. *"Writing" Nation and "Writing" Region in America.* Amsterdam: VU UP, 1996.

Diamond, Irene, and Gloria Feman Orenstein, eds. *Reweaving the World: The Emergence of Ecofeminism.* San Francisco: Sierra Club, 1990.

Diamond, Jared. *Guns, Germs, and Steel: The Fates of Human Societies.* New York: Norton, 1997.

Dike, Donald A. "Notes on Local Color and Its Relation to Realism." *College English* 14.2 (Nov. 1952): 81–88.

Donovan, Josephine. *Feminist Theory: The Intellectual Traditions of American Feminism.* New York: Continuum, 1990.

Dorman, Robert L. *Revolt of the Provinces: The Regionalist Movement in America, 1920–1945.* Chapel Hill: U of North Carolina P, 1993.

Doyle, Helen MacKnight. *Mary Austin: Woman of Genius.* New York: Gotham, 1939.

Drinnon, Richard. "The American Rhythm: Mary Austin." *Facing West: The Metaphysics of Indian-Hating and Empire-Building.* Minneapolis: U of Minnesota P, 1980. 219–31.

DuBois, Arthur. "Mary Hunter Austin, 1868–1934." *Southwest Review* 20 (Apr. 1935): 231–64.

Ecocriticism. Spec. issue of *New Literary History* 30.3 (1999): 505–715.

Egli, Ida Rae, ed. *No Rooms of Their Own: Women Writers of Early California.* Berkeley: Heyday, 1992.

Emerson, Ralph Waldo. "The Poet" (1844). *The Norton Anthology of Literature.* Ed. Nina Baym et al. 3rd ed. Vol. 1. New York: Norton, 1989. 984–99. 2 vols.

Entrikin, J. Nicholas. *The Betweenness of Place: Towards a Geography of Modernity.* Baltimore: John Hopkins UP, 1991.

Etulian, Richard W. *Re-Imagining the Modern American West: A Century of Fiction, History, and Art.* Tucson: U of Arizona P, 1996.

Evers, Larry, ed. "Mary Austin and the Spirit of the Land." Introduction. *The Land of Journey's Ending.* By Mary Austin. Tucson: U of Arizona P, 1983. ix–xxv.

Farris, Sara. "Women Writing Nature: Creating an Ecofeminist Praxis." Diss. Miami U, 1992.

Feld, Steven, and Keith H. Basso, eds. Introduction. *Senses of Place.* Santa Fe: School of American Research P, 1996. 3–11.

Fetterley, Judith, and Majorie Pryse, eds. *American Women Regionalists, 1850–1910: A Norton Anthology.* New York: Norton, 1992.

Fink, Augusta. *I-Mary: A Biography of Mary Austin.* Tucson: U of Arizona P, 1983.

Fishbein, Morris. "The Middleman in Science Literature." *Bookman* 57 (Mar. 1923): 18–21.

Fisher, Philip. "American Literary and Cultural Studies since the Civil War." *Redrawing the Boundaries: The Transformation of English and American Literary Studies.* Ed. Stephen Greenblatt and Giles Gunn. New York: MLA, 1992. 232–50.

Foote, Stephanie. "'I Feared to Find Myself a Foreigner': Revisiting Regionalism in Sarah Orne Jewett's 'The Country of the Pointed Firs.'" *Arizona Quarterly* 52.2 (1996): 37–61.

Ford, Thomas W. "*The American Rhythm:* Mary Austin's Poetic Principle." *Western American Literature* 5 (spring 1970): 3–14.

"Forum on Literatures of the Environment." *PMLA* 114 (Oct. 1999): 1089–104.

Fritzell, Peter. *Nature Writing and America: Essays upon a Cultural Type.* Ames: Iowa State UP, 1990.

Gelfant, Blanche H. "'Lives' of Women Writers: Cather, Austin, Porter / and Willa, Mary, Katherine Anne." *Novel: A Forum on Fiction* 18.1 (1984): 64–80.

Gibson, Arrell Morgan. *The Santa Fe and Taos Colonies: Age of the Muses, 1900–1942.* Norman: U of Oklahoma P, 1983.

Gilligan, Carol. *In a Different Voice: Psychological Theory and Women's Development.* Cambridge: Harvard University Press, 1982.

Gillman, Susan. "Regionalism and Nationalism in Jewett's 'The Country of the Pointed Firs.'" Howard 101–17.

Glazener, Nancy. "Regional Accents: Populism, Feminism, and New England Women's Regionalism." *Arizona Quarterly* 52.3 (1996): 33–53.

Gleason, Philip. "American Identity and Americanization." *Harvard Encyclopedia of*

American Ethnic Groups. Ed. Stephan Thernstrom. Cambridge: Harvard UP, 1980. 31–58.

Glotfelty, Cheryll, and Harold Fromm, eds. *The Ecocriticism Reader: Landmarks in Literary Ecology*. Athens: U of Georgia P, 1996.

Gossett, Thomas F. *Race: The History of an Idea in America*. Dallas: Southern Methodist UP, 1963.

Graulich, Melody. Foreword. Afterword. *Cactus Thorn*. By Mary Austin. Reno: U of Nevada P, 1988. vii–ix. 101–22.

———. Introduction. *Exploring Lost Borders*. Graulich and Klimasmith xi–xxiv.

———. "'I Thought at First She Was Talking about Herself': Mary Austin on Charlotte Perkins Gilman." *Jack London Journal* 1 (1994): 148–58.

Graulich, Melody, and Elizabeth Klimasmith, eds. *Exploring Lost Borders: Critical Essays on Mary Austin*. Reno: U of Nevada P, 1999.

Gressley, Gene M. "Regionalism and the Twentieth-Century West." Steffen 197–233.

Grosz, Elizabeth. *Volatile Bodies: Toward a Corporeal Feminism*. Bloomington: Indiana UP, 1994.

Gurian, Jay. "Style in the Literary Desert: Mary Austin." *Western American Writing: Tradition and Promise*. Deland: Everett, 1975. 71–80.

Hall, Jacqueline, D. "Mary Hunter Austin." *A Literary History of the American West*. Ed. Max Westbrook. Forth Worth: Texas Christian UP, 1987. 359–69.

Handlin, Oscar. *Race and Nationality in American Life*. Boston: Little, 1948.

Haraway, Donna J. *Simians, Cyborgs, and Women: The Reinvention of Nature*. New York: Routledge, 1991.

Harding, Brian. "The Myth of the Myth of the Garden." *American Literary Landscapes: The Fiction and the Fact*. Ed. Ian F. A. Bell and D. K. Adams. New York: St. Martin's, 1989. 44–60.

Harper, Richard Conant. *The Course of the Melting Pot Idea to 1910*. Diss. Columbia U, 1967. New York: Arno, 1980.

Harris, Katherine. "Homesteading in Northeastern Colorado, 1873–1920: Sex Roles and Women's Experience." Armitage and Jameson 165–78.

Harrison, Beth. "Zora Neale Hurston and Mary Austin: A Case Study in Ethnography, Literary Modernism, and Contemporary Ethnic Fiction." *MELUS* 21.2 (1996): 89–106.

Hays, Samuel P. *Conservation and the Gospel of Efficiency: The Progressive Conservation Movement, 1890–1920*. Cambridge: Harvard UP, 1959.

Heise, Ursula. "Science and Ecocriticism." *American Book Review* 18.5 (July–Aug. 1997): 4.

Heizer, Robert Fleming. *The Natural World of the Californian Indians*. Berkeley: U of California P, 1980.

Hergesheimer, Joseph. "The Feminine Nuisance in American Literature." *Yale Review* 10 (July 1921): 716–25.

Herndl, Carl G., and Stuart C. Brown, eds. *Green Culture: Environmental Rhetoric in Contemporary America*. Madison: U of Wisconsin P, 1996.

Hilfer, Anthony Channell. *The Revolt from the Village, 1915–1930*. Chapel Hill: U of North Carolina P, 1969.

Hitt, Christopher. "Toward an Ecological Sublime." *NLH* 30.3 (1999): 603–23.

Hobbs, Glenda. "Harriette Arnow's Kentucky Novels: Beyond Local Color." E. Toth 83–92.

Hoennighausen, Lothar. "The Old and the New Regionalism." D'haen and Bertens 3–20.

hooks, bell. *Talking Black: Thinking Feminist, Thinking Black.* Boston: South End, 1989.

Hougland, Willard, ed. *Mary Austin: A Memorial.* Santa Fe: Laboratory of Anthropology, 1944.

Howard, June, ed. *New Essays on "The Country of the Pointed Firs."* Cambridge: Cambridge UP, 1994.

Howarth, William. *The Book of Concord: Thoreau's Life as a Writer.* New York: Penguin, 1982.

Hoyer, Mark T. *Dancing Ghosts: Native American and Christian Synchretism in Mary Austin's Work.* Reno: U of Nevada P, 1998.

Inness, Sherrie A., and Diana Royer, eds. *Breaking Boundaries: New Perspectives on Women's Regional Writing.* Iowa City: U of Iowa P, 1997.

Jackson, John Brinckerhoff. *A Sense of Place, a Sense of Time.* New Haven: Yale UP, 1994.

Jameson, Elizabeth. "Women as Workers, Women as Civilizers: True Womanhood in the American West." Armitage and Jameson 145–64.

Jauß, Hans Robert. "Aisthesis und Naturerfahrung." *Das Naturbild des Menschen.* Ed. Jörg Zimmermann. München: Wilhelm Fink, 1982. 155–82.

Jaycox, Faith. "Regeneration through Liberation: Mary Austin's 'The Walking Woman' and Western Narrative Formula." *Legacy* 6.1 (1989): 5–12.

Jewett, Sarah Orne. *The Country of the Pointed Firs and Other Stories.* 1896. Ed. Mary Ellen Chase. Intro. Marjorie Pryse. New York: Norton, 1982.

Jensen, Merrill, ed. *Regionalism in America.* Madison: U of Wisconsin P, 1952.

Jones, Llewellyn. "Indian Rhythms." *Bookman* 57 (Aug. 1923): 647–48.

Jordan, David, ed. *Regionalism Reconsidered: New Approaches to the Field.* New York: Garland, 1994.

Kaenel, A. "After the Cold War: Region, Nation and World in American Studies." D'haen and Bertens 73–81.

Kahrl, William L. *Water and Power: The Conflict over Los Angeles' Water Supply in the Owens Valley.* Berkeley: U of California P, 1982.

Kallen, Horace M. *Culture and Democracy in the United States.* New York: Boni, 1924.

Kaplan, Amy. "Nation, Region, and Empire." *The Columbia History of the American Novel.* Ed. Emory Elliott et al. New York: Columbia UP, 1991. 240–66.

King, Ynestra. "Healing the Wounds: Feminism, Ecology, and the Nature/Culture Dualism." Diamond and Orenstein 106–21.

———. "Toward an Ecological Feminism and a Feminist Ecology." *Machina Ex Dea: Feminist Perspectives on Technology.* Ed. Joan Rothshild. New York: Pergamon, 1983. 118–29.

Kolodny, Annette. *The Land Before Her: Fantasy and Experience of the American Frontiers, 1630–1860.* Chapel Hill: U of North Carolina P, 1984.

———. *The Lay of the Land: Metaphor as Experience and History in American Life and Letters.* Chapel Hill: U of North Carolina P, 1975.

Kowalewski, Michael. "Bioregional Perspectives in American Literature." Jordan 29–46.

———. *Reading the West: New Essays on the Literature of the American West.* Cambridge: Cambridge UP, 1996.

Langlois, Karen Sally. "A Fresh Voice from the West: Mary Austin, California, and American Literary Magazines, 1892–1910." *California History* (spring 1990): 22–35, 80–81.

———. "Mary Austin and Houghton Mifflin Company: A Case Study in the Marketing of a Western Writer." *Western American Literature* 23 (summer 1988): 31–42.

———. *A Search for Significance: Mary Austin: The New York Years.* Diss. Claremont Graduate School, 1987. Ann Arbor: UMI, 1987.

Lape, Noreen Grover. "'There Was a Part for Her in the Indian Life': Mary Austin, Regionalism, and the Problems of Appropriation." Inness and Royer 124–39.

———. *West of the Border: the Multicultural Literature of the Western American Frontiers.* Athens: Ohio UP, 2000.

Limerick, Patricia Nelson. *The Legacy of Conquest: The Unbroken Past of the American West.* New York: Norton, 1987.

London, Joan. *Jack London and His Times: An Unconventional Biography.* New York, 1939.

Long, William J. "The Modern School of Nature Writing and Its Critics." *North American Review* 176 (May 1903): 687–98.

Love, Glen A. "Ecocriticism and Science: Toward Consilience?" *NLH* 30.3 (1999): 561–76.

———. "Et in Arcadia Ego: Pastoral Theory Meets Ecocriticsm." *Western American Literature* 27 (fall 1992): 195–207.

———. "Revaluing Nature: Toward an Ecological Criticism." *Western American Literature* 25 (fall 1990): 201–15.

Lueders, Edward, ed. *Writing Natural History: Dialogues with Authors.* Salt Lake City: U of Utah P, 1989.

Lutts, Ralph H. *The Nature Fakers. Wildlife, Science & Sentiment.* Golden: Fulcrum, 1990.

Lyday, Jo W. *Mary Austin: The Southwest Works.* Austin: Steck-Vaughn, 1968.

Lyon, Thomas J. "The Nature Essay in the West." *A Literary History of the American West.* Ed. J. Golden Taylor et al. Forth Worth: Texas Christian UP, 1987. 221–66.

———, ed. *This Incomparable Lande: A Book of American Nature Writing.* Boston: Houghton, 1989.

Macy, John. "Honest American Fiction." *Dial* 63 (16 Aug. 1917): 112–14.

Major, Mabel. "Mary Austin in Fort Worth." *New Mexico Quarterly* 4 (Nov. 1934): 307–10.

Marx, Leo. *The Machine in the Garden: Technology and the Pastoral Ideal in America.* New York: Oxford UP, 1964.

———. "Pastoralism in America." *Ideology and Classic American Literature.* Ed. Sacvan Bercovitch and Myra Jehlen. Cambridge: Cambridge UP, 1986. 36–69.

McCullough, Kate. *Regions of Identity: The Construction of America in Women's Fiction, 1885–1914.* Stanford: Stanford UP, 1999.

McDowell, Tremaine. *American Studies.* Minneapolis: U of Minnesota P, 1948.

———. "Regionalism in American Literature." *Minnesota History.* 20.2 (1939): 105–18.

McGinnis, Michael, ed. *Bioregionalism.* New York: Routledge, 1999.

McGregor, Robert Kuhn. *A Wider View of the Universe: Henry Thoreau's Study of Nature.* Urbana: U of Illinois P, 1997.

McIntosh, R. P. *The Background of Ecology: Concept and Theory.* Cambridge: Cambridge UP, 1986.

McKinney, Viola Wheless. "Mary Hunter Austin: Interpreter of the Southwest." MS Thesis. Kingsville Texas, 1950.

McWilliams, Carey. "A Letter from Carmel." *Saturday Review of Literature* (4 Jan. 1930): 622.

———. *The New Regionalism in American Literature.* Seattle: U of WA Bookstore, 1930.

Merchant, Carolyn. *The Death of Nature: Women, Ecology and the Scientific Revolution.* London: Wildwood, 1982.

———. "Ecofeminism and Feminist Theory." Diamond and Orenstein 100–105.

———. "Women of the Progressive Conservation Movement: 1900–1916." *Environmental Review* 8.1 (1984): 57–86.

Merleau-Ponty, Maurice. *Phenomenology of Perception.* 1962. Trans. Colin Smith. London: Routledge, 1992.

———. *The Visible and the Invisible.* 1948. Ed. Claude Lefort. Trans. Alphonso Lingis. Evanston: Northwestern UP, 1968.

Metcalfe, Dale. "Singing Like the Indians Do: Mary Austin's Poetry." Graulich and Klimasmith 65–85.

Michaels, Walter Benn. *Our America: Nativism, Modernism, and Pluralism.* Durham: Duke UP, 1995.

Mickenberg, Julia. "Writing the Midwest: Meridel Le Sueur and the Making of a Radical Regional Tradition." Inness and Royer 143–61.

Mighetto, Lisa. "Science, Sentiment, and Anxiety: American Nature Writing at the Turn of the Century." *Pacific Historical Review* (Feb 1985): 33–50.

Miller, Elise. "Jewett's 'The Country of the Pointed Firs': The Realism of the Local Colorists." *American Literary Realism* 20.2 (1988): 3–20.

Morrow, Nancy. "The Artist as Heroine and Anti-Heroine in Mary Austin's *A Woman of Genius* and Anne Douglas Sedgwick's *Tante.*" *American Literary Realism* 22.2 (1990): 17–29.

Mumford, Lewis. "The American Rhythm." *New Republic* 35 (30 May 1923): 23–24.

———. *The Golden Day: A Study in American Experience and Culture.* New York: Boni, 1926.

Murphy, Patrick D. *Literature, Nature, and Other: Ecofeminist Critiques.* Albany: State U of New York P, 1995.

Myres, Sandra. *Westering Women and the Frontier Experience, 1800–1915.* Albuquerque: U of New Mexico P, 1982.

Nash, Roderick Frazier. *Wilderness and the American Mind.* 1967. 3rd ed. New Haven: Yale UP, 1982.

Nelson, Barney. "*The Flock:* An Ecocritical Look at Mary Austin's Sheep and John Muir's Hoofed Locusts." Graulich and Klimasmith 221–42.

———. *The Wild and the Domestic: Animal Representation, Ecocriticism, and Western American Literature.* Reno: U of Nevada P, 2000.

Nielsen, Aldon Lynn. *Reading Race: White American Poets and the Racial Discourse in the Twentieth Century.* Athens: U of Georgia P, 1988.

Norwood, Vera. *Made from This Earth: American Women and Nature.* Chapel Hill: U of North Carolina P, 1993.

———. "The Photographer and the Naturalist: Laura Gilpin and Mary Austin in the Southwest." *Journal of American Culture* 5 (summer 1982): 1–28.

Norwood, Vera, and Janice Monk. *The Desert Is No Lady.* New Haven: Yale UP, 1987.

Oates, Joyce Carol. "Against Nature." *On Nature: Nature, Landscape, and Natural History.* Ed. Daniel Halpern. San Francisco: North Point, 1987. 236–43.

O'Brian, Sharon. "Becoming Noncanonical: The Case against Willa Cather." *Reading in America.* Ed. Cathy N. Davidson. Baltimore: John Hopkins UP, 1989. 240–58.

Odum, Howard, and Harry Estill Moore. *American Regionalism.* New York, 1938.

Oelschlaeger, Max. *The Idea of Wilderness : From Prehistory to the Age of Ecology.* New Haven: Yale UP, 1991.

O'Grady, John P. *Pilgrims to the Wild: Everett Ruess, Henry David Thoreau, John Muir, Clarence King, Mary Austin.* Salt Lake City: U of Utah P, 1993.

Ortner, Sherry B. "Is Female to Male as Nature Is to Culture?" *Woman, Culture, and Society.* Ed. Michelle Rosaldo and Louise Lamphere. Stanford: Stanford UP, 1979. 67–87.

Overton, Grant. "Mary Austin." *The Women Who Make Our Novels.* New York: Dodd, 1928. 8–22.

Pearce, T. M. *The Beloved House.* Caldwell: Caxton, 1940.

———. "Mary Austin and the Pattern of New Mexico." *Southwest Review* 22 (Jan. 1937): 140–48.

———. *Mary Hunter Austin.* New York: Twayne, 1965.

Petry, Alice Hall. "Universal and Particular: The Local-Color Phenomenon Reconsidered." *American Literary Realism* 12.1 (1979): 111–26.

Phillips, Dana. "Ecocriticism, Literary Theory, and the Truth of Ecology." *NLH* 30.3 (1999): 577–602.

Piepmeier, Rainer. "Das Ende der ästhetischen Kategorie 'Landschaft'. Zu einem Aspekt neuzeitlichen Naturverhältnisses." *Westfälische Forschungen* 30 (1980): 8–46.

Plumwood, Val. *Feminism and the Mastery of Nature.* London: Routledge, 1993.

Poland, Tim. "'A Relative to All That Is': The Eco-Hero in Western American Literature." *Western American Literature* 26 (fall 1991): 195–208.

Porter, Nancy. Afterword. *A Woman of Genius.* By Mary Austin. Old Westbury: Feminist, 1985. 295–321.

Powell, John Wesley. "Institutions for the Arid Lands." 1890. *Selected Prose.* Ed. George Crossette. Boston: David Godine, 1970. 41–52.

Powell, Lawrence Clark. "A Dedication to the Memory of Mary Hunter Austin, 1868–1934." *Arizona and the West* 10 (spring 1968): 1–4.

————. *Southwest Classics*. 1974. Tucson: U of Arizona P, 1982.

Pratt, Mary Louise. *Imperial Eyes: Travel Writing and Transculturation*. New York: Routledge, 1992.

Pryse, Marjorie. "'Distilling Essences': Regionalism and 'Women's Culture.'" *American Literary Realism* 25.2 (1993): 1–15.

————. Introduction. *Stories from the Country of Lost Borders*. By Mary Austin. New Brunswick: Rutgers UP, 1987. vii–xxxviii.

Quigley, Peter. "Rethinking Resistance: Environmentalism, Literature, and Poststructural Theory." *Environmental Ethics* 14 (winter 1992): 291–306.

Raine, Anne. "'The Man at the Sources': Gender, Capitel and the Conservationist Landscape in Mary Austin's *The Ford*." Graulich and Klimasmith 243–66.

Reiser, Mark. *Cadillac Desert: The American West and Its Disappearing Water*. New York: Penguin, 1987.

Richardson, Robert D., Jr. *Henry David Thoreau: A Life of the Mind*. Berkeley: U of California P, 1986.

————. "Thoreau and Science." *American Literature and Science*. Ed. Robert J. Scholnick. Lexington: UP of Kentucky, 1992. 110–27.

Riley, Glenda. *Women and Indians on the Frontier, 1825–1915*. Albuquerque: U of New Mexico P, 1984.

Rimmon-Kenan, Shlomith. *Narrative Fiction: Contemporary Poetics*. 1983. London: Routledge, 1994.

Ringler, Donald P. "Mary Austin: Kern County Days, 1888–1892." *Southern California Quarterly* 45.1 (1963): 25–63.

Ritter, Joachim. "Landschaft: Zur Funktion des Ästhetischen in der Modernen Gesellschaft." *Subjektivität. Sechs Aufsätze*. Frankfurt/M.: Suhrkamp, 1989. 141–90.

Roach, Catherine. "Loving Your Mother: On the Woman-Nature Relation." K. J. Warren 52–65.

Robertson, David. *Real Matter*. Salt Lake City: U of Utah P, 1997.

Rolston, Holmes. *Philosophy Gone Wild: Essays in Environmental Ethics*. Buffalo: Prometheus, 1986.

Roosevelt, Theodore. "Nature Fakers." *Everybody's Magazine* 17 (Sept. 1907): 427–30.

Rossi, William. "Roots, Leaves, and Method: Henry Thoreau and Nineteenth-Century Natural Science." *Journal of the American Studies Association of Texas* 19 (Oct. 1988): 1–19.

Rudnick, Lois Palken. "Re-Naming the Land: Anglo Expatriate Women in the Southwest." Norwood and Monk 10–26, notes 239–44.

————. *Utopian Vistas: The Mabel Dodge Luhan House and the American Counterculture*. Albuquerque: U of New Mexico P, 1996.

Ruppert, James. "Discovering America: Mary Austin and Imagism." Allen 243–58.

————. "Mary Austin's Landscape Line in Native American Literature." *Southwest Review* 68 (autumn 1983): 376–90.

Sack, Robert David. *Homo Geographicus: A Framework for Action, Awareness, and Moral Concern*. Baltimore: John Hopkins UP, 1997.

Sale, Kirkpatrick. *Dwellers in the Land: The Bioregional Vision.* San Francisco: Sierra Club, 1985.

Schaffer, Jeffrey P. *The Tahoe Sierra: A Natural History Guide to 106 Hikes in the Northern Sierra.* 1975. Repr. Berkeley: Wilderness, 1987.

Scheese, Don. *Nature Writing: The Pastoral Impulse in America.* New York: Twayne, 1996.

Scheick, William J. "Mary Austin's Disfigurement of the Southwest in *The Land of Little Rain.*" *Western American Literature* 27 (spring 1992): 37–46.

Schlenz, Mark. "Rhetorics of Region in *Starry Adventure* and *Death Comes for the Archbishop.*" Jordan 65–85.

———. "Waters of Paradise: Utopia and Hydrology in *The Land of Little Rain.*" Graulich and Klimasmith 183–201.

Sergeant, Elizabeth Shepley. "Mary Austin: A Portrait." *Saturday Review of Literature* 11 (8 Sept. 1934): 96.

Shi, David E. *Facing Facts: Realism in American Thought and Culture, 1850–1920.* Oxford: Oxford UP, 1995.

Sierra Club. "Sierra Club Population Policies." 16 Sept. 2003 http://www.sierraclub .org/policy/conservation/population.asp.

Simonson, Harold Peter. *Beyond the Frontier: Writers, Western Regionalism, and a Sense of Place.* Fort Worth: Texas Christian UP, 1989.

Slotkin, Richard. *Regeneration through Violence: The Mythology of the American Frontier, 1600–1860.* Middleton: Wesleyan UP, 1973.

Slovic, Scott. *Seeking Awareness in American Nature Writig: Henry Thoreau, Annie Dillard, Edward Abbey, Wendell Berry, Barry Lopez.* Salt Lake City: U of Utah P, 1992.

Smith, Henry Nash. "The American Rhythm." *Southwest Review* 15 (1930): vi–vii.

———. "The Feel of the Purposeful Earth: Mary Austin's Prophecy." *New Mexico Quarterly* 1 (Feb. 1931): 17–33.

Snyder, Gary. *The Practice of the Wild.* San Francisco: North Point, 1990.

Spencer, Benjamin T. "Regionalism in American Literature." Jensen 219–60.

Spiller, Robert, Willard Thorp, Thomas H. Johnson, Henry Seidel Canby, and Richard M. Ludwig, eds. "Regionalism and Local Color." *Columbia Literary History* 304–25.

Starr, Kevin. *Americans and the California Dream: 1850–1915.* Santa Barbara: Peregrine, 1981.

———. *Material Dreams: Southern California through the 1920s.* New York: Oxford UP, 1989.

Stauffer, Helen Winter. Review of *Western Trails* and *Cactus Thorn* by Mary Austin. *Legacy* 6.1 (1989): 69–70.

Steffen, Jerome O., ed. *The American West.* Norman: U of Oklahoma P, 1979.

Steiner, Michael, and Clarence Mondale, eds. *Region and Regionalism in the United States: A Source Book for the Humanities and Social Sciences.* New York: Garland, 1988.

Stewart, Frank. *A Natural History of Nature Writing.* Washington: Island, 1994.

Stineman, Esther Lanigan. *Mary Austin: Song of a Maverick.* New Haven: Yale UP, 1989.

Stout, Janis P. "Mary Austin's Feminism: A Reassessment." *Studies in the Novel* 30.1 (1998): 77–101.

———. "Willa Cather and Mary Austin: Intersections and Influence." *Southwestern American Literature* 21.2 (1996): 39–59.

Sundquist, Eric J. "Realism and Regionalism." *Columbia Literary History* 501–24.

Tallmadge, John, and Henry Harrington, eds. *Reading under the Sign of Nature: New Essays in Ecocriticism.* Salt Lake City: U of Utah P, 2000.

Tate, Allen. "Regionalism and Sectionalism." *New Republic* 69 (23 Dec. 1931): 158–61.

Teague, David W. *The Southwest in American Literature and Art: The Rise of a Desert Aesthetic.* Tucson: U of Arizona P, 1997.

Thomas, John L. "The Uses of Catastrophism: Lewis Mumford, Vernon L. Parrington, Van Wyck Brooks, and the End of American Regionalism." *American Quarterly* 42.2 (1990): 223–51.

Thoreau, Henry David. *The Maine Woods.* 1864. New York: Penguin, 1988.

———. *The Natural History Essays.* Intro. and notes Robert Sattelmeyer. Salt Lake City: Peregrine Smith, 1980.

———. *A Week on the Concord and Merrimack Rivers.* 1849. New Orleans: Parnassus, 1987.

Tichi, Cecelia. "Women Writers and the New Woman." *Columbia Literary History* 589–606.

Tompkins, Jane. *West of Everything: The Inner Life of Westerns.* New York: Oxford UP, 1992.

Toohey, Michelle Campbell. "Mary Austin's *The Land of Little Rain:* Remembering the Coyote." Graulich and Klimasmith 203–20.

Toth, Emily, ed. *Regionalism and the Female Imagination.* University Park: Pennsylvania State U, 1985.

Toth, Susan Allen. "'The Rarest and Most Peculiar Grape': Versions of the New England Woman in Nineteenth-Century Local Color Literature." E. Toth 15–28.

Tracy, Henry Chester. *American Naturists.* New York: Dutton, 1930.

Tuan, Yi Fu. *Topophilia.* Englewood Cliffs: Prentice Hall, 1974.

Turner, Frederick. *Beyond Geography: The Western Spirit against the Wilderness.* 1980. New Brunswick: Rutgers UP, 1986.

Turner, Frederick Jackson. "The Significance of the Frontier in American History." 1893. *The Frontier in American History.* New York: Holt, 1953. 1–38.

Van Doren, Carl. "American Rhythm." *Century* 107 (Nov. 1923): 151–56.

———. Introduction. *The Land of Little Rain.* Text by Mary Austin. Photographed by Ansel Easton Adams. Boston: Houghton, 1950.

———. "Mary Austin." *Scholastic* 25 (29 Sept. 1934): 4, 23.

———. "The Roving Critic." *Nation* 114 (29 Mar. 1922): 371.

Van Doren, Mark. "The American Rhythm." *Nation* 116 (18 Apr. 1923): 472.

Veysey, Laurence R. "Myth and Reality in Approaching American Regionalism." *American Quarterly* 12.1 (1960): 31–43.

Walker, Franklin. *A Literary History of Southern California.* Berkeley: U of California P, 1950.

Walls, Laura Dassow. *Seeing New Worlds: Henry David Thoreau and Nineteenth-Century Natural Science.* Madison: U of Wisconsin P, 1995.

Walton, John. Foreword. *The Ford*. By Mary Austin. ix–xvi.

———. *Western Times and Water Wars: State, Culture, and Rebellion in California*. Berkeley: U of California P, 1992.

Warren, Karen J., ed. *Ecological Feminist Philosophies*. Bloomington: Indiana UP, 1996.

Warren, Robert Penn. "Regionalism or the Coterie Manifesto." *Saturday Review of Literature* (28 Nov. 1936): 8.

———. "Some Don'ts for Literary Regionalists." *American Review* 8 (Dec. 1936): 142–50.

Waters, Lena W. "Mary Austin as Nature Essayist." Diss. Texas Tech. U, 1974.

Webster, Beverly. "Owen's Valley's Mary Austin." *The Album: Times and Tales of Inyo-Mono* 5 (Oct. 1992): 42–51.

Welter, Barbara. "The Cult of True Womanhood: 1820–1860." *American Quarterly* 18.2 (1966): 151–74.

Westling, Louise. *The Green Breast of the New World: Landscape, Gender, and American Fiction*. Athens: U of Georgia P, 1996.

Whitman, Walt. *Leaves of Grass*. 1855. Oxford: Oxford UP, 1990.

Wild, Peter. "The Dangers of Mary Austin's *The Land of Little Rain*." *North Dakota Quarterly* 56.3 (1988): 119–27.

———, ed. *The Desert Reader: Descriptions of America's Arid Regions*. Salt Lake City: U of Utah P, 1991.

———. "Sentimentalism in the American Southwest: John C. Van Dyke, Mary Austin, and Edward Abbey." Kowalewski, *Reading* 127–43.

Williams, Terry Tempest. Introduction. *The Land of Little Rain*. By Mary Austin. New York: Penguin, 1997.

Wilson, Charles Regan, ed. *The New Regionalism*. Jackson: UP of Mississippi, 1998.

Wilson, Christopher. *The Labor of Words: Literary Professionalism in the Progressive Era*. Athens: U of Georgia P, 1985.

Witschi, Nicholas. "Sinclair Lewis, the Voice of Satire, and Mary Austin's Revolt from the Village." *American Literary Realism* 30.1 (1998): 75–90.

Wood, Ann Douglas. "The Literature of Impoverishment: The Local Colorists in America 1865–1914." *Women's Studies* 1 (1972): 3–45.

Work, James C. "The Moral in Austin's *The Land of Little Rain*." *Women and Western American Literature*. Ed. Helen Stauffer and Susan Rosowski. Troy, NY: Whitston, 1982. 297–309.

Worster, Donald. *Nature's Economy: A History of Ecological Ideas*. Cambridge: Cambridge UP, 1985.

Worthington, James. "American Patterns Skillfully Woven in Austin Lecture." *Carmel Pine Cone* (17 Aug. 1922): 7.

Wyatt, David. *The Fall into Eden: Landscape and Imagination in California*. Cambridge: Cambridge UP, 1986.

Wynn, Dudley Taylor. "A Critical Study of the Writings of Mary Hunter Austin (1868–1934)." Diss. New York U, 1939.

Young, Vernon. "Mary Austin and the Earth Performance." *Southwest Review* 35 (1950): 153–63.

Zagarell, Sandra A. "Country's Portrayal of Community and the Exclusion of Difference." Howard 39–60.

———. "Narrative of Community: The Identification of a Genre." *Signs* 13.3 (1988):
498–527.

Zitkala-Sä. "Impressions of an Indian Childhood." *Atlantic* 85 (Jan. 1900): 37–47. Rpt.
in Fetterley and Pryse 535–47.

Zolla, Elémire. "Mary Austin, Essayist and Student of Rhythm." *The Writer and the
Shaman: A Morphology of the American Indian.* Trans. Raymond Rosenthal. New
York: Harcourt, 1973. 187–97.

INDEX

Abbey, Edward, 53, 59–60
"Aboriginal Fiction" (Austin), 153, 251 n. 14
Abram, David, 21, 22, 238 n. 2
Adams, Ansel, 11
Alaimo, Stacy, 57, 137, 231 n. 6, 232 n. 16, 248 n. 35
Allen, Paula Gunn, 195, 196–97, 251 n. 13, 260 n. 19
"American Folk" (Austin), 201
American Rhythm, The (Austin): creation of national mythology in, 49–52, 230 nn. 31–33; on evolution of American race, 29–30; Native American culture in, 52, 153, 228 n. 27, 229 n. 27, 251 nn. 13, 17, 253 n. 24, 260 n. 20; performance of, 229 n. 28; on spiritual function of literature, 46–47, 237 n. 39
"American Women and the Intellectual Life" (Austin), 113–14
"Amerindian Folk Lore" (Austin), 154–55
Anderson, Sherwood, 258 n. 10
Apthorp, Elaine Sergent, 184, 224 n. 19, 234 n. 22
Armitage, Susan H., 259 n. 10
"Art Influence in the West" (Austin), 251 n. 14
"Artist Life in the United States" (Austin), 227 n. 11
Austin, Mary: on adult education, 81, 206, 237 n. 42; autobiographical aspects of work, 11, 225 n. 24; biographical sketch of, 10–11; biographies

of, 225 n. 21; bioregionalism and, 26, 218, 238 n. 51, 250 n. 6; on communism, 149, 150, 249 n. 2; on consciousness in nature, 1, 71, 108, 239 n. 8; critical response to, 4, 12–13, 26, 51–52, 61, 128, 229 nn. 27–28; cultural pluralism of, 3, 156–57; on democratic promise of regionalism, 2, 3, 32, 50–52, 146, 206–7, 208, 210–11, 213, 220–21; on economy, 146–50; on environmental determination of national culture, 6, 27–28, 31–32, 49–50, 218, 223 n. 2, 227 n. 10, 230 n. 33; on environmental factors in identity formation, 1, 19–21, 27, 96–97, 218–19; environmentalism of, 4–5, 16, 44, 65–67, 84, 107, 148, 159–60, 163, 167–68, 213, 215–16, 218, 250 n. 3, 253 n. 29, 254 n. 31; on environmental representation, 37–39, 45; feminism of, 2, 16, 60–61, 113–14, 126, 128, 217–18, 241 n. 2, 243 n. 9, 244 n. 17, 247 n. 31, 248 n. 36, 255 n. 37, 256 n. 42; on gender politics of literary market, 54, 60, 217–18, 231 n. 2, 245 n. 23, 256 n. 44; integrates feminist, environmentalist, multicultural concerns, 2, 4–5, 6, 17, 61, 217; interest in folk culture, 51, 201–3, 210, 260 n. 27; interwar regionalism and, 3, 32, 146, 191; mysticism of, 10, 15, 40–41, 45, 98, 99–100, 106–7, 110–11; on Native American culture, 2–3, 16, 30, 50–52, 107, 147–51,

UNDER THE SIGN OF NATURE: EXPLORATIONS IN ECOCRITICISM